The Challenge is in the Naming

A Theological Journey

The Challenge is in the Naming

A Theological Journey

Lydia Neufeld Harder

CMU Press
Winnipeg, Manitoba 2018

CMU Press
500 Shaftesbury Blvd
Winnipeg, Manitoba
R3P 2N2

Cover and interior design: Matt Veith
Image of Paint: Public Domain.

Printed in Canada
by CP Printing, Winnipeg, Manitoba.

Library and Archives Canada Cataloguing in Publication

Harder, Lydia Marlene, 1939-, author
The challenge is in the naming : a theological journey / Lydia Neufeld Harder.

Includes bibliographical references.
ISBN 978-1-987986-04-4 (softcover)

1. Feminist theology. 2. Feminism--Religious aspects--Christianity. I. Title.

BT83.55.H37 2018 230.082 C2018-901929-8

To Gary

Partner, co-parent, friend, colleague, confidant

beloved companion on the journey

Table of Contents

Chapter 6 Power

Chapter 7 Dialogue

Chapter 8 Wisdom

Chapter 9 Ministry

Chapter 10 Discernment

Abbreviations

AMBS	*Anabaptist Mennonite Biblical Seminary, formerly Associated Mennonite Biblical Seminary*
CMBC	*Canadian Mennonite Bible College, a prior college of CMU*
CMU	*Canadian Mennonite University*
MCC	*Mennonite Central Committee*
TMTC	*Toronto Mennonite Theological Centre*
TMTC	*Toronto School of Theology*
GGUC	*Conrad Grebel University College*
ETSC	*Evangelical Theological Seminary in Cairo*
IKERI	*Imam Khomeini Education and Research Institute*
LGBTQ	*Lesbian, gay, bisexual, transgender and queer*

All Bible quotations are from the
New Revised Standard Version.

Foreword

by Kimberly Penner
and Susanne Guenther Loewen

I (Susanne) first met Lydia Neufeld Harder over a decade ago while working as a pastoral intern in Toronto for my undergraduate practicum requirement. I remember feeling honoured that Lydia would take the time to meet with me as a young woman with what were then mere intentions of doing graduate work in theology. She was encouraging, but also warned me to prepare myself, because theology at the graduate level was still very much a male-dominated field and women would be the minority in most of my classes. I was incredulous at the time, but she turned out to be right!

I (Kimberly) met Lydia when I began my doctoral program at the Toronto School of Theology at a scholar's forum hosted by the Toronto Mennonite Theological Centre (TMTC). Monthly scholars' forums at TMTC are an opportunity for affiliates of the centre (primarily current and former Mennonite graduate students) to present a paper or research in progress for conversation. I experienced Lydia's presence as warm and welcoming and her comments and questions insightful. I knew that she was a former director of TMTC and that she and her husband Gary were pastors at the time. I was not familiar, though, with her contributions to theological scholarship.

As doctoral students together, we (Susanne and Kimberly) shared with each other the published and unpublished work of Mennonite feminist theologians who had not received much "air time" at the Canadian Mennonite institutions at which we had both previously studied, at least not compared to male scholars like John Howard Yoder, Harold S. Bender, or even Canadian Mennonite scholars like Harry Huebner and A. James Reimer. Lydia's *Obedience, Suspicion, and the Gospel of Mark: A Mennonite-Feminist Exploration of Biblical Authority* was one of the books we poured over and discussed most often as we navigated studying theology and ethics as Mennonite women at Emmanuel College, a United Church of Canada college in the context of the ecumenical Toronto School of Theology (which includes the Toronto Mennonite Theological Centre). Though she had retired from her official academic role by then, we gladly welcomed Lydia's continued involvement in the TMTC Women's Group, a small community of Mennonite-feminist students, pastors, and theologians which provided a context for us to get to know her and her work, and to put it into practice.

We considered her work groundbreaking because she claims this hybridized identity and method as a Mennonite-feminist theologian. Mennonite scholars had previously engaged feminist theology with varying degrees of interest, but it was always viewed at a distance, from a self-contained and distinctive Anabaptist-Mennonite perspective. Harder was one of the first to claim a kind of "dual citizenship" in these two schools of theological thought. But this is not to suggest that this is a straightforward claim. Rather, it has rendered her an insider/outsider in the Mennonite community,[i] as she does not embrace her Anabaptist-Mennonite heritage uncritically or triumphalistically, but rather allows Mennonite and feminist theologies to mutually critique and inform one another, holding together a feminist hermeneutics of suspicion with a Mennonite "hermeneutics of obedience" or discipleship.[ii] This gives her particular insight into issues of Mennonite cultural/religious nonconformity and understandings of gendered power within the church. She highlights, for example, the way that Mennonite nonconformity to the norms of wider culture and society has often unfolded along androcentric lines, and thus has often actually meant women's conformity to patriarchal norms:

> Biblical exegesis has contributed to making male discipleship normative for the meaning of the term, subsuming female experiences of discipleship. In Mennonite tradition this led to an understanding of discipleship that was largely associated with cross-bearing, self-denial, obedience, and servanthood, characteristics that radically challenged the expectations that a patriarchal society had of men, but which affirmed what was already expected of women.[iii]

Harder's attention to the neglected experiences of Mennonite women has highlighted the ways in which the Mennonite church has critiqued the abuse of power and violence of "the world" without applying a comparable critique inward, to its own communities. As one of the contributors to *Peace Theology and Violence against Women*[iv] and in other essays, Harder takes on what is perhaps the most glaring example of this double standard: the silence around renowned Mennon-

---

i See Chapter 5, pp. 147-49.

ii Harder, *Obedience, Suspicion, and the Gospel of Mark*, ix.

iii See Chapter 3, p. 96.

iv See Elizabeth G. Yoder, ed., *Peace Theology and Violence against Women.*

ite theologian John Howard Yoder's sexual abuse of female students. Elsewhere, she uncovers the ways in which the silence around Yoder's abuse is a symptom of a deeper pattern around gendered power within Mennonite communities, noting that

> Mennonite women have experienced the power of 'brotherly' admonition, as it was usually called, used against them.... Though no comparison has been made between the public confession required of women disciplined for sexual activity resulting in pregnancy and the silence surrounding sexual abuse by male members of the community, it is clear that Mennonites have only recently applied peace teachings to the issue of violence against women. The rule of Christ can therefore be understood as having at least two primary functions within the Mennonite community. It has been used to counter the authority and power of alternative community structures. It has also been used to enforce conformity to community norms that encouraged women's inferior status.[v]

Her suspicion of all unequal relationships of power promotes an intersectional view of oppressions (including, for example, sexism, racism, heterosexism, ableism, classism, and ageism) as interlocking and, therefore, justice and peace as necessarily sought in all relationships—including in gendered and sexualized relationships.

We both drew on Harder's insights for our dissertations, especially as we formulated our theological methods. I (Susanne) used a Mennonite-feminist, dialogical method to formulate a theology of the cross and redemption which does not reify violence nor all forms of suffering as redemptive, taking up many of the incisive questions Harder poses, including, "If Jesus' death was redemptive, is all human suffering also redemptive? Does obedience to God mean that women should negate themselves and willingly accept the violence enacted against them? Is this the path to salvation? These questions are further complicated in a theological framework that asserts that God the Father willed that his child be killed. How does this act model loving parenthood?"[vi] Harder's compelling vision of "the Source of Love who is the centre of our home, our God who has given birth to us, suffered with us in our lack of shalom, challenged us in our injustice and empowered us anew to live the way of love in a violent world"[vii] also fed my

---

v Harder, *Obedience*, 45.

vi See Chapter 9, p. 293-94. Cf. Chapter 8.

vii See Chapter 2, p. 70.

own theological imagination.

I (Kimberly) drew on Harder's method of "obedience and suspicion" for articulating, for example, an ecclesiology and understanding of the authority of Scripture for Christian sexual ethics that remain accountable to those persons most severely impacted by unequal relations of power (e.g. cisnormative, heteronormative patriarchy) in Mennonite Church Canada and Mennonite Church USA. Harder's attention to and critique of gendered relations of power within ecclesial communities influenced me to ask, can the dominant Mennonite understandings and practices of ecclesiology as ethics be transformed and function in liberating, nonviolent ways as a method for an embodied theological ethics and for sexual ethics committed to the experiences of those who are shamed, excluded, or otherwise bear the burden of the current and predominant ecclesial power relations?

Through her work and by her example, Harder has taught us to claim our own agency as disciples of Jesus committed to justice and peace and, at the same time, reminded us to remain self-critical and to leave space for the Spirit to move in unexpected ways and relationships. She has challenged us to resist the temptation to view ourselves exclusively as marginalized since that is to deny our own potential to construct hierarchies of power, whether intentionally or unintentionally. In her own words:

> A minority status does not mean weakness. A minority status, whether Mennonite or feminist, does not protect me from these hard choices…in the use of power. The temptation to deny power and authority that comes with education, economic stability, denominational identity, race or gender is there within both the Mennonite and feminist communities. The gospel would challenge the community to expose my use of political and social power to dominate or control.[viii]

Or as she states in chapter 5 of this collection: "Postmodern suspicion challenges all hermeneutic communities, whether mainline or minority, to subject their theological discourse to analysis by new conversation partners in order to test whether the theological language supports assumptions and prejudices limited to their own narrow experience of God. In this context Mennonites can no longer hide from the admonition of other Christians."[ix] In other words, it is important to remain suspicious of any emphasis on perfectionism or obedience that does not simultaneously acknowledge human vulnerability. Harder's emphasis on disci-

---

viii Harder, *Obedience,* 139.

ix See Chapter 5, p. 147.

pleship as empowering praxis which involves both a commitment to nonviolent resistance to all forms of violence, including gendered and sexualized violence, as well as a commitment to the church community as the context for lived discipleship ethics exemplifies this vulnerability.

In the essays and reflections within this volume, Harder's rich blending of personal, church, and academic narratives and contexts all point to the multiple ways in which her perspective is hybridized: as an experienced scholar and pastor she bridges the divide between church and academy; as a spouse, mother, and theologian she links the personal and the political, overlapping traditional and non-traditional women's work; as a Mennonite-feminist she bridges the divide between biblical studies and theological and ethical reflection. Her work overflows gender alone, speaking also to same-sex marriage, Muslim-Christian dialogue, and Indigenous-Settler relationships from a Mennonite-feminist perspective. In these ways, Harder's work lays helpful groundwork for intersectional feminist, womanist, and queer theologies and ethics, which are increasingly recognized as indispensable for a theology and ethics of nonviolence and peacemaking. The introductions to the chapters and articles in particular reveal in many cases the untold (or unheard) history of Mennonite organizations such as the Toronto Mennonite Theological Centre and the development of Mennonite feminist theology. It is not often that a scholar takes the time to reflect in such detail on the contexts out of which their writing emerges and to share so deeply and vulnerably of the joys and challenges they faced over the course of their career.

This interdisciplinary collection has the potential to become a pivotal resource for the next generation of Mennonite theologians, scholars, and pastors, among whom many women in particular identify a sense of belonging within both Mennonite and feminist circles. As is evident above, the two of us have found Lydia's love for the church and theology to be infectious, and we hope the readers of this volume will, too.

Preface

A TIME FOR NAMING

One way that I often began my classes in theology was to ask my students to introduce themselves by giving us the names they have been given or called and the names they have chosen for themselves. Among names like Gail, Geoff and Charlotte were also names like mother, sister, friend, as well as nicknames like Buddy or Precious. Sometimes the names held special meaning; other names hurt or brought painful memories to mind. I used the poem that follows to bring the question to another level. As the students began to wrestle with the question of how we dared to name the Creator, the One beyond our naming, in our theological studies they caught a glimpse of the risk we were taking and the serious nature of the task. By bringing our own experience of being named together with the challenge of doing academic theology, the students could sense the vulnerability and openness needed to enter deeply into the course's agenda.

The notion of "naming" brings a personal element into the theological work that we do. Theology is not only about objective analysis and factual truth. At its depth theology is also relational, a meeting of the "I" and the "Thou" as Martin Buber put it. Moreover, as we have begun to realize within our twentyfirst-century Western worldview, how we name the "other" in the context of relationship and dialogue also suggests how we understand the power dynamic within that relationship. In addition, theological reflection includes intentionally naming ourselves, who we are, how we have experienced life within the web of intertwining relationships that have shaped us. Theology thus also names the world we live in, its complexity and its beauty, its joy and its pain. It is in that naming, that we draw boundaries, gain new freedom to grow into our identity and welcome others into relationship and community.

The following poem hints at some of the tensions and possibilities that arise if we pay attention to how we name each other and how we name God in our theological journey. I wrote a poem initially to prepare us to meet fellow Christians from around the world at Mennonite World Conference in Winnipeg in 1990 and I have since adapted it considerably for many different contexts.

A TIME FOR NAMING AND A TIME FOR BEING NAMED[x]

Doing theology in community is all about naming
Exploring the names given, the names accepted.
Identifying the relationships and the ruptures
The dreams and the visions

Around us and beyond us.
Reconsidering old names, creating new ones,
Seeking correlations, discovering connections
Encountering the Mystery of the One who first named us.

Names are powerful! Naming is risky!
Names give concreteness to our concepts,

> They bring order to a chaotic world.
> Names can hurt and names can heal,
> Names do something to both the one who names
> and the ones being named.
> Names witness to who we are and to who we can become.

Names characterize and categorize.
Names identify and label.

You shall be called by a new name. (Isaiah 62:2)
But he was called a blasphemer, a traitor…

They were called Protestants
They were called Catholics
They were called Mennonites
They were called Muslims
They were called the quiet in the land
They were called troublemakers
They were called peacemakers
They were called…
 If you are reviled for the name of Christ, you are blessed. (1 Peter 4:14)
Names divide or unify.
Names include or exclude.
I belong to Paul, I belong to Apollos,

x A version of this poem was first published in *Courier* (Spring, 1990).

I belong to Cephas (1 Corinthians 1:12)
Let us make a name for ourselves.... (Genesis 11:4)
By what name shall we be called?
With which name shall we identify?
Rich or poor? Powerful or powerless?
Oppressed or oppressor? Educated or illiterate?
Disabled or talented? First world or third world?
East or West, North or South? Young or old?
There is no longer Jew or Greek, there is no longer slave or free,
there is no longer male and female, for all of you are one in Christ Jesus. (Galatians 3:28)

Names express who we are.
Names hide who we are.

You have a name of being alive but you are dead. (Revelation 3:1)
You are Simon son of John.
You are to be called Cephas (which is translated Peter). (John 1:42)
By what name shall I address you?
Can I really tell you who I am?
Can I share the depth of my experience?
Shall I make myself vulnerable?
Can I get to know you? Do you really want to know me?

Names recognize and give dignity.
Names can be changed.

The shepherd calls his own sheep by name. (John 10:3)
The nameless ones are named.
You are a son of Abraham
You are a daughter of Sarah.
The forgotten ones are remembered,
The lost are found.
Hagar ... where have you come from and where are you going?
Zacchaeus ... I'm coming to your house today!
Mary ... why are you weeping?
Once you were not a people but now you are God's people. (1 Peter 2:10)

How then shall we name the God we meet
In the scriptures and in our experience
In our relationships and in the tradition?

The God beyond all naming
The God of Mystery and Incarnation
The God of Sara and Hagar and Abraham
The God of Mary and Joseph and the women at the tomb
The God who enters our world again and again.

Naming God in theology is a risky endeavor
In the midst of idols, masks, false images and pretenses
Listening to the God who first named us
Hearing our names, remembering our calling,
Seeing visions, dreaming possibilities
Observing the world with new eyes.

Naming God in theology can be an act of worship
A response to a name given, a blessing understood.
But you are a chosen race, a royal priesthood, a holy nation
God's own people, in order that you may proclaim the mighty acts
of the One who called you out of darkness into the marvelous light. (1 Peter 2:9)

One of the articles that I read and reread many times during my years of study, written by the philosopher Paul Ricoeur, was entitled "Naming God."[xi] Until I reread the various articles that I had written, I had not realized how much the challenge of naming God while naming myself, others, and the world is a common thread in my writings. As I reflect now on my journey I realize that intentionally naming the other is always risky and carries much power—whether of blessing or curse.

Naming God authentically is always a response to God revealing God-self to us. The biblical story of Hagar, the first person in the Bible to name God, suggests something about the vulnerability needed to receive a vision of who God is.[xii] Hagar is alone in the desert, rejected by Sarah and Abraham and pregnant with her master's child. And it is in that context that she receives a powerful vision of an angel who asks her to reveal the depth of her despair: "Where have you come from and where are you going?" She responds to the vision and the blessing given her by naming the Lord who spoke to her, "You are *Elroi*" [that is, the God of Seeing]; for she said, "Have I really seen God and remained alive after seeing him?"

Vulnerability and risk is also there for the women at the tomb of the crucified

---

xi Ricoeur, *Naming God.*

xii Genesis 16:7-14.

Jesus.[xiii] On that occasion it is Mary Magdalene who names the resurrected Jesus "*Rabbouni* (which means Teacher)." The story continues with the commission Jesus gives to her: "But go to my brothers and say to them, 'I am ascending to my Father and your Father, to my God and your God.'" The task to tell others continues with every vision of God we may have.

I have chosen to gather into one volume articles and papers of mine that have been previously written and/or published over the last thirty years. Since most of the articles were written in response to specific invitations coming primarily from my Mennonite context they are occasional and specific. The introductions that I have written (printed in italics) describe the questions and experiences and context that occupied me over the years. Readers will be able to judge how much my theology has developed or changed.

Since learning to articulate one's theology is a cumulative effort, ideas and even stories are sometimes repeated in the various articles that I wrote. The repetitions suggest that these ideas and stories have had an important impact on me. A journey is partly about chronology and my reflections do follow the passage of years. However, the *kairos* moments intersect and interrupt a smooth telling of the story. In my reflections, there is a circling back and a circling forward with key ideas and symbols repeated but gaining ever deepening significance for me. This also means that readers can delve into any chapter they wish to find the kernel of my theological convictions and assumptions. Some readers may choose to read the more scholarly articles, others to read primarily the personal stories that give a context to the articles.

Many conversation partners and mentors encouraged me as I stumbled along trying to find my way in the academic and church world. Some are named in this book. My thanks to them. Many others could be mentioned, for there is a large community of seekers and discoverers that has surrounded me and given me hope. The lively conversations at the meetings of the Toronto Mennonite Theological Centre Women's Group have been particularly timely for me as I reviewed my writings for possible relevance to the coming generation of theologians. I have been especially blessed to have the encouragement of Susanne Guenther Loewen and Kimberly Penner who have read my manuscript at several different stages and given important feedback.

My deepest thanks go to my husband Gary, my closest friend and confidant, my companion on the journey for over fifty years. The mutuality that we have experienced in our marriage and in our vocations has given me hope that all people in their unique differences can work toward mutual encouragement and counsel.

My journey in theology is uniquely mine and is only worthy of telling if others can hear in it their own name being called by God. I hope it can encourage

xiii John 20:11-16.

others, whether they engage in formal theology or not, to acknowledge the mysterious presence of God in their lives. I have been richly blessed. These words were written for my children and grandchildren who will name God in their own different and unique ways and to my students over the years, who have blessed me with their questions and insights.

Chapter 1: Vocation

NAMING THE JOURNEY

I page through the collage of memories in a scrapbook that I made during my doctoral studies in theology. The cards, photos, newspaper clippings, and program brochures testify to my growing understanding of myself as a theologian and as a ministering person. When I doubted my calling, I was reminded of the experiences that these mementos represented and was reassured that there was support for me. I named this scrapbook a "theological journey," a journey that was not yet finished but continues even today in my retirement years. My work life has included elementary school teaching, homemaking and volunteer work, scholarly work, teaching at the university level, administration, and finally pastoring. Each of these work situations had its challenges and its rewards. But none of these alone would I name as my vocation or calling.

At this point in my life I resonate most with Parker Palmer when he says, "vocation is not a goal to be achieved but a gift to be received."[1] *I have named that gift "blessing" in some of my writings and named the source of the calling that I have felt throughout my life "God." What I have not so clearly identified is that this calling is intimately connected to the self created by God as good and given to me as a gift to be cherished with my personality, sexuality, and family and community connections. I have been given a specific socio-economic and cultural place within which I need to discover who that true self is and within which I need to find the vocation that will bring blessing to others. The road to accepting the treasure of my true self has meant rejecting some of the expectations others had of me and learning to speak in my own voice and to act using the capabilities given to me by God.*

I have often longed for affirmation from the church community for who I am. The church does have special moments in which they, in a public and personal way, bless and affirm each person as a "beloved daughter/son of God."[2] *In the Mennonite tradition, child dedication and baptism are particularly important as opportunities for this kind of affirmation. For Mennonites, baptism also has an additional meaning—to commission the newly baptized into the vocation of "blessing others," in other words, into the vocation of the church. I look back at my own baptism at the age of seventeen as a special moment in which I was aware of being loved but also cognizant of the responsibility that baptism entails toward others.*

Yet understanding the clues that pointed to my vocation has not been easy. To go beyond role expectations and job qualifications to discovering the place where my own deep gladness meets the world's deep hunger[3] *has required a lifetime of asking ques-*

tions, listening to the potential that others saw in me, and most importantly listening to my own deeper desires and hopes and passions. It has meant reflecting critically on the systems and institutions that tend to control and shape who I am. These systems have included the church and the university. It has not always been easy to make constructive choices based on my own inner convictions and to name and discard that which makes me conform to expectations not related to my calling.

My thinking about my vocation is rooted in the biblical story as well as in the denominational tradition in which I stand. Mennonites freely use the word discipleship to express the response of following the way of Jesus as the faithful answer to God's call. I have struggled with the biblical story and the history of interpretation of that story, a story in which women seem to play a secondary role. Yet I hear the call most vividly through the words of the angel at the tomb speaking to the female followers of Jesus, "Go, tell his disciples and Peter that he [Jesus] is going ahead of you to Galilee; there you will see him, just as he told you."[4] *This promise, that Jesus goes ahead of us and that we will "see" him, is one that I hold on to as I continue on the way.*

I have not entered this journey without encouragement. I am part of a larger ecosystem including the family into which I was born, the community and the church that have nurtured me, and the larger network of relationships that have continued to bless me. Sometimes I could not hear the blessing amidst the critical voices. Yet always the voice of God naming me a beloved daughter has been there assuring me that there is a path to follow, that I am not alone in the struggle, and that Jesus has walked the road ahead of me.

Vocation has thus become a term that describes not only my own journey, but also the journey of the church as it too again and again discovers the gift that it has been given. Much of my journey intersects with the journey of the Mennonite church to which I belong as it struggles to hear the calling of God in the midst of other voices clamouring for attention.

The three articles in this section give hints of the tensions that developed within me as I tried to find my way in the context of a church trying to find its way. The first is a version of my story that I wrote as encouragement for women in their journeys. The second is one I wrote during my most active time as a scholar to explain some of the choices I made in my scholarly work. I have included a third, not previously published article, written after six years of co-pastoring with my husband.

Because these three articles were written many years apart, they overlap in their reference to particular experiences that have become symbolic to me. In the chapters that follow, my story will be fleshed out as I recall the various contexts that led to my scholarly writings. As I continue to ponder and reflect during this retirement stage of life, I am filled with joy and thankfulness for the gift of my vocation and the discoveries I made along the way.

* * *

REACHING FOR A BLESSING[5]

When I was a little girl, I found it difficult to answer questions about what I wanted to be when I grew up. My standard response was "a teacher," an acceptable answer. However, buried deep within me was another answer that I never dared whisper, even to myself. My dream seemed too presumptuous. So I chose between the three vocations that seemed acceptable for women before marriage: teaching, nursing or clerical work. I went to teachers' college and spent several years teaching elementary school children. However, the inner urgings continued.

A Secret Dream Unfolds

Though unaware of it, my family and congregation had nourished my secret dream since early childhood. Playing church was a favorite game in our home. Together with my brother, I planned and led pretend worship services and programs involving younger siblings and neighbours, all to the delight of my parents. I do not know why I did not choose to play the role of my mother who took care of the children in the *Stübchen* (nursery) at the back of the church. Instead, I identified with my father, a lay minister and teacher in the church.

Theology was everyday language in our home. I remember heated discussions about how to interpret Genesis, while we were perched on ladders, picking cherries in the orchard. These debates were interspersed with lively hymn singing, the lead taken first by those in one tree and then those in another.

I listened to stories of Mennonite life in Russia during the terrible events of the Revolution. This gave me a concrete context for my father's strong convictions of non-violence. No wonder that I longed to go to Bible College to be able to indulge myself in these kinds of discussions without the drudgery of farm work.

My home church had encouraged me to commit my life to mission and service. I began teaching Sunday school in my early teens, became involved in daily vacation Bible school and camp programs. Our youth group of about seventy young people carried on an ambitious Friday evening program. I enjoyed the committee work and opportunities for involvement in choir and service projects. At age seventeen I was part of about fifty youth who attended a Canada-wide Mennonite conference in my home town. (Later I would hang the picture of the official delegates, all men, above my desk. When I would get discouraged about the lack of support for women, I would remember with hope how much had already changed since that day!)

A Struggle for Faith

The three years at Canadian Mennonite Bible College (CMBC) were some of the richest years of my life—and not only because I met my husband there. At first I felt privileged to read and study, to reflect on the many questions about life and the Bible in the midst of a community that treasured both worship and critical thought. However, soon my studies took on the nature of a struggle for faith as life experiences and intellectual questions began to overlap. During a vacation break, I came home to a church in conflict over differing views of leadership, styles of worship and biblical interpretation. I heard my father being discredited and disgraced by people whom I had respected and loved. I saw my mother trying to carry on her supportive role as she experienced the rejection of a congregation.

Faculty at CMBC encouraged critical reflection. This allowed me to phrase my questions in theoretical language, without betraying the hurt lying just below the surface. My real questions, ones I never quite dared to speak out loud, were ultimate ones: Where was God if the Bible was produced in a very human process and if the church was made up of sinful human beings? How could I be sure that God was real?

In studying 1 Corinthians, I gradually discovered a God who chooses to communicate to us, not outside of human mediation, but through the human Bible and even through a sinful church. The possibility that God, in God's grace and love, could also use me became a promise that brought meaning and purpose to my life. I remember well singing Handel's "Messiah" with great joy, having rediscovered God's presence in my journey. Now I had a theological foundation for the sense of calling that I continued to feel.

In the last year of study, another theme began to emerge. It was the sixties and the theme of freedom was in the air. Our class chose the motto, "Freed to Obey" for our graduation theme. I spent hours arguing against the other suggested theme, "Obey to be Free." I insisted that freedom from God came as a gift before we could obey and become servants of God. These discussions would be replayed many times in the future in various contexts.

Already at that time I began to experience the subtle but dominating influence that society and the church had over me as I tried to follow my calling. For example, professors were urging my brother to continue studying because of his good grades. No one suggested further studies to me, even though I also had good grades. The equality and mutuality of relationships between students during college days began to change as different opportunities presented themselves to men and to women. Marriage increased these differences, since both my husband and I assumed that his career goals would determine our future.

The tension this created within me climaxed in the year that my husband, Gary, was doing a year's pastoral internship training in London, Ontario, as part of his seminary training. We lived in a small basement apartment with our two infant children. Gary's work was intense. He spent much time in becoming self-aware in settings of small learning groups in the hospital and church where he received supervision. No conscious decision on my part was needed to know that I could not continue to work with him in congregational settings as I had in the past.

My role had become house-keeping and child-care. Depression and unhappiness began to surface more and more. Slowly I began to admit my own feelings of being left out, my jealousy of Gary and his opportunities to study and minister. I realized that we had begun a pattern in which I tried to work through my husband's profession, knowing there would be no affirmation of my own sense of calling. This did not contribute to a healthy partnership. It also did not allow me to do my work joyfully, using my own gifts and abilities.

Several key people encouraged me in the task of self-reflection during this time. One woman from the church offered to care for our children during the Sunday school hour so that I could teach an elective course, the first opportunity I ever had to teach adults. The chosen theme was a study of the book by Lois Gunden Clemens, *Woman Liberated* (1971). This allowed me to explore my own issues in the context of women and men serious about searching for new and more faithful interpretations of the Bible.

Gary's supervisor arranged a small group experience in which interns and spouses could interact, particularly about the effect that the internship experience was having on our marriage relationships. This created a context in which Gary and I could begin to name the dysfunctional communication patterns in our marriage and begin to create new ones. Though this was a stressful time, I began making more conscious choices about my role in the church and in our family.

Toward Mutuality in a Marriage

My struggle to respond to God's call took a different turn when Gary became pastor in Edmonton. In a church where lay involvement was encouraged I was free to be part of many areas in church life. In women's Bible study groups and the adult Sunday School classes I began to articulate publicly my convictions and questions. The central issues facing us during this time included raising children and growth within marriages as well as questions about God's presence during accidental death, suicide, and domestic violence. Volunteer activities included working for a Distress Line, on a daycare board and teaching Sunday school. These broadened my horizons, but also raised questions about the value of my activities when compared to my husband's full-time job as pastor.

The shift to a more mutual relationship in our marriage did not come easily. Sometimes I struggled with feelings of unworthiness and guilt. One such occasion was when I left our three pre-school children with Gary, while I spent a week away in an orientation session to prepare for writing a quarter of the Foundation Sunday School curriculum.

A significant turning point came for us as a couple when we were in Paraguay during Gary's sabbatical year from the pastorate. We decided to each teach half-time at the seminary and shared the parenting and household tasks equally. I began to admit how much I enjoyed the teaching. Meanwhile, Gary realized how much parenting he had missed by his total commitment to public ministry.

Naming the Dream

Back in Canada, I again began to explore various career paths. In my search for direction, I asked advice from a favorite professor. When I told him of my interest in further studies in theology, he encouraged me, suggesting that I was lucky that I could take courses "just for fun."

Somehow I felt crushed and humiliated. Why had I imagined that my gifts could be used to serve the church. However, I cautiously began exploring further studies by applying to enter university to secure a bachelor of education degree. I was discouraged by the lack of credit that I would receive for my past education.

I finally decided to do what I really wanted to do—study theology. Unexpectedly, I received the equivalent of a master of divinity degree for my various undergraduate degrees and occasional courses, a not so small miracle. I could enter directly into a master of theology degree program at Newman College, a small Catholic school in Edmonton.

There I learned to articulate my Mennonite faith in dialogue with Catholic brothers and sisters. I discovered feminist theologians who read the Bible self-consciously as women. I struggled with social justice issues together with a larger ecumenical community. I found role models, such as Sister Lina Gaudette, who taught me to value my own integrity and commitments even in the midst of an androcentric church. After graduation, I was even hired to teach several Bible courses in the same college.

Several key experiences during those years helped me to own my gifts and offer them to the larger community. I remember a weekend retreat with Katie Funk Wiebe, a Mennonite author. She shared the story of how she finally named herself an author, because that meant accepting the responsibility for the influence her books might have on others. It would have been much easier to say that she just wrote a few little articles "for fun."

After that retreat, I struggled for a long time but I finally named myself a Mennonite theologian, albeit secretly. I knew this meant accepting my share of responsibility for the direction that Mennonite theology was taking.

My Mother's Blessing

I remember weeping as I listened to the tape of the ordination to ministry of my brother and my sister-in-law, Doreen Neufeld. Doreen was the first woman ordained in the United Mennonite Conference of Ontario in 1980.[6] What moved me most deeply was hearing my mother's words at the end of the service. My father had been asked to speak, but when he finished, she decided she also wanted to say something. She spontaneously offered her own blessing. I wept because of my mother's courage. I wept because of the many gifts that she had, which had not been used in the church. I wept for myself, admitting that I too longed for affirmation from my faith community. However, I was not left without a blessing. Just about the time that I was finishing my master's thesis, I was asked to speak at a conference on power and authority held at the Mennonite college that I had attended. I still have a vivid memory of standing before former professors and respected church leaders. I wondered if I would be able to get any words out, even after the many hours of hard work that I had put into preparing the lecture.

I received courage from the lines of a song that kept ringing in my ears throughout that weekend. Our choir had recently sung a Bach cantata in which the words of Psalm 115: 12-15 were set to music. Certain lines kept repeating themselves to me: "*Der Herr segne euch…euch und eure Kinder!*" [The Lord bless you…you and your children]. I accepted those words as a commissioning by God for my task, a promise that my children would also be blessed as I responded to the inner call.

Soon I discovered a fact of life: not everyone agreed that women's voices were needed in Mennonite theology. I became discouraged when my tentative contributions were discounted or my ideas attacked. I remember one consultation in particular. I was completely overwhelmed by the political maneuvers that I saw happening, participants completely ignoring women's concerns and exclusive language being used.

At one point I could not hide my tears, so went downstairs to hide in the washroom. There I found the other two women attending this conference of approximately one hundred leaders. They were also crying. What redeemed this conference for me was a letter by one of our male church leaders who encouraged me to continue to speak, despite the suspicious atmosphere and exclusivity that he admitted had been very apparent at that meeting.

"The Lord has been Mindful of Us"

Many people did wonder about the wisdom of my next major decision. Why would a home-maker facing fifty move her family across the country to begin a six-year doctoral program in theology? My husband's commitment to mutuality and his willingness to move for the sake of my studies created this possibility for me. However, to take this step, I also had to overcome a lifetime of conditioning that told me that practical service and theoretical work are separated along *gender lines.* The years of study in Toronto were full, rich years. Intense involvement with a friend who was struggling to affirm her own gifts after years of sexual abuse created a practical edge to my theoretical studies of power and authority. I discovered that theological schools also have political agenda and that women must be able to articulate their own goals and insist on their own sense of direction.

After graduation came the real test on whether I believed in my calling. Gary and I had arranged a meeting with a small group of people to help us discern our future direction. Before the meeting could take place, we received an invitation to come to CMBC to teach there for one year. Rather quickly we assumed that we would say no, because Gary would not be able to arrange a year's leave from the church that he was pastoring.

Surprisingly, the discernment group thought otherwise. They affirmed my gifts and suggested that I go by myself for the first four months. Perhaps Gary would be able to join me for the second half of the year. This created a great inner turmoil for me. I could not imagine going by myself without Gary's support. However, he too urged me to take this opportunity. I finally accepted this as God's leading and phoned CMBC with my acceptance.

Now it was their turn to hesitate. If I were there alone, what message would this give to younger women in their college? I was devastated. However, after reconsidering, CMBC decided to invite me to teach all year, with Gary coming for the second semester. Opportunities to teach and preach have continued to appear for me after that year of working in a Mennonite institution.

Do I now know what I will be when I grow up? I continue to find the question relevant as I begin to think about retirement. Perhaps the call to ministry that I have felt throughout my life was a call to further growth. Perhaps it was really an invitation to be a disciple, following the God who leads us step by step, nudging us on to further maturity amidst the various obstacles, both external and internal.

If this is true, then no human institutions can stand in the way of our becoming all that we were meant to be! For "the Lord has been mindful of us; [God] will bless us" (Psalm 115:12). This is our confidence as women responding to God's call.

* * *

Naming Myself a Theological Scholar in the Anabaptist Tradition[7]

When meeting with prospective students in theology, I often warn them about the risks of standing in this particular scholarly space. From the perspective of a critical analyst standing on the boundary between church and world—that is, from the perspective of a trained theologian—the disjunctions and contradictions with respect to our language about God can sometimes seem overwhelming. At the same time, I cannot help but share with these students my enthusiasm for studying theology. Where else do the discourses of church and world meet so overtly in a dialogue about the mystery of life? What other subject matter is so inclusive of every aspect of experience, both personal and communal? Though long displaced as the "queen of the sciences" in the university, theology remains in the church an integral element of discourse as we listen to the voice of God and testify to that experience. Who would not welcome the privilege of being part of such a constructive and necessary enterprise?

Still, it is the contradictions that first come to my mind. Indeed, as I reflect on my scholarly journey, I realize that it has been the tensions and contradictions in both life and God-talk that first drew me into the formal study of theology. It has been my search for wholeness and unity that has encouraged me to ask ultimate questions and seek universal truth. My journey into theological studies can best be described by focusing on some of the choices I have made as I struggled with polarities and dualities that often seemed beyond reconciliation.

Theological Questions: Theoretical and Practical

Since childhood I had noticed that the teaching of the church and the actual life of church members did not always correspond. My natural response to this disjunction between theory and practice, between knowing and doing, was to name practice as the real problem; indeed, it was relatively easy to label persons "hypocrites" because their walk did not match their talk. When I became more sensitive to the contradictions in my own life, I resolved to try harder to live out what I had been taught.

For me this unity of knowing and doing was "discipleship." My Anabaptist forebears had died because they too believed in this focus on practicing the faith. The quotation of Hans Denck was deeply ingrained in my consciousness: "No [one] can know Christ unless he [or she] follows after him in life."[8]

It wasn't until my second year in Bible college that I began to reflect more seriously on "knowing," the second aspect of this duality. How could I be sure that the knowledge that I was being taught was true?

I had enjoyed my first year of college, thriving on the social life of the community and the rigorous biblical study. Gradually, however, my experiences gave rise to theological questions that could no longer be satisfied by simple answers. My home church was embroiled in a conflict that involved my family and friends. As I watched the congregation play out its power struggles, and as I listened to the name-calling and rejection of persons whom I had considered sincere Christians, I recalled the images of the church that I had just studied. The church was the "body of Christ," the "temple of the Holy Spirit," the "family of God." Honesty demanded that I face the contradiction between the ideal and the real, the theory and the practice.

I consequently began to ask questions that had to do with the very source of my faith. Could I still name this group of people as "church" if there was so much inconsistency between word and deed? If God could not be found in this congregation, would I be able to find God anywhere else? If the church was suspect, what about my own life? To what reality did all our language about God and God's people actually refer?

Even the Bible became suspect for me. After all, I had been learning that it was written by ordinary people and authorized by the church through a long, difficult political process.

These questions focused in a crisis of faith for me the very semester that I had registered for several courses on Paul's epistles. It was these doubts and questions that enabled me to see the realism in Paul's letters (especially in 1 Corinthians), as he struggled with the problems and challenges faced by early Christians. I noted that the sinfulness of the congregation was not hidden or camouflaged in these letters. Yet Paul still dared to name this community the "body of Christ." Where did he find that faith? As I wrestled with these issues, the God of grace who accepts people wherever they are met me in the reality of life. I realized that only God could transform my home congregation into the people of God, the Bible into the Word of God, and me into a Christian.

A subtle change was beginning to happen in my theological beliefs. I started to appreciate that the reconciliation between theory and practice in our God-talk could only come about when God was actively transforming both human theory and human practice. Instead of relying on statements of belief, giving them ultimate authority, I began to trust the God who is beyond human systems of thought. This God encouraged me to explore the contradictions and tensions in our human belief systems in order that I could hear the Word of God anew.

I began to realize that "knowing the will of God" is not self-evident, but rather comes through a process of listening and waiting for the divine voice while exercising our God-given aptitudes and skills. Though raising questions would sometimes create strong objections and fears within the church, I determined not to be afraid to explore the language we used about God. After all, even our most lofty language can never be equated with God.

Gradually I became convinced that the "practice" of critical scholarly work could be helpful to the church in discerning the difference between human idols and the true God. But I also realized that accompanying that practice must be a faith in the presence of the Holy Spirit who could use our limited theological language to witness to the good news of the gospel. These convictions gave me the courage to enter the field of theology with a strong sense of personal calling from God.

A Scholarly Identity: Freedom and Responsibility

After a number of years of elementary school teaching and homemaking, I began to consider graduate studies in the field of theology. When I sought the advice of a Mennonite professor (and former teacher of mine), he encouraged me to begin taking some theological courses—this despite the fact that I was already in my early forties. Despite this encouragement, however, his next words presented me with major decisions, even as they created an identity crisis that occupied me for many years. He suggested that I was lucky that I could study theology "just for fun," implying that my work would not lead to an academic vocation, let alone a calling to serve the church. Rather, it would be a hobby.

I felt crushed and humiliated. Had I succumbed to that greatest of all sins—pride—by wanting to engage in a scholarly vocation? In the Anabaptist tradition, especially in the writings of Menno Simons, there exists a strong suspicion of the "learned ones" who do not have a calling from God.[9] More generally, there seems to be an underlying fear that scholarly activity will rely solely on human knowledge and that it will thereby lead to false teachings, pride, and the wrong use of power. After all, it was the educated theologians and preachers who persecuted the early Anabaptists! With these things in mind, I began to understand the reluctance of many Mennonite scholars to refer to themselves as "theologians" or "scholars," preferring instead the label "teachers."

Of course, my self-doubts were only exacerbated by being a woman. How could I, a woman, presume to have a calling from God to practice theology (a calling that would take me into the public sphere) when service in the domestic area was already my vocation as a female disciple? As I reflected upon the painful conversation with my mentor, I realized that he had accepted an implicit division between males and females, a division that assumed male responsibility for the church's leadership while restricting female responsibility to less prominent forms of churchly service, e.g., nurturing "personal faith" and "service."

This division was further confirmed for me a few years later, at a Mennonite theological conference to which I was invited. By the late 1980s there had been much ferment in the larger society and church about the need for women's voices in public conversations. As this meeting, however, only three of the one hundred delegates were women.

In light of these experiences, I began to search the Anabaptist-Mennonite tradition to understand the roots of the situation. As I did so, I discovered the struggle between various trajectories within the tradition, and even within the Bible itself. Again it was helpful to name these trajectories as human attempts to speak about the will of God, while realizing anew that God often speaks through the marginal voices and minority traditions. On a more personal note, I learned I could not escape the calling of God by bowing to dominant views. Instead, I was directly responsible to God for my theological work.

Thus, after a long struggle to own my interests, abilities, and calling, I (secretly) named myself an Anabaptist-Mennonite theologian. A retreat with Katie Funk Wiebe, a Mennonite writer who told of a similar struggle to name herself an author, encouraged me to accept both the privilege and the responsibility that this naming entailed. What freed me from the attempt to be "god-like" was again the acknowledgment that all theological research was a human enterprise. At the same time, naming theology a human endeavor affirmed for me the conviction that women shared completely in the human task of responsible discourse about God.

A Scholarly Language: Public and Communal

I had almost finished my master's degree in theology at a small Catholic seminary when I was asked to give my first theological paper at a Mennonite conference. True to Anabaptist convictions, the participants at that conference were made up of pastors, scholars, and lay persons. I had read extensively and rewritten my paper many times, using the latest theories on hermeneutics and authority to illuminate my ideas. At the same time, I had reflected on the biblical resources in an effort to correlate my ideas with the scriptures. Afterwards, a number of people remarked that my paper had been helpful.

What I remember most, however, was a critical remark made by someone from my home congregation. He asserted that he had understood nothing of what I had said. Why could I not use straightforward language that could be understood by everyone? Had I forgotten my roots in the congregation?

It is no accident that, in my research since that day, I have focused on the notion of the interpretive body, or "hermeneutic community."[10] According to John Howard Yoder, who invoked that term almost twenty years ago, the early Anabaptists insisted that biblical interpretation was best done in hermeneutic communities that were committed to structuring their communal life and practice according to their understanding of the text.[11] In other words, it was within a church congregation (not a scholarly gathering) that the best biblical interpretation took place, because the members of the congregation were actively involved in discerning God's will in their lives.

Practically speaking, of course, theological conversation in the Anabaptist tradition has usually been limited to persons of the same sex, ethnic identity, and social class. But the notion of a "hermeneutic community" has nonetheless meant that the role and authority of the theological scholar in congregational life has been ambiguous—an ambiguity that is particularly evident in discussions about the kind of language that scholars should use and the kind of accountability that scholars should have to the church.

In response to such discussions, I have found helpful Walter Brueggemann's imagery of a "wall" that separates the community of faith from the larger society.[12] Brueggemann suggests that people of faith, particularly theologians, must learn to be bilingual, speaking different languages in their different conversations. Their primary theological conversations will take place "behind the wall," with other members of their faith community. Here they will use a communal language, a language shaped by the conviction that God is alive and active in the world.

But the wall is more than a boundary that keeps the world out; it is a meeting place where people with different perspectives on reality gather. People of faith must therefore carry on conversations that take place "on the wall," conversations that will need to be conducted in a "foreign" tongue. Indeed, because these public conversations are frequently constructed around outsiders' dominant perceptions of reality, they will often use a language that assumes a different view of the world from the insiders' view.

Sometimes these meetings on the wall will be friendly, creating new insights for both insiders and outsiders. Sometimes, however, these meetings will be controversial or even hostile.

Whatever the climate, conversations on the wall carry with them inherent dangers and tensions. While they may be tempted to do so, the faithful who stand on the wall dare not ally themselves with the powerful in society, who assert that their language is the only universal language and the only grounds for negotiation. At the same time, because this conversation on the wall is a public conversation, the faithful dare not monopolize their sense of truth. The best the faithful can do in this regard is to thoughtfully translate the convictions of the church into a foreign tongue and thereby propose alternative views of reality to those on the other side of the wall.

Of course, even this carries dangers and temptations. Too often those in the church will consider this translating work marginal, even heretical. On the other hand, those involved in the translating process (including theologians) can all too easily forget the more primary language of the faith community and instead bow to the absolute claims of the public view.

I have often become aware of the bilingual nature of theological language, as well as the temptations that come to those standing on the wall. I have realized that I cannot collapse the two languages (the communal and the foreign) into one language without giving up the integrity of my own calling. I therefore stand on the wall, sometimes speaking a foreign language, sometimes speaking in my own primary tongue, but always attempting to witness to the truth wherever it is found.

A Scholarly Method: Suspicion and Obedience

One of the first choices that must be made when one begins doctoral studies in theology is to decide among the distinct departments within the larger school of theology. Since Anabaptists have not been able to imagine theology without a serious study of the Bible, I had assumed that I would enter the biblical studies department.

The director of the program affirmed my choice—until I said that I was interested in the contemporary meaning of the Bible. He quickly informed me that I could not do that in the biblical studies department, because that department concentrated on the historical meaning of the texts. I was therefore told to register in the systematic theology department, where I soon discovered that the basic division between departments also discouraged any connection between the practice of reading the Bible and contemporary theological reflection. In none of my theology classes was the Bible ever used directly or recommended as reading material. My greatest conflict with one of my committee members had to do with her objection to my wish to explore particular biblical texts as I worked on my thesis. That would be "crossing disciplines," she said, and I therefore would not have adequate tools for that task. Moreover, she assumed that my interest in using the Bible as a resource was merely a naive fideistic strategy rather than a rational-critical approach to theological method.

I began to realize that theological scholarship is complicated not only because it is human discourse about the divine. It is also complex because each of the different interpretive communities roots its language in its own authoritative presuppositions, convictions, and methodological approaches.

How does a theological scholar negotiate her way between the contrasting claims of university and church? Can one be detached and objective, as is often demanded by the university, and still be committed to faith perspectives as required by the church? Alternatively, can one do scholarship for the church and not succumb to merely justifying the church and its interests and actions?

It was within these tensions that I began to hammer out my own methodological approach to theology and particularly to the Bible.[13] My rootedness in the Anabaptist tradition, long suspicious of "the world," encouraged me to ask critical questions about the function of departmental boundaries in the university.

Gradually I noticed that one central function of these boundaries was the protection of the interests of scholars in each discipline. This realization gave me the courage to explore a variety of disciplinary approaches to theology despite the objections of my advisory committee. In this process I gained new tools and perspectives from which to analyze my own theological tradition. For example, philosophical studies opened my eyes to the importance of language that can connect past and present, thus making the past active in the present; biblical studies illuminated the truth claims within historical texts, claims that continue to challenge present understandings; sociological studies described the relationship between particular social-political contexts and theological language in both past and present; and systematic theology helped me to understand the networks of beliefs developed over time.

One significant result of this approach was that I became increasingly suspicious when the church justified its beliefs by appealing to biblical proof texts. I had long suspected that Christians feared a critical look at their cherished beliefs because they might not hold up to inspection, and scholarly methods helped me distance myself from my own theological tradition in order that I might assess its claims more critically. This in turn led me to an intensive study of the book of Mark, with a particular focus on the pre-understandings that I myself had been bringing to the text.

It was during this study that I first noticed the difficulty that the disciples had in "hearing" the divine Word in the words of the Jesus, a deafness that was rooted in their political aspirations and strivings.[14] I realized anew that revelation cannot be guaranteed by our appeal to being disciples (the "people of God") or by our insistence that we are the ones who are simply obeying the Bible. Instead, our focus must be on opening our ears by becoming self-critical to hear anew God's self-disclosure. In sum, suspicion of others' claims must always stand side by side with the suspicion of our own superficial claims to truth.

The theological methodology that has emerged for me therefore refuses to accept the polarity commonly assumed by scholars—a polarity that places critical thinking and religious commitment, human endeavor and divine revelation, at opposite ends of scholarship. Both objectivism, with its scholarly detachment, and biased scholarship, with its assumption of the relativity of all truth, are rejected. Instead our prior commitments and interests must be identified to open ourselves to methodological distancing and critical accountability.

Accountability to more than one community encourages self-conscious choices between various claims to truth while, at the same time, opening up a space to listen again to God's disruptive Word. This critical discernment rests on the ultimate faith that the Creator God was active in the particularity of Jesus and continues to be actively present within human history through the Spirit.

A Scholar's Ethic: Power and Vulnerability

It was during my graduate studies that I began to realize that methods stressing logical coherence and rational justification were not enough to legitimate a claim to truth. Indeed, I realized that the constructive task of interpreting the Bible, of finding language to speak of God and the world, is an ethical practice and therefore needs also to be judged by its use within particular contexts.

Correspondingly, I began to struggle with the way biblical language such as "servanthood" and the "way of the cross" had been used within the Mennonite church to justify the marginalization of women and the silencing of victims of sexual abuse.[15] At the same time, I became aware of how society at large had legitimated its treatment of First Nations people by using Christian theological language. My reading of liberation theologians further sensitized me to the political dimensions of language use. And I recognized that, as an Anabaptist, I too was part of a minority theological tradition that had been trivialized throughout much of recent history. I therefore began to turn my attention to issues of authority and power, focusing especially on the power of biblical language as it is used to speak of the divine.

Indeed, as long as theological language is considered only theoretical, it does not have much power to heal or hurt. Only when we begin to understand that language use is a praxis—that is, a combination of theory and practice can we begin to speak of the power of our scholarly work.[16] Moreover, only when we see communication (listening, speaking, writing, and teaching) as central to our churchly task can we understand the need for ethical criteria for those actions.

Having made those recognitions, and desiring such ethical criteria for my own scholarly activity, I looked to the Anabaptist tradition for assistance. Ethics, nonviolence, and peacemaking have always been considered central to Anabaptism, but I discovered that modern-day Anabaptists wrestled more with business decisions, political processes, and personal ethics than with ethics for the idea-oriented professions.

What the Anabaptist tradition did provide, however, was the Bible—more specifically the Bible as a model for a communication salvific for people throughout the centuries. As I explored this text more thoroughly, I discovered a Bible that is vulnerable to misinterpretation because it was formed within human history, a Bible that nevertheless has integrity because it included the voices of many different kinds of people.

I found within the Bible a conversation (and sometimes even a struggle) between traditions that allowed no one tradition to be supreme, since only God was to be worshiped. For example, the Torah tradition of Moses was often challenged and renewed by the prophetic tradition. The wisdom tradition, which included much knowledge from outside of Israel, was challenged by the exodus tradition, which speaks of a unique experience of salvation and election. And the messianic tradition of a warrior king was challenged by the Messiah Jesus, who came in peace and reconciliation.

This shape of the biblical canon, replete with its many voices and perspectives, created a new set of questions for my own theological work. Who was included and who was excluded in the scholarly discourse in which I participated? Were certain people's writings excluded because of race, gender, or political commitments? A quick survey of the books on my shelves testified to a rather limited conversation.

In my reflections I began to focus more and more on the area of dialogue, asking questions of power and authority. What does it mean to listen to the voice of the marginal and powerless? How can theologians speak authentically about their own discoveries and convictions while being open to the views of the "other?"

Reflecting on the Anabaptist tradition with its ethic of justice, nonviolence, and peace has been helpful to me. More and more I have realized that being vulnerable and open to critical dialogue comes first of all with a strong sense of God's active role in the whole world—even beyond the church. I do not need to resort to weapons of destructive words nor appeal to divine justification if l can acknowledge that the knowledge of God is always beyond all of us.

I do not need to defend God, if God will ultimately be the one who reveals truth and destroys falsehood. I can open myself to the dialogue of others because I believe that God loved the world and offers everyone revelation and salvation. I do not need to feel threatened by those with whom I differ; rather, I can be both discerning and open to the words of others. I must therefore acknowledge the power of my words while remaining vulnerable, opening myself to a broad group of critical conversation partners.

Theology's Focus: Process and Truth

In 1987 I was asked to be on the Faith and Life Committee of the Mennonite World Conference. During the three years leading up to the celebration in Winnipeg, Manitoba, a small group of representatives from the broader Mennonite world tried to hammer out a confession of faith that would provide the language for a public act of commitment during the final worship service.

Because we came from radically different contexts, and because we wanted the statement to have integrity, we became very sensitive to the kind of process that we needed to engage in. We attempted to draw many different people into the process, to work at the power issues that were involved, and to look at the different theological approaches that were natural for different groups of people.

While I continue to affirm that sort of careful process, I must also acknowledge my final, post-conference reflection: regardless of the process, the powerful words of the confession mean nothing if they are not true. If God is not active in our history, it really doesn't matter that we have worked out a wonderfully freeing process of theological reasoning. Process must be connected to convictions that have substance.

This has been one of my growing insights. The process of theoretical work is a political process and must have integrity. However, theology is finally of value if God's real presence among us is discerned and named.

This implies some substantive naming of Truth. Yet no naming of God can adequately describe the God beyond names. I have therefore found it helpful to use the term "truth claims" to stress the fact that, when I am convinced of an aspect of truth, it begins to make its claims on my life. I cannot go back to what I have known before without losing my sense of integrity. My worldview begins to shift to include this new insight, and with this shift comes the urge to communicate what I believe to be true.

But which language shall I use to express my limited sense of who God is and what is true? Traditionally Anabaptists have rejected philosophical, symbolic, and more doctrinal language in favor of concrete biblical language (e.g., "following Jesus"). At the same time, we have been influenced by the various streams of theological thinking around us, particularly those that stress literal interpretations of Scripture and the factually oriented language of science and technology. Will our traditional approach to theological language be rich enough to mediate experiences of the transcendent God in this age? Or are there new images, concepts, and metaphors that can speak truthfully in our day?

Recently I have begun to move into the more intuitive language of symbol and image in my public speaking. This overtly multivalent language tends to open us to dialogue and challenges us to rethink our convictions and re-imagine our visions for the future.[17] Instead of using language that communicates supremacy and absolute authority, I search for simple but rich terms that will witness to something larger than the words themselves. Thus, for example, in speaking about the Bible's power, I do not begin with talk of inspiration and revelation. Instead, I use the image of the Bible as our "home." This encourages exploration of the "family" narrative and the various discussions that arise from interpretations of that common story. It also allows us to acknowledge the dysfunctional aspects of how that home has functioned in our lives.[18] At the same time, confessing the Bible as home points to how our very identity as Christians is totally dependent on the one to whom the Bible points with its rich imagery and narrative.

As a "biblical people," Anabaptist-Mennonites have been tempted to focus on factual language to draw boundaries around God. In the process we have sometimes created a God too small to worship. Focusing on the richness of language by multiple witnesses is a new way to point to God, who is beyond our human limitations, even the limits of our theological language. And it is to that God of Truth that all theological language must point.

The Scholarly Agenda: Individual and Communal

The phone call from Mennonite Central Committee (MCC) seemed innocent enough. Would our fledgling institution consider hosting some Muslim exchange students from Iran? The complications of arranging a doctoral program for Islamic students at the Toronto School of Theology, with its Christian commitments and its university affiliation, did not immediately strike me. Instead, I became excited about the opportunity to be involved in interreligious dialogue as part of MCC's larger peacemaking effort. After all, I was aware of how often interreligious conflict was at the root of war.

Soon I realized that a theoretical understanding of dialogue does not always include an awareness of the time and energy needed to ensure authentic conversations with those of different cultures and religions. This realization was driven home again this past year, when my husband and I were asked to visit Iran. There we spent several weeks in a totally Muslim environment. I had not counted on this kind of intensive encounter. In fact, my scholarly research had been going in a different direction, focusing most directly on my own heritage of faith. I had been quite content to stay within a more comfortable Christian (albeit university) context. The new theme of interfaith dialogue felt somewhat intrusive.

This experience raised important questions for me. How do I choose my specific research projects? What motivates me in my choices? How do I discern which projects to spend time on? I realize that often my own interests and curiosity—my questions and suspicions as well as my past experiences dictate my choice of subject. Sometimes the larger church community assigns a topic to me. Usually financial remuneration has not been the largest factor, though I have realized that it is tempting to work in those areas for which research grants are more easily available.

I have learned to say yes to certain assignments within my area of expertise and no to others. Sometimes, however, I am drawn into an unexpected area, as in the cases above. It is then that I need to discern whether this is a call to me to move beyond my own comfort zone. Usually this is a time for self-reflection and reprioritizing my work.

At times I have even called together a group of people from the church to help me in this decision making. If my research is to be of use and relevant to the larger church and society, I must also pay attention not only to my own interests but to what the needs of the community are.

I have discovered that my endurance during the slow, sometimes agonizing work of research is proportional to the degree to which the personal and the communal agendas come together. This means that I must maintain contact with both the church and the university to choose projects that will be relevant as well as interesting.

Choosing a Third Way

Naming myself a theologian in the Anabaptist tradition has been a long and gradual process. The tensions that invariably arise when the words scholar and Anabaptist Christian are placed side by side have no doubt nourished some of my most fruitful and satisfying scholarly work. At the same time, I have discovered that being accountable to both the church and the scholarly community is exceedingly difficult. Again and again I am faced with crucial ethical and faith decisions arising out of these commitments.

Having experienced the reality that neither the church nor the scholarly community fully understands or supports me in this work, I have often been tempted to align myself with one or the other to dissolve the tensions. Yet the place on the "wall" is the place to which I am called. Here I can work out a third way beyond the polarities and dualisms that ask me to reject either the world that God created or the church that is called to witness to God's salvation.

It is here on the wall that I feel I can be most open to God's revealing presence. Indeed, it is through my work as a theologian that I most freely and joyfully witness to the God that I have come to know.

* * *

RECEIVING THE BLESSING WITH THANKSGIVING[19]

I read the litany almost with disbelief. Even though I had been included in many ways in the formal farewell weekend when the retirement from full-time pastoral ministry of my husband was celebrated, I had not expected the words I now read. My friend had given the litany to me, since we now no longer attended the church where Gary had pastored for 20 years. The litany was read on a Thanksgiving Sunday several months after we left the church. It was a way for the church to let go and begin a new journey without letting the past interfere with new directions. It was entitled a "Litany of Thanksgiving"[20] and began with these words:

> Generous God we know that all good gifts come from you.
> We give thanks for the gift of Gary and Lydia's ministry.
> Their giving has strengthened and deepened our common life.
> They have blessed us in many ways for many years.

It was what followed that was totally unexpected. Alternately, there was a celebration of Gary's gifts with my gifts. There was no difference between thanks for the gifts of the ordained pastor and thanks for the gifts of me, a lay member of the church. And what was particularly moving was that these gifts were mentioned by name. In fact, these gifts were the very ones that I had tried to nourish and develop.

The litany began with thanks for the preaching ministry. I had been a part of the lay preaching team in the congregation for several terms. Members of this team preached several times a year, but more importantly they suggested themes and texts for sermon series, they evaluated and tested sermon ideas, they supported and encouraged the pastors in their preaching and they drew in other lay members of the church to also preach. I had thoroughly enjoyed that aspect of church life.

> Gary's preaching was perhaps his greatest contribution to our church
> He loved words, he knew their power; he crafted them carefully.
> He spoke words of challenge, caring and inspiration,
> Refreshing words that shaped and sharpened our understanding
> Of what it means to follow Christ.
>
> Lydia had an enthusiasm and love for the Biblical text.
> She probed deeply, asked hard questions,
> Made discoveries and wanted us to do the same.
> The Bible was not simply the object of her academic study;
> It was a place of life-giving encounter with the Holy Spirit.
> And this encounter was meant to continually refine
> The beliefs and practices of the church.

Another part of the litany touched on one of the inner struggles I had in being the wife of a pastor at a time when there was a shift from lay pastoral leadership to professional leadership, and from more defined roles for men and women to more creative discovery and use of every person's gift in the church. Interestingly, that part of the litany came under thanks for being a "role model."

> She was the traditional pastor's wife supporting her spouse
> Raising a family, feeding the 5,000 at a moment's notice.
> She was the non-traditional scholar/theologian,
> Preaching, teaching, shepherding doctoral students.
> Lydia embraced both roles and we were the richer for this.

As I reflect today on 6 years of pastoral ministry, I recognize that this litany was the blessing I needed to move more directly into pastoral ministry. The last shreds of anger, bitterness, and envy were dissolved as I received these words of blessing from the congregation that knew me best. I could now be a co-pastor with my husband without the burden of unresolved emotions that could easily have affected our work. The naming of the specific gifts that are mine assured me that, yes, I could be a pastor and could use my gifts wisely in a congregational setting. I felt free to tell my husband that no longer would I be a pastor's wife while he did interim pastor pastoral work in other congregations. Instead I wanted to be a co-pastor with him during these few senior years left for us to work.

Our partnership had developed over the years and now both of us felt very comfortable in working together. We have parented and done home-making together but have also co-taught a course on church and ministry at Conrad Grebel University College for over 10 years. I joined him on the preaching team at the church and we stimulated each other with ideas from our reading. We've even led some workshops together. We have used the image of pairs dancing in some of the pre-marriage counselling that we have done together and that image is also a good one to describe our work relationship. For it is in pairs dancing that each dancer makes both their individual dance moves as well as the moves that are made in total sync with each other. I recognize now that I needed the years when I developed my own gifts and confidence just as Gary needed to develop his. I needed to get in touch with my inner self with all of its passions, both its pain and its joys. The years of home-making, of scholarly pursuits and of teaching were years of learning to know myself better and of finding a calling that went beyond a particular job.

The recognition that I was envious of my husband in his pastoral role came very early in our marriage. In those early years, I wrote a piece about being a pastor's wife for a meeting with other wives of pastors. I admitted that I had tried to work out my own calling by giving my husband all kinds of unneeded advice as to who to visit, as to what to preach and as to how to lead organizationally in the church. Because I could not be a pastor in the Mennonite church at the time because I was female, I found unhelpful ways to still work through my husband. As a home-maker I was jealous of the theological discussions and support that Gary got from his peer group and I was angry that women did a lot of the work in the church but received little recognition. Yet I was happy to be a particular pastor's wife, that is Gary's wife. Supporting him in his role, as I would have supported him no matter what profession he had chosen, was something that I would always want to do.

It was many years later that I recognized the pain that had been hidden as I entered the scholarly world and found my own niche in teaching theology. I often attended continuing education meetings for pastors as they overlapped with my interest in teaching in the ministry department. At one such meeting the speaker was Celia Hahn who lectured on how pastors could grow in authority without becoming controlling.[21] She explained the various ways in which we can become persons with "integrated" authority. Autonomy and assertiveness are joined to received authority in a joyful sharing of our power with others. In the small group discussion later, I was suddenly overcome with emotion. I was weeping because I had gotten in touch with an unspoken inner dream of becoming a pastor. For the first time I admitted to myself that I had gifts and abilities and visions that would have helped me to be a good pastor. I admitted the pain that was deep within me because I had been excluded from that profession because I was a woman. I recognized that my interest in feminist theology had much to do with my own experience of feeling excluded from pastoral ministry. Admitting that pain was the beginning of a healing process in which I claimed my own power and my own vocation, thus integrating my theology deeply with my emotional being.

At retirement age, after years in which my primary work had been in teaching and scholarship, I entered pastoral ministry. One of the first questions that came to me from the search committee that was interviewing us was totally unexpected. "How do you justify "biblically" being a woman in pastoral ministry?" I was somewhat stumped at first as to how to respond. Yet I had no lingering feelings of resentment at the nature of the question. I felt it was an honest question by someone who had not been able to reconcile the literal words of Paul with the present acceptance of women in leadership. I was able to respond without being defensive, pointing to the women at the tomb who were given the mandate to go and tell the other disciples that Jesus had risen from the dead. In my later ministry in that congregation I was able to freely engage the women and men who still had doubts about women's roles. I was also happy to learn that they hired a female pastor after we left the congregation.

The years of doing interim ministry in three congregations has felt like "icing on the cake" as I now reflect on my career choices. I have enjoyed many aspects of my career path whether this was in home-making, scholarship, teaching, or administration. But for me, becoming a pastor brought together so many facets of who I am, allowing me to express myself freely through my work. Though the congregations that we pastored had some difficult challenges to work through, I felt energized and joyful. My love of people, my analytical abilities, my theological insights, my administrative capabilities all had a place in this profession. As I worked together with Gary I felt particularly happy that we could so easily live out the mutuality between men and women in our ministry, a mutuality that I had craved earlier.

One of the aspects of pastoral ministry that I particularly enjoyed was the opportunity to use some of the frameworks and ideas that I had gained in my readings for the course on church and ministry that I had taught regularly. I was a teaching pastor and found that the resources that I had gained over the years could easily be used to communicate with adults and children. I also enjoyed the creativity and flexibility in pastoring that is not always appreciated by those who have always done it. One surprise was that I really enjoyed administration, working with committees on overall goals while making sure that care was taken with the details. (This was something that my husband was glad to hand over to me!)

Even before pastoring I had enjoyed discovering the unrecognized gifts of people and assisting them to use them in God's kingdom. Pastoring gave me a unique opportunity to develop a keener eye and ear to hear these hidden desires and to recognize the hidden gifts. Recently a woman (I will name her Sue) came to me at a gathering and thanked me profusely for my presence in her congregation. Sue had a history of mental illness and had always found it difficult to find her place within the church. She recalled a turning point in this relationship. Often she had been asked to do things in the church for which she felt unsuited, which then became a burden to her. In one of our visits she told me how much she loved knitting and crocheting (something she said she would have never mentioned to a male pastor). The prayer shawl ministry that I had only recently heard about came to mind. It took only a small bit of encouragement for the congregation to add this to their caring ministry. I recall the public blessing prayed for the people who would receive the shawls and for those who were knitting prayers into each shawl. Sue joyfully told me how many shawls she had knit and how vital this ministry was to her. These kinds of affirmation confirmed for me that God had indeed called me, with my particular experiences and gifts, into pastoring at that time and place.

However, becoming a pastor was not my vocation writ large. Instead, my vocation has always been larger than any particular role. The calling that I have felt throughout my life continues to be a calling even as I retire from official ministry. Each time that my giftedness and the world's needs come together in particular relationships, or actions or words, I thank the Creator for the gift of life given me, the Spirit for the way she has led me and Jesus who has called me and has shown me the way. I feel richly blessed.

Chapter 2. Hermeutic Community

NAMING THE CONTEXT

"Are you religious?" was the first question that I encountered when I entered the halls of Newman College, a Catholic seminary near Edmonton, Alberta in 1980. Not understanding that I was being asked whether I was a member of a religious order, I naively answered, "Yes." My naivety about persons of faith from other denominations showed itself in other ways. My Bible College studies, finished almost 20 years earlier, had prepared me well for graduate studies in the biblical and historical fields. But I was ill prepared for more philosophically oriented theology, for the focus on doctrine and tradition, or for concern with the official magisterium. I hardly knew what Vatican II was all about with its shocking revolution of thought and worship within the Catholic church. I did not understand the centrality of the Eucharist in Catholic worship. Nor did I get the joke when my classmates chuckled at my reference to "non-Mennonites"—as if the whole world revolved around my small denomination. (Come to think of it, did it really make more sense to speak of non-Catholics?)

I encountered the question of theological methodology in one of the first courses in the Master of Theology program taught by Sister Lina Gaudette. She became a valuable role model and mentor to me with her rigorous demands and probing questions as well as her gentle support. Already in that class I had to write a paper articulating my own approach to theology—an approach I named "neo-Anabaptism," which emphasized a hermeneutical approach to revelation as a way to "hear" the divine voice.

The program that I entered demanded both a comprehensive oral exam in the various branches of Christian theology as well as a thesis that needed to be defended in a public forum (mine reaching 150 pages). My advisor, Father Martin Moser, was well suited to preparing me for both the exam as well as the thesis. He was the kind of advisor who thought through my thesis with me, always bringing one more book for me to read that he just happened to find—right on my topic!

His close involvement also became a problem for me because we both tended to think comprehensively and found it difficult to move into a more analytical mode. Though he advised me to be more focused in order to finish my thesis, our discussions were always wide-ranging, raising more questions than answers. I received a good grounding in Catholic doctrine and passed the exam handily. My thesis explored the notion of hermeneutic community—the notion of a corporate discernment of Scripture within a covenant community—an idea gleaned from the Anabaptist tradition. This topic was congruent with the vision of community I had gleaned from my own church experience, though I already had a niggling suspicion that my experience as a woman in community was different from that of my male friends.

As I reflect back now, I recognize the seeds of future study in these first scholarly attempts to articulate my theological approach. Studying in a Catholic context encouraged me to uncover my own assumptions and differentiate them from those of my fellow students. At the same time, I became more aware of the larger theological world that I was entering with its distinctive vocabulary. To articulate my convictions using the frameworks and language of the academy and ecumenical context was challenging. My definitions of community were expanded and changed in unexpected and liberating ways.

The thesis, "Hermeneutic Community: The Contemporary Relevance of an Anabaptist-Mennonite Approach to Biblical Interpretation," examined the role of the community in the hermeneutical process from three main perspectives. The first perspective, biblical-historical reflection looked at the relationship between text and context in the formation of Scripture to discover the implications of this basic relationship for the hermeneutical process. My conversation partners in this section were well known biblical scholars such as James A. Sanders, Bernard Childs, Norman Gottwald, Walter Brueggeman, and Paul Achtemeier. This was familiar territory from my Bible College days. The second perspective, a broad philosophical and theological one, focused on theories of understanding and reflects on epistemology, ontology, and hermeneutics in order to understand the phenomenon of textural interpretation. This topic was foreign territory for me and I struggled to understand even a bit of what philosophers such as Hans-Georg Gadamer, Jürgen Habermas, and Paul Riceour were saying. This introduction to these conversation partners created a thirst in me for more philosophically oriented knowledge and greatly influenced me later during my doctoral studies. Finally, I included a third perspective, the practical-theological, which relates more to the pastoral situation and to how a community actually reads Scripture. Here various political and liberation theologians were particularly helpful such as Jürgen Moltman, José Miguez Bonino, and Elisabeth Schüssler Fiorenza. All of these perspectives both challenged and confirmed aspects of the Anabaptist-Mennonite understandings.

The interdisciplinary nature of the thesis pointed to the need I felt for an integrated basis from which to do theology. I was looking for something that would bring together my experience in the congregation and in my denominational context with the broader world of scholarship in an ecumenical and academic context. I was also growing uneasy with the many polarities that I experienced within the scholarly world. The basic division between subject and object that modernity had promoted in its search for factual truth seemed to create other dualisms such as the ones between universal truth and particular truth, theory and practice, and even male and female theological writings. Coming face to face with the relativity of knowledge raised many questions around the authority of Scripture. The seeds for my doctoral work were planted in those years at Newman College.

During these studies, I was still primarily a home-maker, involved with Sunday school teaching and helping to establish a day-care within our church. My volunteer work included answering phone calls at a newly established Distress Line (a suicide prevention program), visiting patients in the hospital, and chairing the board of our church's daycare centre. My weekly women's Bible study group kept me grounded in congregational hermeneutics while I struggled with theoretical frameworks. Our three children provided an antidote to my serious work, allowing me time away to delight in joyful play and to solve the practical issues that came with parenting teenagers.

I wrote the thesis in long hand since I had never learned to type. Every day my husband typed out my scribbled notes on his 20-year-old typewriter. Eventually I hired a typist to create the finished manuscript. My family and academic context were still in the pre-computer world in which terms such as "save," "search," "web," and "network" were not technical terms. Encyclopaedias and dictionaries (as in books) were still the primary sources of general knowledge. Index cards were used to gather and sort the quotes from the books I was reading. "Cut and paste" were literal terms and much time was spent on retyping; there was no "insert footnote" mechanism to easily keep track of my sources and no way to "google" for information.

The changes that were happening in my context were both personal and social. Slowly I was becoming conscious of the term postmodernity and the challenge it would bring not only to theology but also to the way scholars access sources and communicate with the church. In addition, I was moving from a primarily domestic sphere to the public sphere, from home and church congregation to the academic and ecumenical context. My identity as wife, mother, elementary school teacher and church member was changing to include scholar, theologian and tentatively feminist. This shift felt risky as well as exciting.

I have included the final conclusion of my unpublished thesis since it illustrates my earliest attempts to define and enlarge the meaning of hermeneutic community, a notion strongly rooted in my own Mennonite tradition. It is a prelude to the articles that follow, as it attempts to apply the notion of hermeneutic community to congregational life from the point of view of feminist theology. The last article, though written somewhat later, includes the way feminist theology has shaped my view of the Bible, especially in the face of violence toward women justified by an appeal to Scripture. These essays point to my doctoral work where I used the term hermeneutic community as a heuristic device to analyze both Mennonite and feminist communities and their interpretive practices. I continue to see it as a helpful tool for identifying the multiple socio-economic and theological contexts that shape our experiences.

* * *

A REDEFINITION OF HERMENEUTIC COMMUNITY[1]

The attempt to examine the contemporary relevance of the Anabaptist-Mennonite communal approach to hermeneutics in my thesis has led to a close look at the interpretive process itself. This has been done in an interdisciplinary context in which the distinct insights of each approach were acknowledged and respected. This recognizes the fact that each perspective comes to its descriptive and analytical task from within a distinct framework and with particular concerns in mind. Each approach highlights certain aspects of hermeneutics while neglecting others. Much of the dialogue between the various approaches is just beginning to happen, and therefore any definitive explanation of the interpretive process is not forthcoming. However, certain commonalities are beginning to emerge.

These trends in recent hermeneutical theory show considerable compatibility with the Anabaptist-Mennonite approach. At the same time, they provide insights which will refine, enlarge, and elaborate on the basic Anabaptist-Mennonite definition of hermeneutic community. The following understandings, arising out of the convergence of the various perspectives, are important for a redefinition of hermeneutic community:

1) There is a general recognition of the importance of the social location of the interpreter and therefore of the interrelatedness of personal and communal tradition. The philosophical perspectives of Gadamer, Habermas and Ricoeur are particularly helpful, for they affirm that both the horizon of the interpreter and the horizon of the text are involved in the hermeneutical process.

2) Several crucial aspects of the communal context of interpretation have been emphasized by the various approaches:

   a. Communal traditions produce the pre-judgements and preunderstandings with which the interpreters approach the scriptural text.
   b. Communal structures and institutions affect the vital communication process which validates the interpretation.
   c. Communal language in its various modes of discourse mediates the meaning of the text.

3) It seems clear that a particular communal horizon can either help or hinder the hearing of the truth of the text. Various levels of community involvement all contribute to this horizon. (e.g. general cultural milieu, scholarly

world, geographical and social community, church congregation.)

4) Because this communal involvement, whether recognized or not, is active in all interpretation, there is a growing realization of the importance of bringing the various loyalties and commitments to consciousness to avoid ideology and false consciousness. This means a realization that we both stand within a given community, as well as choose community loyalties.

5) It is in a dialectical process of critical listening and genuine response to both text and fellow interpreters that personal and communal understanding occur. Dialogue is central to the communal process.

6) The priority of the faith community as a context which contributes to hearing the truth of Scripture has been generally affirmed. The characteristics of such a faith community include a dynamic faith heritage, a rich faith experiential base and an authentic faith praxis.

These understandings of the hermeneutical process imply that, though every interpretation of Scripture is conditioned and influenced by the communal context, a deliberate communal approach to hermeneutics can lead to a deeper discernment of the text. The term *hermeneutic community* thus indicates an approach in which conscious commitment to a community of reference and accountability accompanies an openness to dialogue and critique. It includes identifying with communal tradition, participating in communal praxis, but also being involved in critical communal reflection. It therefore implies a dialectical process between the prophetic voice and the consensus of tradition. This definition of hermeneutic community influences every aspect of interpretation. The implications can be focused by relating this communal approach to a number of polarities existing in the contemporary hermeneutical discussion. By noting positions and counterpositions in the three areas of authority, role of faith and goal of interpretation, the way the communal approach can provide a direction for a resolution or synthesis will be clarified. In this way the contemporary relevance of hermeneutic community will be indicated.

Context of Authoritative Interpretation

In an age of pluralism, the discussion concerning the authority of biblical interpretation is particularly crucial. Two responses to today`s gradual breakup of the orthodox consensus of the past can be discerned. The first tends to appeal to the *absolute* authority of certain interpreters, pointing to the "givenness" of their power and influence because of some quality which gives them inherent superiority. We can note this in the appeal to traditional authority, where power is located in an office or position given by birth, tradition or election. However, absolutism is also evident in the appeals to reason or charisma, where power is given by virtue of skill, training, personality, or education. This type of authority gives the right to persons possessing it to teach, while expecting others to listen and learn from their interpretations. It makes select persons responsible for the interpretation, while releasing others from that responsibility. There is a stress on right and wrong interpretations. Concern with unity, stability and accurate transmission of authoritative interpretations is central.

In contrast, the second approach to authority emphasizes the *relativity* of all interpretation. Plurality is assumed to be positive, and there is a great tolerance for other persons' points of view. Individual freedom and the authority of personal conscience are highly prized. Scripture interpretation that is flexible and adapts to each person's unique needs and concerns, is the ideal.

The definition of hermeneutic community as outlined above, can provide some direction toward finding an alternative to either of these extreme approaches. Though the need for authority is recognized in order that a community can have identity and act creatively, absolutism is limited by the stress on a dialogical communication process. Though the variety of personal experiences and situations are affirmed, individualism is equally tempered by the commitment to community process. Offices, roles, training and abilities become functional, serving a catalytic function as the community works at differences and agreements. Ephesians 4 in its picture of the faith community as the body of Christ, brings together the variety of personal gifts, critical dialogue and authoritative interpretation that shapes and transforms the community. As a description of the faith community in its hermeneutic function, these verses can have particular relevance for the issue of authority today.

> The *gifts* he gave were that some would be apostles, some prophets, some evangelists, some pastors and teachers, *to equip the saints for the work of ministry, for building up the body of Christ,* until all of us come to the *unity of the faith and of the knowledge of the Son of God,* to maturity, to the measure of the full stature of Christ.... But *speaking the truth in love,* we must grow up in every way into him who is the head, into Christ, from whom the whole body, joined and knit together by every ligament with which it is equipped, as each part is working properly, promotes the body's growth in building itself up in love.[2]

Role of Faith in the Interpretive Process

The way the role of faith is perceived in the interpretive process is largely dependent on the way faith is defined. If the emphasis is primarily on faith as *content*, the focus will be on the role of beliefs, doctrines, principles and laws that provide a framework for interpretive studies. Church tradition has crystalized certain interpretations which are considered universally valid. These rest on the sure foundation of the inspiration and infallibility of Scripture. Faith is a response of receptivity to God, who through grace has provided structure and stability on which we can rely in our interpretive work.

The opposite pole emphasizes faith as personal *experience.* The creative, spontaneous aspect of the faith response to God is given prime importance. Interpretation is a dynamic process in which personal appropriation is considered crucial. The Bible speaks anew to each generation, and therefore interpretation can be innovative and creative. Faith is response to God the Holy Spirit, who endows each person with the charismatic gifts which will open Scripture for him/her.

The communal approach to hermeneutics challenges an exclusive emphasis on either direction. The stress on the static content-centred role of faith in the interpretive process is challenged by the recognition that institutions and structures can serve both good and evil. Tradition comes to us as a mixed stream of human sinfulness as well as God's grace. Rituals and language forms can become dead and ideological. The critique of the prophet is needed to help open the traditions to new life.

Those who stress the dynamic, experienced-centred role of faith need to be reminded of their rootedness in communal structure. A creative faith response is only possible because it has been nourished by the symbols and traditions of the past. At the same time, because the danger of false consciousness in the individual response, there is need to critique the content of traditional interpretations.

A dialogical, communal approach to hermeneutics takes both structure and process into account. The apostle Paul models this approach for us in his letter to the Corinthians when he expresses an equal concern for process and for a stable content of faith.

> Let two or three prophets speak, and let the others weigh what is said.... For you can all prophesy one by one, so that all may learn and all be encouraged.
>
> Now I would remind you, bothers and sisters, of the good news that I proclaimed to you, which you in turn received, in which also you stand, through which also you are being saved, if you hold firmly to the message that I proclaimed to you.[3]

Goal of the Interpretive Process

Both revelatory truth as well as personal salvation have been stressed as goals for the hermeneutic process. The search for universal, objective truth puts an emphasis on God's disclosure in the past. What is revealed is who God is in Godself, apart from what God does for us personally. This is usually expressed in a conceptual, dogmatic framework. *Revelation* puts the stress on what the Bible *tells us.*

An approach often juxtaposed to the first stresses the search *for meaning for me.* Here the focus is on subjective truth, on existential meaning, on a personal relationship. Interpretation is oriented toward the future, toward personal transformation and salvation. What is important is what Scripture accomplishes in me as I respond to the call of God.

Interpretation that is centred in a hermeneutic community understands revelation and salvation to be intertwined and inseparable as a goal for biblical study. It recognizes that revelational truth always emerges in concrete, particular contexts. Jesus, the ultimate revelation came within history, to a particular people, at a particular time and place. So too Scripture is *historical* and even today its revelational content is only recognized in saving events that transform the listeners. At the same time, salvation is broadened to include not only personal salvation but also social liberation and transformation. The communal perspective asserts that horizontal communication happens simultaneously with the vertical. Particular knowledge of God's will leads to witness to universal revelation.

Matthew 18 points to this interrelationship of salvation and revelation when it relates the concrete "binding and loosing" process within a disciple community, to heavenly norms. Hermeneutic community reminds us that the faith community, as it studies and responds to Scripture, is the context for both revelation and salvation.

> Truly I tell you, whatever you bind on earth will be bound in heaven, and whatever you loose on earth will be loosed in heaven.[4]

The significance of an emphasis on communal hermeneutics is therefore evident for both interpreter and community. For biblical interpreters it means a realization of the functional nature of their role in the interpretive process. It means an understanding of the limitations and contributions that a particular social location brings to the hermeneutical task. Interpreters will therefore be open to critique and dialogue as they commit themselves to concrete communities of interpretation.

Faith communities, sensitive to their hermeneutical responsibilities will realize that their particular tradition as well as the contemporary experience and praxis both limit and contribute to understanding the biblical texts. This mean taking the prophetic voice of individual interpreters seriously, as well as promoting a process of mutual critique and affirmation, both among its members, and in dialogue with other communities.

Thus hermeneutic community finds it contemporary relevance in that it relates the people of God to the Word of God in a dialectical process of interpretation.

* * *

HERMENEUTIC COMMUNITY: A FEMINIST CHALLENGE[5]

The invitation to give a paper at a special consultation at Associated Mennonite Biblical Seminary (AMBS) in June of 1986 came as a surprise to me. Willard Swartley, who had recently given a number of lectures both at our church in Edmonton and at Newman College, invited me to these meetings. I had learned to know Swartley, an esteemed New Testament professor at AMBS, during my husband's seminary days. He had taken special interest in my teaching of the New Testament at a Catholic seminary and was happy to give a lecture there.

Thirty women, predominantly Mennonite, had been invited to come to the AMBS campus for two days to serve as consultants to three biblical scholars doing research on the theme of "shalom." I was both thrilled and very nervous about accepting the invitation, realizing that this would be my first time speaking specifically not only as a scholar but also out of my new self-consciousness as a woman in theological studies. This gathering was also the first to draw together Anabaptist-Mennonite women with post MA or MDiv education in biblical and theological studies for face-to-face conversation.

I had finished the MTh degree at Newman College in 1984 and was teaching sessional courses at several colleges at the time. Much of my excitement about going to this consultation was to meet other Mennonite women who were wrestling with similar issues. My own growing feminist self-consciousness was being nurtured by my readings for a feminist course that I was co-teaching with an Anglican priest and by the discussions with a group of ecumenical women at St. Stephen's College. I had had the opportunity to hear Elisabeth Schüssler Fiorenza, a feminist biblical scholar, at a special lecture in Edmonton and was excited about reading her controversial books. I had also become part of an informal network of Mennonite women that were actively writing for Mennonite Central Committee's Women's Concern *publication. But in my context in Alberta, I had not been able to have many conversations with Mennonite women who identified with both the agenda of feminism and with theological scholarship.*

The conversation at the consultation was stimulating in a variety of ways. First of all, David Schroeder, a former professor and mentor of mine from CMBC, was one of the biblical scholars. His work focussed on the Bible, revelation, and community, the very topics that I had struggled with in my master's thesis. I respected his work and therefore was very anxious to hear his response to feminist theology. Mary Schertz and Gayle Gerber Koontz were two Mennonite female theologians whom I was meeting for the first time. They were beginning to speak and write publicly from a woman's perspective. To find that my struggle with biblical hermeneutics was shared by other women in my denomination gave me courage to consider entering doctoral studies. I was also challenged by a Catholic woman, Toinette Eugene, who brought the perspective of liberation and black theology into the discussions by questioning narrow definitions of feminism.

It was not easy to insert feminist theology directly into Mennonite theological discussion. Gayle Gerber Koontz, who edited this collection of essays, highlights some of the difficulties and hesitancies that showed themselves during those days.[6] *These can be summarized as follows:*

1) *There was ambivalence about the involvement in the enterprise itself exhibiting itself in disagreement about different forms of feminism but also about the value of academic training, at least in traditional patterns. Was not an active life of reconciliation more in tune with the biblical call to shalom?*

2) *There was uncertainty about whom to fruitfully include in the conversation. This showed up particularly in the confusion between a feminist and a woman's point of view. Not all participants would have understood the specific direction that feminist scholarship was taking and its radical challenge to biblical hermeneutical methodology. This also meant that men were uneasy about their role in the discussion. Certainly the women at the consultation were not in agreement with each other about whether feminist theology was the way forward for women in the church.*

3) *Because there were plural viewpoints and commitments among the women and men as well as varied experiences of sexism, there were also power differences among the participants. This should have meant special care that minority positions could be safely articulated. However, the typical structure of scholarly consultations was followed, a structure that did not give adequate care to the complex dynamics between people, especially women who had only recently entered the scholarly world.*

The following essay was my response to feminism and its challenge to biblical hermeneutics. It represents my "coming out" in our Mennonite seminary community as an academic and as a feminist—a somewhat scary but exhilarating experience.

* * *

An emphasis on the faith community as a hermeneutic community has been central to the way Anabaptist-Mennonites have expressed their approach to Scripture interpretation. This stress on congregational interpretation was a way of saying that the revelatory truth of the biblical text could most readily be discerned within the context of a disciple community committed to following the Lord of Scripture. All members of the covenant community were to be responsible to participate in the process of determining the meaning of the Bible. Not the state, nor specialized theologians, nor hierarchical authorities were to be the final judge of the Bible's meaning. Rather accountability was to the whole community of faithful followers of Jesus. A process of dialogue and mutual counsel was to enable a congregation to live out the practical implications of the gospel message. Faith experience (salvation) was thus closely linked to faith knowledge (revelation). Instead of a sole emphasis on the objective revelation of the past, there was a shift to include the present faith experience as important in the process of hearing the dynamic word of God in the Bible.

Feminist theology in common with other strands of liberation theology also contends that biblical interpretation must arise out of concrete communities.[7] Feminists understand these to be communities of liberation where women and men struggling for equality and mutuality become "prisms through which God's action in the mending of creation is to be understood."[8] They insist that communities whose praxis is liberating for all its members can more readily discern the meaning of Scripture. They agree that theology is not the exclusive prerogative of a select group of people—educated, trained, ordained men—but rather is the province of all persons. They point out that the oppressed who have experienced the grace of God in their new-found liberation and freedom have a particular contribution to make. The emphasis for feminists therefore is on defining more concretely the community best able to interpret the Bible.

Both Anabaptist-Mennonite hermeneutics and feminist hermeneutics acknowledge two poles in the interpretive process. They recognize that in the dialectical movement of Scripture interpretation both past revelatory knowledge and present faith experience are important. However, feminist theology with its strong emphasis on salvation and liberation for all persons presents a particular challenge to Mennonites to spell out more clearly the shape of the hermeneutic community. As the definition of salvation is enlarged and adjusted to include the experience of women, the particular limitations and strengths of a specific hermeneutic community will be evident. This paper will therefore focus on the shape of the hermeneutic community: its traditions, its institutions and structures and its language. The description of the importance of each of these aspects of community in the interpretive process is taken from recent philosophical theory. Specific critique comes from various feminist theologians.

Communal Tradition

Hans Georg Gadamer, one of the most important theoreticians of philosophical hermeneutics at the present time has redefined the role of tradition in the hermeneutical process.[9] He understands tradition to be the historically formed pre-understanding with which an interpreter approaches a text. Tradition is not something over against us but something in which we stand and within which things are perceived and defined. Thus both the context (horizon) of the interpreter and the context (horizon) of the text are involved in a dialectic process of interaction. Understanding takes place when a "fusion of horizons" occurs, when past and present come together to form the meaning of the text. The particular pre-judgments with which interpreters approach the text arise out of the tradition of the community of which they are a part.

Tradition, however, is not static, but dynamic and in motion, changing and moving in the encounter with the text. Unfruitful pre-judgments are discarded, and positive orientations are affirmed and enlarged as horizons interact and fuse. In this dialogical process there is always a partial negation of one's horizon (that is the tradition in which we stand) in order to allow oneself to be questioned as well as to question. Tradition must therefore be brought to consciousness and critically evaluated in order that new insights from the text can emerge.

Church history and tradition have been of central concern to feminists, for they have realized how important they are in providing the orientation with which biblical interpreters approach their task. Feminists have argued that women were shut out of the hermeneutic community for most of the history of biblical interpretation. The foundational tradition arose out of male experience and interaction with the text. As Rosemary Ruether points out, by not allowing women to study, teach or preach, women have not only been excluded from "shaping and interpreting the tradition from their own experience, but the tradition has been shaped and interpreted against them."[10]

As women begin to bring their experience of liberation and freedom in Christ to bear in the dialogue with the text, a critical force is unleashed which questions many traditional assumptions. The limitations of past formulations of the meaning of the Jesus event are clearly seen when female experience of bondage and liberation are taken seriously. A new inspiration is given for a reconstruction of history where research focusses particularly on the marginalized and forgotten women in Christian history.[11]

Feminist theology thus presents a clear challenge to hermeneutic communities to evaluate and test the tradition which informs their biblical interpretation. Have the presuppositions arisen out of a tradition which took women's experiences seriously? Are they being tested by women's experiences of today? Communal tradition will not stay untouched when women are fully included in the hermeneutic community.

Communal Structures and Institutions

The concepts of critical social philosophy focus on a second aspect of hermeneutic community—the crucial communication process between members of the community. It has become increasingly evident that the discovery and sharing of truth can be hindered not only be misunderstanding, but also by systemic distortions caused by particular power relationships. Here we are entering the realm of praxis, the realm of relationships between persons involved in the institutions and structures of communities. Jürgen Habermas, one of the foremost critics of ideology in Europe and America, has pointed out the social and political dimensions of the dialogical process.[12] The emphasis is on the situation of interaction in which the meaning of the text is understood. Habermas stresses the conditions of unconstrained and unrestricted discourse in order that valid truth can be established. All participants in the community must have the same opportunity to initiate and be involved in the discussion. They must have the same chance to express attitudes, ideas and feelings. Barriers which cause a breakdown in communication must be removed. Ideology is thus defined as "false consciousness" or "systematically distorted communication." Self-reflection and critique must occur in order to establish the institutional interests and concerns which influence the communication process.

Habermas insists that no interpretation is value free. The aim of critique is an understanding of social relationships through analysis and explanation of the elements of repression, violence, and coercion within the community, in order to free it through emancipative action.

For Habermas it is important not only to understand the interpretations of the past, but to transform the society of the present. Theory and praxis cannot be separated when we realize that the community is made up of individuals all participating in a vast network of power relationships in both society and church which will influence the hermeneutic process. Attention must be given to institutional structures and their use of power so that implicit ideological biases can be exposed.

Feminist theology insists that of basic importance in realizing how power relationships distort the communication process is to understand the pervasive influence of patriarchy on the church. Patriarchy is "not only the subordination of females to males, but the whole structure of Father-ruled society: aristocracy over serfs, master over slaves, kings over subjects, racial overlords over colonized people."[13] Women have become conscious of how this hierarchical stratification has led to female alienation, marginalization and exploitation. The vital intersubjective dialogue between women and men is basically affected by power relationships which are usually only unconsciously sensed and rarely articulated or taken into account. Feminists thus begin their interpretations with a "hermeneutics of suspicion" which helps them uncover areas of self-interest in the dominant interpretations.[14] They search carefully to see how biblical texts function in the original historical-biblical settings as well as in the ongoing socialization of men and women. They insist on honesty in spelling out presuppositions with their ideological and political implications. And they strive for a hermeneutic community of equality and mutuality where dialogue can lead to a richer understanding of the text because all participate equally.

Mennonites who want to interpret the Bible in community will need to come to terms with patriarchy and its pervasive influence in both church and society. They will have to examine their structures and institutions realizing how they affect community dialogue. They will have to become sensitive to unconscious power relationships which inhibit free exchange of ideas. They will need to work for an end to hierarchical structures, substituting relationships of mutuality and cooperation. Community praxis will then take its proper place in the hermeneutic process.

Communal Language

The philosopher and theologian Paul Ricoeur has pointed out the importance of communal language in the interpretive process;[15] for it is within language that biblical interpretation is made public, and inter-subjectively shared—where religious experience is articulated. It is language that explains and describes, but also inspires and manifests. It is language that mediates the meaning of the biblical texts. Ricoeur has looked carefully at the process of bringing the meaning of the text back into speech which can be understood. He recognizes the various kinds of discourse in our communities that actualize the text for our time—theological reflection and explanation, but also preaching and poetic discourse.

Ricoeur has focused particularly on symbolic language with its revelatory and mediatory characteristics. For symbols represent language in its most intensive level, language closest to the rood of existence. Their interpretation cannot stay at the literal level, but must always go beyond to secondary meanings. These can best be expressed in ever-expanding metaphorical expressions and concepts. He notes the richness of biblical language which includes narrative, prophecies, law, proverbs, prayers, hymns, liturgical writings and wisdom literature. However, when Ricoeur looks at the discourse present in our scholarly communities, he notes a loss of sensitivity to poetic and symbolic language.[16] The ideal language for persons in the twentieth century is scientific language which attempts to eradicate all ambiguity and misunderstanding. Words and sentences are explained and defined to ensure identity of meaning for everyone. Metaphor and symbol are seen as mere emotional embellishment, appealing to subjective understanding, not really having to do with reality.

This linguistic impoverishment in many communities has deprived people of articulating such existential realities as radical evil or grace-empowered hope. Ricoeur recognizes the need for language that can explain and describe, but also calls for language that can release the revelatory power of the text in multiple symbolic and metaphorical expressions. This is particularly true for texts which "name God," for though God is named in diverse ways in the Bible, there is also an incompleteness about all of these namings. Just as the kingdom of God is signified through parables, proverbs and paradoxes for which no literal translations will ever suffice, so no naming of God will exhaust the meaning of that expression.

The area of language has become increasingly important in feminist thought. It is not only one of inclusive language when referring to persons that is important. The most important critiques are in the whole realm of God-talk. Women have begun to recognize the poverty of much of the language used for God in our communities. As they point out the narrow and limited male expressions referring to God which are generally used in our churches and theological communities, they are becoming aware that the traditional doctrinal and historical-scientific language for God is inadequate.[17] It is no accident that feminists are stressing not only expository and creedal formulations of theology but also music, litany, art, poetry, dance, story, and discussion. The use of metaphor and parable are highlighted rather than systematic or syllogistic thought.

Feminist theology is thus making us aware again of the elusive and mysterious nature of truth. It is questioning the validity of the prevalent mode of discourse in both our scholarly communities and church communities which try to define and describe God so literally that many people experience no sense of relatedness to such as deity. Feminist theologians have pointed out how interpreters can so identify God with language about God that one name for God is absolutized, thus excluding complementary models and images. They insist that the relationship between God and human beings is an event, dynamic and alive; therefore, no doctrinal formulation or even symbol or metaphor will be adequate to express its meaning. As the hermeneutic community of women and men dialogue about their grace experiences of God in light of Scripture, new models, metaphors and concepts will appear. Thus feminists are helping theology realize the limitedness of its language. This includes the question of the relationship of language and the experience it can mediate—the relationship between theological God-talk and life's experience of the divine.

Mennonites have traditionally rejected philosophically-based theology and have prided themselves on their biblically-based practical theology. They have rejected symbolic language in favour of the concrete language of "following Jesus." At the same time, they have been influenced by various streams of theological thinking, particularly those that stressed literalistic interpretation of Scripture or the factually oriented language of science. God-talk in our communities, both scholarly and congregational, has tended to become narrow and limited.

As feminists begin to point out the fact that the God-talk is mostly male-oriented, Mennonites will also have to grapple with the mode of discourse best suited for speaking about God. What kinds of experiences of God does our language express and inspire? How meaningful is our language for contemporary women and men? Is there a richness in our language which can mediate experiences of the transcendent? The focus by feminists on communal language can give Mennonites the opportunity to examine our mode of discourse to see whether we have not succumbed to the sin of idolatry as well as the sin of irrelevance.[18]

In speaking about the importance of the community of faith in the interpretive process, Mennonites have realized that revelational truth emerges in concrete particular communities. They have stressed that God's disclosure in the past and God's work among people in the present come together as the Bible is interpreted in the community of believers. They have recognized that salvific experiences can open a community to understanding the truth in Scripture. Women are now beginning to share experiences of liberation and salvation with their faith communities. As they do so, communal traditions, communal structures and institutions, and communal language will be challenged by their insights and critiques. The opportunity is there for us to experience anew the dynamic on-going presence of God who continues to work creatively in our communities of faith.

* * *

OUR GOD-TALK: IMAGES, IDOLS, METAPHORS, AND MASKS[19]

I took the crayons and hesitantly began to draw. The swirl of colour surprised me! I had begun with a deep intense circle of red, red like the coals of a campfire, red like the setting sun in the evening, red like the geraniums that my father loved best. Then without any conscious thought, I picked up a blue crayon and slowly the image began to change. A calmness was introduced into the scene as the blue began to blend and mediate the intensity of the red. Gradually the emerging mauve changed entirely to a clear blue colour—the colour of the sky and the calm sea and my mother's eyes.

"What is your image of God?" was the question that had been posed to us. We had explored this in music and dance and now were given free range with paints, crayons and a large blank piece of paper. We were encouraged to let our imagination go without the usual inhibitions that years of more rational theology had imposed on us. I had begun drawing without any clear idea where my picture was taking me, just letting my hands guide me. I felt a bit rebellious as I saw what I had drawn. Why had I chosen

blue? I knew that red was the more likely choice of colour for my image of God—a colour that seemed to describe my father's temperament with its exuberant expression of emotions. Yet I had introduced the blue into my image, the blue that I associated with my mother and her warm, even temperament. And in that instant I knew that my image of God had changed, had been enlarged and deepened.

It had felt risky to take this workshop with Walter Wink and June Keener-Wink. It was risky because our finances were stretched at that time, but risky also because I was not sure whether I could handle the various approaches to biblical study that were being introduced. Walter had written a book that I found disturbing but also energizing. The small book, The Bible in Human Transformation *(1973), began with the startling statement, "Historical biblical criticism is bankrupt" and went on to talk about how the scholarship of the time could not easily be used to bring about transformation in people or in communities. Wink introduced additional ways to approach biblical study in order to include our whole being in the response to Scripture. In this particular workshop we explored the notion of "son of man," a term used by Jesus as a name for himself. We began to use the term, "the child of the human," as a translation that was more accurate and one that challenged us to think of Jesus in human terms rather than only as divine.*

I remember the prayer I wrote to Jesus the, "child of the human," the way I was able to name my own temptations and challenges in ways I had not done before. I sensed an intimate connection with God that made prayer more like a conversation rather than a wish list. During the months before this workshop I had consciously prayed to God as mother, trying to enlarge my image in a more rational way. But this was the first time that my emotions caught up with my mind and I could sense a mother's warm embrace together with the security of a father's arms around me as I reflected on God's love for me.

As I now reflect on my own use of God language, I realize that I have resorted to gender neutral language. Instead of using many names for God, I tend to use one or two primary names. Generally, I do not use the male pronoun for God and only sometimes do I use a female pronoun. The question has been lying dormant for me in the last years as I have concentrated on other aspects of theology. The language in the church has also followed this pattern. From being a rather divisive issue in the 1980's it has slid below the radar for most people.

I wonder if we in the church and perhaps also in the academy have lost some of the urgency and importance of the question of how we imagine and name God. The loss of the personal in the gender-neutral language, the loss of the awe and holiness in moving to names that are less hierarchical, and the continuing domination of the male imagery in our biblical texts has discouraged some of us even as we saw the need for more intensive work in this area.

I wonder if we need to bring this question to the fore again in our secular but increasingly multi-faith context. The question goes beyond only male language to the larger question: how do we speak about God in this postmodern world? Do we still worship the God named in the Bible? What does it mean to name the God who is the great "I AM" without resorting to idolatry? How can we avoid domination and triumphalism as we relate to other religions and their understanding of God?

I have included a reflection first printed as an editorial introduction to the theme in the Women's Concern Report, *a periodical published by Mennonite Central Committee. It points to the interconnections of our language and our experience in community, something that we must continue to explore as we think about our God-talk today.*

* * *

During my college days I read a small book entitled *Your God Is Too Small* by J.B. Phillips. The author urges his readers to discover a God "big" enough to meet the challenges and questions of the real world. Phillips was convinced that many people carry inadequate conceptions of God, images that are not only irrelevant to their lives, but that also prevent them from glimpsing the true God.

When we ask questions about the picture of God that informs our life we are probing the heart of our Christian faith. No wonder that the recent discussions in feminist and liberation theology about inclusive God-images has spawned so much reaction and response. As at so many times in the history of God's people we are asked to look again at our God-images and answer that basic question: who is our God?

It is time to open the discussion of the names we use to characterize God. By using words such as "idols" and "masks" in the title of this article we are acknowledging the risk and danger involved in any imaging of God. At the same time, we want to express our relationship to God in words that honestly communicate our personal experience. "Images" and "metaphors" are necessary for us to do this.

In my readings and reflections on this theme over the past months several key ideas emerged again and again.

All language about God is limited and inadequate to describe God

The Hebrew people, well aware that God was beyond speech, were reluctant to speak God's name. Stories, metaphors and various substitute names were used instead of the name YHWH to describe their relationship with God and still preserve the sense of holiness and transcendence. God could be characterized as the God of war as well as the God of peace, the God who never changes as well as the God who repents. They sang praises to God as the stable rock of our salvation as well as extolled the dynamic vitality of God as the spring of living water. Jesus was both the Lion of Judah and the Lamb that was slain.

The paradoxes and contradictions in the biblical picture of God push us beyond easy creeds and images fixed in stone to dynamic, fluid images which more fully encompass the ways God relates to us.

Traditional Mennonite theology and worship faces a particular problem in this regard. In its fear of idolatry and in its reaction to the elaborate and symbolic worship of high church traditions, it has rejected the use of physical imagery in sculpture, painting and architecture. Instead it has stressed the simple straightforward, literal language about God. But in this literalness, the distance between language and reality is sometimes forgotten. The ability of metaphoric and symbolic speech to communicate truth is not understood. By using only one or two words and images for God it easily can be assumed that God is already known fully by us. Our view of God becomes static and narrow.

We need to learn again that at the root of our inability to speak adequately about God lies God's transcendence and mystery. An emphasis on neglected biblical images can raise our consciousness to see how we have limited God. Creative efforts to express our relationship to God make us aware of how dependent we are on the thought patterns of our particular culture. Yet all our stumbling and awkward attempts to describe God can only testify to a God who continues to resist our attempts at classification, one who even now says to us" I am who I am" (Exodus 3:14).

Our basic picture of God is formed very early in life in a complex interaction between a conscious and subconscious response to life's experience as well as to the formal teaching we receive.

This week as I sorted old papers while spring cleaning I discovered a picture drawn by my daughter at the age of 5. Entitled "My Family," it showed mom, dad and brothers in rather typical fashion for a child of that age. What caught my eye was the picture of a similar, much larger person hovering over the others with arms out stretched. For Kristen this person was as real as the others. She named that person God.

Psychology teaches us that how we experience ourselves in relationship to God is related to how we experience ourselves in relationship to the world and to other people. In her book about women's spirituality and the gender of God, Sandra Schneiders points out that just as our self-concept may be unhealthy so too our God-image may be unhealthy and need healing.[20]

The therapy needed is not just a rational re-conception of God but a "therapy of the religious imagination": story, art, and music appeal to our emotions and can reach the unconscious level of our beings. An integrated approach involving intellect, will and feeling can bring healing to incomplete God-images. It is important therefore to bring our subconscious image to the surface so that we can allow God to cleanse and redeem that part of ourselves. We must expect our images to change and grow as we relate more deeply to God.

The truth of our words about God must be tested by the way we use the words in actual situations.

In a recent discussion with a woman who was rejected as a ministry candidate expressly because she was a woman, I was struck by the pain in her voice as she said, "I feel like the God who called me into service is a very different God from the God of the ministerial committee."

The decision had been justified by appeal to a God who determines persons of one sex to be leaders and those of another sex to be obedient followers. It made me realize again how the metaphors and images we use for God can be used either to bring salvific experiences for persons or be used to defend situations of oppression.

It is no surprise that the people who are calling for a new look at our God-imagery are persons who have been oppressed by Christian people and nations. Black people are rejecting a white god who condones slavery and apartheid. South American people are resisting obedience to a North American god who allows exploitation of the poor. Women are questioning a male god who calls forth structures that deny full personhood to women and justify patriarchal power of men over women.

Jesus' words, "You shall know them by their fruits" (Matthew 7:16) can be a guide to testing our God-images. What actions, feelings and commitments do our images call forth? Legitimizing unjust social orders as God's will can bring into question whether we have adequately understood God.

The challenge for us is to risk God-talk that moves us beyond the names that have become idols that mask or limit God. It calls us instead to explore metaphors that enrich, deepen and challenge us in our worship and in our actions.

* * *

THE BIBLE AS OUR HOME[21]

Elizabeth Gingerich Yoder called the consultation at AMBS in 1991 a "bold experiment" as it brought theologians and therapists together to consult about the subject of peace theology and violence against women.[22] *The shape of the conference was structured to have theologians present papers and therapists respond to their work. The primary purpose was to "assemble persons from the Peace Church traditions who have dealt with the topic of violence against women and/or peace theology in a scholarly or professional way to identify issues, to shape the future directions of peace church reflections and practice in relation to violence against women, and to encourage further work on the issues."*

Perhaps the "boldness" that was needed was not merely the boldness of therapists and theologians consulting together, but rather the courageous naming of violence within the Mennonite church, a church that claimed to be a peace church. Gayle Gerber Koontz notes that it was only with the most recent wave of feminism in the early 1970's that basic information about violence and violation of women became widely available and noticed in North America.[23]

My own first awareness of the abuse of women came during my early teen years. My father came home very upset one day. I gathered from a conversation I overheard between him and my mother that he had just confronted a church member who had violently abused his wife and that the confrontation had not gone well. More recently I had learned of other such situations within our context in Edmonton and Toronto. But even more devastating was the rape of someone within my own family circle. I knew personally how the secrecy and shame associated with this crime did not encourage healing. In addition, I had also entered more fully into the story of a friend whose rape and abuse had created trauma beyond my imagination. The challenge to accompany her on her healing journey was almost more than I was capable of. But in publically naming myself as a feminist, the door had somehow opened for more and more women to disclose to me that they had been abused. I did not know what to do with this knowledge. This conference was a welcome gathering for me to help me respond more adequately to situations in which many women find themselves.

I realize now that I was only partly aware of the irony of a conference on violence against women being held on the campus of AMBS at a time when the writings of John H. Yoder, a former professor, still spoke the definitive word on peace for many people. Yoder was a former professor at AMBS and it was only during that time that his sexual abuse of students at the seminary and beyond became more widely known.[24]

I had used Yoder's writings in my thesis and though I had challenged his notion of "revolutionary submission" I had not yet dealt with his sexual abuse of women. I discovered some of the hidden pain this had caused some women during the conference but I certainly was unaware of its extent and of his more overt theological justification of this abuse. This was all the more surprising since I had recently become a board member of AMBS. I do remember that in my first meeting of the board, in response to a question about Yoder, we were told that the matter was being taken care of through a church process. Since Yoder no longer taught at the seminary, we need no longer concern ourselves with that matter.

There was a "silence" around Yoder and his theology at this conference as well. I noted in rereading the papers that only Carol Penner directly engaged Yoder's work, specifically on his notion of subordination. It was only when women talked to each other alone after the formal meetings that some of the secrecy was lifted.[25]

What I do remember was a tension between those who used feminist/liberation approaches to the theme and those who did more traditional biblical and theological work. Again the question was raised: whom do we engage as our conversation partners when we do our theological work? Some progress was made by including women and practitioners such as social workers and psychologists in the conversation. But what about the ones who have suffered abuse? The ones who feel shamed and cannot speak without ruining their own reputation? We were still far from creating a safe place for persons who have been hurt by men within our churches and hurt even more deeply by the church who has silenced these voices.

I do remember a rather heated discussion about the "hermeneutical privilege of the oppressed," something strongly argued against by some theologians, while championed by others. Perhaps what was disconcerting to many of the women was how easily men took over the conversation and how difficult it was to speak about this topic with both men and women present.

My own contribution to this discussion came as a response to Mary Schertz, a biblical scholar reflecting on a biblical theology of shalom in the context of violence against women. In my response to her paper I tried to find a way to speak about the Bible's authority that can help us come to terms with its human nature, thus opening ourselves to the human experience within the text. I had also hoped to open us to the stories of violence within the biblical material and help us to see that there is already a struggle going on within the Bible about how to deal with that violence. I wanted to lift some of the silence around our own complicity in this violence by paying attention to only some voices within Scripture as we do to only some voices within our congregations. This paper only hints at the direction that my own thinking about peace theology was moving toward at that time, but the metaphor of the Bible as a "home" and the hermeneutic community as "homemakers" in that home still rings true to me.

* * *

It is always easier to dialogue with those persons with whom one shares basic assumptions and commitments. I am happy to respond to the paper by Mary Schertz because I too stand in that ambiguous place where love for the church and the Bible is intertwined with anger and pain at the way the Bible and theology have contributed to the violence against women. I too am committed to breaking the silence in theological and church circles, a silence which permits us as a Mennonite church to espouse a peace theology while harboring violence in our midst. I too struggle to name the "bad news" in our peace theology while attempting to proclaim the "good news" which God has for us.

Schertz's paper begins by exploring the reasons why we must give serious attention to biblical theology as part of the way of dealing with the issue of violence. This is not self-evident to feminists who insist that theological reflection must begin with experience. I would like to expand on Schertz's discussion by using a metaphor which can help us reflect on our complex and contradictory relationship to the Bible. I would like to reflect on what it means to confess that the Bible is our "home," a home that has at times been dysfunctional, but one which can help us regain a sense of truly being "at home."[26]

There are a number of ways in which we can think of the Bible as our home. It is in the Bible where the stories are told of our origins and where we as Christians were first named. In the Bible those decisive events which formed our identity as family of God are told and retold. Many of the crucial arguments among us were already begun and carried on within the biblical forum. Our most intimate feelings have been expressed within this sphere. We can rebel and leave our home, but it will always be there as we struggle to find a sense of identity in our own time and context.

As with any home, it will be very difficult for us to come to terms with our heritage if we cannot admit its humanness. One way to look at this human factor is to begin to examine the voices which interact within the biblical conversation. Though there are many voices which speak, some voices are loud and dominant; others are almost silenced, hidden and marginalized. The stories of the kings, of male prophets are told more eloquently and with more detail than the stories of mid-wives, of home-makers and of slaves. The male-centeredness (androcentrism) of the Bible needs to be acknowledged so that we can ask a deeper question. Which voices speak the truth, identifying that which is of God and that which holds the members of the Christian family together? Which of the many interpretations of our family experiences express the essence of home for us?

Perhaps our family discussions will become more sensitive and open if we begin to listen to the marginal voices in our home. Perhaps healing will come as we open ourselves to the stories of pain and anger even within the Bible. As every member of the family begins to share in the interpretation of the past we will come to terms with some family secrets which were hidden in the closet. But it is only in taking this risk that marginal persons and even strangers will begin to feel "at home" in our midst.

This shift in the way we listen to the biblical conversation will mean a similar shift in our theological methodology. We will need to become self-conscious about the reasons in our own experience which lead us to emphasize certain biblical passages to the exclusion of others. It is this connection of biblical theology to experience which opens a space for a new look at Mennonite peace theology and violence against women. Biblical theology will change if interpreters with different experiences begin to read and interpret the Bible.

A recognition that interpreter and text form two poles of the dialogical interpretive process means that we must become aware of how our biases influence our biblical theology. The choices of our conversation partners become an ethical issue. We need to become more conscious of how power relationships influence the theological conversations in which authoritative interpretations of the Bible arise.

Schertz's paper struggles to set new directions in biblical theology by speaking from the viewpoint of someone who stands in solidarity with women affected by male violence. In her discussion of the themes of peace theology she points out a number of crucial areas that need more work. I want to speak to several of the areas that she refers to and add a few additional comments.

1. Our creation theology will be greatly affected if we begin with the experience of disharmony and violence between women and men. We will then be listening most closely to those voices within the Bible which speak of healing and of hope. We will not primarily be concerned to describe an ideal state of shalom. Rather we will identify various situations of disharmony in the pages of the Bible and note how God's creative power worked to create new relationships of love and respect between people. The focus will be on recognizing and accepting the gift of God's healing work among us. Part of that gift will include a new understanding of ourselves and the other in the image of a creating healing God, thus challenging us and empowering us to become co-creators in this healing process.

2. Our covenant theology will need to come to terms with the kinds of power relationships which our theological language has idealized. The metaphors of sovereignty for God have included images of power which we experience as dominating and controlling. The metaphors of our human position have emphasized images of subjection and impotence. Thus covenant relationships, whether between God and humanity or between women and men are often understood as oppressive rather than freeing and empowering, especially when God and men are identified as the powerful and dominant partner.

What is needed is another look at the human temptation to see God in our own image, a temptation which was already there in the patriarchal setting of the biblical world. If we begin our theology of God's power by focusing on the way Jesus empowered people like Mary or Zacchaeus or the woman with the flow of blood, we cannot speak of a pattern of relationship where someone orders and the other obeys. Our covenant relationship with God has more to do with God's accepting our "personal autonomy" while continually inviting us into relationship. Living according to the covenant arises out of the empowerment and friendship which God offers to us.

3. Our theology of cult and its role in restoring shalom when it is broken needs to focus more directly on feelings of anger and the notion of forgiveness if we want to include those who have been abused in our worship. When we acknowledge that false guilt and false forgiveness are temptations of the one who has been abused, we will have to look more seriously at how we can legitimately express anger and pain in our worship settings. The psalms which express anger and even a wish for vengeance have often been an embarrassment to Mennonite peace theology. We do not know how to incorporate them into our worship experience. However, when trust is broken, when justice has not been done, when the temple has been violated, the faith community will need to incorporate ways to

express anger into their common life. They will have to find a process which does not begin with quick superficial forgiveness but wrestles with the gravity of sin. This will have to be done in a way that places the community into the presence of God who brings shalom to our relationships.

4. The cross as a major symbol of the power of God in making shalom will need to be re-examined in order to understand its role in the life of someone who is abused. The way of the cross as suffering love looks different if we speak from the standpoint of someone who feels powerless in the face of the abuser.

Perhaps a direction in which to go is to look at the disciples and their struggle with the cross. We would need to examine the temptations of both male and female disciples as they sought to follow Jesus. What was the challenge that Jesus gave to those who felt particularly powerless? Was the way of the cross the same for those who felt weak and inconsequential as for those who felt a sense of worth and authority? What do we make of the failures of the disciples and the response of Jesus to them?

We may also want to explore new aspects of Jesus as model. For example, we can gain a new sense of the need for empowerment when we focus on the times when Jesus needed the support of his friends, when he struggled in Gethsemane for a sense of purpose in the senseless violence around him, when he needed to be strengthened and empowered before he could go the way of suffering love.

Another direction that needs further exploration is to look again at the differences between the cross of Jesus and the suffering of those who experience violence and abuse. Are they really the same? What makes suffering redemptive? Where does resurrection fit in the theology of suffering?

I have indicated a few directions that a Mennonite peace theology would need to explore if we begin to listen to the voices of those who have been silenced or marginalized in our family conversations.

Perhaps we can think of biblical theology as an exercise in "home-making." However, this home-making is not reserved for only one person who is given a role of house-keeping so that everything will be neat and tidy. Instead all of us must become involved in the vital conversation process which does not cover up injustice or abuse in the home but instead deals with them in a healing way. It is then that we will discover anew the Source of Love who is the center of our home, our God who has given birth to us, suffered with us in our lack of shalom, challenged us in our injustice and empowered us anew to live the way of love in a violent world.

Chapter 3: Method

NAMING MY METHODOLOGICAL APPROACH

The initial plunge into the waters is always shocking as well as energizing. Each morning when I wake, I still have to resist the temptation to go back to sleep rather than go to the pool for my morning swim. But when I enter my home after the swim my body and mind are refreshed anticipating the work of the day. This analogy came to mind as I thought about those six years of doctoral study. Plunging into intensive study created in me a new energy for my work. Yet I still had to encourage myself to keep going every day during that initial process of entering a complex doctoral program with its many requirements. It all felt too intimidating for me, a woman nearing fifty, who had spent most of her working life as a home-maker rather than scholar.

Choosing the courses to take was itself a challenging task. I entered my studies hoping to understand the hermeneutical process of biblical interpretation. Beneath that hope lay the question of how God reveals Godself to us in the book we often name the "Word of God," a matter usually stated as the question of biblical authority. At the same time, I was convinced that it was not so much a question of revelation but more a question of reception of that revelation. I had named listening as a hermeneutical process in my master's thesis. Now, I wanted to dive deeply into the questions that had arisen for me in order to understand how God's word becomes present in human history today.

I chose Jürgen Moltman as my primary theologian because I knew he had been in dialogue with Mennonites and was a European political theologian who could perhaps help me with my questions around authority and power. But this pursuit led very quickly into the larger questions of how we know anything at all, that is, the area of epistemology. For that question I had to enter more intensely into the often obtuse and confusing field of philosophy, a field that many women shied away from. I chose to do intensive courses on Kant, Hegel, and Marx, as well as on European Critical Theory. These helped me understand how feminist approaches grew out of the larger philosophical issues of our time, as well as how they challenged each of the philosophical directions led by male thinkers.

At the same time, I took an intensive seminar course on Scripture interpretation. For two semesters a small group of four students and two professors spent time exploring how one Psalm, Psalm 69, had been interpreted throughout history, beginning with changes from the Hebrew text to the Greek text, and moving to various translations and interpretations by Jewish and Christian scholars. My wish to enter this course created some controversy among the biblical scholars. After all, I was not in their department and had never studied Hebrew. I argued successfully that learning from the practice *of biblical scholars would help me understand the* process *of interpretation, that is biblical "hermeneutics," my primary interest.*

For our research paper in that course we each had to choose a text and trace the shifts in interpretation through the centuries. My choice of the Magnificat, Mary's song in the gospel of Luke, was not accidental but arose out of my growing feminist consciousness and my interest in justice and peace. It proved to be one of the most enlightening but also enjoyable papers I wrote during my student days. I discovered the multiple ways in which this poem had connected with people's lives through the ages. This course convinced me that my choice to study the notion of hermeneutic community was the right one. The changes in methodology as well as interpretation that I noted in the study of the Magnificat were linked closely to the changes in the communal context of the interpreters of the text as well as the larger philosophical presuppositions of the time in which they wrote.

I also took a course on the gospel of Mark in which the emphasis was not so much on historical critical approaches to biblical exegesis but rather more on literary narrative methodologies. In my exegesis of the last chapter of Mark I used multiple hermeneutical methods in my own interpretation of the verses. I became convinced that these methods were merely tools and that systematic theologians like myself, who read the text with different questions in mind than the historical critical readers or the literary narrative scholars, could fruitfully learn from all of these methods.

The hermeneutic community of doctoral students and professors interacts in other ways than listening to lectures, reading texts, entering theological conversations, or sharing papers. I entered a theological school with its own sociological, political, and theological assumptions and rules of conduct and had to learn to navigate these in order to grow into a scholar and teacher. First, there was the matter of being of a minority faith tradition, no matter which of the seven schools of theology (which make up the Toronto School of Theology) I studied in. My registration was at Emmanuel College but some of the courses I took were held in the other denominational schools. Learning to ask questions that arose for me in schools outside of my denomination helped me to become aware and to articulate my own assumptions. It also helped my classmates and professors to articulate their presuppositions, creating the opportunity for critical dialogue that had the possibility of being creative and constructive.

Emmanuel College had set up a room with six or seven desks for graduate students. Here several of us gathered and debated many topics that arose for us during our studies. We finally had to make a rule of silence at certain times of the day so we could also read and study there. An important shift in my self understanding took place for me after one of these conversations. Several of us had been complaining that there were too few courses in feminist theology and that women were being neglected in the schools which were dominated by male professors. So we decided to do something about it. We began to plan for a weekend conference with Phyllis Trible, a well-known feminist biblical scholar, as guest. It was empowering to take concrete steps to change our learning environment to suit our needs. The conversations with the various schools to provide money for this venture allowed us to make our larger concerns known. The event was a great success and provided us with much grist for thought as we each worked on our own thesis proposals.

I had learned that I was in charge of my own learning and that I needed to make sure that my goals were met. This also meant that I would encounter the politics of the institution in a direct way. The first barrier to overcome was arranging a meeting of my committee (made up of busy professors from three different colleges) which was to oversee me through the first years of course work. I learned that I had to take the initiative to set up this meeting and to make sure that I was meeting all the program requirements.

But I also had to learn how to work with members of the committee from the various colleges who did not agree with each other about what I needed to learn. When one professor flatly refused to let me take a course that would have fit into my goals, but did not fit his theological approach, I had to learn to make my own arguments and eventually to compromise. When two of the professors argued about whether a course was suitable, l decided to make the "political" move to take one course by each professor. This served me well because each had some valuable expertize for me to learn. Probably my worst experience came when one professor refused to let me be the tutor in his class even though I had received a bursary for that work. He told another student that this was because I was "a Mennonite woman." I understood that this represented two strikes against me. Though I received encouragement from the dean at the time to accept the money without any extra work, I resented the fact that I did not receive the teaching experience that I should have had, because I was judged on the basis of my gender and denominational background rather than my knowledge.

I learned much from one of my professors in feminist theology whose specialty was European critical theory. I enjoyed her stimulating lectures and her incisive critical thinking. She was one of the persons on my thesis committee and I knew she would hold me accountable and would make sure my reasoning was sound. I decided to do an interdisciplinary thesis, that is a thesis that brought together my hermeneutical approach with my interpretation of particular biblical texts. This crossed the disciplines of systematic theology and biblical studies. I remember well the discussion of my proposal that spilled out beyond her office into the hallway. Both of our voices were raised as we argued. She insisted that I would never be able to successfully defend my thesis and graduate since I was not a biblical scholar and therefore not capable of biblical interpretation; I argued that theology for me meant bringing into dialogue the conceptual frameworks of systematic theology with the interpretation of specific biblical texts. Finally, in exasperation I said that I didn't care if I would not graduate, the thesis I wanted to write was going to be written out of my interest and that strict rules between disciplines did not matter to me. Reluctantly she supported me in my efforts and passed my proposal. Since we knew each other well by that time, I also knew that she respected my work.

Probably the best experience of my doctoral studies was with my advisor, George Schner, a Jesuit Catholic professor who encouraged me to write from within my own tradition but also alerted me when I was making assumptions that needed to be explained and explored. I always came away from my meetings with more clarity as to the direction that I could go. He rejoiced with me when something suddenly became clear to me and he suggested options when I met obstacles in my writing and was discouraged. To work against my tendency to postpone writing by reading more books, he chose to diagram where I was in the process and then to point me to specific readings that would take me to the next step. I remember him saying: "You are saying the same thing over and over again but in slightly different ways. I wonder if you are afraid to tackle what comes next?" I mourned the loss of a friend and mentor when he died a few years later.

My thesis was published under the title, Suspicion, Obedience and the Gospel of Mark: A Mennonite Feminist approach to Biblical Authority. *It represents the integration of various experiences and learnings during my doctoral work. I discovered that the notion of hermeneutic community was a useful heuristic tool that allowed me to relate my feminist and Mennonite convictions to each other while also learning from the biblical text. I also began to see discipleship as a key theological notion from within the Mennonite tradition, albeit one that needed further exploration in order to serve as a key identity marker for Christians.*

This section includes two articles that illustrate my growing concern with bringing interpretive methodologies in line with my theological convictions about faithfully "listening" for God's voice in the biblical texts. Both were written while doing doctoral studies when much of my doctoral work focused on testing and refining a methodological approach to theology.

* * *

DISCIPLESHIP REEXAMINED: WOMEN IN THE HERMENEUTICAL COMMUNITY[1]

As I write this introduction I am mourning the death of David Schroeder, one of my favourite professors during my years at Canadian Mennonite Bible College (CMBC). As I reflect on this particular essay written twenty-five years ago to honour Schroeder's academic contributions, I realize that at the time I had only begun to appreciate how much Doc (as we affectionately referred to him) influenced the particular direction I took in my doctoral work. Yet I felt very honoured to be one of two women to contribute to the David Schroeder Symposium in July, 1998.

Schroeder came to CMBC as one of those first Canadian Mennonites who had re-

ceived a doctorate in theology.[2] He began his teaching career during a time of ferment and renewal in the Mennonite church that was spurred on by the scholarly work of a number of young men from USA and Canada in the 1940's and 50's. Before that time there had not been a strong tradition of scholarly work in theology by Mennonites. In Canada, in particular, there was a suspicion of scholarly work in the largely rural communities who had emigrated to Canada in the 1870's. Instead they valued "Gemeindetheologie," the simple but sincere theology rooted in the life of the farm and community. The influx of Mennonite immigrants from Russia during the 1920's meant that the church had to continue to depend on their lay (unpaid) ministers called out from within the congregation, as very few had the opportunity to do any academic study.

The recovery of the "Anabaptist vision," articulated by a group of Mennonite scholars and Mennonite Central Committee workers in Europe after World War II known as the "Concern" group, challenged the church to new faithfulness in service and in its communal life. David Schroeder, though not part of that group, came to CMBC after acquiring his doctorate at the University of Hamburg, having studied philosophy and theology. He represented a new wave of scholarly study of theology by Mennonites in Canada that created unease and disagreement within the congregations. This created tension between the college and the constituency, a tension that these young scholars had to navigate.

CMBC had been established in 1947 to equip young people for church leadership and service ministries beginning with only 33 students from across Canada to nearly 100 during the years in the 1960's that I attended the college. (Near the end of my time there, it became an approved teaching centre of the University of Manitoba and in the year 2000 became part of the federation of colleges now named Canadian Mennonite University.) Together, with a number of other professors, Schroeder was committed to upholding a high standard of academic work as well as a strong commitment to the congregations.

I am not aware of when I realized that the dualities that plague our church life as well as our scholarly endeavors needed to be embraced into a more inclusive way of thinking—one that is not afraid of paradox and mystery, yet is rooted in concrete community living. In reflection, I believe the roots of this conviction were planted by the teaching and example of Schroeder.

Schroeder was deeply committed to the discernment of Scripture in congregations through a process of "binding and loosing" as gleaned from Matthew 18. What he meant by this was a process that holds persons accountable to the community and God, but also simultaneously frees them to joyfully live in accordance with God's will. This latter insight made a big impression on me in the 1960's when freedom was in the air, a time when our culture struggled with freedom movements from Martin Luther King's freedom marches to women's liberation protest meetings. Schroeder rejected the more rule oriented church discipline that was common in Mennonite tradition and instead promoted one that created the climate for voluntary obedience to God by freeing persons from the "principalities and powers" that wanted to dominate the church.

But perhaps what influenced me most was the character of Schroeder himself. His modelling of a person of integrity who accepted both his power and his vulnerability demonstrated to me that keeping together commitment and critical academic work as a disciple following in the way of Jesus was possible. When I was asked to speak at the symposium honouring him I was in the midst of exploring this in terms of my new awareness of feminist theological methodology. The focus of discipleship as a way to hold these tensions together also came out of my biblical studies with Schroeder and became the key theological notion in my thesis. However, living into the mystery of the human/ divine relationship that discipleship names continues to be an ongoing challenge for me and is therefore a life-long journey.

* * *

Twenty-five years ago a group of students graduating from Canadian Mennonite Bible College (CMBC) argued about the wording of the theme for their graduation service. David Schroeder's classes in biblical theology were probably the strongest influence in the choice of the two main concepts we were considering: freedom and obedience. The discussion centered on the way these concepts relate. Should the theme read "Freed to Obey" or "Obey to be Free?" I was one of the students who argued first one way and then another, not convinced that the tension between the two concepts could be wholly resolved. Theological study had told me that according to my Anabaptist heritage, obedience was central to discipleship. Moreover, I had begun to experience something of the freedom God gives to those who follow. Yet I had a vague intuition that obedience and freedom could not be put together as easily as our class was trying to do with either choice of wording.

Today I am struggling with the same tension, but the issue has become larger than a mere question over proper wording of a graduation theme. This tension, as I see it now, is deeply rooted in the experience of many women in our churches and society who obey but do not find freedom; who serve but do not discover abundant life. It finds expression in the ambiguity women feel as they ask how they can authentically and freely communicate their experience within the hermeneutical communities where their voices have been marginalized.

On Method

To address the central issues of women in the hermeneutical community, I will look closely at a process of biblical interpretation which takes into account both the context of the reader as well as the content of the biblical texts.[3] The motif of discipleship will be the central guide in bringing these two foci together.[4] My concern throughout this study will be to understand how women can responsibly and freely participate in biblical interpretation within the church. In this I am partly emulating a process I have learned from my Anabaptist forebears. As expressed by Walter Klaassen, Anabaptists claim that the "text can be properly understood only when disciples are gathered together to discover what the Word has to say to their needs and concerns."[5] This emphasis on the body of disciples as the primary "clue-generating community"[6] for biblical interpretation is important for the church since it makes women and their experience integral to the theological process.

Yet it is not really Anabaptist theology but rather feminist theology that has helped me to understand more clearly how important the relationship between theory and practice actually is.[7] Here I have come to see how extensively theology has concerned itself with abstract truth at the expense of seriously examining the practical function of concepts in the faith community. Hence it is necessary to integrate the theoretical and the practical import of discipleship. We must ask what discipleship has meant for both women and men as they participated in the life of the church. How has it affected the way they communicate their experiences and understandings of the Bible within the congregation?

In the first part of the paper I will make some preliminary observations about the relationship between the community *tradition* of discipleship and the community *practice* of biblical interpretation within Mennonite congregations.[8] In the second part I will concentrate on developing an understanding of discipleship as presented in the gospel of Mark. I have chosen Mark, the gospel of the "way" of discipleship, because I want to begin with concrete *stories* of discipleship.[9] Although the *teachings* on discipleship in Matthew and Luke, especially as presented in the Sermon on the Mount, have been more influential in Mennonite writings, it is significant to begin with a re-examination of the context of Jesus' actions and life. In this way, I am emphasizing the dynamic nature of discipleship which all too easily becomes static as teachings become rules. Because Mark knows of the "paradigmatic discipleship of women"[10] this gospel becomes particularly crucial in examining what discipleship meant for both women and men in the early church.

One final comment on method. An important aspect of theological method is choosing conversation partners with whom to discuss and test ideas. Both my Mennonite heritage and feminist theology have influenced the questions I am asking and the approach I am taking.[11] In addition to consulting biblical scholars of both literary and historical-critical persuasions as I tested and refined my inductive reading of Mark, I also engaged in dialogue with several intentional hermeneutical communities formed for the purpose of giving shape to this paper.

This included not only several meetings with a group of Mennonite scholars and pastors, but also numerous discussions with women who are part of Mennonite congregations. Both aspects of this approach have helped focus my questions and observations about understanding women in the hermeneutical community.

The purpose of this paper is not to outline a conclusive definition of discipleship or of the hermeneutical community, but rather to analyze the process itself. This study seeks to examine the way we search for truth as part of the ongoing journey of life. It is to challenge past formulations by giving a central place to women's realities.

The Historical Context

The ambivalence and tension that Mennonite women feel as they begin to participate more directly in scholarly theological study no doubt has many causes.[12] It is clear that part of this ambivalence arises out of their perception and understanding of faith as taught and practised by their congregations. Included are both the theological tradition and the pattern of social interactions within the community.

Emphasis on the hermeneutical community has been of particular importance for Mennonite women. By implication all members of the congregation are responsible for discerning the meaning of the Bible for both their personal and their communal lives. Neither hierarchical authority, nor specialized theologians are to be the final judges of the Bible's meaning. There is no privilege of the powerful. Accountability is to the whole community of faithful followers. The congregation discovers the guidance of the Spirit through mutual dialogue and counsel.

Practically, this means that women in the Mennonite church have been given freedom to participate in Bible study. Women have faithfully attended adult education classes, Bible schools and Bible colleges. However, not until recently have women become adult education teachers, pastors, writers or theology professors. Their understanding and experience were included only indirectly in the theological heritage which formed the life of the church. Books on Mennonite history and Anabaptist theology were silent about women's participation in the faith heritage. There were almost no female writers of books on Mennonite theology and mission. Issues that especially concerned women, such as family violence and pornography, were not addressed as part of the Mennonite understanding of peacemaking. Other issues such as abortion, marriage and divorce were usually discussed only by men. The boards of congregations and church conferences were usually male-dominated even though women were actively involved in the life of the church. Women's voices were often heard only by other women in women's Bible study groups or in auxiliary organizations in the church.

The silence of women in biblical interpretation has been supported by another aspect of the theological tradition.[13] Discipleship, understood primarily as obedience, service and self denial, supported the silent role of women. These features of discipleship conformed so closely to the characteristics of women as defined by society that their subordinate role was not questioned. A committed disciple was to obey the will of God, that is, to live a life of service and self-denial. This implied being humble, giving up power and going the way of the cross. Love, nonresistance, cross-bearing and separation from the world were all part of being disciples. These expectations also coincided with the role of women in a patriarchal society.[14] Ideal mothers were to love and give unceasingly of themselves. Women who stayed in the home were protected from the world and its evil as these have traditionally been defined. Nonresistance, love and cross-bearing describe the way women were expected to respond to the demands of men who are "the head of the home." Thus the ethic of discipleship has affirmed the status quo for women in a patriarchal society.

This emphasis has affected how women have come to understand themselves. They have developed a personal-domestic as opposed to a communal-public self-understanding. This has grave implications for the formation and articulation of a church theology.[15] In its relationship and institutional structures the church has not challenged the patriarchal separation of the personal-domestic and the communal-public realm according to gender. Women therefore applied the texts to their domestic life and learned to serve the aims of the mission organizations of the church.[16] Men were given responsibility for shaping a "public theology" which directed the church in its social and political functions.

As a result, women have learned that talk of servantleadership did not apply to them. It was not considered the duty or obligation of women to initiate theological conversation in public places. This view has been reinforced by texts from the epistles which stressed silence and obedience. Discipleship was "internalized" to mean submission and support for the structures of the church.

Women have struggled with the roles assigned to them and with an understanding of discipleship that supports unquestioned obedience to this teaching. They were, however, not able to highlight this in conferences or articulate it in Mennonite writings. Even today feminist theologians struggle to be taken seriously because the issues they speak to are considered marginal.

For men the notion of discipleship functioned very differently. Service, self denial and nonresistance challenged the status quo of male roles in the larger society. The demands of discipleship in the complexities of the economic, political and social realm were considered to be primary agenda for theology. Much has been written by men about the issues they face as they attempt to live according to an ethic of servanthood in the community and in public life. It is in this way that the issues related to the use of power in social and political life have been made central to Mennonite theology.

As women have entered public life in their vocations, changes are also coming about in the life of the congregation. Women are no longer content to be on the periphery of the hermeneutical community. Therefore, central theological formulations are being re-examined in order to include women's experience. Areas of life that society and the church have so often separated along gender lines—the personal and the social, the intellectual and the emotional, the domestic and the communal-public—now must be integrated. One way to begin this process is by exploring the biblical text with an openness to reinterpreting important theological formulations so that they can become freeing for all people. Serious engagement with the early Christian faith will invite us to hear again the call to discipleship. For Mennonite women this renewed listening to the text is fundamental as they seek to enter more fully into the hermeneutical community.

Women and the Biblical Story

Since discipleship is clearly an important theme in Mark, a study of this early gospel can guide us to a deeper understanding of what following Jesus meant for the early church.[17] The focus in this section of the essay will be on the women who followed Jesus. We will endeavour a careful reading of the text and ask whether there are not aspects of discipleship that are often missed when the focus is only on the Twelve.

Women as Followers

Before focusing on the women's response to Jesus we must first examine whether Mark includes women when he refers to the disciples of Jesus.[18] Many commentators have simply equated the disciples with the Twelve.[19] Though the term, discipleship, may be used generically to include all persons who follow Jesus, the particular texts used to define its characteristics are about male disciples. We must therefore look carefully at the way Mark speaks of the disciples. Whom does he include and whom does he exclude? Why does he choose certain people and not others in the way he tells the story?

Mark uses the word "disciple" forty-two times to speak of the associates of Jesus and makes specific reference to the Twelve in eleven verses. The word "apostle" is used once.[20] There are a number of different texts which focus on three members, or even one member of the disciple circle, namely Peter. Although "disciple" seems to be a favourite word of Mark's, it is not completely clear how inclusive the term is. Moreover, it is not evident how the disciples are set apart from the crowd, even though the disciples and those with Jesus are distinguished from his opponents, particularly the scribes and Pharisees.

Elizabeth Struthers Malbon suggests that a better understanding of discipleship would include all who meet the demands of following Jesus.[21] The word "follow" is used in the calling of Simon and Andrew as well as Levi. It is used in a number of places in the sense of journeying "on the way" with Jesus.[22] Jesus uses the term when he challenges the crowd and his disciples to deny themselves, take up the cross and "follow" him (8:34). Peter speaks of having left all to "follow" Jesus (10: 28), and Bartimaeus "followed" Jesus on the way (10:52). It is interesting that in the passion narrative the term is used specifically of women. There it speaks of Mary Magdalene, Mary the mother of Jesus, and Salome, who, "used to follow him and provided for him when he was in Galilee" (15:41). Mark writes the women into the story only at the end even though he points out that they were present from the beginning. An important question for us to examine is: how do the stories of women in the rest of the gospel relate to discipleship?

Mark gives another clue to understanding discipleship by the way in which he pictures the relationship between the larger group of followers and the Twelve. Some commentators would use a diagram of two concentric circles to describe this relationship with the innermost core closest to Jesus being Peter, James and John, the next group being the Twelve and the largest circle including all the other disciples, perhaps even the crowd. Women are excluded from the inner circle, unless the women in chapter 15 would be taken as a parallel inner circle.[23]

Perhaps the relationship between the larger and smaller groups of disciples is best seen in the role each fills in Mark's story. Some functions are common to both groups.[24] Both groups travelled with Jesus in Galilee and on the way to Jerusalem. Both received private teaching. Jesus rebuked both for their failure to understand. Jesus called on all to deny themselves, take up the cross and follow. However, several passages suggest a role for the smaller groups which is not explicitly stated for all the disciples. In the appointment of the Twelve we read that they were chosen by Jesus to be with him and "to be sent out to proclaim the message and to have authority to cast out demons" (3:13). This is followed in a later chapter with the sending out of the Twelve two by two with authority over the unclean spirits (6:7). They preached, cast out demons and anointed with oil many who were sick (6:13). It is in this context that we have the only use of "apostle." "The apostles returned to Jesus and told him all that they had done and taught" (6:30).

A more specific role is also associated with the groups of two or three. Peter and Andrew were called to become "fishers of men [sic]." Peter, James and John were witnesses to the raising of Jairus' daughter and to the transfiguration. These three were also asked to be with Jesus in his prayer at Gethsemane. The women were witnesses of the death and received a specific commandment to "…go, tell his disciples and Peter that he is going ahead of you to Galilee" (16:7).

This would suggest that in Mark the smaller groupings are the ones called to specific responsibilities or tasks. They are not insiders who alone receive esoteric teaching so that they will understand Jesus more clearly. This teaching is open to all followers to all who have "ears that can hear." All followers must exemplify their response to Jesus in their actions. However, Mark gives particular functions of public leadership to the smaller groupings of persons who are responsible for participating in the mission of Jesus. In his portrayal of the smaller groupings Mark emphasizes the specific challenges and responsibilities associated with an open acknowledgement of commitment to Jesus and his mission.

In Mark's story then, women remained hidden in the crowd much longer than male followers of Jesus. Although Mark includes stories of women who responded to Jesus, they fade back into the crowd and are not openly part of the circle of disciples around Jesus and they do not directly participate in the mission of Jesus. Nevertheless, it is clear that Mark considered the women followers of Jesus and included them in his use of the word "disciple."

Mark in Historical Perspective

In his narrative Mark most often associates women with the crowd or with the larger grouping of unnamed followers. The primary actors are male. Women are clearly present in his gospel in no less than sixteen contexts, but they do not become the primary characters of the story. They are generally pictured as silent and their direct conversation is seldom recorded. In a number of places they exemplify self-denying service. They are named and specifically identified with the disciple-circle only in the passion narratives. Until then they are presented "as minor characters who make brief cameo appearances and then disappear...."[25] Prior to chapter 15, verse 40, Mark mentions no woman by name except Herodias (who clearly is not one of the disciples) and Mary, the mother of Jesus. A number of commentators have pointed out that in contrast to the Twelve, women exemplified the servant role of true discipleship. The socially accepted role of women and the understanding of true discipleship seemed to coincide fairly well. To be considered disciples of Jesus, women needed to accept the role that society placed on them and remain hidden in the crowd, quietly carrying out their role of supportive servants.

Munro is convinced that this "anonymity and relative invisibility of women in Mark is due in part to the androcentric bias of his culture which viewed women only in terms of their relations to men."[26] There are, however, hints that this patriarchal picture is not completely accepted by the writer of Mark. He begins to correct his androcentric bias by stressing stories that show Jesus' solidarity with the social and religious outcasts of society. The controversy dialogues and sayings in Mark indirectly challenge patriarchal structures.[27] Furthermore, the stories in which women appear do not picture them solely in stereotypical roles. There is a move here to place women into the public realm. A critical impulse that denies male centrality in God's kingdom can be seen in Mark's mention of the "many women" who already followed from the beginning and in the important part women play in the resurrection accounts.[28] In order to understand the importance of these changes we must look more closely at specific women portrayed in the Gospel of Mark.

Mark's View of Discipleship for Women

Even though Mark does not tell his stories from the point of view of women, insight into the issues that they faced is evident in the stories where women appear. It is especially important to note the places of tension in these stories. Women who had internalized the values of their society would have felt some of the same tensions regarding their role as did the male writer. An important clue, therefore, is found in the actions or words of women that created anxiety in the other actors in the stories. Throughout the Markan narrative, when the mystery of the kingdom has implications for their own lives the disciples protest or do not understand or are afraid.[29] Hints of misunderstanding or fear are also important clues in understanding the struggle of women disciples. Furthermore, Jesus' response to the women may provide a clue to the particular challenge laid before them. His praise of a woman's action would point to an aspect of following that is new and important. A closer look at the key stories in which women play a role will highlight the visions and struggles of women followers of Jesus.

Mark 3:31-35. In this short episode Jesus responds to the request of his mother and brothers to see him by placing obedience to God over against the usual primacy of natural blood relationships. Doing God's will creates a new social reality which is to substitute for the requirements usually associated with close family ties. The inclusion of the word "sisters" suggests that the group sitting around Jesus included women who had become part of a new community committed to doing God's will; women who were followers of Jesus. Implicit in this pericope is the idea that family relationships do not confer status or special treatment on disciples of Jesus. The assumption that women understand their place primarily in terms of their household status is shattered in this passage. Women, as well as men, are challenged to follow wherever Jesus leads.

Mark 5:25-34. The struggle of the woman healed of the flow of blood is described by words such as fear and trembling. She attempts to receive healing unobtrusively by touching the garments of Jesus. She is well aware that because she is unclean she is an outsider. Did she struggle with a deep sense of unworthiness and therefore try to reach the healing power of Jesus in a quiet, undemanding way? Her faith is strong and she receives the desired healing. But Jesus takes her a step further. He challenges her to tell the whole truth in a public place in front of the crowd gathered around him. The healing miracle gave her the courage to speak up. Jesus affirms her by calling her "daughter" and telling her to go in peace.

Mark 7:24-30. In this story we have the rare phenomenon of direct conversation by a woman. (The only other such occasions are in chapter 6 with Herodias and in chapter 16 where words are spoken by the women going to the empty tomb.) The dialogue between Jesus and the woman clearly centres on accepted social and religious divisions between Jews and gentiles. The woman challenges Jesus to go beyond these accepted divisions and heal her daughter. It is noteworthy that for "this saying" she can go her way, knowing that the demon will have left her daughter. Her challenge to Jesus was understood by him as a sign of her faith. We can assume that it was not easy for the woman to go beyond the accepted social customs in order to try to reach the Jewish rabbi with her concern.[30]

Mark 10:13-16. This story does not specifically mention women but it is generally assumed that women were among those bringing children to Jesus. The rebuke of the disciples based on an accepted social division between children and adults brings forth both Jesus' indignation and his beautiful words, "Let the little children come to me." Jesus affirms those who recognize his acceptance of the little ones.

Mark 14:1-11. In this story a woman anoints the head of Jesus. By this "prophetic sign-action" Jesus is named and recognized as the Anointed One, the Messiah, the Christ.[31] This passage begins the stories on the passion of Christ just as in a parallel way the narrative of Peter's confession introduces the section on the prediction of the suffering of Jesus. However, here the confession is not made in words but in action. In comparison to some of the other gospel narratives, this woman is pictured as anointing the head, not the feet of Jesus. A hint of boldness arises here which suggests a deep love for Jesus. This is the story of a disciple of Jesus who has understood his Messiahship and is ready to proclaim this insight with her actions. By placing the story of Judas' decision to betray Jesus into the same context the writer of Mark emphasizes the contrast between these two disciples.

We can only guess what this action meant for the woman by noting the criticism she received for it. The money should have been given to the poor. She has broken accepted religious patterns with her action. Jesus, however, commends her and prophesies that her action will be proclaimed wherever the good news is preached throughout the world.

Mark 15:40-47. Here the emphasis is on the women who witnessed the death and burial of Jesus. The women are named and yet are part of a much larger group that has been following Jesus to Jerusalem. Their role until this point had been to "minister" to Jesus, something that fits in well with the accepted role of women.

But here they suddenly enter front stage as primary witnesses to Jesus' death, burial and resurrection. They watched from afar, probably because of a very real fear they had for their lives.[32]

Mark 16:1-8. This story begins by repeating the names of the women. Again anointing is mentioned, thus connecting this story with the one in chapter 14. The direct speech indicates the women's worry—the very practical matter of rolling away the large stone. The story emphasizes the largeness of the stone and the weakness of the women. The women see the young man dressed in a white robe who tells them that Jesus has risen. They receive the command to go and tell his disciples and Peter that he is going before them to Galilee. The women are entrusted with the message for the other disciples. It is important to note how their feelings are described. They are amazed when they see the empty tomb and the young man. This amazement changes to trembling and astonishment when they are given the command to proclaim the resurrection. According to this ending of Mark they do not say anything to anyone because they are afraid. The story ends with the silence, fear and disobedience of the women.

Discipleship Re-examined: Summary Reflections

What then does the call to discipleship mean for women? The women in Mark are generally pictured as part of the larger group of "little people" who have little status in society and often come to Jesus for healing.[33] Their behaviour demonstrates faith and service. This coincides with the orientation to family and home for women in a patriarchal society. However, our brief survey of the main stories reveals that women too struggle with their response to Jesus and that this response requires breaking out of pre-established roles.

In Mark's telling of the story, several clues indicate that the issue for women was whether to become visible, whether to step out from the crowd in order to gain healing or express love. It was not easy to take the initiative for overcoming social barriers in order to gain access to Jesus, whether these stemmed from the Jew-gentile, adult-child, or clean-unclean dichotomies. Renouncing the self meant a willingness to speak in public both about one's uncleanness and about one's healing (as the woman with the flow of blood did); it meant courageously and persistently challenging the barriers which denied them access to Jesus (as the mothers of the children or the gentile woman did). Following Jesus may also have meant that women gave up the security and status of their place in the family social unit to be included in a new social grouping of those who do the will of God. Being obedient to God could mean risking arrest and death.

The last few stories in Mark bring new aspects of women's experience into the open. Women are shown not only as those who need healing but also as those who become responsible. Rhoads and Michie point out that the women and the other "little people" begin to fulfill the roles expected of the Twelve who fail Jesus at the end.[34] The woman who anointed Jesus becomes a model of discipleship in her love and understanding of Jesus. The women who witness the death and burial demonstrate a courage which the other disciples lack. It becomes clearer that, for both women and for men, following Jesus may mean risking or sacrificing money, reputation and even life.

Malbon interprets the focus on the women in the final chapters as a reversal of the historically conditioned expectations which the implied readers would have had of women.[35] The reversal of outsider and insider permeates Mark's gospel and is clearly stated in Mark 10:31: "many who are first will be last, and the last will be first." The historical reality of women's discipleship overturns the expectations of the implied reader who expects little from women. In this context the ending of Mark is particularly crucial. The story ends in ambiguity. The women are challenged to become the proclaimers of the good news of the resurrection. They are asked to accept the responsibility of being the first witnesses to the other disciples and to Peter. But Mark ends the story telling of their failure.[36]

The early church as well as biblical commentators have been uneasy with this ending. The other gospel writers affirm that the women did tell the story, though the disciples did not believe them and thought it was "an idle tale." Several later additions to Mark's gospel also support this version. First Corinthians is the only record which cites the proclamation of the resurrection going through Peter and the Twelve without mention of the women. Church history confirms that both men and women have continued to struggle with the role of women as proclaimers of the good news.

The ambiguity of the ending of Mark's gospel remains if we stay with the question of the author's intention. No clear indication of his purpose is given.[37] However, the unclear ending leaves the decision with the reader who must supply the ending. The narrator asks the reader to evaluate and respond to the silence of the women. Will the women overcome their feelings of weakness and fear? Will they accept the command to proclaim the good news? Will they become full and responsible partners with the other disciples in spite of initial failure?

By bringing the silent women into the foreground, Mark is suggesting a direction in which God is leading the early Christians in their understanding of discipleship. Malbon summarizes the twofold message: "anyone can be a follower; no one finds it easy."[38] I suggest in addition that the women in Mark leave us with the challenge to become free from the social barriers that bind us. In turn we are empowered to step out from the crowd and become involved in Christ's mission. Discipleship means accepting responsibility for the gospel message and following Jesus into the world.

This understanding of discipleship opens our eyes to new characteristics of the Jesus whom we are challenged to follow. The emphasis is now on the leadership of Jesus in his courage to act even at the point of greatest vulnerability. We are struck with the boldness of Jesus as he questions the institutional structures which attempt to define and limit his relationships to people (Mark 2; 11:27-33; 12:13-40). We understand in a new way those stories in which Jesus is not able to do any great work because nothing is expected of the carpenter from Nazareth (Mark 6:1-6). We recognize the leadership of Jesus in his questioning of the traditions and in his breaking out of established social and religious norms (Mark 7). We gain courage by noting Jesus' answer to those who questioned his authority (Mark 11:27-33). We identify with aspects of Jesus' struggle in Gethsemane realizing that the human temptation is to avoid the responsibility and pain of doing God's will (Mark 14:32-42). The way of the cross is understood as a way of courageous suffering which arises out of inner strength and leads to freedom from that which limits doing God's will.

The emphasis in this definition of discipleship is placed on the need to be freed from those institutions and social expectations which limit full participation in the mission of Jesus. The challenge is to step out of the crowd and be willing to confess publicly the need for healing as well as the joy of full acceptance. A disciple is one who is empowered and freed to obey the call into mission.

The Tension within Discipleship

To fully understand the dimension of discipleship that comes to the fore with the women in Mark we must briefly compare their experiences with the stories of the Twelve. These are focused particularly well for us in the narratives following Peter's confession. In chapter 8 Peter is rebuked for having in mind the things of human value rather than the things of God. One must be willing to give up even one's life for the sake of Jesus and the gospel. In chapter 9 Jesus follows up on the discussion of who will be the greatest by taking a child and placing it in the midst of the Twelve. Following Jesus means being willing to be last of all and servant of all. Chapter 10 emphasizes giving up riches in order to enter the kingdom as well as leaving relatives and lands for the sake of the gospel. It also includes the story of James and John who wanted to sit at the right and left of Jesus in glory. This is followed by the teaching of a new way of leadership which does not lord it over others but which willingly serves as Jesus did.

The emphasis in these passages is on following Jesus who gives up his "power," "prestige," and "position" to follow the way of the cross.[39] Jesus is the one who chooses a life of servanthood and ministry. He does not exercise his prerogative to rule by lording it over others but willingly suffers and dies for the sake of the people whom he loves. He chooses to associate with sinners and outcasts, he identifies with the "little ones" and willingly serves, giving his life for the sake of those undeserving of his love. He becomes an outsider so that outsiders may become insiders in the kingdom of God.

If we compare this understanding of discipleship with that gained from the women disciples we note that there is a certain tension between the two understandings of what following Jesus means. One focuses particularly on what discipleship means when one perceives oneself or is perceived as being powerless; the other focuses on what it means when one is seen or sees oneself as having or deserving power, prestige or status.[40] If one is already in the position of a servant, a "little one," the need is to become empowered, to break through the structures which bind to gain healing and take responsibility for the gospel message. However, if one is in a position of power and leadership the need is to become a servant, to willingly give up power which may limit or dominate the other. The paradox in Mark's understanding of discipleship warns us against an oversimplified understanding which is not related to the social reality of life.

Conclusion

How does this study of discipleship set a direction for a re-examination of how women and men are involved in the hermeneutical community? What new questions does it raise for our consideration?

Firstly, this study points to the complexity of the theological notion of discipleship. If we try to understand what following Jesus means in particular social and religious contexts instead of only in an abstract general way, we will be able to see more clearly both the opportunities and temptations that face us as Christians in the twentieth century. We will better understand what it may mean to follow Jesus in the communities in which we are often labelled according to our position in the hierarchical ladder of status and prestige. We will be able to identify how we have internalized false understandings. The theology of discipleship will then challenge our too easy acceptance of the roles that society assigns to us. It asks us to bring together theory and experience, the theological formulation and its concrete function in the community.

Secondly, if this analysis of the biblical notion of discipleship has any validity at all, it implies that we must consciously restructure our hermeneutical communities. We must begin to take women as well as other "little people" seriously in how we plan our discussions and interactions, whether in the congregation or in the academy. We must look for the silent people in our biblical discussions and theological writings and find ways to empower them so that they too can participate in shaping the theology of the church. We must be sensitive to the way our key theological formulations sometimes function to make persons outsiders to the hermeneutical process. We must make discipleship an inclusive word rather than one that renders some persons outsiders.

Finally, this study also challenges us to reflect on the reasons why certain emphases have become more important than others in the teaching, preaching and theological writings of Mennonites. Why has discipleship as obedience to institutions and structures become internalized for many persons even though Anabaptism began with a challenge to many institutions of its day? Why have we so easily identified with the male rather than the female disciples?[41] What threatened the church so that obedience rather than empowerment became primary in its understandings? Why did the church accept the easy division between private and public, personal and social, female and male? Who benefits from these divisions?

Discipleship can function to exclude, marginalize and silence persons in our hermeneutical communities. The paradoxical relationship between freedom and obedience, service and empowerment can remind us that as we listen to each other we will hear again the call to discipleship from the One who invited all to follow in the "way."

***

BIBLICAL INTERPRETATION: A PRAXIS OF DISCIPLESHIP[42]

We certainly were not aware that the small group brought together by Kathy Schantz (representing MCC Women's Concern Committee of MCC USA and Canada) in early 1991 would initiate a series of conferences for Mennonite women interested in "doing" theology. At this informal gathering, Arnold Snyder and John Fast represented Conrad Grebel College (a Mennonite institution associated with the University of Waterloo) while Carol Penner and I (both of us doctoral students in theology) represented women interested in the scholarly study of theology. The idea that was being presented to us was to plan a conference in which women would be both presenters and responders in an exploration of various themes in theology.

As far as we knew this would be the first formal gathering of Mennonite women involved in scholarly theology. We were enthusiastic about the idea but also had some reservations about the usual way in which theological discussions were held. Both Carol and I had experienced academic discussions and felt that their critical orientation was hurtful to women just entering the field. Usually the presentations were long with very little time for audience participation. The respondents worked much harder in finding the deficiencies in the paper than in supporting some of the good ideas. Was there not another way to do good academic work? Could not a way be found in which collaboration was the approach rather than critical analysis alone? Could different practices of theological discussion take place if women took the lead?

In addition, we wanted worship to be integrated with the scholarly discussions. In fact, worship needed to be central, since not all knowledge was analytical and rational, especially if we think about knowledge of God. There needed to also be a way in which our bodies and our emotions could intentionally be involved in the process. There needed to be room for passion and for personal experience not mere abstract detached presentations.

I remember the animated conversation around the title of the conference. "Doing" was not a usual term for the work of theology. For the female members of the committee it was a deliberate choice emphasizing that this was not merely a theoretical exercise but a serious praxis that has implications for the life of the church and academy. The mode of discussion was to bring experience and the Bible, practice and theory, together in a collaborative, non-adversarial conversation. For me this was a chance to look at the question of theological method from a wholly different perspective, a perspective in which the church community was not peripheral.

There was also much discussion about how to make this conversation accessible to more women. Because it is difficult for participants to enter the conversation if they are only hearing the presentation for the first time, the decision was made that the major presentations would be pre-published in the Conrad Grebel Review *so that everyone would have access to the speakers' words. In addition, respondents were encouraged to correspond with the primary presenters so that a collaborative process could be put in place right from the beginning.*

The presentations were divided along the usual academic disciplinary lines such as history, theology, biblical studies, and ethics. However, we included practitioners from various work situations who reflected on issues raised within their context. These included those with experiences with Mennonite Central Committee, in a government social services department, in grassroots peace and justice work, and in the area of domestic abuse.

Our anticipation was high; our fears were also very great! Who would come to such a conference? The brochure gave the purpose in this way: "to provide a forum for Mennonite women to work on theological issues and to provide a meeting place for women and men who are interested in exploring the emerging theological voices of women." About 180 self-selected women representing different branches of the Mennonite church attended this meeting. Very few men were present. This was somewhat disappointing since the Mennonite colleges always gave the lack of qualified women as their reason for not hiring women.. We thought this would have been an ideal place to hear women and to encourage them as prospective faculty members. It seems that there was confusion among the men as to whether they were invited or even welcome!

My husband Gary, who was one of the few men who attended, writes about how it felt to join his bass voice to that chorus of sopranos and altos. "I sailed into the conference in good spirits, looking forward to some good theological stimulation—until we got to the first hymn as we started our worship. I belted out my bass line loudly and with confidence. But amid the beautiful all-female choir with only soprano and alto sounds, my bass voice sounded like an intrusion."[43] *He goes on to use this experience as a metaphor of how women must feel when male voices dominate in the chorus of theological voices. He continues, "I long for the time when the church will invite women's voices as a full part of the theological choir. Till then I will gladly feel exposed and discombobulated in the occasional women's theological choir." His support was especially important to me as I presented my first major paper arising out of my doctoral work. Still, it was comforting that we were among women and male supporters rather than in a critical academic context.*

I very much needed support in the presentation and discussion of my paper. I felt very vulnerable in presenting it as I already knew that one of my respondents, a New Testament scholar, disagreed with my approach. Her response suggested that I no longer opened myself to the revelation of the text because I used a feminist hermeneutic. Instead, she suggested that I sought to direct the process of interpretation to further my own feminist goals.[44] *She identified feminism as an ideology that prevents one from being open to the intent of the writer or to the timeless transcendent truth beyond the writer.*

This reaction raised an important question for me: are the various methodologies that we use in biblical interpretation value-free? Are the questions that historical or literary methods ask more value free than those that feminist scholars or theologians ask? My answer was that methods are only tools for the greater task of listening to the texts, and that by using a variety of tools we can more easily hear what the text has to say. However, the niggling suspicion that we cannot separate our methods so easily from their pre-suppositions was still there for me.

At the time, I felt somewhat defensive. I had thought long and hard about what to say and felt misunderstood by some of the participants. Feminism was and perhaps continues to be a troubling word for many women. At this conference many women were unaware of the various approaches of feminist theology and some women were definitely opposed to any use of feminist language. I had intentionally named my approach as feminist because I define it in its most basic form: women are fully human and made in the image of God, therefore they should be treated as such. I resist definitions that speak about equality with men, as if maleness defines who is human. I wanted to rather speak about mutuality in relationships between women and men.

But in the discussion of the paper I felt caught between those women that wished to address power imbalances and those who would rather speak about "women's ways of knowing," a side of feminism that assumes that women have a more intuitive, "right brain" approach to knowledge.[45] *The more technical theological language that was used by those of us who were academics was also foreign to many. As a result, we spoke past each other.*

In addition, there were other unspoken fears. Katie Funk Wiebe expressed some of the questions that lay beneath these first conversations that we were having as women doing theology. "Can biblical feminists hang on to biblical faith? Can women remove themselves from their own agenda when they come to the text? What if God actually wanted women to be submissive, subservient, yielding, not using their gifts fully?" [46] *Other women spoke openly about their anger at the church institution and articulated their personal questions as to whether they could continue in a male-dominated church based on an androcentric Bible.*

Katie Funk Wiebe was asked to speak at the conference as one of these early female pioneers in doing theology. Though she was not an academic theologian as such, she often reflected theologically on her own experience in her many inspiring books. Many of her thoughts fit with ideas expressed by feminists. She suggested in her own perceptive summary of the conference that the role of experience in theologizing could have been more central in the discussion and would need further exploration. Her summary of what happened when women found their voices expresses well the other side of what I also experienced at this meeting of women.

> *They lifted their voices with joy about the privilege of being a woman who could give birth to a child and nurture it. They spoke*

> *about the privilege of bringing happiness and celebration to other's lives. They spoke as prophets against the physical and sexual abuse of women, of poverty and domination. They spoke in a voice filled with terror. "How can I bring up my children so that they're not ravished and also don't ravish others?" pled one mother. They affirmed one another as disciples who are thinkers, scholars."*[47]

One of the hopes that many women had for this conference was to find colleagues who were interested in the same questions that we had. I remember well my excitement in meeting Nadine Pence Franz who was working on similar themes. The many discussions that happened in the washroom, around the dining room tables, and in the hallways were as important as the formal ones in the lecture hall.

Throughout my studies, I had missed having female mentors and role models from my own denomination who could both encourage and challenge me. This gathering of women created space for mentoring and peer support. It encouraged us to find each other and to use every opportunity for dialogue. Since that time, I have actively tried to initiate and be part of small groups of women interested in theological discussions. I am particularly encouraged by women who gathered at the Mennonite World Conference in Pennsylvania in 2015 to set up a network of female theologians. I pray that these networks can encourage women throughout the world so that they can work side by side with men in providing leadership for our larger denomination in the area of theology and biblical studies.

* * *

Preface

One reason I entered formal theological studies after many years of homemaking was to come to terms with the ambiguous and contradictory way the Bible functions in the life of the church. I have frequently seen the Bible used as the ultimate authoritative weapon in ethical, theological, and political battles.[48] It has legitimized and justified oppressive institutions and practices. Yet I have also seen the Bible used to enable women and men to interpret reality in the light of God's incarnational love. I have seen Bible study empower individuals and communities to initiate significant changes in the world about them—changes which to me were signs of God's coming reign of love and peace.

My primary interest in formal studies was to explore the Bible in order to understand how the same text could function in such contradictory ways. When I registered at a school of theology I assumed that I would enter the biblical department in order to examine questions related to the issue of biblical authority in the context of the actual exegesis of texts. However, a phone call from the director of advanced degree studies made me aware of the strict division between disciplines. Biblical exegesis was done in the Bible department, primarily using historical methodologies. It was the theology department that focused on contemporary issues such as biblical hermeneutics and biblical authority.

I soon discovered that the division between departments also encouraged a basic division between the actual practice of reading the Bible and theological reflection on that practice. In none of my classes in theology and hermeneutics was the Bible ever used directly or recommended as reading material. In a number of classes any reference to particular Scripture passages was discouraged because it meant a "crossing of disciplines." The ethical and theological decisions that were made in the course of scholarly work did not seem to be informed by a continual wrestling with particular biblical texts.

It was my readings in feminist theology which challenged me to return to the biblical text in order to deal with the practical questions which I faced in my scholarly work. For example, Elizabeth Schüssler Fiorenza calls for women to claim their Christian identity in the "discipleship of equals" begun by Jesus.[49] She emphasizes that biblical scholarship, as a "communicative practice which involves interests, values, and visions," is then informed by that identity.[50] In a critical article on feminist ideology, Sandra Schneiders emphasizes the transformation that happens as interpreters accept the "invitation to enter into and inhabit the world of discipleship."[51] Though the historical world described by the Bible is patriarchal, the Bible can mediate a vision of discipleship which transcends that world. These challenges struck a responsive chord in me, reminding me of important discipleship texts in my own tradition.

In Mennonite tradition discipleship has been a way of expressing the unity of "knowing and doing" in a life of following the way of Jesus. Defined largely as self-denial and sacrifice, discipleship has regularly and easily been applied to the traditional life of "doing." For many women this has been assumed to be a career of homemaking and childcare. However, what discipleship means for work focused on "knowing," for the daily life of a scholar, seems much more ambiguous and unclear.

This paper will therefore explore the issues related to the scholarly practice of biblical exegesis and interpretation in the context of a theology of discipleship. The approach will be self-reflective, attempting critically and creatively to bring together theory and practice in our approach to the Bible. Though focused on the issues of a biblical scholar it raises crucial questions about the nature of discipleship for all who are committed to following in the way of Jesus.

Introduction

A. Historical perspective.

Barbara Brown Zikmund's summary of the modem history of American women's relationship to the Bible can be helpful to us in providing a background to a critical look at women's involvement in biblical studies. She has pointed out the challenges which women's new self-consciousness of themselves as women has brought to biblical studies.[52] This history can be summarized in five overlapping stages:

(1) In the early 19th century the Bible was used meticulously to define the differences between men and women, usually in ways which made women both different and secondary in creation and redemption. This hierarchical interpretation was often used to justify women's place in society.

(2) By the middle of the 19th century a rising feminist consciousness called for discrimination between those parts of the Bible which were essential and those which were culturally relative. The masculine bias of biblical interpretation was recognized in the way essentials had been defined in the past.

(3) By the 1880s women recognized the need to do their own serious study of the Bible to counteract the oppressive use of the Bible. During most of the 19th century biblical studies by women attempted to compensate for the inequality, marginality, and oppression which they experienced by glorifying women's place as a special calling to serve God in a unique way. They studied the lives of great women and examined the roles of women in the Bible.

(4) In the early 20th century women's studies programs began to stress not only the differences between sexes but also their equality and common humanity. Alternative images of biblical women were highlighted and stories were remembered which allowed women to claim their history and to emphasize the equality and complementarity of women and men. These studies were considered supplementary, like the studies of other minority groups, and were thus situated on the edges of the academic world.

(5) Feminist studies in the later 20th century have begun to use the material and methods cultivated in women's studies to critique past assumptions and to create a new interpretive framework. This means that not only those texts dealing directly with women but every biblical text must be approached through inclusive questions. The goal for feminists is to reconstruct theology by liberating the faith (including the Bible) from oppressive patriarchal patterns of thought and action.

These five historical stages still find expression in the wide range of ways that Mennonite women relate to the Bible at the present time. In their participation in adult Sunday school, in women's Bible study groups in the churches and in the community, as well as in their scholarly study Mennonite women choose a wide variety of hermeneutical approaches related to their understanding of themselves as women. As they participate more fully in all aspects of societal and church life, Mennonite women begin to ask questions about their involvement in biblical interpretation. Because the Bible has been used to marginalize and silence women in church there is a great deal of ambivalence and uncertainty about their role in scholarly work and how this relates to a life of discipleship.

B. Mennonite women and discipleship.

A closer look at the concept of discipleship reveals an ambiguity that has surfaced more clearly as women begin to participate in biblical interpretation in the context of their own experience. It is clear that as a generic word for followers of Jesus, the term disciple has been used in the Christian tradition to refer both to men and women. Of the 230 instances where the term is used in the Gospels, about 90 percent either are not limited to the 12 disciples or else do not make clear whether they or some larger group is indicated.[53] However, in many exegetical discussions it is assumed that "disciple" refers to the Twelve and that the stories of women are extrinsic to a discussion of discipleship.[54] Our understanding of the joys and struggles of discipleship in the present day has therefore not been illuminated by the stories of women followers of Jesus. Biblical exegesis has contributed to making male discipleship normative for the meaning of the term, subsuming female experiences of discipleship. In Mennonite tradition this led to an understanding of discipleship that was largely associated with cross-bearing, self-denial, obedience, and servanthood. characteristics that radically challenged the expectations that a patriarchal society had of men, but which affirmed what was already expected of women.

The combination of patriarchal culture and this androcentric understanding of discipleship had negative implications for women's involvement in biblical interpretation. Discipleship encouraged women to model obedience and submission to the Bible and its male interpreters. A patriarchal separation of the domestic and public sphere encouraged "servant" leadership roles for men and unquestioning acquiescence for women. Stories of women disciples in the Bible were not examined to give a fuller, more nuanced meaning to the term. Discipleship defined by male experience thus promoted an auxiliary and passive role for women in life and in the hermeneutical process.

If discipleship is to be an inclusive word for us today it must include all who follow Jesus. This means looking again at the Bible to discover the various ways in which discipleship and following Jesus are described. However, this raises the crucial question of how present and past understandings of the term are related in our interpretive approach to the Bible. Sandra Schneiders has pointed out that as Christians have appropriated the biblical text over the last 1900 years an enlarged understanding of discipleship has been generated.[55] How does this tradition of discipleship produced through a historical process of interpretation relate to the study of the biblical text in its historical context?

The commitment to discipleship raises key issues about how we as female disciples understand our involvement in the process of interpretation. These questions in turn take us back to the Bible for a closer look at the truth claims of particular texts about Jesus and his way. We will begin our study by looking at the scholarly process of biblical interpretation and identifying several of the issues that a commitment to discipleship raises for us. Second, we will re-examine two texts which focus particularly on the shift in emphasis that comes if discipleship becomes a truly inclusive term. The conclusion of the paper will give some indication as to how the hermeneutical spiral would continue if our praxis of biblical scholarship was informed by these texts.

The process of biblical interpretation

Theologians and philosophers are raising a number of questions related to the pre understandings within which scholars do their biblical study.[56] Understanding the hermeneutical process as a social process in which the community context has an important place is central to that discussion. Mennonites traditionally have recognized the importance of the social context of biblical interpretation in their notion of the church as a "hermeneutic community" that reads the Bible in community in order to discover God's will. The congregation of disciples gathered for Bible study and prayer was assumed to be the primary social context in which authoritative interpretations of the Bible were discerned and appropriated.[57]

Liberation theologians, including feminist theologians, point to a different aspect of the social context. They insist that every interpretation is inevitably and inescapably contextual and therefore particular and limited. The social, cultural, economic and political nature of the context influences what we discover in the Bible.[58]

The following discussion describes how a particular self-identity, that of a Mennonite female disciple, is related to the communal context of biblical interpretation in church and university. It understands the hermeneutical process as a social process and raises the issues for interpreters from that angle. Several key questions arise about how a theology of discipleship would affect women's participation in this process.

A. How does a theology of discipleship help determine a basic hermeneutical stance toward the authority of the Bible?

Discipleship has been associated with two seemingly opposite hermeneutical stances toward the authority of the Bible. Anabaptist-Mennonite tradition as articulated by John H. Yoder, stresses obedience by insisting that "only he [sic] who is committed to the direction of obedience can read the truth so as to interpret it in line with the direction of God's purposes."[59] This places the emphasis on obedience and on a reading of the Bible in the context of the experience of the church congregation. In contrast, Elizabeth Schüssler Fiorenza points to the dangerous appeal to the authority of the Bible made by a church that is shaped by the remembrance of the "historical winners" and not by the "subversive memory of innocent suffering and of solidarity with the victims of history." She therefore calls for a "hermeneutics of suspicion," a critical interpretive approach that arises out of the experience of women-church, a community that attempts to live according to the vision of the discipleship of equals. Interpreters in this approach evaluate the way the Bible is used to justify oppressive and violent practices of church and society.

Though Mennonite obedience and feminist suspicion appear to be opposite approaches toward the Bible, both speak of authority in the context of communities of experience and practice which emphasize particular commitments and biases. Scholarship has generally taken an approach to authoritative interpretation which questions this emphasis on commitment and subjective experience. In academic circles the exegesis or interpretation which gains authority is said to be objective and free from bias. Here authority is related to reason and factual evidence. The scientific approach which assumes value-free, detached inquiry is paramount in the community of academic scholarship.

This larger difference raises the crucial issue of the relationship of text and reader in the interpretive process. The simple equation of text with object and of individual reader with subject is modified if interpretation is seen as a social process of discernment. Scholarly institutions as well as churches have been authoritative communities which possessed "the power to ostracize or to embrace, to foster or to restrict membership, to recognize and to define what 'true scholarship' entails."[60] Commitment, whether to the canon of the church, to the methodology of the university, or to a feminist community of action can all be understood as decisively influencing the interpretive process. Interpretations are never value free and truly objective. The critical aspect of biblical study is thus shifted to include not only the text but also the interpreter and her/his commitments. A hermeneutics of suspicion which asks critical questions about how social context has affected all interpretations must then be seen in light of these commitments and convictions.

Discipleship understood as commitment to Jesus challenges Mennonite women to articulate their relationship to various interpretive communities in the context of that commitment. The authoritative communities to which scholars see themselves accountable must be identified and placed within a larger theological framework which helps set priorities. The biases which affect their readings of the text must be articulated as clearly as possible, including identifying the limitations of a particular social location. Included in this process is the question of whether gender contributes to particular biases. Is suspicion an acceptable stance toward the patriarchy of the Bible and its past interpretations? Or is obedience the only appropriate stance toward the authority of the Bible for someone who claims to be a disciple?

B. How does a theology of discipleship help us choose our primary conversation partners?

The concept of hermeneutic community describes the companions and partners with whom we interact as we participate in biblical interpretation.[61] Both Mennonites and feminists have spoken to this issue. Mennonites have emphasized the importance of testing interpretations with others in the church congregation in light of their experience as disciples seeking God's will. Feminists have emphasized the distinctiveness of the female experience and urged women to interpret the Bible on the basis of their solidarity with other women. To this has been added the strong voice of various liberation theologians who have pointed to the hermeneutical privilege of the oppressed.

At the forefront of the present-day discussion about communal discourse is the issue of power and powerlessness. Gayle Gerber Koontz suggests that categories such as powerful and weak are relationship-specific and do not intrinsically characterize a person or group as a whole.[62] Women have begun to identify the complexity of these categories in their own experience. For example, Sharon Ringe speaks of the "status inconsistency" of her own social context as a North American, Caucasian, middle-class clergywoman who teaches at a Protestant seminary.[63] Except for her femaleness each of these characteristics point to privilege and dominance in the larger world community. She emphasizes the need to learn the "power of articulation" as a woman who has been marginalized, but also the need to learn "the art of silence" as she seeks to hear the voices of those who have been dominated and oppressed by the people of her social class.

In this context a new expanded notion of discipleship is crucial in helping us re-examine where we have drawn the boundaries of the hermeneutic community. The political context of our scholarly work in the institutions of church and university suggests that we must go beyond the traditional polarity of church/world to understand our own power/powerlessness in relationship to specific discourse partners. A recognition of both the limitations and advantages of our social and political position can make us aware of our personal power as well as intentional about our choice of conversation partners. Dialogue with those who differ from us can show us our own prejudices and can enlarge the experience base for our biblical interpretation.[64] Because power and weakness have often been seen as gender-specific categories, women will have to articulate how their identity as female disciples influences their habitual patterns of listening and speaking as well as their deliberate choices of dialogue partners.

C. How does our theology of discipleship influence the choice and status of methodology?

Katherine Doob Sakenfeld has suggested that the methods which we choose in our scholarly work may have a great deal to do with our understanding of how the Bible may become the word of God for the community of faith today.[65] She suggests that someone using a formal literary approach might be emphasizing the role of the text itself as the mediation of God's word, while other scholars may focus on historical reconstruction because they are emphasizing the mediation of God's word through the experience of the historical faith community. The key theological debates about methodology have thus usually focused on identifying the locus of revelation, whether this is seen to be in the text or in the history which produced the text. Mennonites have tended to focus on Jesus as the locus of this revelation and emphasized historical methodologies to interpret the biblical texts about Jesus.

Feminist approaches to the Bible have challenged these traditional historical and literary methodologies by focusing on the marginal voices which did not gain central place either in the text or in the communal process of forming the canon.[66] A number of feminists as well as other liberation theologians have pointed out that these suppressed voices came from people who did not experience liberation and justice from the dominant group. They have therefore emphasized that revelation is always "for the sake of our salvation."[67] This has shifted the conversation to include not only how God revealed God's will through the Bible in the past but also how God liberates and saves through the way these interpretations are used in the present.

This signifies a major paradigm shift in methodological approaches. The primary key to the meaning of texts has shifted from determining the historical as reference of biblical language in facts and ideas to noting how the language was used in the social setting to transform the community. The emphasis on facts and propositions is being replaced by a focus on the multiple uses of language and the complicated relationship that language has to the world and to speakers and hearers of language. Language is understood not only as a medium for individuals to transmit facts and ideas. It is also seen as a social phenomenon which helps to build a framework for a community's view of reality.[68]

This has meant that there is a greater consciousness that we are reading an ancient text in the 20th century. Every historical reconstruction is still influenced by this new context. Phyllis Trible points out that already in the Bible "context altered text."[69] She illustrates this by showing how a single text in different settings yielded contradictory meanings. Reinterpretation of texts has always freed the Bible to give and take on new meanings for later generations faced with new issues. Interpreters are therefore beginning to recognize that the function of the text in a social context is part of its meaning. Sandra Schneiders suggests that a process of decontextualization and recontextualization by successive readings is the natural process of interpretation required by any text which is fixed because of its written form.[70] She thus wants to point out how the text "mediates the continuity and enables the discontinuity" that there is between the discipleship of the first Christians and our own Christian experience.

Decisions relating to methodology arise out of our understanding of how past and present are related in the reading and interpreting of the Bible. For disciples who wish to follow Jesus this raises the prior theological question of how revelation and salvation can be identified. It asks us about our theology of God and how we understand God's revealing and saving in the past and in the present. Is it always the majority voices which express the truth of God? Or does God sometimes speak through a minority voice? How do our present experiences of God help us distinguish between true and false understandings of the Bible? How can the record of experiences of God in the past contribute to understanding what revelation and salvation are in the present? Will it make a difference if we interpret the Bible in the context of our experience as women? These theological decisions will influence our choice of scholarly methodologies and help shape how we will use availabe methods in our interpretation of the biblical text.

D. *How does the theology of discipleship influence the impression point in the texts that we study?*

Frank Kermode talks about the "impression point" as the moment of interpretation or discovery when some part of the text becomes the key to the interpretation of the whole.[71] This impression point is thus privileged in relationship to the whole text because the gestalt or description of reality which is produced in an interpretation is articulated around it. He points out that this impression point may originate in the text or in the needs and interests of the reader. Clues as to what is most important often come from the text itself. For example, the literary form or genre gives some clues as to what is most important in a text. Narratives, hymns, poems, and sermons all have different ways in which they indicate what is central to the literary unit.. However, the impression point is also related to the questions with which a reader approaches the text. These questions may be more closely related to the social context and personal issues of the reader.

How these two aspects come together in the interpretive moment for a particular reader cannot be predicted. In this sense interpretation can be understood as continuing the creative work of the writer. Traditionally this can also be seen as the work of the Holy Spirit who illuminates the Word. Willard Swartley puts it this way: "In the co-creative moment, text and interpreter experience life by the power of the divine Spirit."[72]

In this context we can note how the impression point has changed for women as they have become self-conscious of themselves as women. Women are choosing texts that were considered unimportant or peripheral in the past. They are focusing on minority traditions, on women characters, or on power relationships within the text. The questions that they bring to the text come from their experience as women, though their methodology may otherwise be similar to well accepted literary or historical approaches.

Arguments about the validity and testing of the various readings of a passage must therefore also ask how gender has affected this process. Women as well as men have a "canon-within-a-canon" which both opens and blinds them to other ways of reading the text. How the interpretive efforts of women will be understood is related to whether women can be affirmed as disciples who are also open to the moving of the Spirit and can therefore participate in a co-creative moment which can bring new life to both the text and the community

The truth claims of the text: Identifying revelation and salvation

In this part of the paper we move more directly to the study of texts about discipleship. I will not attempt a thorough exegetical study of the biblical texts that I have chosen. Rather I will illustrate a feminist shift in orientation and note some of the questions which this brings to the interpretation of the texts. I have chosen a key discipleship text in Mennonite tradition (John 13:1-20) and placed beside it a text about a woman's response of discipleship to Jesus (John 12: I-8). In this way I want to suggest ways in which a feminist reorientation to biblical study affects the language and understanding of discipleship.

The four issues that I raised in the discussion on the interpretive process will provide the framework for my work with the texts. I will do this in the order in which I actually became aware of hermeneutical choices.

A. The impression point.

I was drawn to the above texts when I noticed their close proximity in the Gospel of John during a quick overview of the passion stories in preparation for a Lenten sermon. In my experience the footwashing story was a popular text for teaching about discipleship as service. My new consciousness of women as equal and full disciples opened me to seeing Mary as a disciple. Suddenly the parallelism between the two stories struck me and I began to wonder whether reading these two stories together would help illuminate the deeper significance of the symbol of footwashing.

I observed that the setting for both stories was a supper not long before the death of Jesus. In both stories feet are washed or anointed and then wiped dry; in both there is strong objection to that action by a disciple; in both Jesus responds to the objection by asking the disciples to look at the action in a deeper way; in both Judas is present and his false discipleship is alluded to; in both there is discussion of status differences between people (i.e., poor/rich and servant/master).

Later study confirmed that, while rare, other commentators have also noticed these similarities. In a source critical study M. Sabbe points out the similarity in terminology used in the two stories for the action as well as the analogous perspective on Jesus' death.[73] He finds a close literary relation between the two narratives. He also points to the fact that already in the 12th century the two stories were connected by having two different rites of footwashing on Holy Thursday: " the *mandatum fratrum*, which depicts the footwashing with which the Lord honoured his apostles and the *mandatum pauperum*, which recalls Mary's anointing of the feet of Jesus in Bethany (John 12:1-4) where Christ represents the poor."[74] Several scholars have noticed how elements of John 12 which seem peculiar when the story is understood as an isolated incident gain meaning when viewed in light of the footwashing scene.[75] This is particularly true for the peculiar action of anointing the feet and then immediately wiping off the ointment—which cannot be explained satisfactorily without this parallelism.

A number of feminist scholars have pointed to the relationship between the two stories. Elizabeth Schiissler Fiorenza suggests that the story of the anointing points forward to the scene at the Last Supper.[76] Both chapter 11 and chapter 12 emphasize the love and friendship between Jesus and Mary, Martha and Lazarus. Chapter 12 characterizes Mary as practicing the sign of true agape love by anointing him for his burial in contrast to Judas the unfaithful disciple who later betrays him. Sandra Schneiders suggests that it is "likely that John is deliberately presenting this woman as a disciple of Jesus the Teacher, a role generally forbidden to Jewish women."[77]

It seems possible then on literary and historical grounds to put these two narratives together around a symbolic action of footwashing. The impression point comes primarily from present-day reality but has been affirmed by studies focused on the historical text itself. Thus a story often considered marginal is connected with a central story about the meaning of discipleship to open up new possibilities of understanding Jesus, who is the primary link between the stories.

B. The methodology

Instead of turning directly to exegetical studies, a feminist orientation encourages me to read the text first of all in the context of my experience in my own church community. This reflective reading of the text allows me to articulate the preunderstandings that already influence my reading—preunderstandings which may be challenged by a more careful reading and study of the text. I remember John 13 being used primarily to point to the humble service of Jesus, a model to be imitated by his faithful disciples. The basin and towel continue to be important symbols of service for the Mennonite church. Footwashing is still practiced in some churches in connection with the communion service or love feast. John 13 also seems to be a popular text for ordination services, since it models "servant leadership," a popular concept for pastoral leadership in the Mennonite church.

The story from John 12 was less commonly used. From Sunday school I can recall the story told as a rather embarrassing incident about a woman, a sinner, who rather inappropriately showed Jesus her great thankfulness for forgiving her sin. However, Jesus valued her extravagant gift knowing what was in her heart. This story was also frequently used in women's meetings where the humble gift that women give with their sewing, food preparation, and service projects was being affirmed and recognized.

The story format of these texts invites readers to identify with the main characters of the story. I have usually heard the story retold to elicit certain identifications. In the story of John 13 the primary identification was not with Peter as a person who found it difficult to let someone of higher status—his Lord and Master—wash his feet.[78] Rather it was emphasized that we identify with Peter, who found it difficult to serve others, and with Jesus, who humbly served Peter. In the second story sinners and women were expected to identify with Mary in her feeling of humble gratefulness. However, it was rare to be challenged to identify with Jesus, who welcomed the washing of his feet by Mary, or to identify with Mary's courage in approaching Jesus so boldly despite the audience's disapproval.

In a quick overview of the exegetical studies I noticed how discussions of the meaning of the text were related to decisions about the reconstruction of the tradition history of the text. Fernando Segovia notes the incredibly vast number of scholarly articles which discuss the meaning of Jesus' washing of his disciples' feet.[79] Yet a consensus has not emerged among Johannine scholars with respect to the fundamental meaning of the passage. The overarching division between the various meanings of the text whether focused on cleansing or service is usually based on conflicting views concerning the literary unity of the passage. The story of the anointing receives less exegetical attention in most commentaries. The study is usually concentrated on the complicated relationships between the parallel anointing stories in the synoptics and the historical reconstruction of the incident.

What was notably missing in most of the interpretations, whether those of my church experience or those in the scholarly writings was any in-depth discussion of status and power relationships. Though the difference between master and servant is clearly indicated in John 13 and the difference between rich and poor is alluded to in John 12, scholars have not explored the question of power relationships. However, when the two stories are taken together we can clearly see the mutuality in the relationship of Jesus and his disciples. Mary, in her act of love for Jesus, overcomes any feeling of inferiority which the difference in status between her and Jesus would indicate. Jesus' insistence that he and the disciples are one in the act of footwashing overcomes any difference in status between himself and his disciples. Over/under relationships are not to be part of the Johannine community.

The questions which have been raised for me in my own direct reading of the text have not been answered satisfactorily through a quick overview of the results of current studies using traditional methodologies. I see the need for further historical and literary studies to test the intuitive ideas which my reading of the text have raised. Whatever methodologies are used they will be guided by a basic assumption: Regardless of its tradition history, the text as it now stands communicates both truth claims and possibilities for transforming actions by women and men today. To read the text in a way that will bring these to light would be the over-all goal of any method that I would use.

C. The dialogue partners.

The choice of dialogue partners for a discussion of this passage means acknowledging the power relationships which influence my choices. It is clear that I have chosen to test this interpretation first of all with other women and then with persons on the margins of church and scholarly life because it is in that context where I feel a sense of mutuality. The commentators to which I have paid the most attention have been women who have only recently received the power to interpret the Bible.

What has been most interesting is that much of the discussion of these commentators concentrated on understanding the reasons for the objections to the footwashings. Both Peter and Judas were uncomfortable with the act of intimacy and love whether it came from Jesus or whether it came from Mary. In the story of John 13 it would have made more sense for Peter to wash the feet of Jesus (someone lower in status serves someone higher) than for Jesus to overcome the distance between them by intimately washing the feet of his disciples. In the story of John 12 it would make more sense for Mary to give to the poor (someone who has more gives to someone who has less) than to act so presumptuously as to wash the feet of Jesus. It seems as if Mary assumes her right as a disciple to decide on the use of the money rather than allow the keeper of the purse to do this. Both of these actions challenge the societal roles in which people are frequently placed.

The objections by the disciples sound only too familiar to persons who have been marginalized because of gender, color, race, or economic status. An analysis of power relationships seems important from the perspective of those readers. Other studies will illuminate different aspects of the text which may contribute to a deeper understanding of the dynamics involved in these footwashings. A historical/sociological study is necessary to discover whether footwashing was practised in the Johannine community and what meaning this may have had within that community. A study of the larger literary unit which could include the story of John 11 as well as the stories between the two footwashing narratives is also needed to understand the logical literary flow of the Gospel.

D. The hermeneutical stance

My hermeneutical stance assumes that suspicion of our limited human perspectives must go together with obedience to the divine Word. It encourages me to ask critical questions of interpretations of the text and of communal assumptions which unquestioningly support certain interpretations.

At the same time, it asks me to be particularly attentive to those interpretations that challenge my present ideas and actions. Feminist suspicion has been used throughout this interpretive process. I have been suspicious of the subtle way that the symbol of footwashing has been used to separate people from each other by encouraging service which continues to reinforce status differences. Just as the two stories have been separated in the preaching and teaching of the church so the service of the dominant has been valued differently than the service of the one considered inferior. The Jesus who serves has been separated from the Jesus who gratefully accepts the footwashing of the woman in his time of need. We have been blind to the fact that the objections to both footwashings center on the crossing of societal norms of acceptable relationships between people.

Conclusions

> (1) We all need to confess that we who are disciples (male and female) often understand only partially what Jesus was all about. Our understanding is blurred by our own experiences of being oppressed and feeling inferior or being dominant and feeling superior. The acceptance of the over/under paradigm affects the way we value others' contributions to the interpretation of a text as well as the way we value our own contribution. Power relationships hinder the hermeneutic

> community in its function of discernment. No human process can fully guarantee that we have fully understood God's revelation.
>
> (2) We need to be suspicious of any process of biblical interpretation which separates people from each other, or which reinforces people in their separate spheres of responsibility in the church, even when it evidences itself in the seemingly innocent guise of discipleship or service. We need a way to do biblical interpretation in a collegial, noncompetitive approach. We need mutual respect and service in our relationships within the larger hermeneutic community as well as in our relationships in the congregation.
>
> (3) Love and intimacy with God are connected to love and intimacy with each other. Both are crucial for any knowledge which can be termed revelational (John 14:21). Intimacy always carries with it a certain vulnerability because it means opening ourselves to change, to salvation in its fullest meaning. This is both risky and exciting. It is risky because often other "disciples," especially those who have been safe conversation partners in the past, will be critical of the commitments which we choose. Yet it is exciting because new dialogue partners, new disciples bring insights that can create new life-giving interpretations.

As Mennonite women begin to add their voices to the larger theological conversation they dare not forget their own unique experiences of God's revealing and saving presence. The two footwashing stories can illuminate and challenge us to follow Jesus in a praxis which brings doing and knowing together in a life of discipleship.

Chapter 4. Ethics

NAMING THE ETHICAL ORIENTATION

During my doctoral studies I had become convinced that as theologians and biblical scholars we were doing more work on the ethics of the vocational practices of others and ignoring our own. The ethic of so-called theoreticians such as myself had not been as thoroughly explored as the ethic of so-called practitioners. This was true of the social/political ethic espoused by many Mennonite theologians with its focus on peace-making in the political sphere, justice in the marketplace, and non-violence in relationships.

Elisabeth Schüssler Fiorenza's article, "The Ethics of Biblical Interpretation,"[1] *discouraged me from working on that endeavour as her exploration of the use and misuse of power already said much of what I might have wanted to explore. However, the need to articulate an ethic for my own work was always uppermost in my mind. This came to a head when I began my career after theological studies. Instead of narrowly working on my own research, I now began the serious work of teaching, administering a program, working actively on committees, and participating in the serious dialogue of the church and academy. During the next seven years I entered the vocation of a theological professor, albeit a part-time one. Each of the articles I published in those years speaks to some of the challenges I faced to bring my personal and social/political ethic to bear on one of the aspects of my work.*

I spent the first year after gaining a doctoral degree at the very same college, Canadian Mennonite Bible College (CMBC), where my Mennonite theological orientation was first formed. I was replacing a professor who was on sabbatical. Here I worked beside professors who had taught me and whom I greatly respected. My own self-confidence was put to the test as I entered the power dynamics at work in relationships among colleagues and with students. I continually asked myself ethical questions that arose out of practical situations. What language do I use in my courses on ethics and theology that will enable students in their own reflections rather than dominate their thinking? What kind of hermeneutic will help create a community ethos in which God can honestly be named as author of truth and salvation? Is there an ethic that informs me as to how I use the power and authority I now have as a professor? How do I encourage the viewpoints of the "other" in class discussions?

I spent the next five years at the institution where I received my doctoral degree. I was asked to become the interim director and then the director of the newly established Toronto Mennonite Theological Centre (TMTC) at the Toronto School of Theology.

Here my context was both the ecumenical theological schools on the university campus as well as the small group of Mennonite students doing their doctoral work. My work was part-time but included administration of the centre and teaching several courses each year. I was faced with the question of how to establish TMTC as a viable institution with limited financial resources while creating a vision that could excite students and the supporting denomination.

During these years, my family context changed dramatically. The move to Winnipeg for one year had meant living separately from my husband for one semester. In addition, it meant living again in a student apartment with its simpler lifestyle, immersed in the life of a small college community. With the move back to Toronto came all the complications of living in the largest urban centre in Canada. The daily personal concerns of home-making, balancing schedules (and finances) and participating in the church community overlapped with the larger concerns of visible poverty, discrimination based on race, and abuse of women and minorities, all of which we encountered in our neighbourhood and through our local newscast. Our children no longer lived at home (though sometimes they came back for short times between jobs or school). We were now becoming an extended family circle with in-laws and several grandchildren. Having young adults making important decisions regarding career and marriage meant that there was always a growing edge to our family life. In addition, as a church community, we were attempting to become more welcoming of persons whose tradition was other than Mennonite as well as becoming more sensitized to issues of poverty, abuse, and disability within our midst. At times I felt as if I was being stretched beyond my comfort zone as I tried to navigate between home, church, and work.

The articles in this section focus on ethical praxis, a bringing together of theory and practice, theological language and institutional life, personal character, and relational integrity. They arose out of this multi-faceted context and the ethical questions that arose for me during that time.

***

THE MUTUALITY OF MINISTRY: A DIALOGUE WITH MARK[2]

Much of our ethics as Christians has been framed by the concepts of guilt and innocence. I too struggled with these notions as I attempted to "grow up" in my theological work, that is, to become a responsible theologian within my denomination. This is reflected in a short article I wrote for the Mennonite Brethren (MB) women's network. I wrote the article entitled, "No Longer Innocent" after speaking at a weekend meeting for MB women on discipleship. Since MB women could not be ordained in their denomination at the time, they faced an uphill battle to receive the blessing of the church for working in leadership capacities. The discussions with these gifted women convinced me that despite the obstacles that they faced, women needed to be empowered to change the "scripts" within themselves, those frameworks of thought that told them that they were weak and powerless and sinful. Instead, they needed to take on the responsibility of shaping the future church as beloved women called by God.

For me, this did not mean doing away with a critical look at the institutional structures to see how the androcentric and patriarchal nature of the church had hurt women. Rather, I needed to acknowledge that by accepting the script telling me that I was the weaker sex, I was invariably co-opted into the system that oppressed me. I needed to resist the internalized voice that told me that I did not serve enough, that I would not adequately care for my family while I was pursuing new areas of work, and that I was not obedient enough to the real leaders of the church. In that article I was challenging myself and other women to become an adult in the church, to become an active shaper of the history of the church. I began this way:

> *I can no longer identify with the phrase "innocent women and children!" This is not because I have lost the yearning to be innocent, to be pure and righteous before God and others. Nor is it because I am confessing guilt for a specific crime of which I am accused. Rather, I am facing the undeniable fact that I am not a child. I know the existence of good and evil and must make choices that affect the lives of others. I can no long hide behind a division of labour in which men are held responsible for the good and evil in the "world out there" and women are assumed innocent because of their gender. I must face my own involvement in determining how the church as the people of God lives in this world.*[3]

As I read this article again after these many years, I realize that it does not speak to the pain and sacrifice that many women experience as they enter the public arena. Nor does it speak to women who are innocent and yet have lost a sense of self worth, women who are abused and victimized. However, I believe that the move to becoming a shaper of history rather than an "innocent victim" is a necessary move that women and other people marginalized by our organizations and communities need to make. I felt a need to address that side of who we are as women—for we too are tempted to blame others rather than to become responsible ourselves, knowing that the cost may be high.

The article reflected my own difficulty in becoming an agent of change within a community. One example may suffice. During the year spent at CMBC I was given two courses to teach that created considerable conversation among the student body. The first was "feminist theology" and included both women and men. The discussion was healthy during the classes, creating new awareness within the male students and identifying for female students some of the subconscious fears and hopes that they had. Several incidents in residence life became served as real-life examples that were illuminated by aspects of the course. I was grateful to the administration that they had instituted this course.

The second course created some amount of turmoil, particularly for the male students, was a course called, "Peace Theology: Theological Issues." The text that had traditionally been used by the professor whom I was replacing for the year was the Politics of Jesus by John H. Yoder. The challenge for me was to teach with integrity since by then I knew something about the abuse that Yoder had inflicted on some women. I did this by adding the booklet, Peace Theology and Violence against Women, as a companion text and by naming Yoder's sexual abuse of women in the first classes. Throughout the course I kept the key question before the students: "Is there something in the theology of Yoder that allowed him to justify his abuse?" In the responses to this class there was defensiveness and anger on the part of some of the students. The dethronement of Yoder who had taken on "hero" status was painful for the students and I am not sure how successful it was. I continued to teach Yoder at TMTC in the next few years. I felt his theology was so engrained in Mennonite thinking that I needed to deal with it directly, rather than ignoring it and allowing it to become dominant without the critical examination that was needed.

A reading of the Gospel of Mark informed my own leadership ministry at the time. In Mark I heard the biblical call to mutuality between women and men in leadership. I began to envision a flexible and dynamic pattern of leadership that continually subverts dominant patterns of ministry so that the marginal voices can be heard. This mutuality did not come easily for me as I struggled with how to pursue this in the context of CMBC where I now taught beside esteemed professors from my own college days. I began to look for spiritual advisors who would help keep me honest and courageous in that first year of teaching. Two women from outside of the college were willing to be spiritual guides for me. Their role in helping me reflect on particular situations and in encouraging me to follow my calling was crucial for me during that year.

I spoke about these first experiences in doing public theology in an editorial for Women's Concern Report using the imagery of music:

> Sometimes I remain silent in a choir of only male voices. At other times, like a young inexperienced singer pushed into the limelight too soon, I burst into tears after singing only a few bars. Frequently I feel overwhelmed by stronger voices and so become silent. Sometimes I sing in the shower where no one will hear my own shrill notes and plaintive melodies.
>
> Only occasionally do I feel the exhilaration that comes when my voice spontaneously and without apology enters fully into a choir of diverse voices singing a new song. Only occasionally do I know that I have found my place and entered the rhythm fully. Only

> *occasionally do I know when I must lead and when I must support a different voice as it soars above the others.*[4]

Now, more than twenty years later, I wonder if my ethical struggles still resonate with women today. Some things have changed. "White" women have become more self-conscious of their involvement in the history of colonialism, racism, and abuse of various kinds including the abuse of the earth. They have begun to recognize their own need to be healed. At the same time, Mennonite women can no longer be identified by a common ethnic, linguistic, or racial background. Instead, female voices from many different cultures and races are entering the theological dialogue. Yet I suspect that, no matter what background, many women who are doing theology in the church still long to let their voices soar freely and without apology within the chorus, sometimes leading with a new melody and sometimes providing the harmony for an old tune. I suspect they still struggle with fear as they challenge the church structures, while longing for the mutuality that I envisioned as I studied the power dynamics between disciples in the gospel of Mark.

***

A dialogue with the Gospel of Mark about the nature of ministry begins by listening carefully to the way that Mark tells the story of Jesus and his disciples. The narrative form of the Gospel implies that Mark's theology will not be presented in logical, conceptual form. Instead, readers are invited to identify with the various characters in the story. They are challenged to discern the meaning of the events by an active engagement with the questions that are raised as the plot shifts and as conflicts escalate. Dialogue about ministry cannot, therefore, wait until a theology is abstracted from the story. Rather, reflective reading begins by noting the different ways in which the Gospel writer and the reader evaluate specific events and persons in the story. Questions that open us to Mark's theology surface when similar or differing assumptions are identified. The very act of reading thus implies an exploration of the tensions and ambiguities that arise within us when the horizons of past and present meet in the reading process.[5]

This essay will begin by reflecting on the way that we as ministering persons, standing in a Mennonite faith tradition, tend to identify with the narrative. It will recognize that most of us who stand within a Christian tradition are re-readers of the story and already have fixed patterns of identification that can help or hinder us from hearing the message that Mark wants to give us. The essay will therefore invite us to re-think this identification in line with the direction that Mark gives to us through his telling of the story. In this way we hope to discover a theology of ministry that empowers us to serve effectively and with integrity in the name of Jesus, the Christ.

I. Naming the Traditions of Ministry

When Mennonites look for a paradigm of ministry within the Gospel narrative, they tend to turn very quickly to Jesus as a primary model of ministry and service. Though this presents us with an ideal to strive for, it also diverts us from identifying with the disciples and their entry into ministry. It allows us to focus on a perfectionist vision of what disciples should be rather than a realistic vision of what disciples can become. It introduces a norm against which we can measure ourselves but sometimes fails to give us an identity that can empower us. It may even encourage a false association with divine authority rather than noting our need for dependence on God's grace and empowerment. An immediate identification with Jesus may thus discourage us from exposing our hidden selves to God's redemptive and healing action. The mutuality that is inherent in a ministry that both receives and gives may be concealed from our eyes.

Elizabeth Struthers Malbon proposes an alternative modeling that is present in the Gospel stories. She points to the followers of Jesus who are portrayed in the Gospel of Mark "with both strong points and weak points in order to serve as realistic and encouraging models for hearers/readers who experience both strength and weakness in their Christian discipleship."[6] This approach suggests that though we may look to Jesus' words and actions for an evaluative framework for ministry in the church, we must look to the narratives of discipleship for realistic paradigms of ministry.

As we turn to the Gospel of Mark, we probably remember rather easily the particular disciple group who is explicitly called to the work of ministry—to "fish for people" (1:17), to "proclaim the message, and to have authority to cast out demons" (3:14-15). That story of blessing, temptation, and opportunity is told in some detail, thus leading many of us to identify closely with this official ministering group of followers. However, the twelve disciples are not the only group of followers whose story is told in the gospel of Mark. Another disciple group is entrusted with the message that Jesus has been raised and is told to "go, tell his disciples and Peter that he is going ahead of you into Galilee" (16:7). This less official story also elicits certain identifications—identifications that have become particularly important to women.

These stories of Jesus' followers provide two distinct paradigms describing two ways of entering ministry and service in the community of disciples. What strikes us initially as we compare the description of these two groups of disciples is the way that gender seems to determine who is named and recognized in the story. The twelve men are officially called to the ministry of Jesus on a mountain, a symbolic reminder of another mountain with key importance for the covenant people. Their story becomes public knowledge and receives public recognition in the oral and written traditions of the early Christian church.

In contrast, the women's stories are hidden in the story of the crowd of people around Jesus. Their story almost becomes a postscript on discipleship, a story recounted only very briefly in the public record (15:41). Feminist biblical scholars are beginning to insist that female stories must be named as traditions of ministry even though their story is told with less detail than the male story. They suggest that the marginalization of certain stories of discipleship and the prominence of others need not necessarily imply that God also evaluates the ministry of women as secondary and less important.[7]

If we begin by accepting both traditions as traditions of ministry, we must ask why the women's story is told with less detail than the male story. Does the marginalization of certain stories of discipleship and the prominence of others necessarily imply that God also evaluates the ministry of women as secondary and less important? A number of scholars are suggesting that this way of telling the story fits into the androcentric (male-centered) cultural milieu of the times where men were usually the writers and the heroes of public literature. They are acknowledging that the androcentricism of the biblical text witnesses to the human mediation of God's word and to the historical particularity of the biblical text.

However, this raises a second key question for us. What is the significance of the sudden appearance of female followers in 15:40-41? Why do these disciples become so prominent in the climactic ending of the story? Why does their ministry suddenly become acknowledged in the official story? What is meant by this breaking of a cultural pattern?

In a more careful study of the way the followers of Jesus are named, we note how Mark demonstrates that the term disciple includes others beyond the circle of the Twelve. This inclusiveness is clearly indicated when Jesus asserts that those who are his kin, his "mother, brother, and sister," are those who do the will of God (3:31-35). Elizabeth Schüssler Fiorenza has pointed out that Mark's use of three verbs to characterize the women's discipleship points to their inclusion not only as disciples but as true apostolic witnesses. The women followed (*akolouthein*), ministered or served (*diakonein*), and came up with Jesus to Jerusalem (*synanabainein*).[8]

These verbs remind us of the call and decision to follow, the mandate to serve, and the challenge to go with Jesus to the cross, key experiences which also validate the male disciples as witnesses and proclaimers of the Jesus event. They remind us that though cultural patterns have often determined who can be official ministers, it was not these patterns which brought women into the official story of ministry. Rather, it was God's direct call to the women that subverted and challenged limited notions of who could be effective witnesses for God. The ending of Mark clearly indicates a new direction for ministry, a direction which includes both women and men in the official naming of ministers.[9]

The differences between the two traditions of ministry point not only to the difference between male and female ministry as described in Mark. They also point to a difference in the way disciples of Jesus throughout the ages have experienced their role in the ministry of the church. Some disciples have been publicly recognized as ministers in the church; others have served quietly behind the scenes. The fact that this difference in official recognition has often coincided with gender or class differentiation suggests that we should reconsider how official and unofficial ministry relate to each other. Can mutual respect and dynamic interaction determine these relationships rather than domination or competition between genders and classes?

Though the Gospel of Mark resembles the culture of the time in the way it describes male and female ministry, it also begins a process of subversion of this evaluation by pointing to a new direction for the relationship between official and unofficial ministry. This process is detected if we look more closely at how the narrative describes the temptations and challenges of each of the disciple groups.

If we can acknowledge that gender differences are not the most important differences between the two paradigms of discipleship, both women and men are free to identify with either of these traditions. Throughout history some disciples, both male and female, have been publicly recognized as ministers in the church. Others, both male and female, have served quietly behind the scenes. As we follow the narrative identifying with each tradition in turn, we will be able to note the difference in experience that official recognition makes. We will be able to reflect on the unique temptations and challenges that often accompany official ministry as well as unofficial ministry. We will be able to see how Mark's narrative challenges readers to bring these intertwining traditions together and to supply an ending to the narrative that will allow ministry to continue so that the good news will be proclaimed.

II. The Ministry of the Twelve (the official ministry)

In the Gospel of Mark, the ministry of the Twelve begins almost at the same time as the ministry of Jesus. Peter, James, and John are already called to follow in chapter 1 and by chapter 3 the Twelve are appointed as apostles, sent out to proclaim the message of Jesus, and given authority to cast out demons (3: 13-19). At the same time, the Twelve are described as insiders who are given special explanations of the parables (4:10-11). In chapter 6 their ministry is again affirmed as they are given a particular assignment and a special empowerment. The Twelve are thus pictured as active participants in the healing and teaching ministry, persons commissioned by Jesus and publicly recognized as leaders in the Jesus movement.

As the narrative unfolds, we note how quickly Jesus' ministry, and therefore the disciples' ministry, becomes controversial. The Twelve very soon become aware that authority conflicts arise when divine power is mediated through an unauthorized person and in an unauthorized way (2: 1-16). They soon discover that even a ministry of healing challenges the status quo and enrages the established leaders of the people (3:1-6). As followers of Jesus, the Twelve become involved in symbolic actions such as plucking grain on the Sabbath (chap. 3). At times they support Jesus' interpretations of the scriptures by not observing the ceremonial washings (chap. 7). They thus participate with Jesus in confronting several of the accepted norms of the community. They discover that with their special assignment comes the challenge to state their central loyalties, to discern the direction of God's actions, and to make judgments about the nature of the mission of Jesus (8:27-30).

After such a strong beginning, it is striking that the Twelve do not continue to be described as ideal models or heroes. Commentators have puzzled over the meaning of a description of leadership that is brutally honest about inadequacy and failure. Was this a polemic against the authority of the Twelve in the early church? Or is this description an honest look at the real temptations and challenges that the Twelve faced as they followed Jesus?

As the narrative continues, we note that nothing characterizes the Twelve more than misunderstanding and fear. Though the disciples had seen many wonders done by Jesus, they trembled in fear as the wind threatened to swamp their boat (4:35-40). Even after seeing the miracle of the feeding of the five thousand, they do not seem to know how to go about feeding the four thousand (8:1-10). Jesus himself reprimands the disciples for not understanding the connection between the two feedings (8:14-21). Though Peter speaks out boldly and confesses Jesus as the Messiah, he misunderstands the nature of that Messiahship and rebukes Jesus when he predicts that his kind of Messiahship leads to suffering and death (8:32-33).

Fear is mentioned three more times in connection with these disciples (9:6; 9:32; 10:32). This fear may be connected to awe and wonder as on the Mount of Transfiguration. But it is also associated with the insecurity of the road that lay ahead of them as they moved toward Jerusalem. However, instead of seeking more understanding, the disciples are afraid to ask Jesus to explain, afraid to face the cost of following (9:31; 10:32). For these disciples, fear seems to indicate a lack of faith and trust in the power and leadership of Jesus.

The response of the Twelve to the fear and insecurity of ministry with Jesus is symbolized by several short incidents in the second half of the Gospel. Here we see the disciples arguing about who is the greatest in the kingdom (9:34) and vying for the places of honour at the time when Jesus will come in his glory (10:37). We find the disciples rebuking those who would bring children to Jesus (10:13) and trying to stop those who were healing in the name of Jesus (9:38). We note how conscious they are that they had left everything to follow Jesus (10:28) and how much they have begun to see themselves not as followers but as those to be followed. James' words symbolize this change when he tries to stop others who were healing and speaks of them as those who are not "following us" (9:39).

This change from following to leading is paralleled by a similar change in the disciples from trust in Jesus to confidence in their own ability. This is demonstrated by Peter, James, and John who insist on their own ability to withstand temptation. Their self-confidence is almost amusing. James and John respond to the probing questions of Jesus about their ability to drink the cup that Jesus will drink and to be baptized with the baptism that Jesus will be baptized, with an assured "we are able." Peter reacts almost angrily to the prediction of the desertion of the disciples with a confident "even though all become deserters, I will not." Thus, it is not surprising that Peter, James, and John do not pray with Jesus in the garden of Gethsemane. They ignore not only Jesus' request but their own need for empowerment from God. In Mark's narrative, the Twelve all desert Jesus and do not again re-enter the story as ministering people. Hope for their return comes only indirectly in the form of a command to the women in the story to "go, tell his disciples and Peter that you will see him, just as he told you."

Jesus actively tries to teach and admonish his disciples, pointing to a way for them to again become effective ministers. He points to the need for prayer when the disciples cannot heal the boy with a spirit. He points to children and servants as those to whom the kingdom belongs, challenging them to both receive the kingdom as a child and, in tum, to become a servant in their ministry. He challenges them to change their focus from what they have left for the sake of the kingdom to what they are receiving through the kingdom (10:20-30). He warns them of the temptations to lord it over people and to become a tyrant in their leadership role (10:42-45). He invites them to "keep awake and pray that they may not come into the time of trial" (14:38). He even predicts their propensity to fall away when leadership becomes difficult. And finally, when they fail, the message of the young man at the tomb challenges the disciples to listen to the women and to return to Galilee, for "there they will see him, just as he told you" (16:7).

The story of the temptations and challenges of this official group of ministers ends with failure but also with promise. It ends with a challenge to trust Jesus' words and to receive his empowerment and healing. What is striking is that the promise speaks directly and concretely, suggesting a way to overcome the temptations that have overtaken the disciples thus far in the story. The disciples must receive the message from those often deemed unworthy to publicly proclaim the gospel. They must follow the one who is going ahead of them, for only then will they see him as he is. They will see Jesus in Galilee, the place associated in the Gospel with Jesus' ministry of healing and teaching.[10] Only when they respond in trust, knowing their own brokenness, will they be open to new empowerment that will equip them for ministry in the name of Jesus.

III. The Ministry of the Women (the unofficial ministry)

The ministry of women also begins in Galilee during the early days of Jesus' ministry. We read that "many" women used to follow and serve Jesus there (15:40-41). However, no details are provided, and so we can only imagine that the nature of this service may have been less public. We can assume that this service fitted in well with the cultural norms of the day and so did not warrant an earlier mention in the official story. Women thus represent the unofficial ministry that often does not get public recognition in a community.

Most of the stories of women in the Gospel of Mark fit in with this assumption. They suggest that women serve in the household or through familial relationships. The public contributions of these disciples to the temple or synagogue may have been limited to the giving of alms in support of the public ministry of others. This contribution is, however, highly valued by Jesus as seen in the incident in which he points to the widow, who out of her poverty gave all that she had (12:41-44). The first explicit mention of women's service takes place in a home, a family setting. Here Simon's mother-in-law gets up from her sick bed to serve Jesus and his disciples (1:29). Though not described, we assume that this may have meant preparing a meal or providing clean beds for Jesus and the Twelve on which to sleep.

In several stories women are closely connected to the healing ministry of Jesus. However, they are pictured primarily as recipients rather than as helpers in the healing process. Several stories including that of the hemorrhaging woman are told of women who were given new life through Jesus' ministering presence. Mary Magdalene, one of the three women mentioned as following Jesus already in Galilee, is identified in the longer ending of Mark as a person from whom Jesus had cast out seven demons (16:9). However, we also have some indication that women were active in bringing others to Jesus. Mark includes the story of people bringing children to Jesus (10:13-16). We can imagine that there were mothers in that group. We also have a specific story in which a mother pleads for the healing of her daughter (7:24-30). Here Jesus is described as explicitly commending her for the words that she speaks. "For saying this, you may go; the demon has left your daughter."

The story of women's ministry that is told with the most detail is the story of the anointing of Jesus for burial in chapter 14. The woman is not named, but her sensitive ministry to Jesus who is facing death is commended. Jesus himself names this personal caring as a good work. "She has performed a good service for me.... Wherever the good news is proclaimed in the whole world, what she has done will be told in remembrance of her" (14:9). Jesus publicly defends her ministry since it seems to have become controversial to the people present at the meal. Jesus' answer suggests that personal caring for a friend in need has great value even in the face of the need to give to the poor. This personal service by women followers is again demonstrated in the last story. Here the women gather to go to the tomb to anoint the body of Jesus. This time Jesus is dead and the women are ready to perform the last service to a friend, a service usually assumed by women in the community.

The temptations and challenges of the women who participated in the more unofficial and personal ministry of Jesus have not been recounted in detail. Little indication is given of the choices that these disciples had to make. However, it is clear from the subtle hints given in the story that decisions of faith were also demanded of women. We can assume that it was probably difficult for the widow to choose to give all she had to the temple treasury or for the woman to anoint Jesus in front of disapproving guests. For the women to be present even at a distance at the cross meant taking some risk. Luise Schottroff has pointed out that sometimes the soldiers guarding the cross were given orders to watch for signs of mourning in order to identify followers of the accused.[11] Historically we know that women were also at times crucified.

The fear of the women in face of this threat of persecution is, however, not mentioned. It is not until the women see the young man dressed in a white robe sitting in the tomb that we read of their fear. The young man assures them that they need not be afraid. "Jesus has been raised. Go tell his disciples." But the Gospel story ends with the women's disobedience to the command of the young man. The women went out from the tomb, "for terror and amazement had seized them; and they said nothing to anyone for they were afraid."

Why were they afraid? Why did they not say anything? Scholars have tried to answer this question in various ways.[12] Some scholars try to excuse the women, assuming that their disobedience was not serious. After all, the Twelve will hear the good news from Jesus directly at a later time. Others speak of the awe that the women felt and minimize the fear. What is clear from other accounts, however, is that the Twelve had a difficult time believing the women when they did overcome their fear and when they attempted to give the disciples the message. The disbelief of these disciples is emphasized three times in the longer endings as well as in the Gospel of Luke (16:11, 13, 14; 24:11). Perhaps the fear experienced by the women is not only related to fear of persecution for themselves. Perhaps the fear is more related to the new responsibility given to them, a responsibility that meant that they had to believe and trust their own experience of God. They had to trust a vision and a commission not authorized by more official authorities. They had to overcome the temptation to flee and to stay hidden in the crowd. Fear thus hindered these women from immediate response to a more public responsibility. For the female disciples, just as for the male disciples, fear was the opposite of trust and faith.

IV. The Movement towards Mutual Ministry

Both the temptations of the Twelve and the temptations of the women at the tomb were connected with fear. The challenges presented to them asked both to go beyond the normative expectations that the community had of them—expectations based on gender roles, status, or even official recognition in the community. For the official leaders, the challenge was to give up their need for prestige and their reliance on their own power, and to listen to the message of those who had quietly served in the background. For the unofficial ministers, it meant being willing to go outside of an established role to speak of their own experience of God and to risk rejection and misunderstanding by those whom they may have considered more qualified.

Mark begins the Gospel with the promise of good news. However, for this news to be proclaimed and heard, both groups of followers must overcome their fear and respond to their particular challenge of ministry. Those who had earlier trusted in their own ability had to learn to listen to those who were afraid of the new task entrusted to them. Those who had been too afraid to speak overcame their fear and proclaimed the good news to the despairing disciples. This meeting of the traditions of ministry took place in the early church as male and female disciples each overcame fear and responded to the unexpected challenge placed before them. A new trajectory of ministry had begun in which official and unofficial ministers worked side by side in a dynamic relationship of trust and mutuality.

The dialogue with Mark challenges us as well to describe the present reality of ministry in the church honestly and without pretense, naming the differences in status and the need for recognition of the various ministering persons in the community. We are asked to describe the temptations and opportunities that are there within the present social and political realities for those who are officially named and for those who perform ministry more unofficially. We are challenged to be sensitive to God who frequently subverts the human evaluations and classifications of ministry, whether this means affirming our ministry when we feel that it is unimportant or pointing us to the need for further teaching and healing.

Above all, this dialogue with Mark has pointed us to the need for mutual ministry. The story of Jesus and his followers cannot go on unless there are both those who proclaim and those who listen, those who heal and those who are being healed, those who teach and those who are open to teaching. What is most crucial about this kind of mutuality, however, is that official and unofficial ministry meet in the common need to receive as well as to give. When there is an openness to God's call, cultural patterns are subverted and real ministry happens in a variety of unexpected ways in the community. A dynamic interaction between official and unofficial ministry characterizes such an openness to the challenges that Jesus places before all of his followers.

Using the story of the followers of Jesus to describe several paradigms of ministry has not led us to an idealistic picture of official ministry. Instead, we have been invited to personal identification with the temptations, failures, and opportunities that came to two specific groups of disciples of Jesus. The narrative suggests that ministry is dynamic and changing as persons respond both by receiving the ministry of others and by willingly ministering to others in unexpected ways.

What this means for us as Mennonites in the midst of our particular social and political realities is not clearly outlined for us. However, as we struggle to name analogies to the Gospel story in the realities of our day, we too can be drawn into the writing of an official story that subverts cultural patterns. We too can discover a flexible and dynamic pattern of ministry. We too can overcome the fear that leads to rigid structures that paralyze our ministry. In this way the good news of Jesus will be proclaimed by both official and unofficial ministers working together in mutuality and trust.

***

FORMAL THEOLOGICAL EDUCATION: THE CENTRE AND THE BOUNDARIES[13]

I do not remember struggling much with the decision to accept the job of interim director of the Toronto Mennonite Theological Centre (TMTC) while James Reimer, the founder and director, was on sabbatical. TMTC was founded in 1990 at the Toronto school of Theology (TST) while I was in graduate studies there. Though very small, it was the only Mennonite institution in North America that worked directly with doctoral students and deliberately entered the theological conversation at the advanced degree level on a university campus. The part-time work as interim director would enable me to keep in touch with the larger academic ecumenical community as well as the Mennonite church and its theological institutions, while also doing some theological writing and speaking on the side.

The vision of TMTC was to train theological leaders for the Mennonite church and beyond. But with only one part-time director, a part-time sessional professor and minimal administrative support, it was challenging work. Administrating this centre tested my every ability to be creative and visionary as well as to be practical and collaborative with students and staff. How I used my newly given authority and power intersected with how the institution could most wisely use its minority voice in the larger university context.

The position did not come with adequate financial remuneration. However, it did come with some perks. I was given advanced degree standing by TST, which meant that I could teach courses on the doctoral level as well as be on the committees of doctoral students. Since this was usually reserved for senior full-time faculty, I was particularly privileged. This meant that the courses I taught were small seminar courses of primarily advanced degree students. The conversations were rich, thus encouraging me to continue my own theological thinking. Since I also helped to plan the conversation among Mennonite students as well as the larger Mennonite forums at TST, I could continue the dialogue that I had started as a student.

The reality of limited financial resources for TMTC only hit me the second year when the director position was offered to me. James Reimer came back from his sabbatical wanting, not the role of director, but the role of academic advisor since he was also teaching full time at Conrad Grebel University College. The grant money had run out and the board (made up of deans of various theological schools plus several representatives from Mennonite conferences and agencies) felt they could only support this institution very minimally due to their own financial pressures. Fortunately for us, the larger consortium of colleges, the Toronto School of Theology (TST), continued to offer us office and classroom space since they were happy to have a Radical Reformation perspective on campus. However, the financial short-fall had to be made up somehow and that task now fell to me, including finding the funds to pay myself as director.

The work of administration was exciting for me but also very frustrating. The board, made up of male members, was intimidating to me, as a female and as someone with no experience in administration. I was able to recruit a volunteer treasurer so that I was not the only woman present at board meetings and later one agency appointed a woman to this board! I continually came up against the financial challenge when I proposed new programs. However, this made me more adept at creative solutions which required little financial support.

Two initiatives that I took were valued by the larger community but eventually were understood to be beyond the scope of TMTC's mandate. One was a pilot project in "Supervised Experience in Teaching Ministry." This was to be a partnership with congregations to build bridges between scholarly work and the local church and to give students opportunity to translate their scholarly work into language for the community beyond the university. The project was a success according to students and the congregations, but without a further grant it was impossible to sustain. The other initiative was to establish an Anabaptist-Mennonite network of scholars. A newsletter and a listing of scholars were to help create relationships among these academics. This enceadour successful and eventually became independent of TMTC. Both of these initiatives took quite a bit of volunteer time but were also very rewarding for me.

One of the advantages of the title "director" was that I gained visibility in the larger Mennonite scholarly and church world. This attention came as a surprise to me, as I had not realized the power that comes with an official position at a theological school. One exciting invitation from outside of North America was a consultation on "Theological Education on Five Continents" that took place in India just before the Mennonite World Conference in Calcutta in 1997. At that conference, Daniel S. Schipani gave the primary address on a vision for theological education. I was asked to speak more directly and practically about formal education and its place in the larger mission of the church.

The underlying theological assumption of the consultation was that we "engage in theological education for the sake of the church in the world in the light of God's reign."[14] *This consultation expanded my context for doing theology in many ways. The interrelated agenda and contexts were specifically designated in terms of the church, with its history and tradition, in terms of the world, understood both narrowly and broadly as social-cultural, and in terms of God's commonwealth of freedom, justice, and peace as revealed in Word and Spirit. How these came together for me in these meetings cannot easily be described in words. I came home from India in culture shock, unable to immediately process what I had experienced. In the monthly newsletter I expressed it as having stood on "holy ground" for a while, holy because of God's presence in the multiple conversations, diverse cultural expressions of faith, and the multi-faceted visual, oral and tactile impressions of India and its people.*

This consultation was the first time that I experienced the exploration of theological themes with a group of people in which participants from North America were in the minority. Presenting a paper and listening to discussions with multiple translations created unique settings for reflecting on power relationships among us. But it also strengthened my resolve to move beyond the church/world, sacred/secular, and insider/outsider dichotomies to see the broader work of God in the world. Most surprising to me was seeing for the first time how the Wind of the Spirit seemed to be blowing around the world despite the acknowledged colonialism, androcentrism and Eurocentrism of Western missionary efforts.

I presented the following paper at this consultation and it represents that broader conversation which I was invited into when I accepted the role of director of TMTC. It reflects the challenges of formal education and arose directly out of my experience as director of TMTC and as a board member of AMBS.

* * *

Creative leadership is often done in the space between vision and current reality, between seeing clearly where we want to be and telling the truth of where we actually are. The energy which can move an institution toward a new vision comes when both a compelling picture of the future is accepted and an accurate picture of current reality is given.[15] Daniel Schipani has given us a vision that is inspiring and thought-provoking in its scope and depth "theological education for the sake of the church in the world in the light of God's reign."[16] In a much less comprehensive way, I want to describe my own context of work as part of the reality that must be put into juxtaposition with Daniel's vision. The tensions that are generated when I place vision and reality side by side create the challenges I face in my role, whether as board member, as administrator, or as teacher. I will therefore speak concretely, referring directly to the two institutions to which I relate—Associated Mennonite Biblical Seminary (AMBS) and Toronto Mennonite Theological Centre (TMTC). I hope that you will respond by also describing your own realities and your own challenges.

The Centre and the Boundary

I want to begin by using spatial imagery to describe my context. This imagery is suitable because formal educational institutions are often identified with buildings and campuses which have an inside and an outside separated by a wall or other visible boundary marker. Moreover, this imagery has been used in discussions of theological education by a number of different writers. I will draw on two sources in order to reflect both critically and creatively on the *centre* and the *boundaries* of formal educational institutions.

The first source, Walter Brueggeman, uses the imagery of a wall to describe two kinds of theological conversation that need to take place in a church context.[17] The first conversation takes place "behind the wall" and uses communal language to speak to the insiders of the faith community and to God. In this conversation reality is defined by the faith and conviction that God is alive and active in the world. The second conversation takes place "on the wall" in a "foreign" tongue. This more public conversation uses language which assumes a different view of the world and is constructed around the dominant perceptions of reality by the larger society. In this conversation the contributions of the faith community are often marginal and controversial.

In Brueggeman's way of using this imagery the boundary or wall refers to the place where the differing perspectives of the faith community and the society surrounding it meet. Sometimes this meeting is friendly, creating new insights for both. Sometimes this meeting is confrontational or even hostile. Choices must then be made by both the society and the theological community about the world-view that will guide its life and work. The choices that the church makes in this public arena reflect on the integrity of the language used behind the wall.

In a quite different way, a number of liberation theologians also speak about the *centre* and the *marginal* (those on the boundary). However, in their use of these terms these theologians are referring to differing social/political locations as defined by sociology and political science.[18] This imagery arises out of the insight that our social context, whether within or outside of a particular church setting, influences our theology. Here the centre refers to the dominant group in the scholarly or church community that determines the agenda addressed in theology. The marginal refers to those with fewer resources who are confined to the edge of the community. Their voice is often silenced because no one is listening to them. In liberation theology's use of this imagery, those who stand on the wall are not there by choice but rather are pushed into that place by those in the centre of the community.

Christian educational institutions can be described using both of these frameworks because these institutions not only represent the church but also are concrete social/political entities in themselves. The questions that I will raise have to do with issues of power and authority, the agenda raised by liberation theology. However, the definition of power and authority is more ambiguous and fluid than liberation theology would admit. This is so because definitions may vary depending on where you stand in relationship to the wall as defined by Brueggeman. The ambiguity will become visible as we move from self-evident definitions to a more complex analysis of the challenges facing these institutions.

A Preliminary Description

At first glance it is easy to name AMBS as a school located at the centre of the faith community. As an inter-Mennonite educational institution committed to the Anabaptist heritage it is crucially located in the centre of North American Mennonite church life. It has as its purpose the "preparing of pastors, missionaries, teachers, evangelists, and other church leaders," that is, persons called to be at the centre of church life. The resources of its community include buildings, books, professors, administrators, and a heritage of education for the Mennonite church that goes back more than one hundred years.

In contrast, TMTC, an inter-Mennonite teaching and resource centre at the Toronto School of Theology, can rather quickly be understood as standing on the boundaries of the church community. Its purpose, "to foster reflection on the Anabaptist-Mennonite heritage by graduate students (doctoral level) and scholars in theology within an ecumenical context," suggests conversation that goes beyond the Mennonite community. Though its location on the largest university campus in Canada implies that its language will be public, dominated by the rational criteria of the university its immediate resources are limited, with a budget under $30,000, two part-time faculty, fifteen to twenty students who relate to the centre in an informal way, and a history of less than ten years. TMTC owns no building but instead uses the resources of its host, the Toronto School of Theology. Its constituency, the North American Mennonite church, is largely unaware of its existence, though it represents the only Mennonite institution in North America devoted to doctoral-level work.

In my role as a board member for AMBS and as the director and a teacher at TMTC I have reflected on the significance of boundaries and walls for the identity and work of these two institutions. I have discovered that some of the central issues that have arisen for me in my work have to do with the meaning attached to the walls and boundaries that our institutional communities represent for the larger church community and for the society around us. I have realized that the above characterization of the two schools is inaccurate, largely because margins and walls, inside and centre mean something different depending on where you are standing when you speak.

As I become immersed in the practical decisions that I need to make I realize that formal educational institutions reflect how we understand the church in the world. The choices and commitments that I make in my work affect the way the boundaries are fixed, not only those of the educational institution but also of the church. Therefore, a closer look must be taken to see how the centre is determined and what the boundaries of the community represent to the various members of the church and society.

Choices and Commitments

The choices that each church institution needs to make have to do with its identity. This identity can be described in terms of Schipani's description of the church's three-fold reason for being. I will therefore frame the discussion of boundaries by asking three key questions which these institutions must answer in relationship to the church's worship, community, and mission:

Which language do we use? (The question of worship.)

Brueggeman has suggested that Christians need to be bilingual.[19] They must be conversant in the language of the faith community where they speak in their own "sectarian" language in order to discuss issues of identity and commitment to God. However, Christians who are faithful to a sense of mission in the world must also be ready to enter the public dialogue where they must speak in a foreign tongue, enter into discussion of agenda that goes beyond their own community, and encounter differing and often conflicting perceptions of reality.

Mennonites who have a history of being a minority religion and a separated people have a long tradition of what can be called *sectarian* conversation. This has allowed them to concentrate on being the church rather than accommodating themselves to the dominant culture of the day. There is, however, a temptation associated with this conversation. Sometimes the language of the church has become *exclusive* refusing access to those from the outside who would wish to enter our faith communities. Some people who do not fit the image of a Mennonite church member have been silenced or given no authority to address the community.

More recently another subtle temptation has entered our communities. As we have gained respectability in our society we have begun to seek academic recognition by entering the public conversation. This conversation has put us in dialogue with other theological institutions that have arisen in the larger context of Christendom, a context in which the interpretation of reality by society at large has sometimes been assumed to be Christian. Therefore, the relationship between church and society has tended to be friendly, with only minor tensions arising between theological institutions and the university. The language commonly used in formal theology has more and more become the language of the reigning rationality of the day, whether that be philosophy, psychology, history, or sociology. The temptation for theology then has been to mistake the foreign language for its own mother tongue, thus allowing the public language to determine its interpretation of reality.

Mennonite students often feel that they are presented with a choice that does not allow them to become truly bilingual. Either they can stay with the biblical language of the community and risk withdrawal into a private sphere of social reality which has nothing to say to the broader world or they can use the foreign language of society and risk being seduced by the dominant rationality of the established culture.

This dilemma faces TMTC in a particular way because it is part of the larger university complex as well as part of an ecumenical institution which has fostered friendly relationships to the university. I well remember being faced with the choice of disciplines as I entered doctoral work. I could enter the biblical department where historical norms were dominant and where I would be discouraged from wrestling with contemporary meanings of the Bible, or I could enter the systematic theology department where the Bible was seldom referred to and philosophical considerations were primary. It seemed impossible to study the Bible as a real source for contemporary theology related to congregational life. As a teacher I continue to wrestle with this issue as I design courses and advise students in the context of a theological school whose existence depends on a friendly relationship with the university.

AMBS is also faced with the choice of language. However, because AMBS is a Mennonite seminary with a primary dependence on the congregations for its existence, its temptation may be somewhat different. Students and professors can easily assume that the language of the Mennonite community and its view of reality can be fully equated with divine revelation. They can then fail to notice when their separate existence becomes exclusive and oppressive; they can ignore the prophetic voices on the margin of the community. At the same time, it is often difficult to notice the subtle influence of the values of the society around us which have become disguised in community talk. This creates a situation in which our theology has no unique resources to assist those living and working in the public arena.

The question of language is a question of primary loyalty and authority; therefore, it is an issue of worship. Choosing a language means choosing a view of reality that can determine both the conversation behind the wall and the conversation on the wall. This view of reality must always be based on the reign of God in both the church and in the world. Learning to worship in order to be open to God's revealing and transforming presence is the antidote to the temptations of idolatry that can be found both in the centre and on the margins of the faith community. Only worship can help us maintain our identity without creating false boundaries. Both AMBS and TMTC are struggling to know how to do this with integrity.

Which resources do we draw on? (The question of community.)

In asking the question of resources our minds very quickly move to two kinds of resources that are valued by the educational community, the resource of finances and the resource of leadership personnel. In fact, at AMBS we have used the term "partnership" to describe the relationship between the congregation and the institution. In this partnership the congregations provide the necessary funds to gain a secure financial base for the school while the school provides the training for the churches' leaders.

However, it is exactly in this simply stated relationship that many of the issues related to community lie. This is so because power and authority are often dependent on who controls the finances and who chooses the leaders. Thus it is easy for persons within educational institutions to begin to vie for power and to compete for status. In this struggle the persons on the margins are sometimes forgotten and competition between people and between institutions begins to happen. Several issues could be named:

a) Who defines what good leadership looks like? Is it the congregations? If so, the training of leaders should take place in the context of a congregation rather than on a campus isolated from the issues of the church. Or should it be the knowledge learned from scholarly study whether this is from biblical studies or from psychology or sociology? Then leadership training should have a more scholarly disciplined focus on academic courses. Who decides this question? Is it the professors, the congregational members, the students, or the board who all have vested interest in the answer to this question? How do we bring all of these partners into the conversation while focusing on a vision that goes beyond each person's personal interest?

b) Who decides which institution should receive the most funds? Is it the denomination or the congregations or the individuals who have the most funds to give? It is becoming more evident how difficult it is for institutions to co-operate and how difficult it is to fund all of them. Some institutions will not survive the financial cutbacks that are now taking place. Which ones should survive?

c) Who should receive financial assistance for their theological education? Should it be the brightest of our young people? Or the ones coming from our white middle-class congregations? Or the male members of the community? Or should our resources instead be used to fund education for members of our minority groups who are unable to fund their own education?

Both AMBS, an established seminary, and TMTC, a new institution, are struggling with the relationship between finances and leadership. But perhaps what is needed is to look again at how we define what is included in the notion of a resource. We might discover that our educational communities need those with disabilities, those of non-white races, women and men of all ages and of a variety of social backgrounds. We would welcome the participation of those from other countries, from other denominations and from other races. Decisions might be easier to make if we would look at how we could co-operate together to make our educational communities reflect the rich diversity of the body of Christ.

Whose agenda receives attention? (The question of mission.)

Daniel Schipani has diagrammed the various agendas that interrelate in diverse ways in theological education. He has suggested that there may be a certain tension which arises as these agendas intersect. He has placed the dimension of human emergence, both personal and social, in the centre of the agenda for theological education. What he has not been able to do is diagram the complex nature of this emergence in light of God's reign.[20]

As the church becomes involved in mission it becomes involved in situations of sin and evil. Victims of oppression and domination, persons bound by habits and customs which do not reflect God's reign, cry out for liberation and healing. But rational education alone does not heal. Nor do ecclesial communities long embroiled in conflict and dissension learn shalom by only talking about it. A society that has become insensitive to the poor needs more than prophetic preaching to change. How do theological institutions foster both formation of character and transformation of persons and communities?

One practical question that arises for educators who take mission seriously is the question of requirements and evaluation of students' work. Transformation is difficult to measure and standard tests do not fit each person. AMBS has struggled with finding ways to be more closely involved with each person in the process of completing an MDiv. Integration papers are discussed with peers. Self-evaluations are required throughout the process. But the task of fostering real change continues to be the biggest challenge.

What is needed is finding ways to invite God's transforming Spirit into the midst of the learning community. Perhaps this invitation comes most powerfully through the witness of the Bible and the testimony of changed people and communities. Thus any theological institution must be vitally connected to the centre of its curriculum—the Bible, and to persons and communities that exhibit transformation by the grace of God. Careful discernment is needed to invite this witness into the classrooms and to take the students out into the world to recognize God's work in the world.

At TMTC I have been given the task of finding ways of enriching the curriculum of students studying at the doctoral level by arranging forums and inviting speakers. Many of my daily decisions have to do with building connections between life outside of the library and the theory written in books. Sometimes this connection is made through a new look at our own history in the Anabaptist reformation. At other times it is made by inviting in someone from the ecumenical or global community to speak to us. Our most intense meetings often have to do with the question of our personal relationship to the Bible. The temptation is to stay with safe topics that do not question the status quo and to focus on academic issues divorced from personal commitment. But it is exactly in the personal interactions that students are faced most directly with their need for divine empowering.

AMBS is rich with resources that witness to God's power. What does this mean for the city in which the seminary is located? What does this mean for persons seeking healing within the community? The connections between daily life on campus and the task of empowering for mission are often difficult to find. AMBS has tried to struggle with this by its focus on practical pastoral education and the opportunities that are given for community involvement. However, both receiving God's healing and sharing God's invitation do not come easily to persons comfortable in their own pew in church.

In the Light of God's Reign

Though AMBS and TMTC are very different institutions they share in common their primary context, the reign of God in the world, and a common task, formal theological education. In their vocation of enabling for worship, equipping for community and empowering for mission they struggle with focusing on the centre as they break down barriers and invite persons beyond their boundaries to come and learn of God's grace. To do this they must become bilingual, they must learn to recognize and share available resources, and they must be able to invite vital witnesses to God's transformation into their midst.

Our analysis has hinted that both institutions will not naturally move in the direction of God's reign. Temptations which deny God and God's way of being in the world are there for persons involved in both institutions. In that sense both institutions must affirm again and again their dependence on the larger church's discernment and counsel. They must be ready to change, to live and even to die in the service of God in the world.

As educators we have been given the task to give creative leadership to the churches' task of theological reflection. May God help us to see a clear vision of where the church is to be and to tell the truth about the institutions in which we work.

***

DIALOGUE WITH HAUERWAS[21]

When I entered the academic ecumenical dialogue, I was hesitant but hopeful that I could both contribute and learn. This dialogue is represented most concretely by the annual meetings of the American Academy of Religion and the Society of Biblical Literature (AAR/SBL) that are held annually and draw thousands of theologians and students of religion. They are an opportunity to gather together to talk about our work, participate in workshops, find out about prospective jobs, and meet colleagues and friends. Over one thousand sessions and workshops are available to those attending.

An additional platform for ecumenical dialogue was created for me when in 1992 I was appointed as a representative of the General Conference Mennonite Church to the editorial board of the Believers Church Bible Commentary Series. *Their meetings took place a day before the AAR/SBL meeting. I had been very happy about this appointment for it gave me the opportunity to see how various biblical scholars from the Mennonite, Church of the Brethren, and Brethren in Christ churches practised biblical interpretation. The main task between meetings was to read the commentaries that were being produced and to give critical and constructive responses to them. The conversation was respectful and I felt affirmed even though I was not a professional biblical scholar but rather a systematic theologian.*

Since the 1970's, Mennonite scholars have "found" each other at the AAR/SBL meetings. At first these meetings were informal, but more recently a forum and reception of Mennonites scholars and friends has been held just before the regular meetings of the AAR/SBL. For many years Herald Press also had a book display among the many exhibitors, featuring scholarly works by Mennonites. Various Mennonite insti-

tutions took turns hosting the receptions that at first were arranged by the Institute of Mennonite Studies. Gradually, TMTC took over the responsibility of arranging these meetings and a committee planned the forum. In the next few years my task would be to make sure all this happened.

My first public presentation at the AAR/SBL came as part of a panel at the Mennonite forum in 1993 responding to Stanley Hauerwas's writings. Hauerwas was becoming a very popular theologian among Mennonites and so the forum was dedicated to his work. We met in Washington that year and I was delighted that my husband could take those days off and meet me there since he was still in Toronto while I was teaching in Winnipeg.

Hauerwas, a Methodist theologian, credits Mennonites, in particular John H. Yoder, with his understanding of Christian theology as rooted in a particular community and its tradition that espouses the non-violent love incarnated in Jesus as the basis of its ethics. For Hauerwas, Yoder's theological approach challenged the modern assumptions of universal reason as the foundation for belief and morality as well as many of the political/social realities of Christendom. When such prominent theologians as Hauerwas, Lindbeck, and Frei look to a theological approach that has been marginalized in the past and suggest that it presents a way forward for all of theology in this post-modern time, Mennonites feel vindicated.

However, by this time I had become disillusioned with Yoder and the popularity of his writings among Mennonites. Criticism of Yoder by women was largely being ignored by Mennonite scholars who could not see the connection between Yoder's abuse of women and his theology. Though I was pleased that I had been asked to be on the panel discussing Hauerwas's theological approach, I also carried within me some anger that Hauerwas's writings seemed to affirm the male orientation of Mennonite theology.

My paper included both affirmation and critique as is usual in these kinds of discussions. Hauerwas's written response printed in the Conrad Grebel Review *also included valid points of agreement and disagreement with each speaker. However, in the oral conversation with the panel, there was one remark that made created extreme distress for me. In response to my suggestion that including women as worthy partners in the dialogue would enrich and change the conversation, a remark was made to the effect that, "once women write something that is worthwhile, we will engage them." I left the meeting and spent the hour walking up and down the streets, trying to calm down. My feelings alternated between anger and disappointment with scholars whom I had respected and a self-blaming that I had put myself in this vulnerable position. I was grateful for the support of my husband who assured me that mutuality between men and women was possible.*

On reflection I realize that I had accepted the critical scholarly approach to academic work without myself taking the responsibility to create a better climate of dialogue. However, the kind of "put down" that happens all too frequently at scholarly meetings is ethically unacceptable. As scholars we need to find better ways of conversing with each other. In succeeding years, my role was to chair the meetings of our Mennonite caucuses at the AAR/SBL meetings. I decided to continue to risk entering these discussions because I firmly believed that women needed to contribute to the conversation. However, I regret that I did not speak up more strongly in encouraging us to become a community of mutuality where all are respected and new voices are welcomed.

The following article demonstrates my attempt to find a way into a conversation that does not marginalize my ideas by naming them as fitting into a particular stream or trivialize them by naming them feminist and thus necessarily historicist and suspect. Typologies can be helpful, but they can also hinder our search for truth by the labelling of the other. Thus, this article illustrates my tentative entry into the larger theological arena represented by the AAR/SBL and a peer reviewed scholarly journal, albeit in a "safe" Mennonite enclave.

***

When I was asked to take part in this panel, the organizer suggested it would not be difficult for me to do so because he thought I was sort of in the "Hauerwas camp." I accepted the assignment since I had long wanted to read some books by the person who somehow had captured the attention and admiration of a number of Mennonite theologians.

I soon discovered why Hauerwas is held in such esteem. He has been able to articulate some key Mennonite convictions in categories that are intelligible if not entirely convincing to scholarly communities beyond the Mennonite church. I began to regret that I had not spent more time on his writings while I was doing my thesis. A theology which in some way asserts the reality of *church* over against the *world* is foundational to our identity as Mennonites. A theology which is suspicious of universalism is popular among those of us who have often felt marginalized in the larger theological discussion. A focus on communal identity rooted in biblical narrative is particularly attractive to a community that has long assumed the continuity of its narrative with the Christian story.

I therefore read on with expectation, assuming that the rejection of the Enlightenment dependence on universalism and epistemological foundationalism would necessarily translate into an openness to the particularity of diverse accounts of the biblical story within the church. I assumed that depending on the church rather than Christendom to embody truth claims about God and ethical convictions about the virtuous life would lead to conversations between various construals of that church. Rather excitedly I looked for the "intratextual" dialogue between women in the church and Hauerwas. I was particularly interested in an account of discipleship which would present an alternative to violence between men and women in the church. I was looking for an embodiment of peace in the dialogue of people of the church willing to be "in touch with one another."[22]

Though I have not looked through all of Hauerwas's many books and articles, I was disappointed that I did not find more dialogue with those who feel marginal within the Christian circle. The constructive dialogue about the construal of church and Bible that I had hoped for was largely absent. My feminist "hermeneutics of suspicion" was aroused and I began to wonder whether the authoritative hermeneutic community in which Hauerwas participates is more exclusive than the word "church" implies.

I now remembered why I had avoided Hauerwas in my earlier work. I had reacted against the way some Mennonites could use his writings to legitimate their own hermeneutical approach, which easily dismissed the feminist movement as the supreme example of Enlightenment strategies and ideals. I hope the irony of this use of Hauerwas's writings is not lost on us. To employ his work primarily in an apologetic way is, I think, to fall into the very trap that he is warning us against. For Hauerwas is attempting to help the church "recover a sense of its own integrity" within a liberal democratic society; he is not defending a particular church and its embodiment of the Christian story. (However, this use of his work has confirmed for me something that I have only recently discovered: theological discourse, no matter what its original intention, can always be used apologetically to protect the status quo when placed into another context.)

This brings me to why I think that Hauerwas's writings can easily be used in the Mennonite context to support and legitimate certain unexamined assumptions—assumptions which stand in continuity with the culture and society around us but which are often unarticulated. These assumptions are hidden in the key terms that Hauerwas uses. I would identify this apologetic move, however, not as a legitimation of a false universalism (a temptation of a church that assumes its role is to cooperate with the rest of society) but rather as a legitimation of a false particularism (a temptation of a church that assumes its role is to be distinct from the rest of society). This kind of justification can be used within a church to legitimate practices which favor the dominant in the church community.

I want to illustrate this point by focusing on the way the term "church" is used to hide assumptions that implicitly justify the continued androcentric patriarchal church. These assumptions are not explicitly stated in Hauerwas's books. But because alternative construals of church are not articulated, readers are encouraged to fill in their own presuppositions arising from their own specific context. I will list several of these assumptions.

1. There seems to be an assumption that the public realm of the church is the real church. The term "church" thus hides the male orientation of the community that Hauerwas addresses. Though the scholarly audience may be largely male, this fact does not justify the lack of critique in Hauerwas's writings of the

deep division that there is in most churches between the public, official church of the leaders, and the domestic, interpersonal church of the laity. Women in most churches participate in an unusually high number in the Sunday schools, in the church meals, in community Bible studies, in the service aspect of the church. In contrast they are comparatively absent in the public ministry and decision making aspect of many churches. The real church for women is often centered in the prayer groups outside official structures, the sisterhood which creates a safe place for the healing of the woundedness inflicted by both church and society. Unless scholars seek out conversation partners who are rooted in the domestic arena, this division and hierarchy in the church is not challenged and the priority of the male church will continue to dominate the theological discussion.

2. Another assumption seems to be that the "patterns of domination" by which we in the church are captured are the same for women and men.[23] Thus Hauerwas does not stress the differences which our particular gender socialization makes in the functioning of the politics of the church community. It is not surprising then that he can discuss "Christian social order" without challenging the authority of role definitions based on sex.[24] Nor does he tackle directly the troublesome issue of violence against women in his discussion of the politics of sex. The politics of community can therefore easily become a justification of certain forms of faithfulness between marriage partners which favor the dominance of the male.

3. A further assumption appears to be that the Christian identity which arises from participation and training in the church is the same for men and women. This does not take into account, however, the personal autonomy that is gained by a male simply by being raised in Western society; nor does it take into account the deep community and service orientation most women raised in Western society accept as normal. This incorporation of female identity into Christian identity as defined by males continues to be justified in the naming of God as the "God of Abraham, Isaac, Jacob, and Jesus" rather than also speaking of the God of Sarah, Rebekkah, Rachel, and Christ.[25] It seems to me that the assertion that male Christian identity and female Christian identity are the same must be demonstrated by a dialogue between Christian women and men rather than be assumed by those who have historically been given the role of articulating this identity.

4. The relationship-specific characteristic of power and authority seems to be inadequately recognized in many of Hauerwas's writings. Hauerwas speaks about the church giving up Constantinian power in its relationship to society and thus willingly using the tactic of the weak rather than the strategy of the strong.[26] However, the church is also an institution which represents divine authority and power to those within the church who often feel weak. Thus discipline when it is initiated by the powerful in the church for those who feel weak often feels coercive and violent. This power relationship must also be addressed, because a denial

of the power which comes with an association with the divine only heightens the possibility of abuse and violence.

5. The assumption that discipleship has to do with being trained and disciplined in Christian community does not come to terms with the ambivalent way in which Christian communities shape individuals. The notion that "losing our sense of need" by being grasped by an adventure which is true, compelling, and demanding does not do justice to the narratives of women and men who came to Jesus because they are in pain and anguish due to guilt and shame. As the narrative of Mark testifies, it is not the twelve who were being trained who become the primary examples of faith but the "little ones" who recognize their need for healing—see, for example, Mark 5:34, 10:52. Thus we must learn not only that we are sinners and need to be forgiven but also that we are children of God and can be healed from the pain and suffering caused by those who would deny this identity, sometimes even in the name of God.

In the discussion thus far I have spoken as a Mennonite woman raising some concerns about how the emphases of Hauerwas can be used to support an androcentric church. However, I also stand with Hauerwas in many of his convictions. I therefore want to indicate a greater concern that can turn my critical discussion into self-critique: the whole question of how to speak about the necessary continuity among God, the biblical narrative, and the church without becoming part of the violence against the "other" that has been so much a part of Christian history. Hauerwas raises this concern in the last chapter of his book *After Christendom?*

Most Christians, including feminist Christians, assert the necessary continuity among God, Bible, and church. Hauerwas's emphasis on narrative focuses this continuity in a helpful way. However, the discontinuity must also be clearly acknowledged. It seems to me that, like metaphor, our narrative language is false when it does not at the same time leave itself open to discontinuity and interruption. The embodiment of theological convictions in Bible and church always carries with it the possibility of the embodiment of alternative gods, alternative stories. Already in the Hebrew Scripture we find interruptions of the central embodiment of the story. These interruptions came when new experiences in life or new interpretations of the Scripture interrupted the accepted norms and created space for God to speak anew. Jesus came as an interruption of the official narrative and created a new narrative embodied within the culture of the times. Yet that narrative as written in the New Testament has also been interrupted as women and men have realized that it too contains assumptions based on the worldview of its time.

Hauerwas is well aware of the constant change, the testing of tradition that needs to go on in the church. He asserts that "God comes to this community in the form of a stranger, challenging its smugness, exposing its temptations to false 'knowledge,' denying its spurious claims to have domesticated God's grace."[27] Nothing can therefore guarantee that we stay insiders to God's truth.

What then about Hauerwas's focus on church and biblical narrative? Somehow as Christians we need both to identify the human embodiments of God's narrative in our midst and to be open to the interruptions that new experiences or new interpretations can give to the human construals of that narrative. Thus we must speak both of the Bible as the Word of God and as a human word. We must speak of the church as a sign of the kingdom as well as at times a sign of the world.

To acknowledge that the truths of the Bible and the Church are not yet wholly God's truth is also to acknowledge that God can speak outside of the church and Bible. Thus the interruptions that come to the dominant narrative do not only come from within the community. At times they come from without, as new experiences are brought into the midst of the community or new interpretations of the church and Bible challenge our own.

What I am calling for is both commitment and critique, both a hermeneutics of suspicion and a hermeneutics of openness to God's voice, both an empowerment to speak our own truth and a willingness to be in dialogue with others. For Christian convictions are not mere matters of opinion; however, neither are they absolute truth guaranteed by a relationship to church and Bible.

Chapter 5. Vision

NAMING MY THEOLOGICAL LENS

As I reflect back on the theological questions that permeate my writings, I realize that my life has been lived within a particular shift in worldview in Western society, the shift from modernity to post-modernity. The questions that underlie my writings came about, at least partly, because I was being influenced by this shift occurring not only in the writings of theological and philosophical theorists but also in the popular expressions of language, music, art, and technology. Underlying much of the culture around me was a growing lack of trust in anything universal that could anchor claims of transcendence, truth, or ultimate reality. Thus the notion of hermeneutic community intrigued me for it helped me to understand how every claim I make to truth is ultimately embedded within a particular and limited cultural political context, whether that is church or society, geographical neighbourhood or ethnic kinship group. This context and the particular experiences that I had within that context needed to be named and acknowledged.

Many of the radical differences among theologians during the 1990's were rooted in differing assumptions gained from either modernity or postmodernity. I understood the need for many theologians to argue against the traditional claims of ultimate truth and certainty and to deconstruct the power relationships that undergirded them. But more and more I began to sense a need to not only deconstruct but also to imagine a new vision of reality that included a God who exists and is active in the world today. I did recognize that each "meta-narrative" that we create is a human creation and therefore only a partial narrative. However, I also made a claim that, though limited, every narrative can point to that ultimate reference—a God who reveals and saves. Because of this, I have become more resistant when theology is subsumed by social, political, psychological, or anthropological analysis in which God is not named. Instead, I have begun to state my assumptions around the reality of revelation as well as around the particular sociopolitical location which has influenced these assumptions.

For me hermeneutic suspicion and hermeneutic imagination are tools that can be used to transform and enlarge a particular heritage. I realized that these tools were available in part as a result of the shift to postmodernity. But I do not want to give postmodernity or any worldview ultimate significance. Rather, I want to insist that God can be named in both a modern or postmodern context and we need to continue to challenge every worldview and the methods produced by them in order to expose their limitations.

But how can we name a God beyond our human understanding, a God we cannot ground in universal reason and who also cannot be contained in our particular doctrinal statements nor our particular narratives or experiences? How do we name a God worthy of our worship and trust?

This question occupied me more and more as I encountered the broad spectrum of theological thinking. In my own writing, I began to refer to truth claims and multiple witnesses to truth in order to recognize the limitations of all methods of naming God while continuing to be convinced by these same multiple witnesses of God's presence in the world. I began to see how new construals of reality are created when we invite new conversation partners into our midst. In line with postmodernity we may want to name these as theological "pieces" rather than as a systematic theology which attempts to create a coherent whole. But I continue to insist that it is God the Spirit who can animate these pieces of theology to provide healing and hope for us in this uncertain world.

The three theological pieces in this chapter differ from each other because they initially had different audiences in mind and thus are written in different styles. The first was written for a North American scholarly audience, the second for an international group of Mennonite leaders interested in the Anabaptist tradition, and the third for a worship service for an ecumenical grad student group at the university. What unites them is my new conviction that, though critical analysis is a necessary step in our hermeneutical effort to reclaim the truth in our tradition, imagination may be the tool most needed to envision a future for our faith communities.

***

POSTMODERN SUSPICION AND IMAGINATION: THERAPY FOR MENNONITE HERMENEUTIC COMMUNITIES[1]

The dialogue partners that I engage with most often in my writings come from my own tradition. Though I read widely, enter many ecumenical conversations, and value the input I receive, it is the companions from my particular church community that create the questions and the convictions that occupy me most often. Therefore, most of what I have published has been for Mennonite periodicals.

However, it is the conversation with philosophers and theologians beyond my tradition that have helped me to articulate my unease with some directions that Mennonite theology has gone in the past. In the following article, I deliberately referred to male authors who describe postmodernity in their writings as important sources for their thoughts. I hoped to initiate a conversation with my male colleagues without first of all creating resistance because of my involvement with feminist thought. What was encouraging to me was to see both male and female conversation partners in this particular issue of the Mennonite Quarterly Review (MQR). *This manner of dialogue was in sharp contrast to the way I had experienced most theological discussions in our Mennonite community in the past where the conversations were separated along gen-*

der lines.

For example, women and men's voices were represented in separated conversations in two issues of the MQR just a few years earlier. In June 1994 a conference entitled, "Whither the Anabaptist Vision" was held in Elizabethtown College. Discipleship, a theme running through many of my articles, was central to this vision as articulated by Harold Bender in 1944. Now 50 years later this vision and its power to integrate the variety of Mennonite theological directions seemed to be losing some of its power.

The papers presented at the Elizabethtown conference suggest that Mennonite theologians were beginning to wrestle with multiple understandings of the Anabaptist heritage. Many were beginning to question the adequacy of Bender's vision, with a growing number of voices suggesting that his vision did not put enough stress on God's action (grace, Gospel) as opposed to the human response to God's call (obedience, discipleship).[2] *At the same time, historians were insisting that there was no unitary theological vision among the early Anabaptists but rather that the term Anabaptism described many different origins and characteristics of a diverse movement. The footnotes reveal, however, that female voices were not yet represented in this conversation as recorded in the MQR.*

That same year, the MQR published papers presented at the second "Women Doing Theology" Conference in Bluffton, Ohio.[3] *What surprised me here were the efforts being made to articulate new visions arising out of a critical consciousness and new attention to experience. Forgiveness, the meaning of the cross, and atonement were among the key subjects considered. The footnotes suggest that male scholars were consulted but also that female peers were increasingly being brought into the discussions.*

Sadly, these two conversations were not yet being brought into one forum. However, the ferment in both the larger world and the small Mennonite community provided a stimulating context for me as I tried to find the language of renewal that I felt was needed. I am deeply grateful to the periodicals that accepted my work during these fledgling attempts at doing theology. However, what was still needed was a much more inclusive visioning that went far beyond including women.

The following essay relies on some of the theological "pieces" important to me in my earlier work but brings them together under the framework of postmodernity.

***

The notion of the church as a hermeneutic community has been especially intriguing for me, both as a member of the Mennonite church and as a preacher and teacher in Mennonite institutions. It suggests that theological convictions about the activity of the Holy Spirit in the church's interpretation of the Bible need to be brought together with a more sociological/political description of the particular process of interpretation that happens in congregations and church institutions. However, the meanings attached to this term in writings by Mennonites have not always assisted biblical interpreters in the practical task of choosing methodological approaches and conversation partners suited to the work of discerning God's Word.

According to John H. Yoder, the locating of authoritative biblical interpretation in a process of congregational dialogue and discernment was already a distinguishing mark of the Anabaptist tradition during the time of the Reformation.[4] For Yoder, "hermeneutic community" implied that the text could be understood best when disciples committed to obedience gathered to discern what the Bible had to say to their particular needs and concerns. Sometimes called *Gemeindetheologie* (theology of community), this approach suggested that biblical interpretation was to be oriented to voluntary communities of worship and practice rather than more universally to Christendom or society in general.[5] Thus this definition of hermeneutic community created a space for the active involvement of each member of a congregation in the interpretive process. However, it also idealized the integrity and obedience of the listening congregation and the committed and listening believer. It therefore gave little practical help in dealing with actual power struggles and authority issues in the congregational process. Nor could it identify those instances when unity came about merely because persons of the same ethnic identity and social class, living in close geographical proximity to each other saw things the same way.[6]

Recently, historian John D. Roth has hinted that a more dynamic understanding of hermeneutic community would pay attention to the disagreements, debates, and tensions that have always been part of the discernment process. He affirms that the ideal of hermeneutic community has "continued to provide a source of ferment and renewal in a wide variety of contexts and circumstances" in groups descended from the Anabaptists.[7] However, for Roth the notion of hermeneutic community would perhaps better describe the "common conversation" created by people who enter the process of interpretation precisely because they recognize the importance of an issue that is being debated. The boundaries of the hermeneutic community would then not be determined by the "common mind," which would or would not result from the discussion, but by the actual dialogue partners of a conversation.

Roth's description allows a recognition and naming of differences, divisions, and tensions that have always been evident in the history of Anabaptist/Mennonite churches. However, it does not assist us in discerning when these differences encourage a more careful reading of the canonical text in order to hear God's voice and when they reveal power struggles linked to political or social status in the community.

Missing in both of these definitions is an understanding of the complex authority and power relationships that exist in a hermeneutic community that also identifies itself as a church or faith community. This complexity is increased because interpersonal relationships in a church community are not only interpreted as interactions between people but also seen as evidence of God's Spirit working in the community. Thus numerous questions can be asked. For example, what does it mean when the contributions of some members to the discussion are valued more than others? Does this mean that these members have more spiritual sensitivity, or is the valuing of these contributions related to the economic, academic or social status of the contributor? What does authoritative leadership blessed by God look like, when there are so many different models of leadership available in church and society? What are the explicit and implicit boundaries of the community based on when they mean different things to insiders than they do to outsiders?

Another equally important authority or power relationship in the church must also be explored. How is the power and authority of the biblical text understood and interpreted? For example, is the power of a text attributed to its canonical status, its dominant place in an ancient tradition, or its power to create a new symbolic world view for its readers? Has the community used the text in the past to give ethical guidelines, to inform the identity of the community as people of God, or to justify or bless certain practices and beliefs? What kind of role does the text continue to play in the community? What does it mean when a community speaks about the Bible as the Word of God?

The present intellectual environment of postmodernism with its focus on discourse has given us some significant tools which can help us look more closely at these aspects of the hermeneutical process.[8] By focusing on the use or function of language and recognizing the dependence of language on community tradition, the notion of discourse opens a new way to connect the text, the individual reader and the hermeneutic community.

In this context certain hermeneutical approaches have taken on new significance. Specifically, "suspicion" and "imagination" as described by David Tracy and Walter Brueggemann, respectively, are two postmodern tools that acknowledge authority and power relationships within the community of interpretation and discourse. In this paper I will indicate the importance of attending to these hermeneutical tools by giving a brief description of these approaches and then illustrating their usefulness by referring to specific examples in Mennonite history as well as in my personal experience within Mennonite hermeneutic communities.

I identify these tools as therapeutic, a term associated with healing but also sometimes associated with excessive focus on the self. In this context, I use the term deliberately to express both the possibility of healing and the limitations and partial usefulness of these approaches. Neither postmodern suspicion nor postmodern imagination can guarantee that the power of the Holy Spirit will enliven the hermeneutical process. However, these tools can encourage the users of theological language (particularly theologians, preachers and biblical scholars) to examine the convictions about power and authority that undergird their notion of the church as hermeneutic community. At the same time, they can assist those involved in the hermeneutic community in making practical decisions about their own role in the interpretive process. Thus they can help us to invite God's healing presence into our communities.

Postmodern Hermeneutics of Suspicion

As a description of our times, the term "postmodernity" is ambiguous and complex.[9] In this paper I use the term (much as David Tracy does in his book *Plurality and Ambiguity*) to describe a new awareness of the close relationship between language and understanding, interpretation and truth, meaning and function.[10] In the latter days of this century North Americans are becoming aware as never before that every description of reality is finally hermeneutical and rhetorical. The notion of complete objectivity is becoming more and more suspect. We have begun to doubt that the self is capable of apprehending reality in a direct, unmediated way. Instead, we accept that what we name reality is constituted through the interpretations that, through argument and discussion, have gained the status of truth or fact at this point in history.

This awareness implies that we understand through language. Language as a social and historical phenomenon is thus not peripheral or only instrumental to the way we see reality. As David Tracy puts it:

> Language is not an instrument that I can pick up and put down at will; it is always already there, surrounding and invading all I experience, understand, judge, decide, and act upon. I belong to my language far more than it belongs to me, and through that language I find myself participating in this particular history and society.[11]

Individuals can therefore not abstract themselves from the society in which they live. The very use of the language of a community implies a participation in its understanding of reality. Entering a discourse includes accepting particular arrangements of power and knowledge, values and prejudices.[12] These arrangements have entered the discourse of a community through a long historical process in which some discourses were excluded and repressed in order to create common understandings of what is true and what is false. However, these common understandings or assumptions usually function unconsciously for users of a particular language by authorizing certain authoritative interpretations.

Tracy suggests that a hermeneutics of suspicion is crucial for theologians in our day because of its function in interrupting these common understandings. It creates space for constructive involvement in reforming the community's sense of reality. This approach allows a kind of "linguistic therapy" which can expose fundamental illusions that we have accepted in our familiar accounts of knowledge, reality and language.[13] A hermeneutics of suspicion is thus intended to help us not only to name the errors in discernment that we continually make but also to probe for the deeper underlying sin, the "unconscious systemic distortions" which may be hidden in our theological language.[14] Suspicion is based on the assumption that the communal praxis of speech, the communal use of language, is in need of constant transformation and healing.

A series of critical thinkers from Nietzsche, Freud, and Marx to feminist and liberation theologians have insisted that this therapy is necessary.[15] They have highlighted for us the fragile and precarious nature of our modern faith in our own autonomous rational consciousness. They have questioned the obvious relationship that has been assumed between so-called objective scientific knowledge and theological language, and have suggested that our subjectivity in all its frailty can never be abstracted from the language we use. As perhaps never before we are aware of how easily sin can be disguised, how quickly we can rationalize our own complicity in evil in the accepted language of a community.

As theologians, biblical scholars and preachers who work with words, we sense with some fear that we are now moving into a postmodern time when the focus of ethical practice is more directly on us. The charge of imperialism and domination is no longer reserved for the missionaries who imported Western culture under the auspices of the gospel or for those who physically abuse their victims. Too often we have unconsciously participated in the prejudices and sins of our own community and its culture by our very participation in language. For the power of language to form the world we live in is more readily acknowledged today than ever before. We sense that we can no longer deny the existence of ideological distortions built on selfish interests or on hierarchical systems inscribed in the very structure of our language.

Tracy points out the dilemma that we now face as we leave behind any confidence we had in the power of our own rational thinking to eliminate error:

> The fact is that we have left modernity behind. We have left any belief in the transparency of consciousness to itself. Reality and knowledge are now linked to language. And with a heightened sense of language, the interruptive realities of

> history and society have entered consciousness anew.[16]

Tracy thus suggests that our easy assurances, our sense of innocence, our unconsciousness of our own complicity will be interrupted when we pay attention to the context of our language use, to those who speak and those who have remained silent. What is new in postmodernity is that this kind of suspicion receives its critical impulse not from some transcendental ideal or from some objective criteria based in the confidence of foundational truth abstracted from each of our particular historical situations. Rather, postmodern suspicion arises when the historical conversation partners change, when new voices are heard in the interpretive community. These voices bring new insights and convictions into the conversation—insights and convictions that disrupt any sense of truth which had previously been regarded as self-evident and transparent.

A change of conversation partners is often hard to accept for those who stress hermeneutic community. It implies that traditional spokespersons no longer have control of the world of discourse. Rather, "the victims of our discourses and our history" direct their suspicions against us and bring to our awareness the ideological distortions hidden in our language.[17] However, this letting go of control of language is necessary in order that our patterns of discourse can be opened to transformation.

This process creates a new context for theological work within the hermeneutic community. The confident position in the conversation assumed by some in the past has now become precarious and ambiguous. At the same time, the subordinate and marginal position assumed by others has gained in power and authority. The victims of dominating discourses and the voices of the marginal challenge any selfish interests or the will to power which may have been hidden in the unconscious of the spokespersons for objectivity. The naming of domination and oppression challenges any reluctance to speak based on a false subordination to those deemed superior. Thus a hermeneutics of suspicion opens the way for the healing of interpersonal relationships within the community.

Suspicion in the Mennonite Context

Neither the notion of suspicion nor a critical focus on the conversation partners in the theological enterprise is new to Mennonites. As marginal members in the larger Christian world, Mennonites have often been suspicious of the theology of other churches and denominations. This is already evident in the Anabaptist movement, where much of the critique of the theology of Catholic and other Protestant teachers and preachers was based on a suspicion of their use of theological or biblical language to justify their actions. Pilgrim Marpeck, for example, suggests that these teachers are "false prophets who, in a deceptive fashion, employ the witness of the scriptures against the devoted and submissive hearts."[18] Menno Simons warned against the "learned ones" who think they have "the keys of heaven and are the eyes and the light of the people" but instead "teach and promote the word, ordinances, and commands of the Antichrist."[19] Anabaptists frequently charged that the consensus reached in the conversation between Reformers and the princes was used to support the status quo assumptions of the state or the church institution rather than to transform the church. As victims in these discourses Anabaptists were sensitive to how theological language could be used to dominate and oppress.

Modern Mennonites have continued in this suspicion. For example, John H. Yoder's writings have articulated many of the suspicions that members of the Mennonite church have directed toward the majority church in North America. Yoder suggests that the writing of church history and theology by mainstream theologians has accentuated a "framework of normalcy" which frequently has fused the power of the state or secular society with the power of the church.[20] By appealing to a doctrine of divine providence that blessed the present political regime, mainline Christians have accepted the notion that the church is responsible for the direction of society. Yoder calls this the "Constantinian temptation." He thus points out aspects of the theological language of mainline churches which support a fusion between the two social/political entities which are on different sides in the apocalyptic battle as described in the Bible.

As a minority voice in a society, theologians and preachers of the Mennonite hermeneutic community have rather easily accepted the role of critic of the mainline churches and of the larger society. They have accepted the view articulated by Yoder that the "wider world" has no privileged place from which to speak.[21] The wider world's language is also only insider language and thus can only speak from within a limited framework.[22] This has given them courage to witness to their own understanding of Jesus and the church. In the latter half of the twentieth century Mennonites have begun to speak in the public domain with new confidence in their ability to make a contribution.

However, there is a difference in the suspicion that Anabaptists and modern Mennonites have employed and the suspicion that Tracy describes. For Tracy suggests that the suspicion that is needed is one that can illuminate the systemic distortions and sin in our own theological systems. This implies that it is important to admit our own rootedness in a particular community's pattern of language and to admit our own difficulty in seeing the distortions in our own pattern of discourse. We are called to admit that we also participate in a kind of "framework of normalcy" which we justify through biblical interpretation.

In Tracy's model, not only is the wider world relativized by the suggestion that every community expresses its own "framework of normalcy" in its own particular linguistic systems. But the "smaller" world is also relativized and thus not able to claim infallibility. A minority church is not saved from prejudice and ideology by its minority status in Christendom or in the larger society. Postmodern suspicion can also interrupt its "framework of normalcy," which may include distortions, ideologies and sin.

Postmodern suspicion challenges all hermeneutic communities, whether mainline or minority, to subject their theological discourse to analysis by new conversation partners in order to test whether the theological language supports assumptions and prejudices limited to their own narrow experience of God. In this context Mennonites can no longer hide from the admonition of other Christians.

Personal Experience with Suspicion

Any illusions of my own rational capabilities to be objective have been destroyed in this postmodern situation in which I find myself. As I enter this precarious place, aware of the limitations and insecurity of my own position in the theological discussion, I realize that the crucial question facing me is accepting those dialogue partners who can assist in making me more open to God's revealing and saving presence. This means opening myself to the disruptive presence of those dialogue partners who can help me see my own involvement in a new way.

This task is made more difficult by the ambiguity of my own sociopolitical position in society and church. For I am both a member of a dominant middle-class white community as well as a member of a minority religious tradition. I have experienced the power given to a scholar privileged to have an education as well the marginalization and subjection assigned to me because of my sex. In my biblical reading I have alternatively identified with the dominant strands of tradition as well as with the marginal and suppressed voices in Scripture. Sometimes I feel the autonomy of a modern individual and at other times I feel completely determined by the manipulative power of a social community.

Faced with the choice of dialogue partners, I recognize the fear that paralyses me as I enter the various conversations. The fear of being ignored and left out of the conversation alternates with the fear that I may be dominating the dialogue. The recognition that I am a "privileged insider" alternates with the realization that I am sometimes a "trivialized outsider."[23] This split within me has become more of an issue as I have gained institutional and academic power within the Mennonite community and within society. It has also been heightened as I have become aware of many persons, including other women, who feel oppressed, rejected, or silenced within the Mennonite community itself.

A narrative retelling of my theological journey in the last number of years would include a variety of conversation partners. These partners include feminist and mainline church theologians, persons who have left the Mennonite community and persons who wish they could become part of the Mennonite community. They include poets, writers, and artists who observe Mennonite communities from the margins as well as women and minority persons who stand within our communities but feel marginalized. These conversation partners have challenged me to name the sins in my primary hermeneutic community and to be more careful in my use of theological language. They have asked me to accept the vulnerable place that preachers, biblical scholars and theologians must assume in this postmodern age in order that the interpretive process may be healing for our communities. They have pointed out the need for a constant reexamination of my own particular framework of normalcy within which I think and write my theology.

A concrete illustration comes from my struggle with the framework of discipleship, which was given to me by the language of the Mennonite community in which I grew up. My basic identity, my foundational convictions and experiences could most easily be expressed by this notion. For me, discipleship included the related terms of obedience, servanthood, nonconformity, and nonviolence. These formed a pattern of beliefs that provided a sure foundation for my faith. Both my conscious theology and my unconscious prejudices were contained in this linguistic system of convictions and beliefs.

To be suspicious of the notion of discipleship as defined by Mennonites has been difficult. It has been difficult because these definitions have been based on biblical passages and have been verified through theological discussions which placed Jesus in a foundational place into the argument. This language has provided the basis for some of the communal choices of Mennonites in their relationships both among themselves and with those outside of the boundaries of the community. It has also legitimated many of my own personal choices.

However, I can no longer ignore the voices that suggest that Mennonites have also used discipleship language to protect the status quo of Mennonite community life. I can no longer resist the voices that challenge us as a Mennonite community to seek transformation. I can no longer dismiss the possibility of my own compliance with a sinful system. I recognize that the voices that question me from the outside articulate the split within myself. They point out both my personal need for wholeness as well as the communal need for healing.

This process of self-reflection created through interactions with a broader hermeneutic community has gone through a number of stages. I can note only a few crucial turning points in my writings.[24] My conversations with other women, especially with those who had been abused by men in our communities, alerted me to the way in which obedience to God and obedience to leaders could easily be equated in our language of a discipleship community. I also began to note how often our theology has polarized the individual and the community, giving priority to the community. This meant that undue power was given to community leaders and that dominance of more marginal people could be justified by appealing to community needs.

Through reading an autobiography by a Metis woman I became aware of the way servanthood language by our service organizations could hide subtle oppression and domination. I began to suspect that Mennonites too find it easier to give from a position of power than to work at mutuality in relationships. Through my conversation with members of other denominations I began to understand how easy it is to collapse divine authority and human authority in our notion of the Mennonite church as a hermeneutic community. A Catholic colleague questioned my use of the term "non-Mennonite," thus alerting me to the fact that even minority communities can become self-centered rather than God-centered. I began to realize how even our much-loved language of church identity, our image of ourselves as "body of Christ," can become idolatrous when we forget the metaphorical nature of the biblical language and exclude other Christians. I began to wonder why our understanding of discipleship avoided wrestling with the descriptions of actual disciples in the New Testament. Could it be that we would rather identify with Jesus, the divine actor in the stories, thus forgetting how similar we are to the human disciples in the stories?[25]

These insights were unsettling for me. However, they also freed me for new relationships within the church as a hermeneutic community. No longer did I need to justify our Mennonite institutions or our language of faith because it excluded others. Neither could I criticize Mennonite institutions or language from outside the community without clarifying my own commitments. Instead I could more clearly see how my position in particular power relationships within the community could skew the conversation so that I could not hear or respond to the admonition of others. Perhaps even more important, I rediscovered the language of historical witness and testimony, both as contained in the scriptures and as contained in the words of present day disciples. This discovery has allowed me to see all of our theological language as partial and limited and therefore as less than absolute. It has freed me to name the distortions that I see built into our theological language. But it has also encouraged me to speak with greater freedom and joy out of my own experience in the community of faith. To describe that latter process, I want to look briefly at the act of imagination as described by Walter Brueggemann.

A Postmodern Imagination

A hermeneutics of suspicion, as I have been using it, is only one step in the process needed to open our hermeneutic communities to healing. Suspicion of oneself can easily result in a paralysis of speech based on guilt and fear of being wrong. Instead, we need a new freedom to speak and listen to each other in order to enrich and enlarge the convictions of truth that we all have. A hermeneutics of suspicion is therapeutic only when it becomes the invitation for deeper consideration, discernment, revision, and re-imagining of our theological texts and contexts. As argued by Brueggemann, the postmodern shift invites us to a new kind of knowing,[26] which consists not in settled certitudes demanded by Cartesian anxiety but in the actual work of the imagination—in a new imagined construal which can be proclaimed and lived with conviction and authority without being legitimated as absolute.

Brueggemann is convinced that our postmodern situation gives language a new role in creating the framework in which we interpret our existence. Reality is not a "settled matter" which language can describe objectively.[27] Instead of giving authority to abstract, objective, and universal descriptions of the world, we now listen to all theology as perspectival and thus particular. We accept that theological language is not only descriptive but also rhetorical, that its real purpose is to persuade others of a particular paradigm of reality. Postmodernism acknowledges that the authority and power of particular texts, with their particular claims to truth, will be accepted as true in particular moments in time, within particular frameworks of reality. All interpretations must be regarded as partial understandings.

Theologians and preachers are becoming more aware than ever before that they are entering the public square of competing construals of reality. However, they must now confess more clearly than ever their own rootedness in a particular community and in a particular understanding of God. They can no longer appeal to objectivity and universality buttressed by rational argument. However, neither can their words be trivialized by others without considering the world that the words propose. Thus a "reordering of social power" becomes possible as previously marginalized persons witness to their understanding of truth as learned in their particular community of experience and interpretation.[28]

In this climate of postmodernism, theological language is tested by more than reason. Postmodernism "openness" is symptomatic of a yearning for a new world, a new construal of reality, a new future. The transformation of present reality becomes the ultimate goal of theological rhetoric. Members of the church search for a "counter or reconstrual of reality" that does not only justify the present reality but gives new vision and thus new hope.[29] Brueggemann reminds us that the witness of the Bible presents such a counter-world, through a variety of witnesses and through numerous narratives.

The materials for this reimagining come from particular community traditions. However, Brueggemann clearly states that these materials come not as a total overarching system that can claim a formal advantage, but rather piece by piece, retrieved from the tradition through a slow and sometimes painful process of reinterpretation.[30] Repressed or neglected experiences and convictions of God's intervention are illuminated and interpreted in a new way, providing new models, images, and concepts. Familiar experiences and central convictions are reinterpreted in a different framework, creating new visions to direct our lives.

The resulting construals of reality are not stable nor unified, nor do they aim primarily at protecting the community status quo. Rather they are dynamic and diverse, freeing the community by presenting new options and new possibilities from which to choose. The role of biblical scholars, theologians and preachers in "funding postmodern imagination" is to provide new material for the ongoing building of community. Brueggemann regards this as "therapeutic talk" that challenges the "presumed world" by its vision for the future.[31]

Imagination in the Mennonite Context

Perhaps an example from recent Mennonite history can illustrate the need for ongoing imaginative interpretation in the Mennonite community. Bender's Anabaptist Vision is perhaps the best illustration in recent years of a scholar/preacher retrieving materials from the past for a reimagining of the future.[32] Bender, who confessed a rootedness in the Mennonite hermeneutic community, also witnessed to truth as he saw it in the public square. His work created the space for a reimagining of the Mennonite community that stimulated other members of the Mennonite hermeneutic community to begin to look toward a new future. His use of terms such as "discipleship" testified to his conversation with biblical material as well as church tradition.

At first Bender's readings became a stimulus for exciting new interpretations of biblical texts, using the tools of inductive biblical study. Rather quickly, however, Bender's ideas were frozen into a normative system in which the focus was not on a dynamic hermeneutic process aimed at nourishing the Mennonite community or witnessing to the ongoing experiences of God in its history. Rather, this systematization began to serve two functions in the Mennonite church. It could very quickly identify "outside influences" foreign to "Anabaptism" and it could justify the existence of an alternative community striving for respectability in the modern world by giving it an objective base in historical studies.[33]

In this process, Mennonite theological identity began to be a subject of discussion and argument by scholars using the tools of rational analysis. At the same time, Anabaptism became the normative framework through which the Bible was read. For those who accepted this identity, Anabaptist theology provided a foundation for building the church and its institutions. However, for others who continued to question, this formulation seemed to legitimize repression of their questions and marginalization of their insights. Imagination for further revisioning built on the retrieval of the Bible and tradition was often stifled. One example may be the way the New Testament focus on discipleship in Bender's formulation subtly hindered a full appreciation of the Old Testament in all its variety.[34]

New visioning is taking place today at the same time that a reordering of social power is taking place in our churches and schools. The argument for one Anabaptist vision or one understanding of discipleship will not gain much credibility in this postmodern world. Rather, the witnesses who will be heard will be those who can present an alternative from a restrictive past while giving new insight into the present and suggesting new possibilities for the future. The community needs a variety of witnesses in order for it to be enriched. For an authoritative divine Word will come only when each of our human construals is seen in all of its incompleteness.

That community identity may be lost in this process is a real fear for a minority community. Unity around a common confession can assist the community in identifying those issues that need discussion. However, creativity and imagination are lost when these common confessions become a static normative vision that stifles the process of reinterpreting the Bible and the community tradition. The language of belief can stay alive only when a dynamic process encourages the gleaning of new theological understandings from the Bible and from our theological tradition in the context of the witness of present experiences of God's transforming power.

Personal Experience with Imagination

The freedom for me to imagine discipleship anew came quickly on the heels of suspicion. Suspicion freed me from both a sense of inferiority as a woman in the theological discussion and a need to defend my Mennonite community. However, this freedom did not encourage me to leave my community and search for other communities.[35] Instead it helped me make a new confession of my rootedness in the Mennonite community with all its limitations. It also gave me the courage to invite others into the conversation and to speak more boldly out of the insights given to me by my experience within my primary community. Thus discipleship gained new definitions and new depth in an enlarged hermeneutic community.

A crucial step for me was to reaffirm the conviction present in Mennonite tradition that all are invited to read the scriptures themselves and to test these interpretations in the context of the faith community. That represented a radical challenge in the context of a theological school where the assumption was that theologians must depend fully on the biblical scholars to do the biblical interpretation. At the same time, I began re-reading the Bible with new lenses—lenses that had been sensitized through the variety of dialogue partners that now joined the conversation. What most triggered my imagination in this re-reading of the gospels was my sudden realization that the women in the gospels could be named disciples, in spite of the fact that the early gospel writers did not explicitly do so.[36]

This insight made a big difference in my interpretations of specific texts. First, it shifted my theology of discipleship from an exclusive focus on Jesus as an ideal to Jesus as the healer and source of power for the disciples. I began to notice how my identification in the narrative with Jesus rather than with the disciples satisfied my need for perfection and for divine authorization of my views. Second, the shift also helped me see all the healing stories as discipleship stories standing alongside the stories of the male disciples. Particularly, in my study of the book of Mark I noted how our Mennonite theology of discipleship had largely ignored the many healing stories of the first half of the gospel and had instead concentrated on the last half with its focus on self-denial and the way of the cross. New empowerment came as I realized how much my ability to follow Jesus depended upon opening myself to the healing touch of God.

Several new "pieces" have thus entered my imagining of discipleship that must now dialogue with my past understandings. I hope they can contribute to the community's language of discipleship in such a way that all of us can become more open to the divine voice calling us to follow.

Conclusion

The terminology in the title of this paper was deliberately chosen. Postmodern suspicion and imagination are not enough for constructing the church as a hermeneutic community. A church can survive only if it witnesses to the truth of God's presence in its midst. However, suspicion and imagination can be therapeutic for a community standing in this time in history, for they can help us acknowledge our need for the active presence of the Holy Spirit to renew and recreate our communities. Just as in the time of Jesus members of the community needed to hear that their ears needed healing so that they could hear and that their eyes needed healing so that they might see so we need to heed that same message (Mark 4:9-12). The church—the discipleship community as described in the Bible—is not an ideal community. Rather, it easily becomes dysfunctional unless God's revealing and saving presence continues to create it anew.

I propose that this view of the church is congruent with the view held by the writers of the letters which later became the New Testament. Paul, Peter, and James did not mainly write in order to make universal statements supported by rational arguments, nor did they attempt to ground the community in absolute norms. Rather, they wrote because the community needed constant transformation, needed healing. They were writing to and about real churches and real people. Their various visions and mandates offered opportunities for the church to grow and mature as it made day-to-day decisions about its life and message. The letter writers witnessed with power to their particular understanding of God.

Postmodernism has given us tools to aid us in becoming more sensitive to how power and authority relationships can distort our hearing of God's Word. By admitting the partiality of our interpretations, we can open ourselves to the witness of "the other," both in our communities and in our biblical tradition. However, postmodernism can also encourage us to affirm again the power of the biblical word to heal us. It can give us new confidence to witness to our particular understandings of truth. Thus postmodernism affirms the need for the church to see itself as a hermeneutic community in which power relationships must be acknowledged and explored.

***

MENNO'S VIEW OF JESUS: THE FOUNDATION OF A NEW REALITY[37]

The invitation came unexpectedly. Mennonites from the Netherlands had initiated a Menno Simons Symposium in 1996 commemorating five hundred years since the birth of Menno Simons (the 16th century priest/Anabaptist pastor from whom Mennonites have received their name). The over-all theme was discipleship, the theme that had been resonating with me throughout my studies. But the paper I wrote for this consultation was to be connected to the writings of Menno Simons. It was also to answer the questions: "Can the writings of the 16th century farmer's son and ex-priest also be of importance to congregations existing in a society which has experienced a totally different cultural and social development? Could Menno Simons still inspire Mennonite congregations in South America, Africa, and Asia?"[38]

Just over 30 participants from around the world gathered at a retreat grounds in the Netherlands to talk together both formally and informally. As I look at the photo of the participants I remember two events: the trip we took to the area where the early Anabaptists lived out their faith, and the communion service that we shared at the end of our talks. Perhaps the experience of a shared faith among persons steeped in different cultural contexts was as important as the actual dialogue on our particular heritage of faith.

The paper I wrote for that occasion was my opportunity to reflect critically on the strong tradition of Christology that inspired "incarnational ecclesiology" often named as discipleship in Mennonite tradition. I was intrigued with the many names Menno used for Jesus and was inspired to reflect again on the human/divine mystery present in Christ Jesus. It was also a chance to enter a premodern worldview with its challenges and opportunities by reading the writings of someone influential in the tradition that I claimed as my own. My imagination needed to be activated, not to provide new vision for the future, but to capture the visions of the past embodied in language that assumed a very different world-view. This dialogue across the ages continues to be necessary so that we can see the limitations of our own worldview and thus open ourselves more fully to the Wind of the Spirit that blows where it wills.

Introduction

> Christ is our King, Prince, Lord, and Messiah, the promised David, the Lion of the tribe of Judah, the strong One, the Prince of Peace, and the Father of the age to be; God's almighty, incomprehensible, eternal Word and Wisdom, the first born of every creature, the Light of the world, the Sun of Righteousness, the true Vine, the Fountain of life, the true Door and Shepherd of the sheep, the true Foundation and the precious Cornerstone in Zion, the right Way, the Truth and Life, the promised Prophet, our Master and Teacher, our Redeemer, Saviour, Friend, and Bridegroom. In short our only and eternal Mediator, Advocate, High Priest, Propitiator, and Intercessor; our Head and Brother. [39]

> For no one can lay any foundation other than the one that has been laid; that foundation is Jesus Christ.[40]

In the litany of names in the first quotation we hear Menno at worship. Definitions, doctrinal systems, conceptual schemes are inadequate to describe who Jesus is. Only an extravagant naming gleaned from the biblical literature will point to the one who is beyond any name that can be given. Menno's response to his own spiritual resurrection is expressed in an overflowing stream of language expressing his joy, awe, and praise. This proclamation cannot be stemmed by opposing human tradition or by threat of persecution and death because it is the only response possible for one who has experienced God's Spirit at work in his own life.

In the strong assertion expressed in the second quotation we hear Menno as a spiritual leader of a struggling faith community. His concern is to clearly identify the true church of Jesus Christ in the midst of conflicting understandings and embodiments of the church. His descriptions of Jesus as foundation are almost always set against the backdrop of false teachers, representing false Christs who offer faltering foundations on which to build. Menno draws a clear image of Jesus, one that can both provide an example to be followed by faithful disciples as well as provide criteria for discerning the true and the false. Menno thus begins to create a theology which will undergird and defend a particular understanding of Jesus and a particular understanding of the church.

Both quotations begin by understanding Jesus primarily from the viewpoint of soteriology and ecclesiology, rather than Christology in its traditional form. That is, Menno is concerned first of all with salvation and empowerment for both individuals and the church as community. He wants to point out how Jesus is active in the world on behalf of humankind rather than explore doctrinal understandings of Jesus' ontological being in a theoretical way. He focuses on the direction Jesus' life points for the nature of the church rather than debating the nature of Jesus' incarnation as a philosophical possibility. He thus chooses to describe Jesus in biblical language given depth and concreteness by his own experience of new life in Christ.

However, in the climate of debate and conflict of the sixteenth century Menno cannot refrain completely from explaining Jesus' work in terms of who Jesus is as an ontological being. He does this in language learned from his contemporaries as well as from the Bible. Thus Menno begins to build a system of theology which makes sense of his particular view of Jesus. His more speculative Christology provides an implicit foundation for the soteriology and ecclesiology which he has embraced.

In this paper we will move from exploring the image that Menno draws of Jesus embodied for us (soteriology) to the image that he draws of Jesus as an incarnation of God (Christology).[41] This will help us to see how the dense network of names for Jesus that Menno weaves in his worship is filled with particular content and meaning. It will also help us to enter into Menno's struggle to keep the tension alive between Jesus who is beyond all human definitions and therefore worthy of our praise, and Jesus who is embodied in human words and therefore suitable to become the concrete criteria of theological truth.[42]

A. Jesus Embodied For Us

As we read more deeply into Menno's writings we are immediately struck with the prominence of Jesus Christ as the foundation of the kingdom of God and therefore the foundation of any reality that really matters. The question of who Jesus is, is linked very closely to descriptions of the kingdom of God, a kingdom that can already be entered into in the present even though its fullness will only be experienced in the eschaton.[43]

Though Jesus is understood as very much present in the world, Menno does not describe him as sacramentally available in the bread and wine of the Eucharist as had been assumed in the Catholic context of his times. Nor is Jesus described in the triumphant apocalyptic language of the Münsterites who tried to bring in the kingdom by force. Rather Jesus is described as joyful good news of grace to those who repent and change their lives, to those who walk according to the Spirit, not the flesh. The polarity between Spirit and flesh which is very evident in Menno's writings suggests that Jesus' dynamic presence in the world will also need to be examined in the context of this framework of reality.[44]

I will give some focus to the complex picture that Menno paints of Jesus embodied for us by describing this image in terms of three interrelated but distinct clusters of terms. Each of these describes concretely one aspect of how Menno understands Jesus' presence among us. Thus we will explore what Menno meant when he speaks of Jesus as Teacher, as Redeemer, and as Bridegroom.

1) Jesus, the True Teacher from Heaven

We must hear and follow that which Christ Jesus, God's first and only begotten Son Himself, brought from heaven and taught from the mouth of His Father, and confirmed by signs and wonders, and finally sealed with His crimson blood. The decretal stands; stands, I say, and can never be demolished or altered by any gates of hell.[45]

This passage taken from one of his earliest writings *The New Birth* identifies Jesus as the teacher from heaven, a term that we find sprinkled throughout Menno' s writings. Related terms which refer to Jesus as the witness of the truth from heaven, the mouth, and word of the Most High God, or the Father's eternal Truth and Wisdom are set in sharp contrast to human teachers with their human wisdom and knowledge.[46] By his usage of these terms Menno clarifies his stance on the important issue of the source of his own authority.

In the passage above Menno insists that Christ's authority is based on its origin in heaven as well as on his life and death on earth. This must be stated clearly because there were other authorities which claimed allegiance and other motivations which were more carnal.

> Therefore, be not intent upon the usages and customs of the fathers, not upon the worldly wise and the learned ones, for it is deeply hidden from their eyes.… It is that wisdom which is not to be brought from afar nor taught in colleges. It must be given from above and be learned through the Holy Ghost.… Therefore be intent upon God's Word, the testimony and example of the holy prophets, the Lord Jesus Christ and His apostles. Let these be your doctors and teachers in the matter and not the ambitious preachers of this world.[47]

Adjectives such as true, dependable, trustworthy, unadulterated, reliable, and pure are used throughout Menno's writings to describe the teachings of Jesus and are contrasted with human doctrines, lies, pretense, deception, fiction, fables, perverted glosses, simple idolatry, and dreams. The latter, according to Menno, are based on the teachings of the antichrist, the master of deception.[48] As such they appeal to human pride and ambition, personified in the ambitious preachers, in the doctors and teachers of the colleges, and in the traditions of the fathers. Menno begins his evangelical preaching by pointing to a new authority. He relativizes every other human tradition, creating a sharp dualism between those who listen to Jesus Christ and those who listen to the antichrist, those who understand only human wisdom and those who know God's wisdom.

As pointed out by Bornhauser, this claim allowed Menno to begin to differentiate between the laws of the Catholic church and God's laws, to begin to question some of his own basic acceptance of commonly assumed truth and to rethink his understanding of God's judgement of human sin.[49] But perhaps just as important this claim gave Menno a norm that could be referred to, a concrete book that embodied the teachings of Jesus and that could not be replaced by human traditions or by new revelations.[50] Voolstra states it this way: "Christ as the incarnate Word and as the summary of the New Testament doctrine and ordinances was the perfect and exclusive embodiment of God's commandments."[51] Thus Jesus, embodied in the words of Scripture, became for Menno the foundation of the anticipated kingdom of God, something that Menno testifies to by placing 1 Corinthians 3:11 on the title page of each of his writings.

In the later writings the often repeated phrase "example, commands, ordinances, prohibitions, and usages of the Lord" points to the importance Menno places on Jesus' literal teachings in the areas of both doctrine and practice. The goal was not only to have the mind of Christ but also to walk as he did.[52] Both personal morality and church ordinances were to be ordered by the teaching of Jesus as inscribed in the Bible. For Menno this implied that there was a unity within the Bible, a unified teaching that connected the prophets with the apostles. This unity of biblical teaching and practical living could be discerned if the response to the teacher from heaven was repentance and a new birth by the Spirit.

In Menno's writings Spirit and Word belong together. Menno insists that the gospel is the only "right and proper Seed from which the true believing and obedient children of God are born."[53] But these children will be genuine children of the Spirit when the gospel is preached "without admixture of leaven and perverted glosses" in the power of the Spirit. For Menno there is a unity between the embodied Word in the Bible, the historical, incarnated Jesus, and the Spirit of Jesus who makes the gospel message alive today.

The understanding of Jesus as teacher is thus basic to all of Menno's theology. In faithfulness to his own norm, Menno pleads with his readers in words "drenched with the phraseology of the Bible" for he does not wish to go beyond his teacher.[54] For Menno it is the embodied Word of Jesus in the Bible which creates a foundation of truth on which he can stand. This biblical Jesus became the basis for judging between the divine and human in all of life.

2) Jesus, the Powerful Redeemer

> He has taught and left unto his followers an example of perfect love, and a perfect life. He has conquered the mighty one, destroyed the power of the devil, has borne our sins, abolished death, reconciled the Father. He has earned for all the chosen children of God, grace, favor, mercy, eternal life, the kingdom, and peace. And He has been ordained by His eternal and mighty Father as an omnipotent King over the holy mountain of Zion, as the Head of the Church, a Provider and Dispenser of heavenly blessings; yes, an almighty Sovereign over all, in heaven and earth.[55]

Jesus' authority has already been indicated in the picture of Jesus as the true teacher. In this passage in the *Foundation of Christian Doctrine* Menno continues his elaboration of who Jesus is to include other aspects of Jesus' power. Jesus is able to offer heavenly blessings to us because he has reconciled and redeemed humanity to God. The dynamic verbs in this passage point to an active Redeemer who conquers, destroys, bears our sins, abolishes, reconciles, and earns God's grace and favour. Jesus is both the one who justifies us before God and the one who energizes us with new life.

Jesus is able to do this because he has been ordained to be King, Head, Provider, and Dispenser of grace by God, the Father. With his designation of Jesus as King, Menno seeks to ground Jesus' saving activity in the eternal God as well as to indicate the victor in the battle between God and the devil. In this utopian vision Menno anticipates a universal kingdom where kings and magistrates, preachers and common people are called to shun Babylon and enter Jerusalem where Jesus reigns. Faith and humble obedience are the only response worthy of such a king.

Menno appeals directly to the princes and governors to acknowledge Jesus' sovereignty as one acknowledges human superiors. He warns that God's kingdom cannot be usurped by any human king (including John of Leiden). Neither can it be brought in by any use of violence (neither that of the Münsterites nor that of the established governors of the land). Thus Menno calls on all who have power in their office.

> Do not usurp the judgment and kingdom of Christ, for He alone is the ruler of the conscience and besides Him there is none other. Let Him be your emperor in this matter and His holy Word your edict, and you will soon have enough of

> storming and slaying.... Therefore, fight no longer against the Lamb and His elect.[56]

When Menno calls Jesus the ruler of the conscience he is asking the human rulers to acknowledge the personal faith of the Anabaptists. He is asking them to respect the witness of the Anabaptists that their authority is of God and to cease the fight against them. Thus an acknowledgment of God as King would result in concrete decisions which would exclude the use of physical force in matters of faith.

The invitation to repent comes with a wonderful promise to all who respond in faith. Jesus will be the powerful comforter for the troubled heart. In a moving passage, in which we hear Menno's voice as he preaches to his flock, Menno uses the first person singular to paraphrase Jesus, the comforter of those who weep over their sins. Again the active verbs stand out, verbs taken from the prophecies of the Old Testament.

> I will not punish nor chastise you, but will heal you, comfort you, and give you life.... I will seek that which was lost and bring back that which was driven away and will bind up that which was broken and will strengthen that which was sick.... By the kindness of my heavenly Father, I am come into the world, and by the power of the holy Ghost, I became a visible, tangible, and dying man; in all points like unto you, sin excepted.... I am the lamb that was sacrificed for you all. I take away the sins of the whole world.[57]

What is striking in both of the above passages is the reference to the lamb in a context of speaking about the power of Jesus. For Menno insists that it is Jesus as an innocent Lamb offered as a sacrifice for humankind who is able to redeem humankind.

Menno is clear on this point. It is because Jesus has his origin in the heavens that his sacrifice is acceptable. Jesus as the incarnated Christ, as a visible, tangible, and dying man, entered history in order to be the innocent sacrifice which justified human persons before God. This could only happen through the kindness of the Father and the power of the Holy Spirit. Redemption has come about through the unity of purpose of the Trinitarian God.

There is therefore no other remedy for sin, neither "indulgences, holy water, fastings, confessionals, masses, pilgrimages, infant baptism or bread and wine."[58] No earthly, human sacrament can be a substitute for this gift given through the grace of God. Even baptism is only an external sign of obedience. Jesus is the true sign, the sign of grace who alone renews, regenerates, and strengthens us in our inner being.[59] It is this strengthening in our inner being by Jesus which allows us to bring forth the fruits of the Spirit and allows us to walk according to the "witness of a good conscience before Him."[60]

But the lamb is also a picture of the one rejected and killed by humans who do not respond to God's grace. Jesus is the "lovely, peaceful, innocent, and obedient Lamb" who will continue to receive rejection until he appears as "an Almighty Sovereign, a Conqueror, and a glorious king before all the tribes and peoples, unto the last judgment."[61] In the meantime, Christ Jesus the Lamb continues to suffer through those who are his own, through the suffering of Christians persecuted because of their faith.[62]

Christ as the powerful Redeemer entered history as the incarnated Lamb able to reconcile humans to God. He continues to be present in the experience of those who respond to his offer of grace, those who are regenerated into new life.

3) Jesus as the Loving Bridegroom

> The Bridegroom, Christ Jesus, through Solomon addresses His Bride, the church, saying, Rise up, my love, my fair one, and come away.… Elect, faithful children, you who with me are called to a like grace, inheritance, portion, and kingdom, and are named after the Lord's name, oh, hear the voice of Christ, our King; hear the voice of your Bridegroom, O thou bride of God, thou friend of the Lord. Arise and adorn thyself to honor thy King and Bridegroom.[63]

Menno uses the language of the Song of Solomon to talk about the union of Christ and his bride the church. Christ is the heavenly bridegroom who invites his bride to come apart and adorn herself for her groom. Those who are regenerated are the new Eve, "made by God to be His [Christ's] bride in the Spirit and made of them His most holy and life-giving flesh…."[64] Jesus as the new Adam gives Himself by pure grace, and makes the regenerated partakers of His righteousness, merits, cross, blood, and bitter death, yes His whole life, love, and Spirit; for they are one body and one Spirit with Him; so that they willingly fulfil, by this spirit of love which they have received of Him (for God is love), all that which the merciful Father by His saving truth, Christ Jesus, has commanded.[65]

It is in the experience of regeneration that a new heart and spirit are received by the Christian. Now they bury their sins in Jesus' death and rise to new life in him. Menno' s frequent use of the Pauline language of being "in Christ and Christ in us" expresses this union as personal. Yet in his later writings the union between Jesus and the corporate church seems to predominate. The church as body of Christ shifts the metaphor into an even more intimate picture of unity.

In this context, the Lord's supper is seen as the marriage feast of the Lord where the unity that comes about through the love of Jesus Christ is expressed in the love between members of the church.[66] The imagery of the one loaf and many grains used in the context of communion also speaks about this unifying effect of love that happens when believers are joined into one body.[67] But not only love is expressed in this imagery. The unity is also a unity in purity and holiness. Jesus the bridegroom sought out his bride in love to be bone of his bone and flesh of his flesh. There is

> but one Eve in the spirit, but one new Rebecca, who is His spiritual body, spouse, church, and bride, namely, those who are believers…pure chaste virgins in the spirit, holy souls, who are of His divine family and holy flesh of His flesh, and bone of His bone.[68]

In contrast, those who "have no communion of the most holy flesh and blood of Christ Jesus" still partake of the flesh of the old Adam and therefore also inherit the curse of the old Adam. They cannot be part of the church, the body of Christ. Over and over again Menno exhorts the believers, insisting that all impurity and sinfulness must be excluded for they must become one with Christ in Spirit, faith, life, and worship. The ban was practiced out of this sense of oneness of Jesus and the church, a oneness that could only be maintained by excluding those who were still of the old nature. Though Menno acknowledges that remnants of the old nature still cling to those who are joined to Christ he maintains that they "fight daily with their weak flesh in the Spirit and in faith," knowing that union with Christ "will beget righteousness and piety unto life according to the will of God."[69]

Menno makes it clear that Jesus is to be the initiator of the relationship. This means that the church must "conform" to Jesus, not the other way around. The church must become the "amiable, obedient bride" who seeks nothing but heavenly things.[70] This new ethical life also results in similar suffering to that which Jesus also endured. Christians will not be spared the cross for they are of one flesh with him. They will be persecuted by those still living according to the lusts of the flesh.[71] However, the inner union experienced by members of his body results in a completely new way of being in this world, a way which is visible in the fruits that can be seen by all.

B. Jesus as the Incarnation of God

A perspective which focuses on soteriology also includes assumptions of a more philosophical nature articulated as a Christology. Menno has not only described how Jesus functions in the world; he has also begun to name who Jesus is. Though Menno attempts to stay with simple assertions about Jesus' work on behalf of humankind, he is drawn into explanations about Jesus' person that go beyond the literal words of the Bible. Though he only attempts to explain his doctrinal position, he also gives explanations that include his self-understanding and his view of the world. Theology, anthropology, and philosophy thus come together in his view of Jesus.

The conviction that Jesus in his incarnation brought about a new way of being human in the world is at the centre of Menno's worldview. He was convinced that the incarnation of the divine was necessary both so that Jesus could atone for our sins and so that Jesus could become the prototype, the pattern, of a new human reality in the world. This prototype is spiritual, yet visible because Jesus was visible as a human person.[72] In Menno's understanding this created a tension in the understanding of who Jesus was as divine, yet incarnated as human. His anthropology told him that to be human meant to be sinful. However, to accomplish redemption it was necessary for Jesus to be wholly divine. Therefore, there needed to be a way of explaining how the demands of the perfect will of God were met by Jesus in his human nature.

This tension in Menno's thinking can be highlighted if we look at the key convictions that were consistently articulated in the soteriological view of Jesus described in the first part of the paper. In each of the three key convictions there is a strong need to avoid misunderstanding by explaining explicitly what Menno has stated implicitly.

1) Menno believes in a strong dualism between the realm of Christ and the realm of the antichrist, between Jerusalem and Babylon, between flesh and spirit, earthly and heavenly. He found this dualism in the biblical writings. However, this radical difference between flesh and spirit needed to be expressed in a climate in which the rejection of the material was being argued as the only way to be spiritual. At the same time this difference needed to be expressed in relationship to the apocalyptic expectation that Jesus was setting up his spiritual kingdom right now in Münster in a visible social, political way. Menno needed to explain how a historical Jesus fit into this dualistic worldview.

2) Menno believed that the only source of spiritual reality is God and that this reality is of one piece from eternity to eternity. It is therefore God who must in his grace extend this spiritual reality to humanity. This meant that Menno needed to explain how Jesus remained divine in his incarnation.

3) Menno believes that this spiritual reality is an inner one but is embodied

or expressed in external visible reality. In Jesus there is a unity between the inner spiritual and the outer empirical. For Menno this unity must also apply to the Bible (the word of Christ) and to the church (the body of Christ). Menno must therefore explain this unity in Jesus in such a way that it can also be applied to the Bible and the church.

A quotation from the Foundation of Christian Doctrine points out the consistency between Menno's Christological assertions and his view of reality as described in the convictions above.

> We teach and believe, and this is the thrust of the whole scriptures, that the whole Christ is from head to foot, both inside and outside, visible and invisible, God's first-born and only begotten Son; the incomprehensible Word, by whom all things were created, the first-born of every creature. We teach and believe that He became a true man in Mary, the pure virgin, through the power of the Almighty, eternal Father, beyond the comprehension and knowledge of man. He was sent and given unto us by the Father out of mere grace and mercy; the express image of the invisible God and the brightness of His glory.[73]

Menno is a child of his times. The notion that original sin was passed to the child through physical procreation was accepted in the medieval milieu in which he lived. The fact that male seed was the determinative factor in creating new life was also accepted. The common theory of atonement that insisted on an innocent sacrifice given to atone for human sin was not questioned. The tension between the need for Jesus to be sinless and the conviction that he was born of human flesh needed some explanation.

The Medieval theologians had a number of different ways to decrease this tension, including protecting Jesus' divinity through the theory of the immaculate conception of Mary. However, both Casper Schwenkfeld and Melchior Hoffman, who together with Menno rejected the materialization of salvation in the Eucharist sought other solutions which protected Jesus' spiritual nature. Menno chose Melchior Hoffman's focus on a new body created by God as a framework for his own explanation. This allowed him to assert the humanness of Jesus without moving with Schwenckfeld into a wholly spiritual direction. As pointed out by Depperman, Melchior taught that "Christ could only have been a spotless sacrificial offering if he had brought his body with him from heaven and had passed through Mary like water through a pipe."[74] The key verse for the Melchiorites was John 1:14, "The Word became flesh and dwelt among us," thus emphasizing the new human reality represented by the incarnation.

The connection that was perhaps most important for Menno can be symbolized by a coin minted in 1534 by the Münsterites. John 1:14 is printed on one side, but John 3:3 on the other, thus connecting the new birth with the incarnation.[75] Menno, like Hoffman before him, was convinced that the new birth meant that humans too could receive a new nature. This new nature was not of the same flesh as the old Adam but rather was flesh of the second Adam, of Jesus. Thus all dimensions of human life were changed for the believer, both personal and social. No longer were the clergy the privileged dispensers of grace. No, Jesus would give this new reality directly to all who enter a new covenantal relationship with him.

Menno's own theory of the heavenly flesh of Jesus was dependent on Hoffman's thinking. In his understanding Jesus became flesh *in* Mary, not *of* Mary. The eternal Word of God is heavenly seed planted in Mary to produce the heavenly fruit, Jesus the heavenly man. The entire Christ became flesh in Mary, suffered and died in the flesh.[76] However, he has risen in the Spirit and now invites believers to also rise with him and become a new creation.

The connectedness of the believer with Jesus created the possibility of a radical change from the burden of creatureliness and sinfulness.[77] An ontological change was possible through regeneration which again gave to humans the power to live according to God's will. Jesus could thus become a true example for humanity because humans too can be empowered to live in this new reality. This new reality could be discerned by others because the incarnated Jesus had become the criterion for what it meant to be a spiritual human being.

Menno continued to have some anxiety about this doctrine for a number of years.[78] However, as is clear in his disputations with the Reformed preachers, the explanation seemed necessary to him to ensure the prototypical function that Jesus had in ensuring the new life in Christ which Menno himself had experienced. Several tracts attempt to justify this theory through an appeal to reason as well as to Scripture. Menno was convinced that his view of Jesus and his power to save was dependent on his particular explanation of how the incarnation of Jesus came about in Mary.

Conclusion

> We must be in Christ and Christ in us; we must be moved by His Spirit, and abide in His Holy Word outwardly and inwardly. Otherwise we have no God.[79]

Menno was convinced that God had become present to humanity in Jesus Christ. Even now God was present in the incarnated Christ, that is, in the Christ embodied in the words of Scripture and in the believers of the true church. This Christ was inner and spiritual but could be externally defined by the fruits of the inner life. Thus the Bible as an authoritative book and the Anabaptist community as an authoritative church received new power. The Bible and the church could become powerful new vehicles which mediated salvation and new life to those who responded in faith and repentance. They could become the context in which discipleship was inspired and substance was given to following Jesus. They created the support needed to give comfort and strength to those who were being persecuted for their faith.

Because this authority was so powerful in their own lives it was easy to forget that the Bible and the church as they were defined by Menno were still human. The temptation was there to equate the Bible (as the word of God) and the church (as the body of Christ) with Jesus incarnated in the world. The close connection between the new flesh of Jesus and the new flesh of the Christian served to cement a relationship between Bible, church, and the incarnate Jesus which allowed no questioning of this authority. The God that Menno now proclaimed was not only contained in human vessels but became more and more identified with human words. The statement that "otherwise we have no God" could also come to mean that there is no God outside of the literal definitions and the human embodiments as described by the Anabaptists. Menno's claim was then in danger of becoming idolatrous.

Maintaining a worship of God in Spirit and in truth is the best antidote to idolatry. However, this becomes difficult when our views of Jesus must also be embodied enough so that Jesus can be seen walking ahead of us in this world. This tension is however necessary in order for our theology to lead to discipleship arising out of the worship of God. Definitions and explanations of Christ's nature must always be held loosely enough so that an openness to God's dynamic Spirit can be maintained and embodied enough so that discipleship is possible. Menno struggled to understand and live according to the revelation and salvation which he saw embodied in Jesus. A study of Menno's writings is worthwhile if it will encourage us also to both worship the God who is beyond our naming as well as live as disciples following the Jesus who makes himself known to us in concrete terms.

***

WHAT'S IN A NAME? (LUKE 7: 36-50)[80]

I enjoy preaching! I particularly enjoy preparing a sermon. I delight in reading a passage of Scripture over and over until some question or vision surfaces that leads me on a path of discovery. A question is triggered when I become suspicious of the usual meaning of the text because it is too superficial, too comfortable, and so acceptable in my com-

munity that I do not have to change my mind about anything! The vision is sparked by a word or phrase or action in the text that catches my imagination, encouraging me to connect that biblical word with my own context. This first stage of sermon preparation usually takes place over a week or two before I sit down and begin the more intensive work of exegesis.

In the second stage I begin to use Bible dictionaries, translations, and commentaries. In this stage I feel like a detective following the clues until the various parts of the text become alive to me and I can see the connections between the individual words and the whole text. Since I do not know the original Greek and Hebrew well enough to translate the text, I rely on a variety of translations to get the sense of a passage in its original context. Wider reading to gain a historical perspective creates some distance between the text and myself so that I can step back a bit from my own views to enter another world and its assumptions. It is after this work that the writing of the sermon begins (of course, I must confess, that sometimes the serious study does not happen as thoroughly as suggested here!).

The writing of the actual sermon is an imaginative art of bringing the text and the present congregation into a conversation with each other. I understand my role as preacher to be a kind of mediator who will encourage further imagination and reflection in the listener. I can do this best if the text has become alive for me in all of its transforming power and if I am familiar with the listeners and their questions and concerns.

Homiletical theory has experienced a shift in its approach as our worldview has shifted and changed. From a strong emphasis on expository preaching devoted to explanation and exhortation from the text it has moved to a more dialogical style with attention to text, context, and listener. Recently I have begun translating some of my father's sermons and noted how different his approach is to mine. I can see the shift in culture affecting the style and content of preaching. Still, I know that the preaching of the past created some of the assumptions of my own work, albeit transformed by my own suspicion and imagination.

I include a sermon in this chapter because it is in sermon preparation that my love for study and my creative imagination have most easily come together. In my academic work I learned to write logically without much thought about how to engage the reader as an embodied person with feelings as well as thoughts. Rather, I was most conscious about the critical readers who could easily challenge whatever I wrote with their own superior analyses. I needed to make sure that every idea was supported by an appropriate foot-note. However, in sermons, the direct engagement with readers whom I could envision sitting beside me in the pews, my neighbors and friends, some of whose stories I knew, was uppermost in my mind. Slowly I began to change my style of writing to a more conversational style, to using metaphor and symbol, letting my imagination enrich the reasoning. I particularly enjoy working with the biblical narratives because they give so many spaces for our imagination to fill, yet challenge us to place our personal story into the biblical story, creating a dissonance and harmony that can lead to new stories.

The sermon I have chosen was one that I preached at an early morning "Wine Before Breakfast" meeting of graduate students at TST. This eucharist worship service was an opportunity provided by the chaplaincy service at Wycliffe College for university grad students in many different disciplines to centre themselves in their Christian identity while they were doing their studies. The sermon is an example of my efforts to bring my sermons more in line with my hermeneutical theory.

***

Luke 7: 36-50

What struck me first, as I began to study this passage, was the variety of titles given to this story in the various translations of the Bible and in the commentaries that I read. These titles, which help to focus our attention on a central element in the story, have been added to the biblical passage by the editors of the particular version of the Bible that we are reading. They try to be simply descriptive, but in that very description, they make a judgment about what the story is all about.

In my limited survey, I discovered that the most consistent element of the titles was the term "sinful woman." But the variations from there show the variety of emphases that have been given to parts of the story. Some connect the story with Jesus, entitling it "Jesus forgives the sinful woman," (thus focusing on Jesus' action) or "Jesus is anointed by the sinful woman" (thus focusing on Jesus as the recipient of the woman's action). Others talk about "The Pharisee and the sinful Woman," thus pointing to the relationship between them. But the title that fascinated me most was the shortest and simplest. One commentary entitles this story: "The sinner."

Titles are important! As students we are taught to be careful with our language so that we can accurately describe and label that which we are studying. This is basic to the use of scholarly language which tries to be methodologically objective. In fact, each discipline tends to define and develop its own terms in order to communicate as accurately as possible within its own context. Naming and classifying is basic to scholarly work; it involves critical thinking and careful judgment.

The question that these titles immediately raised in me was: Is there only one sinner in the story? From one perspective, this question can easily be answered. Luke calls the woman a sinner and calls Simon a Pharisee, suggesting that these names are common classifications which everyone would have understood. Luke reemphasizes this when he gives us a look into the Pharisee's thoughts: "If this man, that is Jesus, were a prophet, he would have known who and what kind of woman this is who is touching him—that she is a sinner." To Simon it was obvious: there are different kinds of women, those who are sinners and presumably those who are not. And everyone understood the kind of actions that made a woman into a sinner. This was a common social classification that every Pharisee would have instinctively understood.

What about the term Pharisee? Luke identifies Simon as a Pharisee, naming him that way three times in the first 3 verses, thus pointing to the significance of this naming. I think for most of us, as re-readers of these gospels, the term Pharisee is connected with hypocrisy and therefore sin. In fact, it is difficult for us to think of the Pharisee as someone righteous and therefore sincere in seeking God's will. However, in the first century, Pharisees were respected for their rigorous obedience to the law and their vision and hope that the whole People of God would live out the Torah someday so that God's reign could fully come on earth. Saul, the Pharisee, whom we meet in the book of Acts, is the best example of this rigorous spirituality. Compared to the Sadducees, who more easily collaborated with the Roman overlords, and the Essenes who lived in separate communities, the Pharisees were much more involved with the ordinary people in their daily struggles. In that first century the term Pharisee would have indicated someone who is generally honoured and respected for his religious fervour and his devout life.

The story previous to this one in Luke, was also all about titles and naming. However, there the question was about Jesus and how he should be named. John, who is in prison, has begun to wonder if Jesus is really the promised one. He sends messengers to Jesus asking him to give himself a name: "Are you the one who is to come or are we to wait for another?" People have named Jesus as prophet when he healed the sick, as Master when they observed his power, and as rabbi when he taught with authority. But they have also named him as blasphemer, a mere son of Joseph, a glutton, a drunkard, and a friend of tax collectors and sinners. No wonder John was confused.

Jesus refuses to name himself, instead asking his followers to name what they had seen and heard—Jesus giving sight to the blind, healing the lame, cleansing the lepers, raising the dead, and preaching good news to the poor. He challenges John to make his own judgment and give him a name that arises out of what he has seen and heard.

Just like in real life, we too, as re-readers of the story, have already made some judgments about the three main characters in this drama unfolding before our eyes. But as we read the story today, let us set aside some of these earlier pre-judgments. Instead let us open ourselves to seeing and hearing something new, something that may confirm, challenge or enlarge our earlier naming.

This story in Luke 7 begins simply with an action of hospitality. A Pharisee has invited Jesus to dine with him and Jesus has accepted the invitation. We begin to expect something positive from this meeting. After all, inviting persons into our home is a way of signaling our openness to a deeper relationship. Here two persons, deeply concerned with the coming of the kingdom dine together—a rich possibility for the future of the people of God.

But immediately there is an interruption. A woman from the city, that is from outside of the home of the Pharisee, has learned that Jesus is dining in that home. Luke introduces her by naming her a sinner.

The dinner was probably taking place in a porch open to the outside so that the woman could come and touch Jesus from behind while he was reclining at the table. She was able to weep over his feet, wiping them with her long hair and anointing them with costly perfume.

In that culture this intimate, rather sensuous action was usually reserved for family and very close friends. In this story the socially accepted boundaries between men and women were being crossed without even an apology or explanation. Loose hair, kissing feet, and passionate weeping are not the usual ways in which respectable men and women relate to each other, especially when they have not even been invited to the feast. The woman has intruded on a private meal, she has transgressed the social codes that are understood by everyone. Luke lets us in on Simon's private thoughts. "If Jesus were a prophet, he would know that this woman is a sinner." In fact, one does not need to be a prophet in order to see that this as an inappropriate action. Luke and Simon are agreed. The label fits.

But this is where the story takes an unexpected twist. Jesus addresses Simon, here named for the first time, and asks Simon to make a simple judgment. Will a debtor, who has more debts cancelled, love the creditor more than the one who has a smaller debt cancelled? Simon probably does not know what this is all about. It makes sense that the one who had the most debt cancelled should also be most grateful. What does this have to do with anything?

Then Jesus becomes very direct. He compares the hospitality of Simon with the hospitality of the woman. Think about it! Jesus dares to name the actions of the woman actions of hospitality rather than inexcusable rude and embarrassing breaches of normal social relationships. Commentators have pointed out that Simon's hospitality was probably not really lacking according to the usual customs. Perhaps Simon could have brought water so that Jesus could have washed his dusty feet. However, washing, drying, and anointing the feet of someone else with your own hands, went beyond the usual polite customs of the day. This would have only happened in intimate settings between close family members or between esteemed Rabbis and their students. Her action in this setting could not be compared to that of Simon's.

But Jesus does not accept this judgment. What he sees is a woman who loved Jesus so much that she dared to bear her heart in front of a condemning group of people. And so he attempts to reinterpret her action so that we can all rejoice in this show of love. And in case Simon doesn't catch on, Jesus very pointedly refers to the way Simon has labeled the woman in his own mind. Yes, she has many sins, but these sins are forgiven. Therefore, she is more correctly characterized by her deep love. Only those who have few sins forgiven have a small love.

Luke does not indicate the response that Simon gives to this challenge. We do not know whether he is ready to see beyond the label? Instead Luke turns our attention to the woman. "Your sins are forgiven.... Your faith has saved you. Go in peace." No admonition to sin no more. No censure of a better time and place to show love. Just a simple affirmation of what the woman's actions had already indicated. She was a woman of love and faith. She could go in peace, for her loving actions were accepted.

Again the response by the woman is not recorded. Instead the attention of the story teller moves to the other guests who have watched these exchanges. But their attention has shifted to Jesus. "Who is this who even forgives sins?" The shift happens because it is Jesus who has now stepped across the socially and religiously accepted boundaries! How can this person believe he can wipe away the sins of another, just like that? How dare he rename the woman as a woman of love and faith? It is not up to him to give a woman dignity, defying the usual labelling by society, giving her new hope and peace. Is this acceptable, even for a rabbi?

And at the end of this short story we are left to decide what this story is really about. We are left to make a judgment and give this story a title.

In these past months, I have become more aware of what happens when a whole society labels persons in certain ways. We have a daughter whose skin colour and natural features give away her First Nations heritage. She is becoming more and more aware of the deep shame that she has felt throughout her life, a shame placed on her by a society who has dominated, oppressed and stolen the heritage of her people. I have had conversations with persons whose sexual orientation is different from the majority. The label of sinner has been placed upon them without any real knowledge of their Christian commitments and actions. I have talked with persons who have been abused and who have suffered much emotional anguish. I am aware of how deeply they feel the censure of our society on anyone who has been labelled psychologically damaged, even if it is through no fault of their own. One of my friends is often totally ignored when we go to a restaurant. After all, she is in a wheelchair and therefore the waiters assume that she would not be able to order the food (though she is a registered psychologist with a doctoral degree).

But I am even more aware of how easily names like theologian, pastor, scholar, or Christian hide secret sins under a cloak of respectability. It is not often that someone like Jesus comes along and so directly faces respectable leaders with their inner emptiness, with their lack of real love, compassion, and hospitality to others.

Choosing a title for this story means that we must make a judgment about what we think this passage is all about. We must decide how to identify with the characters in this story. This judgment is not an objective descriptive statement. It cannot be a detached scholarly titling of a story. Just as Luke gives his judgments, just as Simon makes choices, just as the woman must decide what to do, so we too must name what we have seen and heard. We must decide who we will be as we dine with Jesus at the table.

Perhaps those of us who know what it feels like to be publicly named a sinner, who have felt shame and censure from our communities about our very nature, will want to give this story a new name. Think a moment about how you would name this story.

Perhaps those of us who have always lived a socially acceptable life, fully included in our own faith community, who may have named others as sinners, may want to focus the story more on Simon. How will we entitle the story?

Or some of us may focus on Jesus and ask how Jesus names us. What does Jesus see as we gather at the table? What do our interactions with each other at the table reveal about our innermost feelings and thoughts? What name does Jesus choose for us?

As we gather for our "wine before breakfast" today, let us look each other in the eye and accept God's amazing hospitality and love. We can be assured that Jesus welcomes us and names us "beloved" even as he sees the dark secret thoughts that may be hidden in our hearts. Our tentative gestures of love reaching out for a healing touch will receive what they need at this table. You are all invited to come, eat and drink, and be healed. Let us rejoice in the name that Jesus gives us as we name each other sisters and brothers through Christ Jesus. Amen.

Chapter 6 Power

NAMING OUR POWER AND OUR VULNERABILITY

The consultation was unique and I was pleased to be invited to be a listener/responder to the discussions.[1] *The question posed to all presenters was the same: "Does the fact that we have a distinct Mennonite theology affect the way we carry out our roles of authority and how we wield power in both our professional and church lives?" The themes discussed were power and authority in three distinct areas: business, academia, and non-profit organizations. Those invited to this day of discussion were leaders and persons with official power from across various sectors within the North American Mennonite Church, including executive directors of church institutions, politicians, accountants, and many more. Power was defined simply as having "the capacity to do" rather than "power over." Authority was differentiated as referring to power conferred by others, manifesting itself within a communal context.*

I remember well the conversations by these leaders at that meeting. The struggle to bridge the divide within themselves, the divide between their work in the "secular" world and their commitments in the "sacred" world of church, was also my struggle. I sensed the yearning of some of these leaders to find a place within the church community in which they could be vulnerable with their struggles, a place where they could test their ethical values without judgment, and a place where they were not given too much authority because of their money, knowledge, or prestige nor were judged more harshly than other members when they were successful. I sensed that our Mennonite theology of self-denial and servanthood had not given those with power the tools that they needed to use their authority wisely. Yet I was somewhat disturbed that the consultation did not include those who were most affected by the power of the presenters. Did the leaders not feel "safe" enough to include persons who felt powerless in these same institutional settings?

A very different discussion took place at a "Women Doing Theology" conference where I presented a paper on the theology of service. Instead of reflections on power and authority by those who understood themselves as having power, women were reflecting on service as persons who often felt excluded, vulnerable, or pushed to the margins of power. The history of service by women provided a backdrop to a discussion of how Mennonite theology, particularly biblical interpretation, contributed to women seeing themselves as servants and not as leaders despite a theology of "servant leadership." However, I wondered if at times the term power was avoided because it was most safe to assume that we as women had no power.

While I was doing these theological reflections, I was also teaching a number of courses at the Toronto School of Theology (TST). I chose courses that I thought could contribute uniquely to the ecumenical dialogue while also stimulating Mennonite doctoral students to re-examine their own tradition. At first the courses were primarily on biblical authority or on hermeneutic community. However, as I explored the theme of power more directly, I began to offer courses on the sociopolitical nature of the church beginning with the "free church" tradition which was not represented in the various colleges at TST. My primary conversation partners for an ecclesiology course were Jürgen Moltman, Elisabeth Schüssler Fiorenza, and John H. Yoder. I hoped the students would begin to understand the differing approaches to the power and authority of the church. But I also hoped that they would self-consciously reflect on their own place in a church that is not only a spiritual body but a historically situated social, political, and economic entity.

The personal and the political are not often related in our theological reflection. My teaching of courses needed to be supplemented by discussions with individual students who felt vulnerable pursuing doctoral studies and navigating the complicated nature of the requirements of TST. Jobs after graduation were not assured, misunderstandings of their need to analyze critically the church and its institutions and authorities (including the Bible) felt hurtful, and the academic world left little room to talk about their own faith crises. At the same time, these students were beginning to gain power as scholars and often were not sure what this meant for them.

These struggles with power and vulnerability were not absent from my own life. At that time, I was still a "pastor's wife," not sure of my role in the local church. My theological degree created a new situation in which everyone seemed unsure whether and how I could offer my gifts. I was asked to be on the education committee in our congregation and even to chair it, but there was an unspoken rule that I could not be on the church board as that would represent concentrated power in a "pastoral couple." I fully respected that concern but wished that a conversation about my place in the church could have been created. I was nominated to be on the preaching team and enjoyed that position very much. However, when conflict arose within the team, I recognized that the power imbalance that was created by my theological degree and my marriage to the pastor deflected some of the discussion away from the real causes. I sometimes resented that I could no longer be an "ordinary layperson" as I had been before I began my studies, offering my gifts freely wherever I saw a need.

Dealing with both my official power and my feelings of vulnerability took several practical shapes. I began to volunteer my services primarily outside of my own congregation. Thus I accepted positions on committees within our denomination such as the AMBS board and the Believers Church Editorial Committee. There I was among peers, though often in the minority as a woman among highly qualified men.

Secondly, I tried to find a way in which I could be "licensed" or to be officially named as a Mennonite teacher and scholar so that I was accountable to some group or institution for my teaching within congregations. This was particularly crucial when I left TMTC and no longer had an official title from a recognized Mennonite institution. I became a founding member of "The Teaching Circle," a kind of guild that offered courses to congregations within the Mennonite conference in our area. It gave me support, counsel, and opportunities to teach in congregational settings for several years, but as an experimental approach it ultimately failed to receive adequate financial support to continue.

Thirdly, I began the work of setting boundaries for my scholarly work by being more deliberate as to when it was appropriate for me to speak as a scholar within the congregation. I tried to become more conscious of the weight that could be put on my words in congregational settings, especially since I tended to speak a bit too enthusiastically about my ideas and thus could easily intimidate others. I strived to be more vulnerable in speaking my convictions by sharing my experiences, not only my theological thinking, and using more accessible language. But perhaps most importantly, I began to see my need for community worship with its components of praise, confession, proclamation, affirmation of faith, prayer, and witness, something that a university context seldom gives. There I learned to depend on the power of the Spirit while gaining confidence in offering my gifts where they were needed most.

The two articles in this section are written from two perspectives: the first treats the theme of power historically while the second is an exercise in biblical interpretation on the theme of service. They are united in wrestling with the theme of power and authority in the context of Anabaptist theology—both when one has gained power and when one feels vulnerable and powerless.

***

POWER AND AUTHORITY IN MENNONITE THEOLOGICAL DEVELOPMENT[2]

I was asked to write a chapter in the book Power, Authority and the Anabaptist Tradition *by one of the editors, Benjamin Redekop, whom I had met at various theological consultations. In rereading my article, I am surprised and disturbed by the fact that I did not speak more about Mennonite feminists and their challenge to the notion of power and authority within the Mennonite tradition. In this reflection, I did not yet fully consider the women in Anabaptist history who also shaped the theological "game," though perhaps not in the usual ways. At the time there was still very little written by Mennonite women that I could use as a resource. However, I was pleased that a chapter by Dorothy Yoder Nyce and Lynda Nyce on "Power and Authority in Mennonite Ecclesiology: a Feminist Perspective" was included in the book.[3] It should be read in conjunction with my chapter.*

The opportunity to write an article on the theological development of Mennonite theology allowed me to explore the topic of power and authority more historically. The dilemma of how to renounce "earthly" power while needing power in order to live and act within a sociopolitical context is particularly crucial for persons in our Anabaptist tradition.

If I were writing the article today and extending its scope to 21st century theological development, I would write more directly about the various protest movements within the Mennonite church such as those by women and those who have suffered abuse. I would include the voices of persons from a non-European tradition, from colonized and indigenous groups, and from the LGBTQ communities, all seeking a voice within the Mennonite community of faith. I would not seek out only the more prominent and influential theological voices but also those who have been ignored in the conversation. I would listen to voices who speak out about sexual abuse by theologians speaking about power and would ask critical questions about the lack of awareness that many Mennonite theologians have about their own power. I would also seek out those voices that strive for "truth and reconciliation," attempting to bring the various experiences that we all have into dialogue with the biblical and Anabaptist witness of faith.

For me the crucial question continues to be: why is the playing field so restricted and why are boundaries the primary way we define our faith?

***

Power and Authority in Mennonite Theological Development[i]

The metaphor of theology as a game provides a useful framework for describing power and authority in Mennonite theological development. A game, whether soccer or cards, usually includes a variety of players, diverse strategies, shifting interpretations of rules, and an often elusive goal. Using this metaphor to describe Mennonite theologizing suggests that there is a complexity and plurality in Mennonite theology that contributes to making the game a dynamic and ever-changing reality.[4] But games also have underlying rules that establish the basic framework distinguishing one game from another. So too there are "family resemblances" and regulatory principles that help distinguish Mennonite theologies from other similar Christian theologies.[5] In this chapter I concentrate on illuminating the basic rules of the game by describing the strategies and moves made by individual players in a variety of circumstances.

I have chosen the writings of Menno Simons, the sixteenth-century reformer from whom Mennonites received their name, to illustrate the rules that defined

i Redekop, Benjamin W., and Calvin W. Redekop, eds. *Power, Authority, and the Anabaptist Tradition*. pp. 73-94. © 2001 The Johns Hopkins University Press. Reprinted with permission of Johns Hopkins University Press.

the game during a crucial period of its conception. The definitions of power and authority that began to be assumed by this group of Anabaptists created basic strategies for a game played during a time of social unrest and upheaval. The second part of this analysis moves into the twentieth century. The focus on a different time and setting allows us to evaluate the degree to which the basic rules were still intact several hundred years later, and the degree to which subtle changes and adjustments were made to fit new circumstances. The writings of two influential theologians will demonstrate some of the adjustments made to suit a new time. The conclusion will suggest that the definitive word has not yet been spoken in Mennonite theologizing—new players are continually being invited to join the game. These bring ambiguities and tensions to the surface, but they also introduce new vitality and energy into play. The future shape of the game is thus open, awaiting involvement by many players as the rules are debated, adapted, and reapplied.

Menno Simons

Menno Simons' theological approach to issues of power and authority grew out of a long personal struggle, as a member of the Catholic clergy, to live a life of integrity and to speak an authentic word of truth. This latter task was not easy during a time when a unified tradition based on the political stability of Christendom and the religious mediation of the sacraments by the church could no longer be assumed. The gradual breaking apart of this unity created space for various dualistic worldviews to emerge and thrive. Thus, divisions between the spiritual world and the material world can be recognized in the various debates among Reformers around polarities such as spirit/letter, invisible/visible, gospel/law, or the inner/outer word.[6]

These were not only theoretical debates for the Reformers; rather, the struggles between various theologies were also political struggles between religious leaders seeking to reestablish authority on a firm basis. A focus on the authority of the Word of God did not do away with a merging of the power of the state with a newly reformed church. Paramount leaders such as Luther and Zwingli did not hesitate to use the power of the state to enforce the authority of the Word. However, the use of the "sword of righteousness" was not limited to these Reformers. Figures associated with Anabaptism led the seizure of the city of Münster, proclaiming it to be the New Jerusalem of the last days.[7] Those who resisted were executed or expelled. The failure of this vision, based on a wedding of spiritualism and apocalypticism, led not only to a time of disillusionment but also to persecution for the Anabaptists in the Netherlands.

In this volatile and dangerous context, Menno Simons found a point of integration that allowed him to proclaim a new kind of kingdom with Jesus Christ as its authoritative foundation. Though there were many shifts and changes in Menno's thinking, the notion of radical regeneration was fundamental.[8] In his view, baptism signified a transformation of human nature in the individual, a dying to the old life of sin and a rising with Christ to a new life in anticipation of the heavenly Jerusalem. The Lord's Supper celebrated the coming together of the new people of God as the body of Christ. The church proclaimed a new way of truth as it sought to be light and salt in the world.

The anticipation of God's kingdom in the *Fundamentboek*, Menno's most complete attempt at theological writing, is, according to Helmut Isaak, "universalist and holistic."[9] The time of God's grace includes all people and all nations, and it affects all areas of life. Thus Christians can already be citizens of the New Jerusalem in anticipation of the kingdom coming in its fullness because Christ is already Lord and King over heaven and earth.

This holistic worldview, based on God's grace in Jesus, did not do away with all dualisms. In fact, the dualisms that are found sprinkled throughout Menno's writings reflect the notion of the "new" breaking into the "old" and creating a radical division between people. Thus Menno insists that,

> there are two opposing princes and two opposing kingdoms; The one is the Prince of peace; the other the prince of strife. Each of these princes has his particular kingdom and as the prince is so is also the kingdom. The Prince of peace is Christ Jesus; His kingdom is the kingdom of peace, which is His church; His messengers are the messengers of peace…; His body is the body of peace…our weapons are not swords and spears, but patience, silence, and hope, and the Word of God. With these we must maintain our heavy warfare and fight our battle…with these we intend and desire to storm the kingdom of the devil…the other prince is the prince of darkness, Antichrist and Satan. This prince is a prince of all tumult and blood. Raging and murder is his proper nature and policy. His commandments and teachings and his kingdom, body, and church are of the same nature.[10]

Though these divisions are starkly stated, they do not coincide neatly with the dichotomy between spirit and matter. Rather, Menno understands both the spiritual kingdom of God and the fleshly kingdom of the devil as embodied realities. Both include an inner and an outer nature. Both include a visible church, a concrete message, weapons to defend themselves, and methods to pass this message on to others. Both are games, although played by a different set of rules.

As we read Menno's writings in more detail, we may be surprised at their polemical and argumentive tone. His descriptions of the kingdom of God are almost always set against the backdrop of false teachers, representing false Christs and false churches who offer faltering foundations on which to build the kingdom. For Menno is not concerned primarily with speculative theology, nor is he only striving for logical consistency. Rather, he is seeking to empower and encourage those struggling to live in peace in a world in which the church, whether Catholic, Reformed, or Anabaptist, could be the initiator of violence and bloodshed. His suspicion rests on the experience of persecution and violence, which he cannot name as the fruit of the Spirit.

The concern that spiritual reality be of one piece from eternity to eternity permeates Menno's writings. It is often expressed by the hermeneutical principle that "the same brings forth the same" or "every tree beareth fruit after its own kind!"[11] This implies that only the Spirit of God is able to establish a spiritual kingdom here on earth. Because Menno rejected the mediation provided by the sacramental system of the Catholic Church in which the material sacraments literally became Christ's body on earth, he had to enter the more theoretical discussions about the nature of God and of human beings, and the mediation between them. For him, the incarnate Christ became the vital clue to a kingdom that was spiritual but visible on earth.

Menno interpreted John 1:14 to mean that Jesus embodied the Word of God in his very being, a being in which the inner life and the outer visible reality were unified in one spiritual body.[12] Thus, Jesus was not a sinful human born of Adam's seed but rather a new creation, a new Adam, the Word of God made flesh. He was the perfect Lamb, able to atone for all sin, but he was also the one who initiated a new way of being human in this world. Menno thus insists that "the regenerate…have received a new heart and spirit. Once they were earthly-minded, now heavenly; once they were carnal, now spiritual; once they were unrighteous, now righteous; once they were evil, now good, and they live no longer after the old corrupted nature of the first earthly Adam, but after the new upright nature of the new and heavenly Adam, Christ Jesus."[13] In this optimistic view of regenerated human nature, the church, the bride of Christ, literally becomes "flesh of his flesh and bone of his bone!"[14] The church became a kind of sacrament, the literal body of Christ in this world, charged with the mission of representing God's grace.[15]

This theology of incarnation allowed Menno to connect God's authority and power to human authority and power when it was exercised within the true church. The Bible as Word of God and the church as body of Christ received their essential nature from God through Jesus Christ. Thus the power of God's revelatory Word in the Bible and the authority of a church that would incarnate in a visible way the mind and spirit of Christ were placed under the grace of God active in the world. This intimate connection resulted in "heavenly" power, which makes the regenerated active, confident, and joyful, able to bring forth good fruit. No longer are Christians "bound by any person, power, wisdom, or times but we must be governed by the plainly expressed commands of Christ and the pure doctrines and practices of His holy apostles."[16] Christ's life of love, service, suffering, and death becomes the measure of any embodiment within history that is empowered by the Spirit.

For Menno these convictions grew out of a personal experience of conversion and transformation. Before he could teach and preach to the scattered flock eagerly waiting for a word of truth, he had to give up all his own ambitions and dreams of financial security and power, and become instead a man slandered and persecuted, accused of being a heretic and false prophet. But these convictions also contributed to a new notion of the visible community named "church." A leveling of social hierarchies under God greatly limited the power of the educated, the aristocrats, and the clergy over the "common people." Thus, Menno can say, "Before Him, the great and the commoner are alike, the rich and the poor, the strong and the weak, the learned and the unlearned, the wise and the foolish. With him is no respect of persons; all who do not fear Him, do not conform to His counsel, doctrine, spirit, and example, whether emperor, king, doctor, or licentiate, he must bear His punishment eternally and be subject to His judgment and wrath."[17] Menno Simons' motto, "No other foundation can anyone lay than that which is laid, which is Jesus Christ" proved to be a "provocation for all who based their religiosity on human resources, whether tradition and human convention, learned understanding or worldly power. It smashed the foundations of the powerful and laid bare the one foundation that could sustain a Christian existence."[18]

The effects of this understanding of power and authority soon became evident within a number of the early Anabaptist communities. Non-ordained persons such as women began to gain a new authority through prophetic gifts, members in need received aid through sharing within community, and the power of official leaders was limited by empowering all to be involved in biblical interpretation.[19] The hierarchies, which had been assumed to be God-given or in the nature of divine order and creation, and the offices, which gave authority to certain people, were challenged when measured by the standard of Christ. But not all issues of power and authority in Anabaptist communities were solved through this radical theology of the kingdom of God and the incarnation of Jesus in history.

In the World, but Not of the World

Within the Anabaptist community the dynamic associated with equality before

God and the understanding of nonviolence as the way of discipleship created a shift in patterns of power and authority. The only power that members of the church were to have over each other was that of "fraternal admonition." Physical violence should not be used to discipline those who go astray. Balthasar Hubmaier, one of the most articulate theologians of the Anabaptists, states this rather clearly in his "baptismal order." In baptism new members of the church voluntarily submitted themselves to the church in order to learn to live according to the law of Christ.[20] Through the use of the ban (excommunication) and shunning (social avoidance of those walking in sin), members were encouraged to repent and renew their covenant with God. This process of "binding and loosing" based on Matthew 18 and John 20, was seen as necessary to maintain the moral integrity and unitary authority of the church.

It did not take long before the need for leadership and oversight emerged as small congregations struggled for unity. However, Anabaptists insisted that sacramental ordination, apostolic succession, or education were not adequate legitimations for leadership.[21] They generally agreed that only an upright person who lived a pure Christian life and who was taught by the Holy Spirit could be considered a true shepherd of the sheep. The measure of the spirituality of leaders was to be the congruence of their life with the Word of God.

This appeal to the Word of God did not solve the disagreements about authoritative biblical interpretation and the designation of leaders. Should authority be vested in illumined "apostles," ordained preachers, biblically learned teachers, or everyone in a congregation? There were those such as Conrad Grebel and Michael Sattler who emphasized letter over spirit, those such as Hans Denck who emphasized the priority of spirit over letter, and those such as the Melchiorites and the prophetesses Ursula Jost and Barbara Rebstock who focused on both prophetic spirit and prophetic letter.[22]

As churches began to focus more and more on their own purity, leaders were chosen who demonstrated the external, legislated marks of spirituality, marks more easily discerned than the inner, experiential side of Christian faith. Menno Simons' optimistic anthropology and his growing insistence on obedience to the literal word of God in order to ensure a church "without spot or wrinkle" greatly contributed to a tendency toward a harsh, legalistic approach to church discipline. The weight of leadership began to fall more and more on officially designated leaders; charismatic and prophetic leadership within the church became difficult. Boundaries thus became important as the church moved from emphasizing the gracious empowerment by God through the work of the Spirit, to judging the moral integrity of members of the community who were to embody God's holiness. Differences could not be tolerated when unity and conformity within the community were the signs of obedience to God. Offending members were thus "sent out of the church, God's kingdom, into the world, the kingdom of Satan."[23]

The issue of power and authority as related to governance in the larger society was complicated during a time when the legitimacy of the Anabaptist churches themselves was being contested. In the early years it was not yet clear how the established church would respond to the small communities of Anabaptists, whose advocacy of various shifts in social and religious patterns of relationships threatened to disturb the stability of church and society. Menno appealed to the magistrates to become true Christian rulers and admonished them to use their powers for the good in words such as the following: "Your task is to do justice between a man and his neighbour, to deliver the oppressed out of the hand of the oppressor; also to restrain by reasonable means, that is, without tyranny and bloodshed, manifest deceivers who so miserably lead poor helpless sons by hundreds of thousands into destruction!"[24] Menno did not consider these powerful rulers to be outside of the perfection of Christ simply by virtue of their office, the external sign of power. He suggests that the "calling" of the magistrates was to "enlarge, help and protect the kingdom of God." He calls them to rule wisely and to exercise justice and accountability for the stewardship of their resources. At the same time, he accuses rulers of seeking "fat salaries and a lazy life," wanting to be called "doctors, lords, or masters" and thus abusing their authority. As one of the oppressed and persecuted, Menno calls for the conversion of rulers, to be expressed as toleration and protection of the Anabaptists in the name of Christ and the gospel. Integrity for Christian magistrates implied that the weapons used must be related to the kind of kingdom that was being established. This meant that the Christian's weapons were not to be "weapons with which cities and countries may be destroyed, walls and gates broken down, and human blood shed in torrents like water."[25]

Menno soon admitted that he could find only a few who demonstrated that they truly feared and loved God in the way they used their worldly power. The key marks of Christian faith identified by Anabaptists did not fit well with the political reality of the times. Anabaptists soon found themselves on the margins of society. As the clash between differing views of power and authority became stronger, choices had to be made by both the magistrates and the Anabaptists. Would they accommodate to each other's views by moderating their positions, or would there need to be a strict separation between them? Snyder suggests that there were, in fact, five different political arrangements that occurred during the sixteenth century.[26] These ranged from Anabaptism as the official religion, to toleration of Anabaptists, to outright enmity between Anabaptists and the governing power in a region.

Separation increasingly came to be seen as the best option, especially when the rejection of the sword and the oath became normative in Anabaptism. The

Schleitheim Confession (1527)[27] already states this unambiguously: "It does not befit a Christian to be a magistrate: The rule of the government is according to the flesh, that of the Christians according to the Spirit.... The weapons of their battle and warfare are carnal and only against the flesh, but the weapons of Christians are spiritual, against the fortification of the devil."[28] This implied that a commitment to the kingdom of God made visible in Christ's body could easily be distinguished from the visible manifestations of a commitment to a false kingdom. Authority and power in society became disconnected from God and began to be considered outside of the "perfection of Christ:" Therefore, Anabaptists did not consider positions of authority in the broader society to be proper for their members. They became more and more suspicious of anyone holding an office in the government or the established church. The position of the church on the margins of society became the normal one for a faithful community.

The conviction that the eschatological kingdom of God was already becoming a reality on earth became the basis on which both the goal of the game and the criteria for legitimate moves was based. There were two opposing teams or sides, only one of which could be identified with God's coming kingdom. For the early Anabaptists the goal of the game was to participate in this kingdom (now and in the hereafter), but how to know who were the true players? Identification with God's kingdom could not center on the uniform of the players (the outer ceremonies or the words spoken), since some of the false prophets were also "baptized with one and the same baptism, and were one with us in appearance."[29] Instead, the congruence between the inner and the outer, between the uniform and the play, became the primary criterion. This created a visible church with definite marks identifying it as God's church, but the marks were taken as outward expressions of an inner reality. In this game Mennonites had to wrestle with questions of power and authority by seeking to incarnate the unity of inner and outer in their play. The measure was Jesus, the Word becoming flesh, who embodied true authority in his very being. The use of power became valid—authoritative—if it moved the church toward the goal of embodying the Word of God.

However, over time standardized uniforms and a sharper delineation of the boundaries of the playing field became primary marks of membership on the team. Different interpretations of the game created new suspicions, separations, and competition among team members. Disunity, domination by a few, and new hierarchies began to threaten a game whose goal was to embody the rule of God on earth. The tension within the game centered on how to participate in God's transforming power in the world without using the false strategies of the world, which created worldly power plays and domination. The answer seemed to be a game in which players united in small enclaves on the margins of the larger society, determined to at least bring together word and deed on their own team and within the boundaries of their own communities. Obedience to the norms established by the community became the signs that identified these teams as faithful representatives of the kingdom.

Twentieth-Century Approaches

Over the next few centuries, Mennonite confessions of faith revolved around ecclesiology and mission, with the focus on the inner life of church membership and the outer life of Christian discipleship.[30] A keen sense of boundaries, together with a long history of deprivation in a world that was often hostile, created a faith community with a strong sense of separation from the surrounding culture. However, as societies changed and Mennonites began to depend on friendly governments to protect their traditional beliefs and practices, a crisis in Mennonite identity developed. Hans-Jürgen Goertz suggests that in the twentieth century "a way of life patterned on gestures of resistance against a past age" produced a crisis of historical depth and increasing intensity. The outward markers of membership in the Mennonite side began to be eroded as hostilities with the outside world were replaced by often close collaboration. Mennonites found it increasingly difficult to tell one side from the other as boundaries between sides became permeable. The Mennonite "cognitive center" had dissolved, creating a vacuum that needed to be filled if Mennonites were to continue to play in the same game.[31] It was time for a restatement of the rules.

Harold Bender, a historian and church leader, sensed this need. His 1943 presidential address to the American Society of Church History, entitled "The Anabaptist Vision," was only in part an effort to convince other Christians that Anabaptism was a valid part of the Reformation.[32] His voice was also directed to the Anabaptist-Mennonite church and its need to be revitalized. In Bender's eyes, Anabaptism had taken the Reformation to its proper conclusion by emphasizing the practice-oriented nature of the Christian faith. Discipleship, the church as a brotherhood, and the ethic of love and nonresistance were identified as the common core of beliefs that were characteristic of "evangelical and constructive Anabaptism." Bender summarized the essence of Anabaptism in this way: "The whole life was to be brought literally under the lordship of Christ in a covenant of discipleship, a covenant which the Anabaptist writers delighted to emphasize. The focus of the Christian life was to be not so much the inward experience of the grace of God, as it was for Luther, but the outward application of that grace to all human conduct and the consequent Christianization of all human relationships!"[33] Bender hoped that the institutional Mennonite Church would regain its vigor while finding its own place in the larger context of denominational Christianity.

According to John D. Roth, the renewal of the "Anabaptist Vision" sparked by this speech served as a symbolic theological anchor, a source of identity and renewal within the Mennonite Church during the era following World War II, "as Mennonites became increasingly acculturated into the mainstream culture of North America."[34] Two theologians influenced by this vision significantly shaped Mennonite understandings of power and authority in the next half-century. Their way of intertwining the rules into an integrated approach of their own created some shifts and adjustments. However, the influence of the basic rules as set out by Menno Simons can easily be discerned in their theological approach to power and authority.

Guy Franklin Hershberger

Guy F. Hershberger's *War, Peace, and Nonresistance*, first published in 1944, was based both on the historical consensus that had arisen in Anabaptist Mennonite experience over the centuries and on biblical interpretation focused on the teachings of Jesus in the Sermon on the Mount.[35] The impetus for his writings came from the experiences and challenges facing American Mennonites during the first half of the twentieth century. Interestingly enough, Hershberger did not see the greatest temptation for Mennonites at this time coming from the opponents of the way of peace as it was defined by Mennonites. Rather, he saw the greater challenge coming from the subtle temptation to compromise with a society that had begun to tolerate Mennonites and their convictions.[36] The boundaries between Mennonites and the rest of society were becoming blurred; therefore, issues of identity and authority were coming to the fore. The need, as Hershberger saw it, was to focus on the visible difference between the kingdom of God and the kingdoms of this world. This difference could best be stated in the clear principle of "nonresistance."

Hershberger begins his book with a definition of war as "social conflict in which one party endeavors with the use of force, to compel the submission of the other."[37] Because he recognizes that physical and armed force are not the only kinds of coercive power, he speaks about conflict not only between nations but also between races, political parties, social classes, and even families and individuals. His notion of nonresistance, the strategy that he connects with the kingdom of God, excludes all kinds of force. "Force" includes the nonviolent resistance of Gandhi and the tactics of organized labor and organized agriculture as well as the oppressive methods of the employer class, organized capital, or big business. Pressure groups that operate for selfish ends use methods that become vicious in their attempt to impose justice, violating the greater ethic of love and nonresistance found in the Bible.

Therefore, Hershberger makes a clear distinction between "doing justice" and "demanding justice,"[38] Christians seek to obey the principle of love, not to compel the enemy to comply with their wishes against his or her will. Social changes that are brought about for personal, class, or national advantage are not primarily motivated by obedience to the divine will. They are therefore not rooted in the experience of regeneration through the atoning work of Christ. For Hershberger the church is to be a "colony of heaven" that is neither a human institution nor a mystical phenomenon but a society of regenerate Christians, a Christian brotherhood that belongs to the true kingdom of God.[39] Christians who really follow Christ will live a non-conformed life, a life on a "different level" than those of non-Christians. This is so because through the coming of the Holy Spirit they have access to a source of greater power, the power of love. Because of Jesus, who gives freedom from the passions of "natural man (sic)"; Christians live in a new covenant relationship that allows them to become "the salt and light of the earth."

The New Testament is "entirely unpolitical" for Hershberger because it has nothing to say about how the affairs of state should be conducted.[40] Rulers may be agents of God to maintain order in society, but this only allows the "law of cause and effect" to be administered in society. While Christians must be subordinate to the state's purposes (unless it requires disobedience to the higher law of love), they do not need to be involved in administrating this lower law. Therefore, they should not feel obligated to fill the office of police officer or magistracy. Others who live on a "subChristian" level can aspire to those roles. Christians should aim for the higher place that only they can fill.

Hershberger moderates this radical separation between the two realms when he stresses that Christians must be creatively engaged in witness and service to society by offering alternatives to conventional political activity. They will provide leadership for a "curative" not a "political" mission, which can bring healing to human society and prevent further decay through consistent witness to the truth.[41] Hershberger spells out some of these implications in a discussion of practical service such as relief work and creative initiatives in mental health services. But he insists that ideals such as freedom of religion and loving community are best modeled by the faith community. Thus Hershberger includes a chapter on personal relationships in his subsequent book, *The Way of the Cross in Human Relations* (1958). In this world of family and friends, the spirit of cooperation and love should permeate all relationships. There is no room for attitudes of superiority, but all must think of themselves as "brethren [sic] in the faith, not as high or low, leaders or followers, rulers or subjects:"[42] Only with this kind of humility can relationships function according to the will of God. Cooperation and community come about through "mutual forbearance, and love, and the doing of justice; not by means of self-assertion and the demand for justice."[43]

Though Hershberger is usually thought of as a clear spokesperson for a two-kingdom theology, he bases this division on an integrated ethical principle derived from Christ's teaching in the Sermon on the Mount. History has taught him that it is difficult to live out this principle of love in a world that operates by coercive power. He is suspicious of the blurring of principles that will happen as Mennonites become more fully integrated into society. Therefore, he emphasizes not only the distinction between church and world but also the different levels of morality by which people can choose to live. In doing so, he creates a theology in which new dualisms threaten to divide people from each other, hierarchies are created in which Christians can easily assume their own superiority, and God's presence is removed from whole spheres of life.

Hershberger's theological perspective continued to stress that living according to God's criteria will create separate teams. However, Hershberger goes further, emphasizing that separate playing fields are necessary in order to remain a team faithful to the kingdom. In order to strengthen the team, Hershberger emphasizes the unique and higher mission of God's team while admitting that the other team has its own, though inferior, place in God's overall plan. This allows the tensions between the Mennonite community and the rest of society to be alleviated somewhat, because each participates in its own variety of the power game without interference. At the same time, suspicion of the other team's strategies is nourished in order to encourage nonconformist strategies faithful to the standards demonstrated by Jesus.

The overall goal of the game is not forgotten by Hershberger. In fact, the principle of love and nonresistance stresses the need to bring the inner and outer, word and deed, together. This encourages the players of the Mennonite team to work at this integration within their own community while occasionally moving "to the other playing field" in order to visibly model and witness to Jesus' self-giving way of the cross. This approach is based on confidence in God, who will use this witness to move the game in the right direction.

John Howard Yoder

In the context of a Mennonite identity that seemed increasingly shaped by establishment culture and indiscriminate borrowing from mainstream Protestantism, John H. Yoder sought to find a theology that met two primary goals. He hoped that his theology would bring about repentance and renewal within the church, while at the same time leading to a greater witness by the church to the larger society. He therefore insisted in his writings that the mainline Protestant labeling of Anabaptist theology as inherently separatist (as demonstrating a "Christ against culture" stance as classified by H. Richard Niebuhr)[44] is inadequate and misleading. Instead, he pointed to the transformational dynamic of the embodied nature of the church in culture, patterned after Christ's incarnational presence in history.

In his popular book *The Politics of Jesus,* first published in 1972, Yoder spells out the relevance of Jesus to social ethics and therefore to the broader society.[45] In the chapter entitled "Christ and Power," he concentrates on "power structures" or "patterns" that transcend or precede or condition the individual capacity to make things happen.[46] In line with Hendrikus Berkhof, he suggests that the "principalities and powers" spoken of in the New Testament refer to somewhat the same phenomena that we call religious, intellectual, moral, and social institutions or structures. He suggests, therefore, that the biblical narrative points to the sinfulness of these structures as well as to the continuing providential control that orders them according to the divine will. He thus describes human sin as obedience to these rebellious powers of the fallen world.

The Bible testifies that Jesus has broken the sovereignty of these powers by living a restored and genuinely free human existence, "not the slave of any power, of any law or custom, community or institution, value or theory."[47] That Christ is Lord is "a social, political, structural fact which constitutes a challChatperenge to the Powers.... It is a declaration about the nature of the cosmos and the significance of history, within which both our conscientious participation and our conscientious objection find their authority and their promise!"[48] Thus, Jesus has brought about a radical shift in the human relationship to power by liberating Christians from "the way things are" and creating the possibility of a radical new kind of social order.

Yoder does not focus primarily on the liberation or transformation of the individual person or deal directly with the inner psychological or spiritual factors that have created a loss of autonomy or sense of powerlessness in a person. Instead, he focuses on helping Christians understand external structures and institutions so that they will not be seduced by them. His analysis concentrates on identifying a particular sociopolitical pattern that he names the "Constantinianization" of the church in which a fusion happens between the authority of the church and the power of structures of governance. These create a "framework of normalcy" in which particular power relationships are evaluated on the basis of reason, the orders of nature, common sense, or generalizations arising out of observations of social processes, instead of by the will of God as revealed in Jesus Christ.[49] He insists that when these secondary authorities are fused with the authority of divine providence, the church is not able to see the radical challenge of the gospel of Jesus Christ.

Yoder suggests that Anabaptism, in its attempt to break with this fusion, demonstrated a model of the church as a "messianic community" of reconciliation and agape love under the exclusive lordship of Christ. Because Anabaptism broke with the "fallen powers," creating a visible alternative, it had a revolutionary impact on society. However, the present church has not been suspicious enough of these powers. It has readily accepted the definitional categories of the "world." Therefore, judgment and renewal, rather than gradual reform and nurture, are most necessary.

This revolutionary impulse in Yoder's writings is softened by notions of subordination and obedience. Even though the church knows that the final victory has been won and that Jesus is now the new Lord, it must not impose this new order upon the larger social order violently. It cannot use unworthy means even for worthy ends. Instead, it is "revolutionary subordination" as demonstrated in Jesus' own life, in the early church's attitude to the state, and in the household codes that characterizes the biblical response to domineering power.[50]

This subordination is characterized by servanthood, a radical giving up of the need to control the direction in which society is moving. For those in superordinate positions, this implies a giving up of all domineering uses of their status. For those in subordinate positions, this implies an acceptance of life within a given status without resentment. Following the way of the cross means accepting the cost of social nonconformity, living the life of servanthood, self-giving, and even "self-abasement" in order to demonstrate the reality of the confession that Christ is Lord.[51] Thus Christians can participate "in the character of God's victorious patience with the rebellious powers of his creation."[52]

Yoder's efforts to disentangle the authority structures that determine how we live often focus on the language we use to talk about power. He suggests that there are three different kinds of language built on differing assumptions of authority.[54]3When the church speaks in "marketplace semantics," it must use the ordinary definitions set by the establishment. Thus it will use the terms of sociology and politics to describe the governing structures of society. When the church speaks constructively and critically to the governing power in society, it can make use of the self-justifying language of the rulers to call them to accountability. Then it will speak of responsibility and integrity. But when speaking within the church, Yoder wants to use the covenant language of ministry and service, which claims "the authority of incarnation for the content of messianic servanthood."[54] Instead of the language of power and authority, the church will therefore speak about the gifts of the Spirit, about servant leadership, and about love for the enemy.

In the use of these different languages, Yoder is most concerned about the substantial difference between the language of legitimation, by which power is justified, and the language of prescription, which authorizes the way of discipleship, since both are based on claims of truth. He is concerned that the absolute claim of revelation by which the church is to live should not be polluted by norms drawn from other sources. At the same time, he does not believe that the church should coercively try to control society with its prescriptive language. Instead, the church can demonstrate an alternative social order, thus producing changes within the larger social structure.

In Yoder's theology the notion of two playing fields is rejected. The two kingdoms are not understood to be on two separate levels that therefore cannot clash directly; instead, Yoder understands the time of the church as a period of "the overlapping of two aeons" that exist simultaneously in time. "They differ…in nature or in direction; one points backward to human history outside of (before) Christ; the other points forward to the fullness of the kingdom of God, of which it is a foretaste. Each aeon has a social manifestation: the former in the 'world,' the latter in the church or the body of Christ. The new aeon came into history in a decisive way with the incarnation…the new aeon involves a radical break with the old."[55] The different goal toward which each team is moving can be seen most clearly if one examines the strategy used by the church. Those identifying with the reign of God will accept the place given them on the margins of society, confident that their leader will win the game in the end. They will insist that power or control not be used to move the game in the direction of the goal as they see it. Instead, they will concentrate on proclaiming their leader's power, identifying false authority, and attempting to bring conformity to the team by stressing the proper strategy. This strategy, based on obedience to Christ's lordship, is expressed in the language of servanthood and the way of the cross as modeled by their leader. Yoder assumes that this strategy will not result in social withdrawal, but rather will encourage a unified move toward the proper goal by a team united by a common strategy.

Seeking God's Kingdom Incarnate

The writings of Menno Simons, Guy F. Hershberger, and John H. Yoder illustrate both the variety of ways in which the Mennonite theological game can be played and the boundaries of the game as they have been established through time. They also illustrate that the goal and basic strategy of the game continue to be debated as the players change and the game shifts to various parts of the playing field.[56] Anyone entering the game in the early days of this new millennium quickly realizes that the game is already well under way. However, the basic challenge continues to be discerning the direction the game should go to reach the goal while reinterpreting the criteria that characterize the strategies used by God's team.

Howard Loewen has suggested that there are two primary directions that are being debated in the Mennonite theological game.[57] The first, arising out of the heart of Mennonite theology, is a "strong sense of the incarnational reality of the Gospel in culture." This creates a "transformational grammar" strongly linked to the "paradigmatic way of Israel, Jesus and the early Church." This seems to be in accordance with the rules of the game captured by Menno Simons' understanding of the newness of the kingdom of God and the importance of regeneration. It is also caught by Hershberger's emphasis on the non-coercive power of love in a church that creatively seeks alternatives to the normal power games that are a part of most social institutions. And it continues to be expressed in the freedom that comes with the knowledge that dominating powers are already under the authority of Christ as stressed by Yoder. All of these point to the empowerment of individuals and the church through God's grace, and they name the goal of the theological game as a transformation of the team into God's people.

This emphasis leads to a game in which the team is constantly changing as new members are invited into the game and existing members confess their need for transformation. The focus is not on competition between players, but rather on the transformation of strategies that destroy and damage into strategies that heal and transform. Thus, any truth claim that is made is tied to the empowerment and freedom gained through Christ by the power of the Holy Spirit. In this model of the game, God is seen as the ultimate source of power and authority. Human power that moves toward the goal is always power that is in the midst of being transformed. God's revelation becomes embodied in salvation. Thus, the church "is the world being transformed".[58] Though this may result in nonconformity to the strategies of society, it also allows cooperation with society when it moves in the direction of healing and salvation.

Loewen also points to the other direction that the game can go by admitting that sectarianism and separatism have been a part of the Mennonite ethos during much of their history. He suggests that this direction came about because the transformationist center was overshadowed "internally by the social reality of physical separation from culture and moral deterioration in the community, and externally by the theological definition given to this separatism by mainstream religion."[59] The problem, as Loewen sees it, was that the transformationist ethos at the heart of Mennonite life was not applied to the broader spheres of surrounding culture and not lived out in the moral community itself.

While the external definitions during the early time of persecution as well as in more recent times did support unwanted separations, and Mennonites did not always live up to their best moral understandings, this brief overview of power and authority in Mennonite theologizing suggests that the impulse for separation was present in the theological articulations themselves. Menno Simons' understanding of the church "without spot or wrinkle" already contained the seeds of a dualistic theology that polarized people, thus creating domination and oppression. This perfectionist impulse expressed itself in strict criteria that could easily be used to judge other persons and institutions as unworthy of being the church. Thus the Schleitheim Confession could draw a boundary suggesting that being a magistrate was already outside of the perfection of Christ because the rule of government is by nature "fleshly." So too, Hershberger could draw another boundary placing resistance to injustice outside of the church's mandate because any resistance is by nature selfish and therefore not motivated by love. Yoder's boundaries are more subtle. However, his insistence on a particular language and institutional form to express the lordship of Christ allows him to put strict boundaries between the faithful church and the unfaithful church, between prophets and other Christians. A church that is not Anabaptist according to his definitions is suspected of Constantinianism and therefore of being unfaithful.[60]

Separation is rooted in suspicion and obedience, two hermeneutical approaches or strategies that at first glance seem opposite to each other. They are, however, similar in that both are responses to authority and exhibit themselves in a community in both word and deed. Suspicion of the "world" and its idolatry has been basic to Mennonite theology since the time of Menno. This suspicion has created an important and necessary understanding of nonconformity that has encouraged the church to question society's norms and to work creatively at discernment in its involvement in the larger culture. However, it has also separated Christians from each other and contributed to a division between the secular and religious exercise of power. Banning ideas and people who do not conform to the accepted norms of the church to the sphere of the "world" has therefore been justified theologically.

Suspicion of the 'other'; the one different from the self, continues to permeate much of Mennonite theological literature even when the issues of the separation of church and state are not central. This separation is not expressed so much by overt articulation as by the absence of a variety of voices present in the churches. It is still difficult to find theology written by women or by persons from non-European ethnic and cultural backgrounds. Though the voices of these persons may not have been deliberately silenced, they have heard the subtle message that names them outsiders to the theological game. This silencing has correctly been named as a subtle form of domination.[61]

The emphasis on the primary obedience to God as ultimate authority is biblically grounded and creates a church committed to finding God's will. However, obedience to God and obedience to human authority within the church can easily be confused. The language of obedience and servanthood has also made it easy to ignore the mediation of human leadership and to deny its exercise of power.[62] Moreover, an idealistic view of authority within the church has discouraged it from wrestling with the needs of leaders and with the various power relationships that are present within every community. Several examples: Mennonites have identified with Jesus and his life and teachings, creating in the process an ideal model for discipleship, but they have failed to include the fallible disciples in that model. They have written an ideal Anabaptist history while ignoring many of the actual Anabaptists. They have promoted an ideal theology of ministry that has hesitated to name the political patterns of relationships in church institutions. Thus, the existence of domination is denied, and necessary authority is undermined.

Suspicion of, and obedience toward, authority can easily become partners in a game, creating an ethos of domination and submission within a community. This is so when these strategies give or take authority from the other on the basis of stereotypes or truth claims that are considered absolute and therefore not open to further insight. These static truths become the justification for creating clear boundaries around the team and for insisting on unquestioned conformity to norms of behavior and belief for all members of the team—a rigid set of rules. Attention is diverted from the variety of ways in which authoritative relationships can be experienced, to a unified ethical system based on obedience to one norm. Thus a game is created in which the dynamic transformation of the team itself is stifled.

This struggle between a transformative impulse and a separatist impulse must be traced back to the understanding of God that informs this theology. Not only is the notion of a uniform church evident in Mennonite theology, but so also is a view of God that can be described in terms that are absolute and uniform. For example, Waldemar Janzen has suggested that the Mennonite tendency to see the Old Testament as superseded by the New Testament is based on the church not wanting its inner tranquility to be disturbed by the "realism of the Old Testament in which God's activity cannot be disentangled from history, war and judgment!"[63] At times even the picture of Jesus has been stylized in Mennonite theology so that the complex nature of the authority and power of Jesus is hidden in the image of a nonresistant man who willingly gives up power. Jesus' powerful healings and his authoritative leadership of his disciples tend to be ignored when speaking about the "way of the cross." In addition, the dynamic work of the Holy Spirit has often been separated from a static understanding of the Jesus of the Bible. Strong dualisms can often be traced to an oversimplified image of God.

J. Lawrence Burkholder and Gordon Kaufman are two Mennonite theologians who have questioned the separatist direction of the Mennonite theological game. Burkholder, in his discussion of the moral ambiguities created by his strong sense of social responsibility, and Kaufman, in his insistence on the human aspect of all theology, encourage a solidarity with others in the search for strategies that embody positive power and authority.[64] These thinkers have encouraged a dynamic theological game that must grow and change as it engages with a world searching for more humane modes of power and authority. The contrasting directions of transformation and separatism have opened a number of options to players of the game today. Naming the Mennonite theological game "In Search of God's Kingdom Incarnate" might be helpful, for this slogan can remind us that "thy kingdom come on earth as it is in heaven" is a prayer more than a truth claim, and that "the Word become flesh" happens at God's initiative more than ours.

***

SINGING A SUBVERSIVE SONG OF HOPE[65]

The language that I hear in church today has changed rather dramatically from the language that I grew up with. The words "obedience" and "service" were some of the most used words in the theology that I heard from the pulpit in my growing up years, albeit in German. These were the right response to a God who loved us and saved us. Mennonite Central Committee (MCC) with its motto of "service in the name of Christ" was held up as the goal of all of life, not only for times when we formally worked for that organization. These were strong biblical words that Mennonites used to describe our response to God and that were often misused to insist on the same response to persons of authority. Today I only seldom hear the word service, and obedience is generally only heard in the older hymns that we still sing. Now many Mennonites speak more of love, justice, peacebuilding, and hospitality as ways to follow Jesus. How has this change come about?

Generally, we assume that changes in language come about very slowly. For example, the language for God continues to be very male, even though there has been a growing consensus in theological circles that God is not male. But we also know that certain words that were once popular or over-used quickly lose their charm and are discarded. Even terms such as inclusivity are beginning to lose their significance because they do not adequately express the fullness of what is meant.

In our postmodern world, words such as obedience and service have been associated primarily with a hierarchal world view which our culture has rejected, at least theoretically. The question that was uppermost for me when I wrote this paper was: can our theological language be redeemed or must it be changed completely? A second question was equally important for me: what do we do with Scripture passages that have undermined the mutuality between women and men? Do we ignore these passages, reinterpret them, or formally excise them from our theology?

I have become more and more convinced of the power of language not only to change ideas and attitudes but to help dismantle dominant social structures and to envision new ways of relating to each other. The term subversive is chosen deliberately for the title of this paper to speak of the way some of these terms that we use without thinking can be changed or used in a different way. Subversion implies a reversal or overthrowing of something in order to transform the social order and its power, authority, and hierarchy. Today as I reflect on these terms, I wonder what happens with the loss of these words. Should obedience be taken out of our vocabulary completely in terms of our response to God? Is there never a time to "trust and obey?"

This paper was written for a "Women Doing Theology" conference that was attempting to envision an inclusive theology of service. I meant it to be a creative response to the dissonance that we find in our theological language and our experience. The use of the metaphor of music was an attempt to relate to the many ways in which change comes about: through music, art, dance, and, perhaps least of all, rational language about God. I continue to wrestle with how to bring our complete selves into the theology-making that we all do as we seek to name God in our experience.

***

Introduction

The overall title for these conference presentations intrigued me: *Embracing Hope: Envisioning an Inclusive Theology of Service.* I immediately noted the way it "embraces" both feminist theology and Mennonite tradition. After all, inclusivity has become a code word for feminist theological convictions, an ethos of that community of dialogue. At the same time, no Mennonite will likely question my statement that "service" is still a politically correct term in Mennonite circles. But the title also hints that there is a certain discomfort when inclusivity and service are put into the same sentence. Inclusive service is not yet a reality in either feminist or Mennonite circles. Thus these conversations among women who feel caught between opposite convictions are intended to create a new vision and theology of service. Perhaps this dialogue may yet lead to a song of hope and joy.

Two overarching methodological moves frame this paper. Part I is a critical analysis of the experience of service. New aspects of service are visible if those who serve step back for a moment from the immediacy of their experience in order to ask questions about what is really happening in those interactions. My observations come primarily from my own experience from within the Mennonite church. Thus when I use the term "we" I am referring to Mennonite women. However, all women and men are invited to reflect on their experience of service.

This analysis can lead to a second methodological move, a re-examination of the theology that supports our notions of service. Mennonite theology has primarily been based on biblical texts heard over and over again in the preaching and teaching within our churches. Many Mennonite women, however, feel alienated from this theology. For example, they struggle with theological notions such as understanding service as a "giving away of one's self," holding up martyrdom as the ideal of service, and evaluating any admission of one's own needs as selfish. The discussion at this "Women Doing Theology" conference confirmed this alienation. In Part II of this paper, we will reread key biblical texts with eyes more aware of the complexities of the notion of service in order to begin the process of rethinking our theology.

The title of my presentation, "Singing a Subversive Song of Hope," uses the imagery of music to help us envision service in a different key. Music includes both consonant and dissonant chords. When we place our experience and the biblical text side by side, we can hear the dissonant chords most clearly. Sometimes we wonder if the song that is produced can ever become harmonious again. Yet I believe it is in paying attention to the tension and discord that we can again hear the voice of God. The discernment of this voice of God must come from an inclusive community that is ready to begin by listening. At first we may hear only songs of domination and servitude. But perhaps, as we listen closely, we will find the familiar pattern of notes and rhythms disrupted. The pattern that has been practiced endlessly will slowly give way to a new rhythm, a different harmonization, or even a new melody line. Though the first notes of our new composition may be sung with hesitation, I hope we will find the courage to sing and dance together, each of us contributing to the whole. The song will be one of hospitality and of freedom, of receiving and giving, of justice and communion because it will be based on the kind of love that God has shown us.

I. An Analysis of the Experience of Service

The term "service" is overused in our society. When I read the daily newspaper, a textbook, or the church bulletin, I note that all of them use "service" as a kind of short-hand for actions and practices assumed to be related to each other by some common core. My dictionary suggests twenty basic meanings, ranging from work done for a master or superior to a branch of the United States Armed Forces. In its ideal meaning, service is something a person does for someone else, thus at least temporarily preferring the other's good to one's own. Sandra Schneiders suggests that service is essentially an act of self-gift, of love in its purest form, since the ultimate preferring of another's good would be giving one's life for another.[66]

Rarely, however, do we experience service as the pure self-gift of another. Other models of service have been created that allow many variations on this theme, yet continue to convey the image of self-giving and caring for the other. Service has become a slippery term, used glibly to sanctify various actions, practices, and institutions. Thus we are confused, often not sure where love for the other and love for ourselves overlap. In addition, the ambiguity of the term allows meanings from one realm of life to contaminate or erode ideal meanings in another realm. For example, how exactly is serving as CEO in a corporation related to serving as a volunteer in a nursing home?

I want to illuminate the complexity of our uses of the term "service" by examining three models present in our society and churches from a simple phenomenological point of view. [67] Underlying all of these is service as a relationship between persons or institutions—a relationship that includes elements of power and authority.[68] I will pay particular attention to the boundaries assumed in each model that separate people from each other. This will help us decide whether and how each model is inclusive or exclusive. Of course, "inclusivity" and "exclusivity" have their own problems of definition. Inclusivity can range from mere tolerance to indifference to a hearty welcome of the other. But inclusion and service overlap in their common focus on relationships and their common entanglement with power.

1. Service arising from a condition of inequality (servitude from "beneath")

In this model the servant must perform a "service" for the other because of some basic right or power which the latter is understood to possess. For example, a child in relation to parents, a slave in relation to a master, a laborer in relation to the boss. In every case the service arises because of a basic condition of inequality, and the service rendered tends to re-enforce this inequality in status. A child washes the dishes because her mother demands it. A woman serves coffee during breakfast because her husband claims such service is his right, a mother on social assistance works as a volunteer because the government forces her to do so in order to receive a basic income. All of these arise out of a structure of assumed rights and duties. Though the demands may be benevolently intended, the inclination is for exploitation to take over. This is because the one higher in the hierarchy has the freedom to choose what the service will be and how it will be done. In addition, coercion and violence may be used to enforce this service from the one deemed subordinate. Whether overtly or subtly, pressure is put on the one beneath in the social hierarchy to conform to the will of the one above.

In this model the boundaries between people may be part of external institutional structures. More often, however, they are part of an inner class structure we have incorporated into our subconscious mind. Usually external and internal structures re-enforce each other and both persons accept the invisible boundaries that define this class system. A woman assumes her husband has the right to be served his coffee first, the man assumes it is her duty to serve him. Persons of European ancestry assume they have the right to the best hotels, persons of African ancestry assume they will serve in these same hotels. Laws of apartheid or patriarchy are not needed when such class structures are internalized.

In this model exclusion and inclusion are determined by how well people stay within the expected roles, how well they give up making their own choices. All can be included—if they respect the role that is given them. If the poor serve the rich, all can live together in harmony. If the uneducated comply with the will of the educated, there will be no hassle.

Sometimes there is an attempt at making these structures seem more equal by paying the one who serves or by naming the service something else. However, then the inequality is only more subtle and possibly more cruel. I may leave a tip at the restaurant, but I have clearly conceded to an invisible class system in the high-handed way I have addressed the waiter. The boss may name his secretary his "administrative assistant," but this does not change the possibility that she will be fired if she questions any of his demands. In addition, the remuneration given for her work only underlines the low value placed on her service.

In North America, it is an assumption of equality that makes this kind of service particularly open to exploitation. In our society, equality really means that everyone is equally welcome to compete for the top positions.[69] The competition is however already rigged to exclude those regarded as lower on the social scale. Someone who is disabled is welcome to apply for the higher position, but the demands of the job must be fulfilled in the same way as before. An aboriginal person can apply for any job, but loss of dignity stolen through centuries of abuse, lack of a formal education, and subtle prejudices keep most indigenous people in lower paying jobs. Since the ones on top have the power to determine the norm, exclusion happens.

This model of service breeds competition and power struggles as well as domination and oppression. Those on a lower social scale do all they can to please those higher up, often compromising their own ethical standards so that they can climb up one rung. In this model we compete for status and prestige, not always realizing that even when we succeed, we have only succeeded in becoming an oppressor as well. Most of us will recognize our involvement in this model of service. The crucial question, however, is whether and how this model can be transformed into service that is truly a freely chosen gift of the self to the other.

2. Service arising because of the need of the other (service from "above")

In this second model, service denotes "what the server does freely for the served because of some need perceived in the latter which the former has the power to meet."[70] This is the service a professional renders to a client, a parent to a child, the rich to the poor, the healthy to the sick. Often the appeals for charity that we hear from the church are built on this assumption. The need is so great! You have the ability to meet this need. Be compassionate! Come and serve!

Doesn't this model realize the ideal of service—the unforced seeking of the other's good? And isn't it built on a notion of equalizing assets? Giving to those who do not have by those who have? At its best, this model does suggest a sharing of resources that can lead to deeper relationships of equality. The choice to serve can be free, because the power to choose is given to the one doing the serving. However, it is within this inequality that the subtle temptation of this model lies. What seems like unselfish service contains the seeds of corruption, because the one who serves can easily seek her own good by "detouring" through service to the other. As a parent, I use my child to satisfy my own intimacy needs, as a pastor I view congregational members as needy sheep because this feeds my ego. We even give away our clothes to the "needy" so that our consciences won't bother us when we get new and better clothes for ourselves. No wonder this kind of service is sometimes rejected or at least resisted.

Domination happens in this model when people are stereotyped or placed in the static roles of either "giver" or "needy." Those being served begin to see themselves as dependent, as helpless victims, not recognizing what resources they do have. Those serving view themselves as magnanimous givers, not admitting their own needs. Being rich or poor, educated or uneducated begins to indicate the kind of value accorded one's personhood, one's status on a social scale, rather than simply the kind of resources one has to share. These temptations are particularly dangerous in cases of chronic need. When dignity is taken away, power-plays based on stereotypes begin to happen. Domination, by the supposedly stronger person, partners with manipulation, by the supposedly weaker person, to destroy any kind of healthy relationship that could develop.

The term "servant leadership" that has recently become popular in management and organizational theory recognizes that most people in this model serve via institutions that facilitate or restrain their service.[71] We serve as elders or pastors in a church, as teachers in a school, or as nurses in a hospital. Our service is dictated by the institution rather than only by the particular needs of someone else. However, here too the institution tends to enlarge the power of the one serving rather than that of the one being served. "Servant leadership," with its focus on the one assumed to have the strength and power to facilitate change, can thus easily mask oppressive strategies. This is possibly why boundaries are much talked about in this model. The misuse of power has created the need for strong guidelines for professional conduct. It is now understood that the lack of choice given to those being served provides opportunities for abuse, including sexual or physical abuse. Learning self-care is also a popular notion among professional caregivers.

Learning to express one's own needs and finding ways to care for oneself is crucial when one's vocation consists primarily of giving to others. Women, who have been socialized to be givers and have also internalized low self-esteem, are particularly prone to put the need of others before their own.[72] However, the notion of self-care can also hide an unwillingness to see the "client" as more than a receiver of service. It can cover up the power of the professional who refuses to draw on the gifts of the larger community, preferring instead to be the hero in the good Samaritan story. Thus, self-care can move into two directions: it can open us to receive as well as give; or it can create barriers to more mutual relationships in our service.

Inclusion in this model is determined by the people serving, since they have the power to determine both what is named as legitimate need and how that need should be met. Thus the church can decide who to serve in the broader community and what kind of service will be provided, while recipients of the service must quietly (and thankfully) accept what is offered. Again, a kind of artificial equality can be created by paying the server for the service, as in that provided by a professional such as a doctor, nurse, or lawyer. However, the basis of this model is still inequality, with the professional in charge of the interaction.

Exclusion happens in this second model when patterns of relationship develop in which some are exclusively named as givers or as self-sufficient while others are named as receivers or needy. This is readily illustrated by our response as a church to people with a different sexual orientation. To a specific need for acceptance and dialogue as expressed by homosexual persons, the church has responded by stereotyping all those who are homosexual as needy of conversion and salvation, implying that the rest of the church is healthy. This allows the church to exclude gays and lesbians from service through the church without looking at the gifts and commitments of individuals. Consider other general terms, such as "handicapped" or even "senior citizen," that are used to characterize people so that their individuality is lost and thus their individual choices are precluded. The temptation to stop the movement toward equality in the guise of service is real, because being on top has its benefits.

This model of service is probably the most prevalent in both the contemporary church and the larger society. Can it be transformed, so that service can truly be received as an expression of love and caring rather than experienced as dominating power?

3. A model of solidarity and friendship (service based on equality)

Sandra Schneiders suggests that friendship is the one relationship based on equality. If friends do not begin as equals, they quickly abolish whatever inequality they discover or they make their differences serve mutual goals within the structure of the relationship. In interactions between them, the good of the other is truly the good of oneself. But this self-fulfillment is not the result of a singular pursuit of one's own goals; rather, by receiving love as well as giving it, the happiness of both is assured. Service in this model is freely chosen both by the giver and the receiver. Therefore, it is liberating and freeing. At its best, service between friends affirms equality and promotes mutual dignity, is not demanded and creates no debts, expects no return but freely evokes reciprocity. Perhaps that is why true friendship is so rare and so precious.

Can this third model be extended to persons with whom we cannot naturally share the intimacy we experience within a freely chosen friendship? Can it be extended to institutional relationships? The term "solidarity" is sometimes used to express the kind of relationship we have with another based on the equality and dignity of each person. We stand with another, not above or beneath. Solidarity characterizes the relationship that puts all the gifts of individual persons at the service of the community or institution for the good of each as it is needed. Solidarity describes an interdependence of everyone, where the dignity of each is enhanced, and where coercion and violence are not needed to call anyone to serve.

Service within a relationship of equality cannot easily be institutionalized. Instead, barriers and boundaries are overcome when deliberate moves are made toward equality in status. Many of us have seen how a hierarchical relationship between a so-called boss and his administrative assistant begins to shift when both are involved in setting goals and making decisions that affect both. Even while responsibility is divided so that a diversity of gifts is recognized, the solidarity created can overcome status differences. Even service which might be considered servile and menial can be transformed into a loving action when friendship is at its basis. The seemingly one-sided service given by a loving daughter to her aging mother attests to this fact.

This model is not something that is achieved once and for all; rather, it must become a dynamic force that works itself out in practice. We can recognize solidarity when competition is lessened, co-operation increases, and stereotypes disappear. We see it blossom when decision-making is extended to everyone concerned with an issue. In communities where solidarity reigns, service is dynamic, continually creating new opportunities as gifts are discovered, developed, and used for the good of all.

What about exclusion and inclusion? Because service in the third model is freely given and freely received, it cannot be coerced or forced. Both partners in the relationship must be involved in establishing the mutuality on which solidarity and friendship depend. Thus service here invites and welcomes others. However, the rate of refusal is high, because it is costly to give up seeing oneself in terms of rights, duties, power, or needs. Thus those who do not wish to risk refusal of their gifts, or to accept the dependency inherent in receiving, never experience the gift of true friendship. They are excluded from this model because the cost of interdependency seems too high.

This model of service emerges when relationships between people and institutions are open to dynamic growth and transformation. Hope comes as individual examples create new possibilities for the transformation of institutional structures. There is always the danger that the ensuing conflict and tension will result in a call for a more stable model of service, one that will continue to dominate, oppress, and exclude many while espousing love and goodwill. Yet hope can be sustained when we see the signs of dynamic movement toward mutuality among us.

II. A Rereading of "Service" Texts

It seems to me that many Mennonite women have learned to sing a song of service that affirms subservience and submission or else duty and guilt.[73] This song is made up of a variety of melodies that communicated to us that our service was inadequate and meaningless, that we were not doing nearly enough nor denying ourselves enough. Or alternatively we were doing more than we should, creating dependency or interfering in another person's life.

This song is constructed from a variety of scriptural texts that have been connected to each other to form a complete hymn—a song that, though unsatisfying even to ourselves, we continue to sing for other people. We have forgotten that we have access to the raw materials, and that we too can contribute to the composition of the hymn we sing. We have forgotten that change need not come about by having an "ideal" song imposed from "above." Instead, each individual can initiate change by changing her own contribution to the song. One new note or different rhythm can disrupt a whole pattern of music. As others in the choir begin to hear the disruptive melody being inserted, as they note a different harmonization or recognize a unique rhythm, they are invited to respond to those changes. Hope for a new song begins with that first small change that is deliberately made. Improvisation by others must then follow, because the music cannot go on as before.

In this section, I want to examine our old patterns of singing and to ask whether a new theology of service can be composed. I will reread key Scripture passages that have formed the pattern of notes we name our song of service, but in the context of our experience of service and in light of the models of service just examined. This step begins the formation of an alternative theology of service by disrupting our usual interpretations. It invites women to continue the process of interpretation by participating in the detailed historical analysis that is needed as well as in the ongoing hermeneutical process and conversation. As we do this we may be able to recognize the patterns that don't fit, or to discover new notes that should be included even when they at first sound dissonant. Perhaps we can yet compose a song that welcomes others into a choir of spontaneity and joy.

(1) Masters and slaves, husbands and wives, fathers and children, leaders and

followers: Singing a subversive note in relationships of service "from beneath"

> Be subject to one another out of reverence for Christ.... Wives, be subject to your husbands as you are to the Lord.... Husbands, love your wives, just as Christ loved the church and gave himself up for her.... Slaves, obey your earthly masters with fear and trembling, in singleness of heart, as you obey Christ: not only while being watched, and in order to please them, but as slaves of Christ, doing the will of God from the heart. Render service with enthusiasm, as to the Lord and not to men and women, knowing that whatever good we do, we will receive the same again from the Lord, whether we are slaves or free. And masters, do the same to them. Stop threatening them, for you know that both of you have the same Master in heaven and with him there is no partiality. (Excerpts from Ephesians 5-6)

> But you are not to be called rabbi, for you have one teacher, and you are all students. And call no one your father on earth, for you have one Father—the one in heaven. Nor are you to be called instructors, for you have one instructor, the Messiah. The greatest among you will be your servant. All who exalt themselves will be humbled, and all who humble themselves will be exalted.... But woe to you, blind guides...hypocrites! (Excerpts from Matthew 23)

> "Greetings, favored one! The Lord is with you." ...Then Mary said, "Here am I, the servant of the Lord.... My soul magnifies the Lord and my spirit rejoices in God my Savior, for he has looked with favour on the lowliness of his servant...for the Mighty One has done great things for me." (Excerpts from Luke 1:26-56)

Usually the words "be subject," "obey," and "service" jump out at us as we read the passage from Ephesians. We have often read those verses assuming that the writer is speaking primarily to the ones "beneath," telling them to obey and serve. Probably no passages have been used more often to ensure servanthood than this passage from Ephesians and parallel passages in Colossians and 1 Peter, often called the "Household Codes." Clearly, these imperatives fall into the "servitude model" since they assume a hierarchy where service happens from beneath, service in which women obey husbands, children obey parents, and servants obey masters. Throughout church history, those above have used these household codes to ensure service by those below. And that was easy to do, since the hierarchical pattern of relationships was assumed to be blessed by God, who took the highest place on this ladder.

Yet a more careful reading of the passage uncovers a subversive note that begins to disrupt the all-pervasive tone of servitude.[74] The assumption of ultimate loyalty to the one above is questioned. The passage suggests there is only one master whom you need to reverence and obey—that is God, shown in Christ Jesus. By implication this means that other so-called masters do not make the final evaluation of service you render. Though God is clearly understood as above humans in the divine/human relationship, this does not imply a God who demands service because it is his right. Instead, service is to a God who came to us in Christ, the very self-gift of God. This God shows no partiality to any one class of humans. Both masters and slaves, both women and men must answer to God directly. Therefore, the phrase "be subject to one another" also begins to subvert the competition associated with the first model outlined in Part I. Climbing to the top by trying to please the one above does not yet solve the problem of servitude.

However, is this enough? Has the writer understood the essence of service? Is he only describing the usual social hierarchy or is he justifying it? Is his relocation of ultimate loyalty strong enough to create a shift in these institutional relationships, especially if God is also seen as a Lord and Master whom one must obey without question?

The passage from Matthew is taken from one of the most angry, scathing speeches of Jesus. Over and over, he lashes out at the leaders, the Pharisees, who place burdens on people while they themselves seek honour and privilege. So angry is Jesus that he suggests that naming someone "boss" (whether a rabbi, a father, or an instructor) creates a situation in which that boss can rule over you. Instead, Jesus insists that only God is your master. Under God's reign all are students, all are children. Moreover, under God's reign the usual hierarchy will be turned upside down; the one on top will serve, the one at the bottom will be honoured.

This passage disrupts the dominant social hierarchy much more radically than the Ephesians passage but does it with similar logic. Only God is above you, therefore you are equal. This implies that the usual categories of status and privilege no longer apply. Woe to those who insist that privilege based on status still applies when God is the ruler! Woe to those who are blind, who do not see the new, social/political situation that God is bringing! Woe to leaders

who build their status in order that others should serve! But even more than that, this text assures the ones serving that, in the final analysis, the last shall be first and the first last. Insiders shall become outsiders; outsiders, insiders. In the longer view of Christ's eschatological reign, justice will prevail. And because we can begin to envision this new reality we can live without earthly masters. Is this enough to inject hope in those who live in servitude?

The third passage is a personal testimony of the joy that comes with true servanthood of God. According to Luke, Mary is overjoyed to be counted among the Servants of God, those to whom God has revealed Godself in a special way, those who have been chosen and empowered to serve God. Just as the kings and prophets were called servants of God—she too would receive the power to do the task God had called her to. I believe her acceptance of the invitation to become the mother of Jesus was not coerced or forced. Instead, the Magnificat testifies to God's role in overthrowing the usual hierarchical relationships. Somehow she has experienced that in her calling to be the mother of Jesus.

As I reread these passages, I felt a sense of despair that throughout history, the Mennonite church has not listened to the subversion begun in them. Instead, the church has often used these verses to support the social patterns of a dominant culture by appealing to the Lordship of God. Leaders have insisted that menial service is for those at the bottom of the social scale, that sacrifice and the way of the cross are for those already serving from beneath. Service to God has been interpreted as part of this hierarchical pattern: God as the great "boss" in the sky insists on our service because it is his right to do so. Is this because masters were in control of the interpretation? Is it because it has been too difficult for slaves to live according to an inner freedom? Is it because personal autonomy can be reached only if status is bestowed by other humans? In any case, it seems that the revolutionary notion that only God the Creator is beyond us, that Christ is Lord, has not yet upset the hierarchies of servitude in the church.[75]

Perhaps a change of masters is not enough if we continue to serve "from beneath" with God on top of a domineering hierarchy. However, a subversive note sung by those considered weak can still be powerful enough to change the way God is described in the song. If those in servitude begin to sing this new description of God loudly even for themselves, they will begin to subvert the whole song. We know of the power of the songs of slaves who succeeded in moving toward external freedom by first claiming their own inner freedom and God's promise of the upside down kingdom. Giving our loyalty to God can relativize all other claims to superiority, beginning a larger song of liberation.

(2) Rich and poor, strong and weak, adults and children, healthy and sick: Singing a subversive note in relationships of service "from above"

> "If any want to become my followers, let them deny themselves and take up their cross and follow me.... Whoever wants to be first must be last of all and servant of all." Then he took a child and put it among them; and taking it in his arms, he said to them, "Whoever welcomes one such child in my name welcomes me and whoever welcomes me welcomes not me but the one who sent me...." John said to him,

> "Teacher, we saw someone casting out demons in your name, and we tried to stop him, because he was not following us." But Jesus said, "Do not stop him; for no one who does a deed of power in my name will be able soon afterward to speak evil of me.... For truly I tell you, whoever gives you a cup of water to drink because you bear the name of Christ will by no means lose the reward.... You know that among the Gentiles those whom they recognize as their rulers lord it over them. But it is not so among you; but whoever wishes to be first among you must be slave of all. For the Son of Man came not to be served, but to give his life a ransom for many." (Excerpts from Mark 8-10)

> Then the righteous will answer him, "Lord, when was it when we saw you hungry and gave you food, or thirsty and gave you something to drink? And when was it that we saw you a stranger and welcomed you, or naked and gave you clothing? And when was it that we saw you sick or in prison and visited you?" And the king will answer them, "Truly I tell you, just as you did it to one of the least of these who are members of my family, you did it to me." (Excerpt from Matthew 25)

> But wanting to justify himself, [the lawyer] asked Jesus, "But who is my neighbor?" Jesus replied, "A man was going from Jerusalem to to Jericho, and fell into the hands of robbers, who stripped him, beat him, and went away, leaving him half dead... a priest...passed by... a Levite...passed by.... But a Samaritan while traveling, came near him and when he saw him, he was moved with pity. He went to him and bandaged his wounds. (Excerpt from Luke 10)

I was surprised at how differently I read this set of passages when I realized which model of service they assumed. If read in terms of the first model, by those who have little choice and are already at the bottom of the social scale, terms like "deny yourself," "take up your cross," and "become a slave and servant" enforce servitude and suffering and justify domination and oppression. However, as I reread the verses in their larger literary context, I realized that these words are not addressed to those at the bottom of the social scale. The texts in Mark and Matthew are addressed to an inner circle of followers, particularly to the leadership group of twelve disciples, who had been empowered to heal and teach. The passage in Luke is addressed to a lawyer, someone with high status within his community. These words are spoken to leaders, and they address the temptations of those who would help the so-called "needy." The model assumed is service "from above." The passages in Mark are particularly interesting because small, seemingly insignificant incidents are placed side by side with comments by Jesus, that help us see the impact of those incidents. The disciples argue about who is the greatest, they send away children who wish to be blessed by Jesus, they are jealous of others who are also healing in the name of Jesus, they ask to have the highest places in glory. Jesus responds in a number of ways that subvert this view of service.

First of all, Jesus suggests that the kind of service he calls for can only be done through a denial of one's own selfish goals, such as gaining crowns in the kingdom or climbing higher on the social scale. Secondly, Jesus renames the "needy ones" as first in the kingdom. Welcoming a child is like welcoming their master, Jesus. Feeding the hungry or visiting those in prison is like doing this for a king. He also renames those doing the serving. They are not the ones usually named the servants of God, the Priests or Levites. Instead, they are the outsiders, the Samaritans, who recognize the neighbor in the wounded person from Judea. Stereotyping persons as "needy" or "givers" is rejected. Third, Jesus suggests that givers must also be receivers. I had always thought that the motto "in the name of Christ" came from a Scripture passage suggesting how followers of Christ were to give. Here Jesus turns this saying around and suggests that whoever gives a cup of cold water to us—to the ones who bear the name of Christ, to the disciples—will not lose a reward. Here the disciples are the receivers who should respect the givers. Finally, Jesus addresses the temptation to control the service, to keep power within one's own circle, to exclude others from ministry by suggesting that we become as slaves. Be willing to serve in menial ways. He thus turns the values of leaders upside down, and asks them to truly serve others according to their need instead of only according to what the leaders wish to give.

Thus in a variety of ways, Jesus unmasks the face of service "from above," allowing us to see the power abuse that is possible in a ministry to those who have less. So, why have these verses so often been used to enforce servitude, rather than to unmask power moves? Maybe we need a different term which will not so easily hide the power dynamics involved in this kind of "service from above."

Does it make a difference if we understand these words as addressed only to those who serve because they have received much? Does it make a difference if we name the power they have to choose and make decisions about who is needy and whether they will meet that need? Will anything change if we reject the stereotyping that often accompanies this kind of giving? Can these stories be subversive enough so that those who have the power to exclude others from service or from being served will see themselves and their own need? Will it make any difference if the particular temptations that leaders have to misuse power, under the guise of altruism, are named? Perhaps I am most skeptical that this model can be changed because I can identify with it most readily. I know how difficult it is to be transformed at the core of our being so that the resources and power we have can be truly shared. However, I also know that a compassionate sharing of resources can begin to shift systems of oppression and domination.

Possibly the most subversive note that can be sung by those who serve from above is giving up the right to define the need of the other. Instead, true vulnerability comes when resources and need are named through conversation and dialogue in which both the one serving and the one in need can participate. This is a radical notion. Can you imagine the rich and poor together going through our closets to see which clothes should be shared? A song of mutuality can grow when room is given for this conversation. Melodies of service that truly meet the need of the other can then be composed. Perhaps solidarity can come from this kind of compassionate and vulnerable service.

(3) Perfume and hair, basin and towel: symbols of mutual service within relationships of equal status

> Mary took a pound of costly perfume made of pure nard, anointed Jesus' feet, and wiped them with her hair.… Judas Iscariot, one of the disciples, …said, "Why was this perfume not sold for three hundred denarii and the money given to the poor? (Excerpt from John 12)

> He [Jesus] poured water into a basin and began to wash his disciples' feet and to wipe them with the towel that was tied around him. He came to Simon Peter, who said to him, "Lord, are you going to wash my feet? … You will never wash my feet." (Excerpt from John 13)

> This is my commandment, that you love one another as I have loved you. No one has greater love than this, to lay down one's life for one's friends.… I do not call you servants any longer, because the servant does not know what the master is doing; but I have called you friends, because I have made known to you everything that I have heard from the Father. (Excerpt from John 15)

The basin and towel have long been important symbols of service for Mennonites. These symbols have been used to suggest that we "let go of pride and worldly power" and that we "take on the role of servant" and "humbly" wash each other's feet as Jesus has done.[76] These symbols have been powerful for me as well, though with a slight difference in interpretation. Nine years ago at the first "Women Doing Theology" conference, I suggested there were actually two foot washings in the gospel of John.[77] The first occurs when Mary washes Jesus' feet with perfume and dries it with her hair. The second occurs when Jesus washes the feet of his disciples and dries them with a towel. It may be helpful to look again at these stories in terms of the models of service that we have outlined.

The best clue to the model that underlies these stories arises from the objections to the foot washings in each story. In the first one, Judas objects because Mary should have given the money to the poor. In other words, Mary is seen as a benefactor of the poor, as someone who normally serves from above. We know from the gospel of Luke that rich women gave of their resources to the disciple community around Jesus. Mary, Martha, and Lazarus seem to be from this group of benefactors—a comfortable arrangement for Judas who kept the books. But here Mary disrupts the comfortable social scale. She has recognized Jesus' need for love during this dangerous time in Jerusalem. She takes the perfume and washes Jesus feet, suggesting that this leader can also be needy. Even more daringly, with her intimate action Mary boldly enters the inner circle of disciples. Hierarchical boundaries between men and women are freely crossed. Though female, she claims her place as a disciple right beside Jesus. Mary serves from a place of equality, ignoring the status that others want to give her. And Jesus responds by receiving this love as it is given.

In the second story, just a chapter later and also at a supper, Jesus pours water in a basin and begins to wash his disciples' feet. Again there is a strong objection. Again it is a male disciple who objects. This time, Peter vigorously objects to the foot washing. To understand why, recall the customs of the time. Slaves usually brought in the basins and water, and the guests would wash their own feet. However, sometimes one person would voluntarily wash the feet of someone else, for example, a beloved rabbi, as a sign of deep love and respect. Again this was in intimate action, one reserved for close friends. Why did Peter object to this foot washing? Was it really because he did not want to do the same? Or was it because he had put Jesus on a false hierarchical pedestal, and was uncomfortable with the shift in an established social pattern that Jesus was suggesting? Peter has a model of relationships where there is a clear "above" and "below," each with clearly defined roles. Clearly, Jesus is above and Peter below. For Peter to wash Jesus' feet would have been fine in this situation. The model of service from below would be intact. However, Jesus upsets the expected normal roles. Peter cannot handle this confusion of social order, nor the level of intimacy suggested by this model.

These two stories together contribute to a model of service that is mutual. In these chapters in John, Jesus is described as deliberately moving from servanthood to friendship in his relationships with the disciples. Jesus is pictured as freely receiving service and freely giving service, both extended as a gift of love. "I do not call you servants any longer…but I have called you friends" (John 15:15). Jesus is saying: My love for you has meant that I willingly give myself to you as a gift. I have shared my knowledge of God's will with you freely and lovingly. We are now in communion with each other, a communion in which service is not commanded but embraced. I long to receive this same kind of love from you. In fact, my hope is that this kind of mutual love can become the norm of service relationships within the community of followers, even after my death. Again, a deep sadness fills me as I observe the hierarchical barriers dividing those within the church from each other, even when they serve. Yet I continue to hope. The symbols of perfume and hair, basin and towel continue to feed my imagination so that I can begin to envision a community in which solidarity and love overcome objections based on false social norms.

Conclusion

I wonder if the experience of mutuality in caring communities, pointed to by the symbol of foot washing, could prepare us to sing a subversive note in the many situations in which we find ourselves. Perhaps the predominant models of service can yet be disrupted and transformed. Perhaps the glimpse of God we have received through Jesus can move us to sing again of service as hospitality and freedom, as receiving and giving, as sharing and communion. It will take courage to sing that first tentative note, because that note will produce dissonance in the monotonous and mournful song of servitude and domination that we are used to. But perhaps, as we sing, we will be joined by others and the melody of service can create a dance of joy. May we embrace this hope as we invite each other to sing a song of friendship and solidarity.

Chapter 7. Dialogue

NAMING THE CHALLENGES OF DIALOGUE

The year 2000 represented not only a new century for me but also a shift in context and perspective. I spent the first six months of that year in Egypt and Iran, and they became the impetus for a year of reflection and reprioritising the direction of my vocational pursuits. The following is an excerpt from a sermon that I preached which reflects the looking back and looking ahead that was happening to me that year.

> *Picture this scene if you can! A plum orchard in a small village half way up a mountain just outside of the desert city of Kashan in Eastern Iran. The village, also known as the rose petal water capital of Iran is pleasant and cool on this hot day in May. Rose petal water—a refreshing drink, well known for its medicinal properties—is the reason many people take this winding drive up the mountain. A colorful Persian carpet is spread in the middle of a grove of plum trees; platters of food, including barbequed shish kabobs with rice and vegetables, small green cucumbers, flat crisp Iranian bread, and jugs of cool rose petal water tea are placed into the middle of the carpet! Seated on the carpet are several people. One is a Muslim clergyman dressed in a long grey robe. Next a woman in the traditional black hijab that must be worn by all women in Iran, even visitors—a veil that covers everything except the face. The third person you will probably recognize as a Mennonite pastor, dressed in casual pants and short sleeve shirt, typical North American style—he has admitted just a touch of jealousy on this trip of the more exotic dress of the other two, and has fantasized that he is an Anglican priest in full vestments. And last, a Turkish Muslim chauffeur holding down the fourth corner of the carpet. Now you look more closely at the woman and yes, you think you recognize her. Her difficulty in sitting on a carpet for any length of time betrays her as a foreigner, somewhat unsure of how to manage her flowing robes while she eats eagerly of the delicious food.*

> *The meal is finished and it is time for the afternoon nap. Each person takes a corner of the carpet, stretches out, and relaxes. The Muslim clergy man has hung his white turban on one of the plum trees and is stretched out, already asleep. The woman cannot sleep, despite the soothing chirping of the birds, the almost intoxicating smell of rose blossoms, and the gently gurgling of a small stream near by. She looks up in the branches above her and remembers other orchards. Peach and cherry orchards in Niagara! Crab-apple trees and choke-cherry bushes in Alberta. And two lone apple trees in a back yard in Toronto. "How did I ever get from the peach orchard in Niagara to this plum orchard in Iran?" she wonders. "What am I doing here?"*

The last few years as director of the Toronto Mennonite Theological Centre (TMTC) had been intense and I had become discouraged and unsure of where my best energy should go. I was feeling burned out, knowing I had given my best to TMTC but realizing that my hopes and dreams were not in tune with the financial realities nor with the hopes that board members had for TMTC. I continued to find it difficult to understand the power dynamics among the board members, all of whom represented other higher educational institutions, and to negotiate with them the place of TMTC in their visions of their own schools. I had become resentful of the role assigned to me with its minimal financial remuneration, a role that focussed more and more on administrative details and fund-raising than on visioning and interacting with the students and the larger Toronto School of Theology (TST) community (we could no longer afford an administrative assistant, so I had to do that work). James Reimer, the academic advisor, was putting energy into the teaching, advising, and TST relationships, a role that he had developed over the years and that he did exceptionally well. My official role was becoming less important. As I reflected on all of this, I knew that it was the "volunteer hours" that went beyond what was expected of me by the board that really energized me. I needed to find ways in which I could focus on them rather than on what was frustrating to me. This precipitated the decision to resign and enter a cross-cultural experience with my husband who had been granted a sabbatical leave from his position as pastor.

Quite unexpectedly, through connections with the Mennonite Central Committee (MCC) unit in Cairo (which included our son who was teaching English there), I was given the opportunity to teach New Testament Theology at the Evangelical Theological Seminary (ETSC) in a new MA program that they had just begun. We were acknowledged as MCC-related volunteers in Cairo and thus were able to enter an intensive cross-cultural experience with some support and advice from other more seasoned volunteers. Besides the teaching, we studied Arabic and learned to navigate the transportation system and the daily shopping for food. Each day in Cairo brought us new sights, smells, and sounds as we explored that complex and interesting city. We were invited into many homes of Egyptians, climbed Mount Sinai with Coptic students, visited ancient churches and mosques, sailed the felucca on the Nile, celebrated festivals with friends of our son, and spent a weekend in the home of one of my students in upper Egypt. We experienced Presbyterian worship—Egyptian style—but also Coptic worship and Bible studies and visited a monastery with an Egyptian friend. During those six months, we saw the ruins of Egyptian, Roman, and Greek cultures, the latter on a brief trip to Greece during a vacation week. We snorkeled at Dahab, saw the Suez Canal, and of course visited the markets and the pyramids. Enough grist for many months of reflection!

But perhaps the most intense experiences took place during the last two weeks of our sabbatical when we visited Iran as guests of the Imam Khomeini Education and Research Institute (IKERI). This institute is a graduate school in Shi'a studies that tries to include all the social sciences in its curriculum in dialogue with philosophy and theology. Its leaders had expressed their need for theology professors trained in the West to help them better understand Christianity and its approach to knowledge. MCC, who worked together with the Red Crescent Society on earthquake relief in the region, had responded to this request by suggesting a student exchange where a "dialogue of life" could be part of the theological exchange. TMTC had agreed to host the doctoral students. Thus, my work at TMTC in the last number of years had included helping the two students settle into TST as well as creating other opportunities for dialogue and interaction. The invitation to visit Iran came as a result of that involvement.

Several days were spent in Qom, the scholarly centre of the Shi'a branch of Islam in Iran. Qom has several seminaries and other schools where people from around the world come to study. We had the opportunity to visit with several of the clergy and spent a delightful evening in the home of one of the professors. The days touring various places of interest such as Esfahan with its many bridges and Shiraz with its university and Persian ruins gave us new insights into the life of Iranians. We visited ancient mosques and colourful markets but also university campuses, cemeteries where the martyrs were buried, and various libraries and museums. We were graciously hosted by professors of IKERI and had a formal visit with the director who welcomed us warmly. The second week was spent with the Red Crescent Society who showed us their work, including their preparatory work for the many earthquakes that come to Iran every year. We also spent time with the Armenian Christian church and heard of their experiences.

My worldview expanded exponentially through these intensive encounters. I had spent many years exploring the Bible with my primary questions arising out of my personal and communal experience as a white woman in a Mennonite Church and a Canadian university context. Though the questions had been broadened through my ecumenical interactions and my experiences in the larger Mennonite world, I had never been challenged to move out into another culture and another religion as I had during those months in Egypt and the two weeks in Iran. Perhaps most important for me was the experience of looking at life from behind the veil (even visitors to Iran are required to wear a veil). I discovered that in some ways this makes women anonymous; Iranian women insisted that it also allowed them to walk freely and more safely in the streets. I learned to appreciate the veil as a sign of resistance to the undue influence of the West. After all, it was the Shah who was so influenced by Western culture that he had required that women could no longer wear the chador—something that created much consternation to women who had to give up something that was engrained in their culture and religion at the time.

In the next few years I continued to work both theologically and in practical ways to relate my past convictions and the new understandings gained through my Muslim friends. A number of opportunities arose for me, including participating in several conferences organized by TMTC. Being the academic advisor to an Iranian woman who did her thesis on Letty Russell and feminism was one of the most important interactions for me as it created the opportunity to learn much about the relationship between men and women in Iran. I was also able to participate in a week-long session for Iranian women on "A Mennonite Theology of Peace" at Canadian Mennonite University in Winnipeg. I was invited to attend the sessions and relate informally to the women. That was a very enjoyable week without direct responsibility but with an opportunity to become acquanited with female Islamic theologians.

The two papers that follow have very different audiences in mind. The first was presented at a formal Shi'a-Mennonite dialogue in Iran, the second was presented in a Mennonite context in which the focus was more on self-reflection on our partnership in dialogue.

***

THE BIBLE AS CANON AND AS WORD OF GOD: EXPLORING THE MYSTERY OF REVELATION[1]

I look at the photo of the Mennonite and Shi'a scholars on the cover of the Conrad Grebel Review. *I see the faces of my fellow Mennonites whom I got to know quite well during my second trip to Iran. There were eight of us who were part of the delegation including Susan Harrison (the doctoral student who had partnered with me in hosting the students) and myself. The Mennonite men stand out because they do not have a distinctive dress, while Susan and I with our head coverings fit in very well with the eleven Islamic scholars, mostly in turbans and flowing robes. It is February 2014 and we are in Iran for the second Shi'a Muslim-Mennonite Christian dialogue.*

This rather unusual inter-religious dialogue grew out of the student exchanges between IKERI and TMTC. Phase one of the dialogue, sponsored by TMTC, MCC, and IKERI, took place in Toronto in 2002 and focused on "The Challenges of Modernity." What was unique about that conference was not only that were there the intel-

lectual exchanges but also that there were more informal exchanges sparked by visits to a Mennonite church service, a visit to a modest Old Order Mennonite farm, a visit to a modern urban Mennonite home, and, of course, a visit to Niagara Falls. At that conference I responded to one of the presentations and also helped provide a hospitable welcome as the director of TMTC.

For this second conference we were invited to Iran and again the two-week visit included more than the formal discussions. We arrived just in time to observe the celebration of the 1979 Islamic revolution and at the end of our visit were able to observe the elections for Parliament. We took various tours to places of tourist interest as well as places commemorating political events. Most important to me were the palaces of the former Shah and the simple dwelling of the revolutionary leader Ayatollah Khomeini, as that contrast represented some of the political and religiously important values of the clergy. Our group was led by James Reimer, the director of TMTC at the time, and included several people who had spent some of their career interacting with Islam as well as two doctoral students from TMTC. As in Toronto, there was an attempt to keep the dialogue mutual with a similar number of persons from each religion represented. The theme for this dialogue was carefully chosen because both religions have worked at the relationship between "Reason and Revelation" but have done it somewhat differently. Most of the Muslim scholars had received their doctorates from western universities so English could become the common langague.

My memories of this conference are very warm, for by this time we had begun to develop some trusting relationships with our Iranian friends. I remember the laughter in the van and hotels as we travelled together. I think with fondness of the visit with the parents and relatives of our exchange students and how much we enjoyed getting to know their extended families. I began to understand these students better as we heard much about a parent of one of the students, an honoured Islamic thinker who was assassinated three months after the revolution. I recall the many meals we shared and the respect given to us as women by the Islamic scholars even though there were no Islamic women who were part of the formal dialogue.

My own contribution was a paper on our own sacred text, the Bible. I felt free to speak and converse about this important topic and the way it relates to our understanding of who Jesus is for us. During the discussions, I was profoundly moved by how some of the Islamic scholars spoke about Jesus, who is considered an important prophet in Islam, particularly by the remarks of one professor who teaches Christianity to Muslim students. He had memorized the four gospels and referred to Jesus as "our Lord Jesus Christ," in the kind of respect and honour that Muslims reserve for their prophets. We were also humbled and challenged as Christians in the way space for prayer was reserved in the midst of their scholarly reflection.

As James Reimer put it, "the purpose of these dialogues is to promote mutual understanding and mutual conversion."[2] *By conversion he didn't mean Muslims to Chris-*

tianity or Christians to the Islamic faith (though this could be legitimate in some contexts) but rather to convert one another to a "deeper understanding and commitment to one's own faith, to aspects of one's tradition that have been perhaps overlooked." In the final session we were able to pray together with a Christian leading the prayer and the Islamic scholars saying, "Amen."

One of the enlightening aspects of this conference for me was to understand how privileged we were as Mennonites to be invited to be part of these discussions. Both groups had decided to make this a Shi'a Muslim-Mennonite Christian dialogue to preserve the particularity of each faith. When we toured the library of IKERI I noticed that many of the books on Christianity were Mennonite authored books. This was surprising given that few Mennonite theologians have written books. Though IKERI was branching out to begin dialogues with other Christian denominations, this was still at the beginning stage. I remember that one of our exchange students only realized that Mennonites were a minority Christian denomination after some months studying at TST!

The following paper is probably my most rationally argued understanding of the authority of the Bible. It includes many of my philosophical assumptions as well as theological ones because it is these that often create the different dialogue styles among Muslims and Christians. In contrast to my earlier discussion, this paper speaks more about how I understand God's self-disclosure than how I understand our human response to this revelation. Certainly, the general Islamic view of the authority of their Scripture is very different from my own. For Muslims the authority placed in the original language of the Koran is of such a nature that even translating the words into other languages creates a problem.

These conversations made us realize that we did not understand God's revelation nor "spirituality," the human response to that revelation, in the same way. Thus spirituality became the theme for the next conference. I came back to Canada with a growing conviction of the importance of inter-faith dialogue for all Christians but particularly for those of us who are Christian peace theologians. Understanding each other can lead to deep respect for the differences as well as the commonalities among us.

***

Introduction

The focus in this paper will be on the Bible and the way Christians speak theologically about its authority and function. This will be an exercise in systematic theology—that is, a rational exploration of revelation and authority from within the Christian faith. Thus my first purpose is not apologetic but doctrinal, concerned with exploring issues that arise for Christians in trying to understand the authority of the Bible. My hope is that this will raise questions for us all and that a fruitful discussion can happen as we gain a deeper understanding of each other's Scripture.

I want to begin by rejecting two philosophically oriented approaches to the theological theme of revelation that have developed within Modernity. Both of these restrict the notion of revelation too much for my purposes and thus do not allow full expression of the truth that Christians confess.[3] Firstly, revelation is often understood as a feature of a generally theistic metaphysical outlook, which could be explored generically without reference to the particularities of the Christian community's beliefs about God. In this approach, biblical revelation is usually evaluated in terms of this independent general definition, and the process of reading the Bible easily becomes one of separating the revelational or universal from the specific aspects of language and history. Revelation is then understood as a deposit of knowledge about God, which must by definition, be universal. This creates a dualism between the particular and the universal that tends to undermine some of the most powerful teachings of the Christian faith, such as the incarnation and the sacraments. Both of these are relational notions that bridge the universal and the particular through the action of God.

A second closely related direction taken by many contemporary theologians is to start with epistemological warrants accepted in philosophy in order to justify the possibility of revelation. In this model, revelation becomes the foundational teaching on which all subsequent teachings are erected. Deductive reasoning from that premise establishes the other teachings. When the Bible is then equated with revelation, its authority is directly dependent on epistemological reasoning rather than on the acknowledgment of God's life-giving presence within the worshiping and witnessing community in the power of the Spirit. This makes the apologetic question more basic than an understanding of the God of the Christian faith who determines the community's own identity and mission.

Instead of these directions, I wish to explore the network of beliefs about God that are illuminated when Christians claim that the Bible has authority. Authority in this context refers to "that which (or the person whom) one has reason to trust," that is, it is a relational word.[4] When we are convinced that someone or something will lead us to truthful action and honest speech in tune with the true nature of reality, we accept that person or thing as having legitimate authority. This definition moves us toward an exploration of biblical authority within an understanding of the larger divine-human relationship.

I will begin with the notion of canon in order to focus on the "creaturely reality" of the Bible. I begin here, not because it is the most important way to begin, but because the natural way that people of all religions meet the Bible for the first time is as a set of texts written by humans. Much attention has been paid in the age of Modernity to the historical process of canonization as well as to the final shape of the biblical canon. However, the theological implications of this fact have not often been explicated. I will suggest some of the implications for the theme of revelation and authority.

Secondly, I will explore the term commonly used of the Bible, "Word of God." I will suggest that this term is a metaphor. Again much attention has been paid in Modernity to language and the way it is used to give meaning to experience. I will explore the metaphorical nature of the linguistic term in order to help describe what is implied when I suggest that the Bible is a "sacrament" of God.

The Bible as Canon

"Canon" used as a formal literary category, is not unique to sacred writings. The term originates from the Greek term *kanôn*, a measuring rod or reed or standard. In classical Greek, it was applied to collections of authoritative writings and to several kinds of lists and tables. Its formal use as a designation for the collection of Christian biblical books began in the fourth century when the parameters of the collection were being settled by official action of the church. However, lists of books used authoritatively in the church have also been discovered from as early as the second century CE. The notion of canon implies boundaries around a particular book designated for a particular normative purpose. The focus on the canonical process during Modernity has highlighted the need to look again at that process and ask what it means theologically. A brief overview of how this collection came to be will highlight some of the important transitions in how Scripture was viewed.

We begin with the formation of the Christian Scripture in the first century CE.[5] The church inherited a canon from Judaism, the Hebrew Bible (later named the Old Testament), made up of several different collections of writings including the law, the prophets, wisdom literature and the Psalms. Central to the notion of authority of these writings was their connection to the formation of a covenant community through God's saving intervention in the events of the Exodus from Egypt and the receiving of the law at Sinai. The foundational notion of Hebrew scriptures was as Torah, understood as divinely issued decrees and commands, mediated through Moses and intended as a normative guide for the people. These laws were placed within a narrative context, which firmly tied these writings to the community and its experience of God's saving presence at different stages of its life.

These decrees required interpretation, traditionally given by scribes and based on applying the law to present circumstances. But it was the prophets who carried the authority of divine speech more directly. They were recognized as inspired by the Spirit of God, speaking as God's messengers for specific situations. The collection of their writings was second only to the Torah in authority. The rest of the Hebrew Scripture was made up of a miscellaneous collection of writings of multiple genres and voices. Included were practical wisdom teachings, needed by the community as it interacted with the society around it, as well as Psalms of praise and lament that testify to the close relationship between God and people.

Thus Christians inherited a diverse and dynamic group of texts, read and interpreted within a "text-centered" community.[6] These scriptures were not handed down from heaven or created in a single moment, but were made up of texts selected over time amidst controversy about exactly which books should be considered sacred Scripture. Regardless of where the boundaries were placed, the Hebrew scriptures were viewed as witnessing most centrally to the one eternal, unchanging God, within the dynamic of the history of God's revelation to and salvation of God's people. The unifying factor of the Bible as canon was not a theme or concept but rather the "Integrity of Reality, the oneness of God, to which all the parts, in one way or another, when joined together, point and testify."[7]

Christians accepted this view and saw the function of these writings as a witness to God's active presence among them through the inspiration of the scriptures which were therefore useful in learning how to live a God pleasing life as individuals and as community. 2 Timothy 3:16 in the New Testament supports this view:

All Scripture is inspired by God and is useful for teaching, for reproof, for correction, and for training in righteousness, so that everyone who belongs to God may be proficient, equipped for every good work.

But with the coming of Jesus the notion of Scripture needed to be transformed in order to witness to this startling new reality. The book of Hebrews in the New Testament suggests that God had spoken in a new way through Jesus.

> Long ago God spoke to our ancestors in many and various ways by the prophets, but in these last days he has spoken to us by a Son, whom he appointed heir of all things, through whom he also created the worlds. (Hebrews 1:1)

For early Christians the primary agent of divine revelation was not Scripture per se, but Jesus Christ, to whom the scriptures bear witness. They were convinced that they were living in a new age of the Spirit, that God was not just a God of memory of the past but rather a God who was active in the present through Jesus. Although the earthly Jesus was no longer present, these Christians were certain that the risen Christ, the living voice of God among them, was still there through the apostolic witnesses and the preaching by the early leaders. The collections of narratives about Jesus, the sayings of Jesus, and the pastoral letters written to groups of believers, were circulated as testimonies to the presence of the living Christ through the Spirit. The notion of the inspiration of these witnesses made explicit a comparison to prophetic literature, that closely associated the authoritative reading aloud of the scriptures with prophecy spoken by God through the Holy Spirit.

It wasn't until the time of Iranaeus (180 CE) that we can speak with any confidence of a Christian Bible understood as a selection of authoritative writings which incorporated the new understanding of God's will through Jesus Christ directly into the existing Scripture. The involvement of the Christian community in the selection process is clear. Phyllis Bird suggests that "Truth in representing the tradition and suitability for meeting the current needs were the twin tests of authority in the creation of the Christian Bible."[8] This is not to deny that official recognition included a political process of human decision making.

As we move to a theological account of this activity, we will not deny this human, creaturely process. We will admit that it is vulnerable to abuse and misuse. However, we will focus on God and try to understand this process within the larger context of how Christians see God's relationship to the creaturely world. The central question for us is this: Who is this God who would trust a human community and a human process to be the witness to the eternal presence of God in the world? Or put another way, What is it about the canonical process that would make Christians trust it to be a faithful witness to God's activity in the world?

The answer Christians give to this question is congruent with the description given of God in the substance of the Bible itself. The Christian picture of God is not of invulnerable divine power, of a God without passions, committed only to control and judgment of creation. Instead, both the content and the shape of the canon witness to a God whose perfect love makes God vulnerable and willing to be rejected, a God who invites reconciliation but does not force this on humanity.[9] This is characteristic of love, which is willing to put itself in danger for the other. This kind of love is most clearly embodied in Jesus, who endured suffering and the cross in order to make God's love concretely present in the world. This is a radical, surprising idea, a notion that we as humans would not have naturally assumed to be true. This picture of God could come about only through God's own self-disclosure.

Christians confess that God has always chosen to make God-self present through particular revelatory actions. Revelation is regarded as self-disclosure through divine presence. "To speak of revelation is to say that God is one whose being is directed toward his creatures, and the goal of whose free self-movement is his presence with us."[10] Revelation is not so much information, though it includes that. It is rather God presenting God-self as outgoing and communicative, willing to address the creaturely reality of humankind. Thus revelation is cognitive but also moral and relational. The trinitarian formulation of the one God is a way that Christians speak about this mystery. They confess the origin of this self-presence in the free action of the Creator God, the actualization of this presence through the incarnated Christ, and the ongoing effective presence of God within human history through the Spirit, who will bring all things to an eschatological and eternal perfection.

This revelation is purposive but also mysterious and beyond human comprehension. Its purpose is the overcoming of human opposition, alienation and sin and their replacement with knowledge, love and fear of God. It creates the possibility of communion between God and God's creation by positively inviting reconciliation through the removal of human barriers such as ignorance, self-centeredness and a sinful rejection of God's way. Yet, it is not direct or without ambiguity. The revelation of God is not merely a means of dealing with epistemological questions but is rather a divine action of mercy throughout time and eternity directed toward reconciliation of God's creatures. It is a "setting apart" or "sanctification" of creaturely reality (including the Bible) to serve God's particular disclosive purpose.

Authority of the Canon

How then do we speak about the canon's authority? Perhaps one of the best terms is as "testimony" or "witness" to God's presence in particular moments within a larger context of relationship. As testimony, the Bible points to a reality beyond itself, that is to God. But as testimony it is also a fitting creaturely servant of God in its vulnerability. It witnesses to a God who has chosen not to dominate human creatures but to invite their free response in loving obedience to God's loving actions.

This ties the Bible very closely to the community of faith, the church. This community confesses its purpose is to listen expectantly for the Word of God as the Bible is read; rejoices in worship as God's presence becomes a reality among the people through the Spirit's activity; and discerns the particular word for the present time and place through the activity of the Spirit among the people. This creaturely activity of hearing continues the human role of recognizing God's revelation and salvation, much as was done through the canonization process. However, this too cannot be spiritualized; it includes reading the Bible using all the usual tools—constructing the meaning of words and sentences, following arguments, grasping relationships, and making reasoned judgments about the truth of the statements and their relevance for the present situation.

At the same time, the expectation and hope is affirmed that God will bring all creaturely reality and activity to its fulfillment within God's eternal purposes, because God has chosen to be in relationship with God's creation. All of this is part of the larger human response to God that we call discipleship, that is, a faithful following in the way of Jesus.[11]

At least two important consequences follow this way of looking at the authority of the canon:

1. The inherent authority of the canon will always be somewhat unsettled, never completely secure or totally exclusive because it admits that there is divine disclosure beyond what can be enclosed in a human book. This will always make the Bible less than absolute, because it can only witness to God's presence within history, but not control it. God is free to extend God's presence within history when and where God wills. The temptation is to try to make the Bible totally secure by insisting that it is a divine book and thus that it has absolute authority. The church has often used external means such as coercion, domination and suppression to ensure the Bible's absolute authority. As Christendom became a reality, church and state joined hands in ensuring that the Bible's authority was extended to all nations. One aspect of this domination was the forced conversion of the so-called barbarians. Later, both the Inquisition (with its authority to stamp out heresy) and colonial expansion (with its authority to impose Christian rule) sought to spread the Bible's authority using coercive methods. The sixteenth Century Anabaptist, forebears of the Mennonites, experienced some of this violent oppression in the name of Biblical authority. So did many Muslims at various times in history.

As a result of the Enlightenment and its focus on humanistic approaches to knowledge, the Western church has struggled to find ways to express the relationship of God to the Bible. As the church splintered into various communities it began to develop confessions of faith arranged systematically and comprehensively in order to secure and defend the divine voice against what were considered heretical interpretations. Timeless truths were abstracted from the multiple voices within Scripture and given absolute authority. Gradually new terms such as "inerrant" and "verbally inspired" were used to insist on the technical accuracy of the biblical words. The work of the Holy Spirit was now seen as primarily securing the accuracy of those words. As John H. Yoder shows, these attempts were all ways of making the creaturely Bible as secure as God.[12] They became idolatrous when they insisted on boundaries that were too fixed and static, unable to point beyond themselves to the God who was using the Bible for God's own purposes.

2. The nature of the canon as testimony means that it will always invite further interpretation as God's activity of self-disclosure is continually being extended into human time and space. The ambiguity and complexity of the narratives, commands, wisdom and prayers in the biblical material means that no

one text can be allowed to overpower all others, nor can one interpretation be the final one. As Brevard Childs puts it, readers of the Bible, fully aware of their own frailty, await "in anticipation a fresh illumination through God's Spirit, for whom the Bible's frailty is no barrier."[13] The Bible becomes the arena where God continually invites humans to be transformed into loving people responding in obedience to God's presence. The Bible is not a fixed, frozen, readily exhausted read; it is rather a "script," always reread, through which the Spirit brings forth new possibilities to live life in God's presence. There is an open dynamic in the text itself, so that nobody's reading is final or inerrant. God is always beyond us in "holy hiddenness."

The multiple interpretations of the Bible were threatened in Modernity by a new locus of interpretation, one largely outside of ecclesial control whether Catholic or Protestant. The Enlightenment gradually gave authority to the secular university, where the biblical book was treated much as any other historical book. Historical critical studies threatened to undermine any divine voice at all within the scriptures. Attention was on historical fact, attempting to separate it from interpretation and to find the one meaning intended by the original author. One disastrous legacy of the Enlightenment was the new confidence that humans could stand outside of the stream of time, and with clear rationality distinguish truth from error and light from darkness. The focus was now not on recognizing God's self-disclosure but on analyzing the human events behind Scripture. Various exegetical methods were employed to get to the original historical events, including those of Jesus' life and death. In that context, the authority of the Bible for faith became more and more elusive.

Yet, throughout this time many churches kept on testifying that the living God became present in their midst as the Bible was read within a community committed to hearing the witness to God through the Bible. Also, those formerly excluded from biblical interpretation—for example, women, and persons from a variety of different cultures and languages—began to lift up passages that had long been ignored. The living God continued to be present with God's creatures through a variety of interpretive activity, as God's dynamic Spirit moved among God's people.

What then can we say about biblical authority that arises from a theological understanding of the canon? We are left with the particularity of human interpretive activity within history, which can never guarantee God's presence, but which witnesses to God's promise that God will again and again reveal and save. According to John Howard Yoder, that is precisely where we ought to be, "since that is where God chose to be revealed in all the arbitrariness and particularity of Abraham and Sarah, Moses and Miriam, Jeremiah, Jesus and Pentecost, Luke and Paul, Peter and John."[14] As Christians stand within that large tradition of receiving God's revelation, they are continually tested and judged in terms of the witness of the past. Thus the Bible's authority is expressed most often in terms of challenges for transformation and renewal. The God who has chosen to reveal God-self through the particular mediation of creaturely beings made useful through the Spirit is the same kind of God who was vulnerable to human rejection on the cross. What seems, at first glance, to be weakness is strength, because God's willingness to be vulnerable calls forth a willing human response of love. Within that relationship of love people become convinced of the inherent authority of the Bible. They recognize its congruence with the way God's presence always comes to God's people, not as overpowering or domineering but inviting, moving us beyond our present understanding into God's mysterious presence.

The Bible as "Word of God"

Faith affirmations such as affirming the Bible as God's word are of a different nature than merely scientific or philosophical truth statements. They are more akin to poetic discourse, which arises from the experience of historical reality, but moves to the realm of the unseen. The term "sacrament" is a traditional way in Christianity to speak of these realities.

The expression "word of God" is first of all metaphorical. It cannot be taken literally, for God is Spirit and therefore it is absurd to suggest that divine speech is the same as human speech. Recent semantic studies of metaphor have helped us see its potential in religious language about God. Since understanding metaphor and symbol will be helpful in understanding the notion of sacraments, I will briefly summarize the work of Sandra Schneiders (based on that of Paul Ricoeur) to point out some key characteristics of this kind of language.[15] Metaphor is not merely a contracted simile or a literary ornament, an illustration or a substitute for a literal meaning. It is a powerful form of language in its own right, a power gained because of the irresolvable tension within the term itself. In a metaphor, an affirmative proposition is given, but simultaneously a negation is implied in the likeness between the two terms. For example, in the terms of the metaphor "The Bible is the word of God," the tension implies that the Bible is, but also is not, the word of God. This tension makes the metaphor alive and calls forth its strong meaning.

Riceour has explored what happens when one makes a proposition in a sentence such as "the Bible is the word of God." The sentence makes sense grammatically but does not make sense literally. Thus the imagination must be engaged in a cognitive and affective exploration of the two terms in order to move to a different level of understanding. That is when a new meaning emerges. We therefore resort to metaphor in an effort to bring to speech something that cannot be expressed in literal speech. If either the "is" or the "is not" is suppressed, the metaphor becomes only literal or is an exercise of sheer fancy. Though most metaphors are unstable and become banal and trite through repetition, some retain a perennial power to evoke response. They are root metaphors that draw out rich understandings of the most complex realities of our life.

It is helpful to understand that we are dealing with metaphor in order to explore the referent of the sentence, "The Bible is the word of God." This referent is divine revelation, a revelation that is not restricted to the confines of human language. For some people, this metaphor is dead because they can only see the Bible as another religious book. The "is" has seized to function for them. For others, the metaphor becomes literalized. They have ceased to hear the whispered "is not" that a live metaphor always carries in its affirmation. They regard every word as equally and fully divine and thus absolutely true. Interpretation is reduced to finding this literal meaning of every word, suggesting that then they can perfectly understand the divine meaning. The mystery of divine revelation is impoverished and distorted by limiting it to a human proposition.

Because of the metaphorical nature of the Bible as word of God the language of the Bible invites and indeed requires interpretation and translation. The object of interpretation is revelation in all its richness and complexity. The significance of revelation always overflows the boundaries of our own language. Therefore, we are free to translate the Bible into many tongues and cultures confident that God's disclosure is not limited to one particular articulation of it. In addition, if we define revelation as self-disclosure we realize immediately that the word of God cannot be only rational but must be more holistic than that. In personal disclosure we share with another something of ourselves, whether physical, emotional or intellectual. Language is the symbolic medium of that self-disclosure. So too with God's self-disclosure, something true is shared, but the disclosure goes beyond rational discourse alone.

Symbol and metaphor are related in that both include the affirmation and the negation within themselves. What is important to understand is that symbol is a perceptible reality that points to that which is otherwise imperceptible. A symbol embodies and brings to expression reality that it can never fully say. It moves into the area of the unseen and the inexpressible. Thus symbols hide more than they reveal and there is always ambiguity about a symbol's meaning.

We use expressions such as, "nature speaks to us" or "history teaches us" knowing that these are symbolic expressions putting into language that which is often inexpressible. Thus our theological expressions are at their linguistic level symbolic.

Theologically, we also say that to be accessible to us, God approached us symbolically, through perceptible reality. God opened a locus of encounter through created nature, through historical events, through oracles of the prophets, wisdom of sages, and prayers of the people. Christians recognized Jesus, the living Word, as the definitive revelation of God, the very presence of God in human form. The proclamation of this event by the early witnesses was itself revelatory because it invited those who heard the preaching to respond to God's self-disclosure. The term "word of God" embraces and integrates this whole range of God's symbolic self-disclosure.

Christians believe that Jesus as "Word of God" is the "paradigmatic instance of divine revelation" and the scriptures are the privileged medium of God's gift of God's self to humankind. Historically, the church has used the term "sacrament" to denote this particular kind of symbol. A sacrament articulates the mystery of the divine encounter in a particularly clear and powerful way. As a visible sign of invisible grace it witnesses to the presence of God. Therefore, the church as worshipping community as well as the Bible as witnessing Word can be understood as the sacrament of God to the world. The proper reference of the church as "body of Christ" (a term the New Testament uses) and the Bible as "word of God" is the presence of God with God's people.

Bible as Sacrament

The tension noted earlier when discussing metaphor remains when we speak of the Bible as sacrament. The Bible is not revelation in its fullness, but a symbolic witness to the self-gift that has been taking place since creation and will continue to the end of time. Because symbols are inherently ambiguous, interpretation will always be a challenging work, simultaneously revealing and concealing. Perhaps that is why, within the Bible, the focus of concern is not on whether God reveals, but rather on human openness to hear and believe that revelation. The gospel of John puts it this way:

> But these (signs) are written so that you may come to believe that Jesus is the Messiah, the Son of God, and that through believing, you may have life in his name. (John 20:31)

Throughout his life Jesus continually challenges his disciples to hear the word at a deeper level: "Let anyone with ears to hear, listen" (Mark 4:9). Hearing and seeing are used metaphorically for the disciples' sensitive openness to the gospel message and their obedience to it. The Bible is a medium of God's self-revelation in this sense, so that those who have ears to hear will encounter the living God. Yet, this also means that revelation is inaccessible to those who are not open to hearing the "unseen reality" there to be understood.

Jesus as a human person could be perceived by everyone. However, Jesus, as the revelation of God, the living Word of God, was only "seen" and "heard" by those who were open to that reality. The kind of authority that the Bible as Word of God has is therefore authority within a divine-human relationship that transforms our hearing ability to an openness to the unseen. To respond to God's word is to be changed, to be initiated into a reality that one can participate in, at deeper and deeper levels. Thus we do not speak only about the Bible's normativity as a source book for dogma or commandments. Instead we affirm that the Bible is a primary symbolic invitation into relationship with the divine being. It is a sacrament by which God's grace is made present through the Living Word.

The Bible can be studied as a human text without the transformation of the human person that results when the Word is truly heard. The anti-sacramental views of the early Anabaptists, the forebears of the Mennonites, had to do with the way the sacramental actions of the church were being set apart and used by the hierarchy of the church in order to control access to God. These Anabaptists insisted that there was no power in the physical elements themselves. The bread used in a ritual was just ordinary bread. So too, no one group of people should be given authority to control access to God; nor should the Bible be seen as a supernatural or exclusive book. However, the Bible does become a sacrament of God when persons faithfully interpret the words and the congregation is open to God's presence through the Word.

The Bible can also be spiritualized so that the actual ordinary meaning of the words in the Bible are unimportant for what individuals understand as spiritual interpretation This was a temptation for the spiritualists among the early Anabaptists. This would suggest that God cannot enter the created world in order to communicate with creation but must remain separated from creation. Mennonites in their own ongoing history have struggled with this view as well. What Mennonites have insisted on is that God does not force a response of faith but issues an invitation to those who would listen. God's authority is like the claim of a friend to fidelity and love—always on the level of an appeal, which can be responded to or resisted. The "word of God" as sacrament implies that the Bible is the word of God but can also be used so that it is not the word of God. The Bible as sacrament therefore points to God's willingness to become vulnerable to human response. Yet it is that vulnerability that creates the willing and loving response of God's people.

Conclusion

I am not sure how the term "canon" and the expression "word of God" resonate with Muslims. However, whether these terms have parallels in Islamic writings is not the most crucial item for discussion in a Mennonite-Shia dialogue. Instead, I hope we can focus our discussions on our understanding of the attributes and activities of God that we see in our respective scriptures and that we associate with revelation. In addition, I hope we can begin to address those times when our misuse of our scriptures has led to domination and abuse of the other.

I have tried to say that there is a vulnerability about the way Christians speak about the Bible as canon and as word of God. This vulnerability is there because the Bible is human, historical and linguistic; but that has not always been understood and this has led to misuses and abuses. Yet this very vulnerability contains within itself a powerful witness to the kind of God that Christians worship and obey. It testifies to God's revealing and reconciling presence in history, a presence that calls forth a free response of love and obedience by God's people. By acknowledging the authority of the Bible, Christians witness to what they consider the most basic truth of all: that the powerful, omnipotent, and merciful God initiates relationship with God's creation through God's revealing and reconciling presence. I hope this paper and the discussion to follow will help create mutual understandings between Mennonites and Shi'a Muslims. May God be acknowledged and praised through this dialogue.

***

CAN THESE "ABRAHAMIC COMMUNITIES" DIALOGUE WITH INTEGRITY?[16]

My relationship as a theologian to Mennonite Central Committee (MCC) has several different strands that came together in the Shi'a Muslim-Mennonite Christian dialogues. First of all, as a member of a Mennonite church, I had long been deeply committed to the work that MCC does in relief and development work in other countries. I was very aware that MCC began with a response by Mennonites in North America to fellow Mennonites in Russia during the time of famine after the Revolution in the 1920's. My parents were saved from starvation by that effort. In addition, members of my larger family have been active volunteers for that organization in various countries. However, my own volunteer efforts had been restricted to participating in quilting blankets, participating in relief sales, or supporting other fund-raisers.

However, the six months in Cairo in 2000 helped me become more aware of the development and relief work MCC does in attempting to be a reconciling presence within a large city such as Cairo. Volunteers were teaching English to students in two seminaries; others were participating in resourcing partner organizations in various peace-building efforts, including training young people in conflict resolution skills. Still others were resourcing families and communities in their education efforts. Our own participation as volunteers in the Evangelical Theological Seminary in Cairo helped us understand how these cross-cultural relationships can lead to greater understanding of what is needed to build peace in particular contexts.

Secondly, MCC had become an official member of the board of Toronto Mennonite Theological Centre (TMTC). In my early years as director of TMTC I had wondered who should be invited to be part of the board. The initial partners were all educational institutions or denominational committees related to higher education. Because I was committed to bringing theory and practice together I felt strongly that MCC should be invited to be a partner in this effort. MCC with its focus on practical efforts in peace building around the world was an ideal partner to help us think through the implications of the kind of theology we were teaching and learning. To have someone from MCC on the board would give a somewhat different perspective on what we were doing at TMTC. On my invitation, they accepted this role.

When we were asked to host students from Iran, this partnership became much more important. MCC and TMTC partnered together in a very significant way in this student exchange with Iran. The conferences that took place first of all in Toronto (2002) and then in Qom (2004) had strengthened this co-operation. By the time the third dialogue took place in 2007 various changes had happened. First of all, TMTC had become part of Conrad Grebel University College (CGUC) in Waterloo. CGUC and the advisory board took on a less direct role in TMTC. In addition, new links had been made to other Mennonite schools who were ready to enter these dialogues. At this third dialogue, CGUC and MCC jointly sponsored the interfaith dialogue. Soon after MCC as an organization decided that since TMTC was no longer directly relating to the Iranian exchange it would not send a representative to be on the advisory board. I lamented that change as I had highly valued MCC's involvement in the academic theological dialogue.

Thirdly, I had become a member of the peace committee of MCC International in 2001. This committee met bi-annually as a "think tank" to reflect theologically on the various programs of MCC by responding to questions and concerns from practitioners as well as administrators. I was thrilled to be asked because I felt here was one place where I could concretely enter into theological conversations that were not purely theoretical but eminently practical. Since this was a long term commitment I had the opportunity to reflect theologically on most of the programs of MCC during my term of 8 years. I have chosen to include the unpublished paper that I wrote for one of these meetings because it illustrates the way experience and praxis raise the theological questions that an organization faces in its quest for integrity.

The focus for that meeting in 2008 and my paper in particular was on MCC's presence in Iran. Several important events had triggered the need for theological reflection. First of all, the inter-faith bridge building that MCC was doing had become controversial. The strained political relationship between Iran and Canada and the possibility of US military action against Iran at the time affected the MCC constituency and there was a need to examine again the objectives for MCC in these relationships. The relief effort of MCC in Iran had taken an unexpected turn through the various academic encounters that resulted through the scholar exchange program. MCC wanted to ask again what its role was in these encounters. In addition, in 2006 MCC was invited to facilitate some meetings of American religious leaders with Iranian President Mahmoud Ahmadinejad on his visit to the US and to send delegations of religious leaders to Iran. Did these engagements fit into MCC's mandate of peacebuilding?

Personally, I was happy for the opportunity to reflect on my own involvement in the academic dialogues. The third Shi'a-Mennonite dialogue had some surprising and unexpected twists and turns. I had been asked to provide over-all leadership for planning that conference. Susan Harrison, the MCC assistant in this endeavour, and I worked through many questions as we tried to plan a conference that included input from our Iranian theologians as well as from scholars here in North America. Our goal was to be as mutual as possible despite the power dynamics that were always present. For example, after the topic of "spirituality" was chosen we asked each group to circulate questions that they wished to ask their counterparts about spirituality and then topics were chosen and papers assigned according to these questions. We wanted worship to be an integral part of this conference and many hours were spent thinking of what this would mean. Finally, we decided that each day would have a time of worship led alternatively by Shi'a and Mennonites in their own fashion. When prayers were said each group could decide to say "Amen," if they felt that this was possible. This proved to be a good way to both learn practically about each other's spirituality and to honour the God whom we all worshipped.

Both groups had decided that for a sustained theological conversation there needed to be continuity so the persons invited were primarily those who had participated in earlier formal dialogues. However, we had also decided to include a few new participants from some other Mennonite schools to ensure that a broader involvement could happen in the future. This proved to be valuable when a school such as Canadian Mennonite University in Winnipeg took on the role of sponsoring the next conference.

We decided to invite an outer circle of observers in addition to the inner circle of partipants so that we could also invite a small group of local Muslims and Mennonites who were particularly interested in this exchange. However, this became a problem when the dialogue became politicized and the Muslims who were invited were hesitant in coming because they feared the media and the disapproval of their fellow Iranians. During and after this conference we learned many new things about the conflicts between Iranian clergy and the diaspora community. The public meeting held on the first evening made this very evident, threatening to end any dialogue that we might wish to have.

Preceding the conference MCC and CGUC had begun to get hints that some members of the expatriate Iranian community were attempting to stop the dialogue in any way they could, including trying to block visa entry applications, sending petitions to various agencies, and finally publicly protesting these meetings. The attempts to meet with protesters before the first public meeting failed and so the University took it into their hands to provide protection for the conference participants—an irony for Men-

nonites and their peace building efforts! About 50 protesters shouted down the initial meeting in the Conrad Grebel Great Hall when the first scholar from Iran was introduced. The protesters, some of whom had been reportedly driven from Iran amid the brutality of the 1979 revolution and the ouster of the Shah, displayed graphic pictures of Iranian victims and shouted "Down with the Islamic Republic." The public meeting had to be shut down since order could not be restored.

There were attempts made to engage the protesters before, during, and after that first meeting. However, as Arli Klassen, spokesperson for MCC explained, "Our challenge was that, by providing a listening ear to the protesters, our Iranian clerical guests felt unsafe; and yet by dialoguing with our Iranian clerical guests, the Iranian-Canadians felt that their concerns were being ignored.... Our challenge in the future will be to find ways to continue conversation with multiple dialogue partners about Iran, and to see if we can get to a place where we can help the different groups find ways to hear each other."[17] This event created some hurt and lack of trust between Mennonite and Muslim participants that needed to be repaired in the next few days of the conference.

The conference itself then continued as a closed conference with no more incidents occurring. From my own perspective, this "incident" created the opportunity for a more "real" dialogue to happen with each group realizing the risk that was being taken to dialogue with persons whom our respective governments considered enemies. The following truth quoted by Susan Harrison in her recollections of the conference is particularly apt:

> *Whether they like it or not each party in dialogue is revealed to the other. Everyone should be aware of this as a risk to be taken.... It is even good to experience times of suspicion and of frustration which will oblige the interlocutors further to clarify to themselves the reasons for their encounter and the motives of their cooperation.... This requires a severe pursuit of truth and a true love for people, along with a faith that has been tested and a generous amount of spiritual wisdom.*[18]

The paper that follows was first presented at a peace committee meeting and is printed here with only small revisions. It is an example of the kind of theological reflection that was sparked by my involvement in an institution dedicated to peace-building in its many forms. Because it is designed for self-reflection by MCC personnel, it is largely written in the form of questions that can guide the discussion—questions that are real and not merely rhetorical! The examples mentioned are concrete and therefore also dated. However, the answers that we give to these questions are highly theological and need ongoing reflection as we seek to practise peace-building in our conversations with other faiths.

***

Two experiences of mine in recent years illustrate the complexities of our relationship as Christians, living within so-called democratic states, to Shi'a Muslim Iranians, living in a so-called religious state.

1. **A. Celebrating the Anniversary of the Revolution in Iran as Guests (2004)**

Imagine this scene. You are sitting in special bleachers set aside for military officials, diplomats, representatives of other governments, and the leaders of several religions including leaders of the Armenian church. The date of your visit was planned so that you could be present at the annual celebration of the 1979 revolution. Your Iranian friends are proud of the accomplishments that the revolution has brought to their country. There is music, and there is a long speech by the president. And there are the crowds of people listening to the ceremonies. You watch as "death to America" leaflets are showered from helicopters onto the people. You watch and listen to the cheers. You notice particularly the effigy of the Shah (dressed in an American flag) being burned. You are surprised by the tension that arises in you. Who are you in this scene? American? Canadian? Participant? Guest? Citizen? A builder of bridges of understanding? A Mennonite Christian? What does your presence signify? How do you relate your presence here to your own July 4 or July 1 celebrations? What is different and what is the same?

You also ask: Who are our Iranian hosts in this scenario? Citizens of Iran? Shi'a Fundamentalists? Fellow scholars? Instruments of propaganda? Or fellow believers of the one God? You ask the question: Why was it important for our hosts that we attend this event? And you ponder: how should I respond to this gesture of welcome to Iran?

2. **Hosting our Iranian Guests at a University in Canada (2007)**

Imagine this scene. You have been watching the campus police and the fifty extra police from Toronto preparing to protect the dialogue that has been planned between Shi'a and Mennonite theologians. You have seen the police tactical units on the roof, you have read some of the letters of protest sent to the organizers, you know that the hospital is on alert, ready if there should be violence. As a Mennonite, with a card of invitation, you were allowed to enter the Great Hall first, filing past people with large banners, depicting torture victims and calling for an end to this cooperation with the Iranian leaders. Yet you are convinced that freedom of speech is crucial and that these lectures should be public.

You note that the police have allowed some protesters into the hall. Free speech in Canada means that public spaces are open to all. The protesters surround you and your friends, primarily Mennonites from the area. The Iranian guests, whom you have invited, file in after their Mennonite hosts. There is a feeling of suspense in the uneasy silence during the opening words. But when the first guest begins to speak, the shouts begin as well. The words, "Down with the Islamic Republic" become louder and louder. The chair attempts to outline the rules of dialogue that have been established. But the shouts only get louder. Eventually the chair, in consultation with the police, decides to shut down the dialogue. You sit quietly, yet with tension building within you, while the protesters are led out.

Who are you in this scenario? Canadian? American? Participant? A builder of bridges of understanding? A Mennonite Christian? A host? Who are the Iranians? Guests? Fellow believers? Representatives of a repressive government? Or colleagues and friends? How do you interpret your response to this situation? How do you interpret the discomfort of your guests with you even allowing this scenario to happen? How do you respond to the vulnerability that your guests feel to being publicly identified and slandered, knowing the political tensions within Iranian society?

I will not answer these questions directly but I believe these questions of identity need answering, since MCC's program is built on the foundation of relationships. Instead, I want to do three things:

1) remind us of *theological convictions* that may help us reflect on our involvements in Iran

2) name and explore briefly several inter-related *arenas* of life in which our relationships with Iran are experienced

3) conclude with several *questions* and comments that arise out of our identity as an Abrahamic community that further identifies itself as a community of followers of Jesus, the Christ.

Theological Convictions

I want to begin with a summary of the theological background that informs my response to questions about MCC's role in Iran. The traditional Mennonite position on church/state relationships has been a matter of discussion for us here in

MCC circles rather often, most recently in our discussions on human security. I will be referring to a section from the book *At Peace and Unafraid*[19] as well as leaning rather heavily on a paper by Gerald Schlabach.[20] I want to suggest that we can reflect on our work in Iran through two different frameworks or lenses that are intertwined in a notion of the church as Abrahamic community. In this I am following a suggestion by Gerald Schlabach, that we need to move beyond the opposition between two kingdom theology and one kingdom theology that is present in Mennonite tradition. I will briefly separate these strands to help us think through our work in the context of both the state we live in and the state in which we are guests.

a) The gift and challenge of two kingdom theology

Separation of church and state is deeply engrained in American and Canadian Mennonite ethos and is justified by a long theological tradition beginning with the Schleitheim Confession and continuing through the writings of scholars such as Guy Franklin Hershberger and more recently John Roth. This tradition insists that the kingdom of God cannot be equated to or be brought in by any government no matter how religious it is. The state is part of the "kingdom of the world" that uses coercion and force in order to enforce its social and political values. Christians belong to a different order, Christ's kingdom of peace, and the values of that kingdom are lived out by faithful disciples.

This dualistic worldview has several advantages. It *emphasizes* the different logic that Christians use to establish their priorities, a logic that insists on the way of righteousness and peace-making instead of the way of social, economic and political power calculations. The alternative community, the church, is seen as God's preferred strategy of working in the world through concrete embodiments of the gospel message in communities of faith. State and church are viewed as distinct social/political realities. The primary relationship between church and state in this view is advocacy for the church in its concerns. Thus the church pleads its case before governments in order that the witnessing, healing, and humanitarian relief work can continue. The church does not see itself as responsible for bringing in justice through public policy but rather assumes that justice will be a side effect if non-resistant communities follow the way of peace. It realizes that the church in its very presence within a state can become a prophetic voice calling the state to its primary duties of order and justice.

This view suggests that we live as pilgrims, recognizing that no state is our home, that we will always live in *tension* with the dominant culture. Its prophetic voice is largely directed inwardly toward the church community itself, calling it to repentance when it explicitly or implicitly supports the government in its violent or unjust actions or when it falls into "Constantianism" calling on the "empire" to be on its side protecting and supporting it. This view also warns us that trying to manage history is not our role, though our prophetic presence may assist the state to be more just in its actions.

There are implications for our relationships to the people of Iran if this is our primary orientation. Two kingdom theology would reinforce that we are guests in Iran. Theologically, however, the context of our work would not be substantially different than in our American or Canadian context. For wherever we are we see ourselves as pilgrims and foreigners in the land, focussing on a different agenda than the state. Our primary responsibility would be the embodied presence of the gospel message in solidarity with our brothers and sisters in the Iranian community. Therefore, our relationship to Iran and its government would be one of advocacy, particularly for the minority church in Iran and for our humanitarian efforts in cases of disaster.

The question that this perspective raises is how we respond to Muslim believers, especially those who are part of a theological institution like IKERI. Our two kingdom theology has contributed to the distance that many Mennonites feel between the religious lives of Muslims and themselves. They have often not taken the religion of Islam very seriously or interacted in any depth with Muslim convictions, unless they have viewed Muslims as people to be evangelized. A new question for us is this: Do we recognize these believers as part of the larger pilgrim community of God's people? That is, are they part of the larger community of believers named the Abrahamic community? Or do we see them primarily as representatives of the state of Iran or as enemies of the church? Do we primarily note the tensions that arise between us or do we also trust our Muslim friends as fellow believers?

One large difficulty with a strict two kingdom perspective is that we as MCC related persons are not nearly as independent of the state as we pretend to be. We are dependent on the two governments (ours and the Iranians) for visas, for protection, for order so that we can even visit Iran. We also bring our own political power with us, a power dependent on the state in which we hold citizenship. Thus we may be seen as representatives of our state and often unconsciously bring aspects of our own citizenship with us, even though we profess this homelessness. In addition, a two kingdom perspective sometimes suggests to Shi'a believers that we are not interested in all areas of life including the public, political area but are only interested in private spirituality (a view that is clearly evident in religion in the West, influenced as it is by secular liberal notions). If a two kingdom perspective becomes a static conclusion about how we view the world, rather than an open eschatological vision, it can lead to a triumphalist and exclusive vision of who we are, suggesting that we as Mennonite Christians are the only witnesses to God's goodness and care. This can lead to a Christian identity that is shaped by its anti-Muslim attitudes rather than its commitment to a Christ who loves the whole world.

b) The Gift and Challenge of One Kingdom Theology

A second worldview, suggested by persons such as J. Lawrence Burkholder and Duane Friesen is also present in the Mennonite ethos. It is the notion that God created the whole world as meaningful with a purpose in mind. The course of all institutions including the state is still shaped providentially by God who yearns over them and seeks to lead them to conform more closely to the values of the kingdom of God. God loves and cares for the entire cosmos and is active through the creative and liberating Spirit bringing in the *shalom* that God desires for everyone. God thus judges all powers and principalities according to the ethic engrained in the universe and embodied in Christ's cross and resurrection. God's work in the world is understood to be broader than any church institutions. However, the church is invited to enter God's kingdom and learn to identify and participate in God's redemptive work in the world. Thus the church looks for the movement of God's Spirit in various arenas of life and becomes actively engaged in God's work of "blessing all nations." It understands its calling to embody God's *shalom* in its relationships with others and to actively seek the peace of the "city in which it dwells," whether that is the US, Canada, or Iran.

In this perspective we more easily admit our citizenship in a state and realize that there are many ways to be responsible to seek the peace of that state. Therefore, we do not deny our involvement in the larger political sphere but try to be faithful and wise in our engagements in the halls of power, repenting for the times when we are implicated because of our enmeshments in the systems of which we are a part. Our prophetic voice is part of the witness that we bring to our government and our civil society, a voice that seeks to be just and merciful in all its actions.

There are also implications for our relationships in Iran if this is our primary perspective. In one kingdom theology, we recognize that though our identity is rooted in the kingdom of God, it must be lived out as citizens and guests wherever we may go. The primary challenge is discerning how and when to collaborate with various movements and institutions. This means that we must be self aware and clear about kingdom values and must judge critically ways to be involved in educational and civil institutions, governments and churches, whether these are Canadian, American, or Iranian. MCC would then see itself as one of the social/political groups that God uses to witness to God's reign in the public sphere, rather then seeing itself as the primary or only one. However, it would be important not to use our power as North Americans to bring about our own visions of social community but rather to live and interact vulnerably and truthfully amidst others in the public sphere. Our strategy would eschew all competitiveness and hostility between religions and would move us instead toward openness and receptiveness to the views of others in order to discern wisdom and truth.

In this view peacemaking, justice, truth-telling, and other life-giving processes would be seen as primary values that are part of the kind of *shalom* that we hope for in the various communities to which we relate. However, care would have to be taken that these would not be confused with our Western expressions of these values. Building relationships with both the minority church and the Shi'a leaders will be very complex and will require a humble and respectful spirit. Because the church is a very small minority in Iran we would have to be deliberate about our need for relationship with the various Iranian churches as sources for support and counsel. We may too quickly forge alliances with Iranian institutions of power forgetting our unique identity as Christians. It would be helpful in this context to remember that historically both Christians and Muslims have been the victims of persecution and also the perpetrators of persecution and that even now we have the potential for both within us.

The key challenge that one kingdom theology puts before us is identifying God's movement so that we can align ourselves with it. Is God asking us to help facilitate Muslim/Christian dialogue? Is God asking us to witness more directly to God's way of peace-making? Should we be most concerned with public policy in our own nations and public attitudes toward Iran? Or is God asking us to struggle together with our Muslim friends to overcome the stereotypes that create enmity between nations? This means naming the tentative signs of the kingdom that we see and courageously and humbly following God's leading.

In summary, MCC as a church-related institution is trying to bring together the best within these two theological strands in order to live under the reign of God, both as *pilgrims* in every state in which we move, and as responsible *citizens*, seeking the peace of the state in which we dwell. Thus MCC is called to be an Abrahamic people in this world praying for and living in such a way that God's reign may come "on earth as it is in heaven." This implies that the very presence of MCC can be a *prophetic* witness to the gospel of Jesus Christ as it lives out its own identity as a called-out people of God both as citizens of countries in North America and as guests in Iran. At the same time, this vision challenges MCC to live *wisely*, discerning the direction of God's action and aligning itself with those institutions and people that call for justice and peace. This includes solidarity and dialogue with others who also see themselves as part of the Abrahamic people of God, including the minority church and the majority Shi'a community of believers in Iran. It is with this stance that our organization can live into the promise of God to bless it in order that it can become a "blessing to every nation."

Living as an Abrahamic Community in the Various Arenas of life

The visual model in *At Peace and Unafraid* names various overlapping arenas of life, all of which have been touched in some way in our past involvements in Iran.[21] In this next section I wish to explore these arenas and point to some of the excitement that MCC has felt in its work and some of the hesitation and discomfort that also arise as we become more and more engaged with various communities within Iran. This exploration is not exhaustive, since it comes primarily out of my limited experience, but it may bring some concreteness to our discussion.

1. Caring for creation (countering exploitation)

Perhaps we have never looked at our interactions with Iranians in terms of caring for creation. Yet our involvement in Iran began as a response to a natural disaster. In 1990, a severe earthquake killed 30,000 persons in northern Iran. MCC responded by helping residents rebuild their infrastructure after that disaster. In that context MCC worked with the Iranian Red Crescent Society, a strategic alliance that has produced many conversations and ongoing dialogue about preparation for responding to large scale disasters.[22] The exciting aspect of this relationship is the potential for these conversations to branch into other areas of care for the earth. I can think of several, including the whole area of air pollution that is very severe in the city of Tehran. This common concern allows us to work cooperatively pooling our knowledge with that of Iranians.

But there is another whole agenda that is present at the margins of our discussions with leaders of Iran. This is an area that we are somewhat uncomfortable with, knowing our own national interests as citizens of Western nations. This is the area of oil and nuclear power, resources of the earth that are limited and need careful and responsible use. Throughout Iran's recent history, questions around these resources influence the political and strategic conversations among the nations. Iran itself has felt vulnerable in its particular geographical location and has jealously protected its rights to make decisions according to its own national interests. We are naïve if we do not recognize the gravity of the competitive grasping for power among our nations and others, one that threatens to destroy the earth.

Any engagement with Iranian officials has this as an underlying agenda. What discernment do we need in view of the larger question of care for the earth? Can we find ways to speak of our concern as Christians without being implicated as instruments of the American state? Or is this an area that is too politically charged for us and we do best to avoid the conversation as best we can? What might it be to confess our own culpability as North Americans in this competition and our own fear of a nuclear holocaust? How would this change our relationship with Iranians?

2. Restoring right relationships of justice and righteousness

My own involvement with Iranians began with a simple request from MCC. Would we at the TMTC host several Muslim students from Iran? My immediate response came out of a strong theology of hospitality to strangers rooted in our biblical texts. I knew that these relationships could become a growing edge for the students and faculty of our institution; I also knew I would be changed by this encounter. The surprise for those of us most engaged in this hospitality is how it has grown and multiplied like the loaves and fishes in Jesus' day. We have been hosted beyond any expectations we had, we have discovered in our guests the face of God and we are slowly learning what it means to live in right relationship with each other. But we have also discovered how the systems of which we are a part bring barriers into our relationships, whether simple barriers, like not knowing how to overcome the food regulations that Muslims deem very important, or more complex barriers, like our reluctance to use our power in North America to counter public stereotypes of Muslims.

Probably one area that North Americans are most uncomfortable with is the role of women in Iranian society, especially as expressed in the dress code that is embedded in the law. We bring our own interpretations of this dress code with us and easily become judgmental without understanding the larger context. Slowly we are learning how uncomfortable our guests are with the immoral attitudes and revealing clothing that we have accepted without much question from our secular society. Much more conversation is needed to discover ways to mutually learn from each other. This mutuality is hindered by our own unawareness of how our relationships are coloured by the various social and political systems to which we relate. For example, at the last theological conference, our public justification of dialogue with theologians from Iran was to argue that Jesus had asked us to love our enemies and therefore we needed to do this through this dialogue. However, our Muslim friends found that quite disappointing after our ten years of relationship. Why were we still naming them as enemies in the public sphere? Have we not become friends and neighbours? Why are they being identified through the lens of politics rather than the lens of theological colleagueship? Are we still viewing them through the lens provided by the American media?

It may be important for us to realize how our personal and political relationships are intertwined and that both need more justice and righteousness than has been possible thus far. Because our inter-faith dialogue is a dialogue of life, we often feel vulnerable, knowing that our lives witness not only to our Christian faith but also to our inadequacies in living righteously and witnessing to justice for all. Perhaps a notion of accountability between religious communities would help us be hosts and guests that converse with respect and openness and righteousness.

3. **Truth telling and truth listening (unmasking lying and deception, discerning/witnessing to truth)**

In any good relationship we must trust each other to be truth tellers. I remember on my first visit to Iran, our first audience with the Ayatollah who was the head of IKERI. Gary and I were saying some polite and nice things about how the Muslim community had welcomed our first MCC'ers into their midst. The Ayatollah interrupted us, exhorting us in a gentle way to be more honest. "I know that they had a rough beginning here. You do not need to cover this up." He went on to talk about why Gary and I were invited into the seminary, the first Christian "clergy" to have this privilege in the history of Qom. "It is all because we have learned to trust Ed Martin (country representative for MCC) and MCC that you are here," he told us. Our conversation continued after the necessary reminder by our host that honesty will build trust much more quickly than well meaning polite rhetoric.

In the Iranian context, suspicion and distrust arose during the years when the Shah and America were too closely related thus destroying elements of traditional civil society. The revolution created a chaotic time and when the war with Iraq killed many people more distrust of each other was created. For many Iranians, the present is more stable and has given space to learn to trust again. Therefore, it behoves the West to listen to interpretations of history different from our standard Western ones, particularly of stories like the Iran hostage crisis.[23] This may mean acknowledging the violent past of the Western world with its Christian justifications. We may need to become more aware of the dissidents within Iran and North America and learn to speak honestly when we differ. An awareness of our own stereotypes and fears, as well as the stereotypes and fears that others have of us can help us enter dialogue honestly. Most importantly, we will need to be transparent and open about our own interests in the formal dialogues and in Iran more generally.

Mutuality and honesty imply that we must be willing to let go of the notion that we should always be the ones to determine the substance of our dialogue. In genuine dialogue this substance emerges as we find common ground in the very practice of listening and speaking and discovering particular differences. Therefore, there is always a risk in dialogue—a risk that requires us to be open to change and transformation. We know that suspicion and distrust are also there among our fellow Americans and Canadians, including many Mennonites. MCC is accused of being naive, trusting too soon in the rhetoric of our Iranians friends. In addition, we are asked to be accountable to the expatriate community of Iranians here in Canada and the USA who tell different stories. I am reminded of the history of many Mennonites who escaped from a violent Communist government in Russia in the 1920's who were very uncomfortable when MCC began work in Communist governed countries. As MCC, we are asked to decide where the truth lies in a context that is often very confusing and very muddled and very emotionally charged.

Our response is to be both truth listeners as well as truth tellers. This will continue to require Spirit-led discernment. We have much to learn about the kind of Christian dialogical stance expressed by Jon Hoover who suggests that "we make room in the heart for others and the worlds they inhabit, but do not align ourselves uncritically with powers that cut at the root of that very openness by seeking to harness it for the benefit of one part of humanity to the exclusion of another."[24]

4. **Plurality and homogeneity: recognizing the processes that lead to reconciliation and kingdom living**

As Mennonites we generally view the plurality of ethnic, religious and political groups in our midst as positive, and we value the tolerance that is needed for diversity to flourish. We are comfortable in this space that post-modernity has opened for us since we can now more easily enter the public sphere with our witness. For example, that is why MCC feels comfortable having an office at the United Nation and speaking to various issues from within a plurality of non-governmental agencies. The excitement that we feel about our work in Iran includes excitement about an increasing pluralism that allows us to speak freely within Iran. This is true especially in our theological dialogue. We have been able to be part of a mutual exchange of theological understandings, both receiving and giving of ourselves to those who have had a very different religious, intellectual and political history. The strength of our dialogue has been based on two basic premises. First, we would enter a dialogue of life, not only a dialogue of words, and second, each of us would share as honestly as we could about our own faith, while listening with interest and respect to the other. Through this encounter we have learned that reconciliation can come to us, as we respect our differences and allow the similarities to emerge in those moments that come when we converse deeply with each other. One of these moments came to me on the last day of our Shi'a Muslim/Mennonite Christian Dialogue in Waterloo in 2007. I was moved to tears when one of the Muslim clergy prayed a free and spontaneous prayer with the group and we could all say "Amen." So too, one of our exchange students has talked about how the death of his Catholic professor moved him in a way that he had not expected. As he explained to me, "I never thought that I would sorrow so deeply at the death of a Christian."

But we also have some discomfort in this arena. Are we losing our own identity when we so freely interact with Shi'a Muslims with a different Scripture and a different response to who Jesus is? Should we not more actively witness to the divinity and truth of Christ? Should our more primary task as MCC be in solidarity with Christians? In the same vein, Muslims also feel some discomfort in the dialogue. Are they betraying the truth to which they are committed?[25] Both Muslims and Christians need to discern when plurality becomes a danger to us, when the relativism rampant in our society takes over and we are in danger of losing our own identity and our own passionate convictions. This is an area in which we still have much to learn. Can we be open to hearing how Iran too has struggled with plurality? Can we be open to a pluriform understanding of the good, whether this is good government or good earthquake relief or good freedom or good religion?

5. Peace-building processes that reject violence and coercion.

The excitement that we feel in this arena comes from the many opportunities that we have had to speak about MCC's approach to peace-building. As J. Daryl Byler explained it: "When nations are threatening rather than talking to each other, MCC plans to redouble its advocacy effort and increase people-to-people contact with Iran. Face to face relationships have been the core of nearly two decades of MCC work in Iran."[26] We have discovered openness to this concern among our Shi'a friends and have begun to struggle together to find new ways to relate to each other on concerns for peace building. Several recent experiences testify to these opportunities.

a) The dialogues with Dr. Legenhausen and other Shi'a theologians on peace-building. Dr. Legenhausen has been one of the academic leaders who has hosted the Mennonites in Iran. (Note a recent article he wrote on this theme.)[27]

b) Invitations from Iranians that arise out of the academic dialogue like the one for Susan Harrison, a Mennonite doctoral student, to go to Iran to speak at a conference held by women of different religions in Iran, all working toward peace.

c) The opportunities within our schools such as Eastern Mennonite University (EMU) and Canadian Mennonite University (CMU) to include Muslims in peace-building courses.

d) The learning tours of North Americans going to Iran in which they can overcome some of their own fears and prejudices.

e) The opportunity for MCC to interact with government officials in facilitating conversation between the President of Iran and the churches in the US and Canada.

We feel excitement about these opportunities. However, we also feel some unease. Sometimes we feel that we need to be more careful or we will not continue to be welcome in Iran or in the US or Canada. We know that we are associated with some powerful persons in Iran and we are not sure what this means for us.

We wonder if we have chosen the right conversation partners, if we are only naïve and are treading on dangerous ground. We feel vulnerable and uneasy, wondering if we have gone too far into the unfamiliar ground of political engagement. Do we have the virtues needed to be in a mediating position in the conversations taking place among religions? We need to discuss this question more thoroughly.

6. Calling the powers to their life-giving purpose

This arena brings us into the most direct relationship with government, with law and public policy, with structures of decision-making in both Iran and our own state. As guests in Iran, we do not expect to have direct input into this arena. Yet we feel uneasy when we do not respond adequately to images of torture and victims of state violence. At the same time, we cannot ignore the fact that we are citizens of countries whose policies produce their own victims, who sometimes perpetuate violence and terror around the world. It is often difficult to know how to challenge any of these powers.

One of the powers that we have probably not paid enough attention to is the power of speech, of media and communication technologies that largely shape our worldview. Iranians have been very concerned about the distortions that they see in our media, including our Mennonite press. They do not understand why we allow our own press to continue to communicate false stereotypes of Muslims. (In Iran there are institutions that discern what images are allowed and presses are shut down if they do not follow the rule!) We are uneasy because we do not know how we think theologically about freedom of speech, something that we assume is foundational in a democratic state.

It was an disturbing experience for us at the recent theological conference to be the object of protests rather than the subject of protests. We began to see how much we assume in a democracy about free speech and proper processing of issues. We were horrified that the protests could shout down speakers, before they even had a chance to speak. We recognized our inability to judge what made for unhealthy disorder and what kind of protest against violence was needed even in our own country. We began to see that encouraging dialogue could be dangerous and that it sometimes brought conflict to the fore.

One of the questions that our Iranian colleagues have posed to us as Mennonites on more than one occasion receives only a stumbling response from us. They ask: How would we rule the country if we were suddenly in the majority? How would we keep order? What would we do about the kind of protests that we have observed? Would we use coercive measures to bring about a stable society? Because we already have some political power, we know that calling the powers to their life giving purpose may be the prophetic task that will continue to challenge us the most.

Summary

There are several practical questions that need to be answered by us so that the future direction of MCC will be intentional and arise out of our basic stance as pilgrims and citizens of the kingdom of God. The following are urgent for us at this time:

1. How do we honour MCC's commitment to work with the local church if we decide to also accept Shi‘a believers as part of the larger Abrahamic community?

2. How do we respect and wrestle with the Islam presented to us by the Iranians we meet, while also being aware that other Muslims may well present their religion differently?

3. How do we present our own Mennonite faith perspective without competing with other Christians?

4. How do we keep in balance our listening and speaking with the "powerful" and our solidarity with the more marginal and weaker in society?

5. How can our dialogical practices avoid colonial and proselytizing approaches while including proclamation and witness?

6. What practices of spirituality are needed for those who engage in theological and political dialogue with Iranians so that they may be strengthened in faith and grow in character?

7. How do we deal with the different theological streams in our own constituency and in the larger ecumenical context? What theological framework or image allows us to articulate the mandate of MCC in its relationship to Iran in the best and most honest way?

However, my summary cannot only contain questions. Instead I want to affirm that our interactions with our Shi‘a fellow pilgrims have not been mere talk but can easily be named a "dialogue of life." These interactions have been rich and deep and multifaceted, touching many aspects of life. They have also been "life giving" and we have experienced mutual transformation. Therefore, I want to insist that no state can interfere when the basis of our dialogue is our common humanity before God and our mandate is the peace of the cities in which we dwell. Several words from the scriptures of our Shi‘a friends and from our own can be instructive to us as we continue in this dialogue.

> Hold fast all together to Allah's cord, and do not be divided into sects. And remember Allah's blessing upon you when you were enemies, then He brought your hearts together, so you became brothers with His blessing. And you were on the brink of a pit of fire, from whence He saved you. (Qur'an 3:103)[28]

> For this reason I bow my knees before the Father, from whom every family in heaven and on earth takes its name. I pray that you may be strengthened in your inner being with power through his Spirit, and that Christ may dwell in your hearts through faith, as you are being rooted and grounded in love. I pray that you many have the power to comprehend, with all the saints, what is the breadth and length and height and depth, and to know the love of Christ that surpasses knowledge, so that you may be filled with the fullness of God. (Ephesians 3:14-19)

Chapter 8 Wisdom

NAMING THE NEED FOR WISDOM

My son-in-law Fred interrupted my laundry day activities with the urgent request: "Turn on the TV!" It was September 11, 2001. There we stood, unable to comprehend the magnitude of what was happening to the American nation as we watched the twin towers fall in New York City. In the next days, the comments and responses that we heard intensified our unease and fear. The possibility of violent retaliation was a theme in public meetings, entertainment events, and informal social gatherings. As Mennonite Christians espousing a non-violent ethic we struggled to think of alternative approaches to military intervention.

However, in those early days of the new century, another underlying fear threated to overcome us. For many church attendees, the church itself seemed to be in disarray. The church no longer knew who it was when faced with changing ethical approaches and changing theological certainties. How could an identity be created and shaped when the whole Christian world seemed to be in great upheaval? Could we maintain an identity without the usual boundaries that kept us separate from each other? No wonder that "discernment" became one of the most used terms at congregational meetings and broader church assemblies.

The mood of that time can easily be illustrated by reading the editorials of our church papers together with those in our daily newspapers. In reflecting on the similarities, I realize how much the concerns overlapped with each other. Concern for law and order. Concern around exclusion/inclusion of particular groups of people. Concern for creating community amidst the threat of both individualism and collectivism. Concern about guns in our communities and the culture of violence that seemed to be threatening us in North America. Fear of terrorism in our global community. Fear of people of other religions. We in the church were not alone in our loss of identity and our fear of the other. Yet the uniqueness of the church is that it has a heritage of faith within the Bible to draw on as it discerns direction and addresses its fears.

The questions I struggled with during that time were both personal and communal. They were theological but very practical. They were about reconciliation and peacemaking, but also about finding an identity as God's people, an identity that is not based on our own socio/ethnic background but rather one that is based on God's hospitality and on respect of the other.

As I look over the last chapters, I realize that I have not written a longer article about one of the concerns that has involved my heart and mind the most in the last decades. Yet this concern illustrates directly the crisis we are in as individuals and as churches. The need for a robust peace theology that can address both our insecurity and fear as well as our loss of identity as peace-builders is seen most clearly in our relationship with First Nations people.

My husband and I have three children, one of whom is an adopted Indigenous daughter. When we adopted our daughter at the age of two, we were unaware of the larger community dynamics that would influence our family life. We had decided to adopt to ensure a sister for our two boys; our extended families majored in sons. Also, we were concerned with world population at the time and thought it most responsible to adopt a child that was largely "unadoptable" because of age or a disability. We were unaware of the "1960's scoop" as it is called, in which First Nations children were deliberately adopted into white homes to assimilate them by taking the "Indian" out of them. We rather naively assumed that we could just adopt a daughter, that she would feel equal to our other children, and that she would become like us, feeling the same sense of self-worth that came more easily to our two sons.

As we look back now we realize that subconsciously we assumed her Indigenous heritage was not as important as ours. During her growing up years we made little effort to acquaint her with her own people and her own traditions. Not surprisingly she always felt like an outsider with her brown skin and black hair and found self worth much more difficult to achieve.

We did support her in her later teen years to help her find her family roots. What we discovered was a trail of oppression by government, churches, and ordinary citizens like us—residential schools, physical and psychological abuse, broken treaties and promises, and much deception. For example, the government took First Nations reserve land (our daughter's home reserve) without permission to build a dam that brought prosperity to the Mennonite community in which my husband grew up. We began to realize that as a member of an Indigenous group in Canada our daughter has not been given the dignity that every child of God needs, and this lack of dignity could easily contribute to further broken relationships.

Slowly we have discovered how much we can learn from the resilience of First Nations communities. Our daughter has blessed us in so many ways. We are fortunate to live close to her and her husband and our four Indigenous grandchildren. Our larger family circle has experienced some wonderful moments of reconciliation with our First Nations friends. To be welcomed into a sweat lodge, to participate in an Indigenous wedding ceremony, to sit at a campfire with our children and grandchildren: these are undeserved privileges. Yet there is much need for further reconciliation.

The questions of our own identity must now include the brokenness and need for forgiveness that comes when we acknowledge that we are settler people, people whose privilege was brought about through the domination of others. We must acknowledge how the "Doctrine of Discovery" and the "Indian Act" have served to give us land, home, and security.[1] *And so we are left with the questions: Can God still use us, a broken community, in its relationship with First Nations people? Can God help us to listen more carefully and to find ways to undo the wrongs committed by us as a community? How can we as families and as a church be part of the process of supporting the claims of our Indigenous neighbours and friends, overcoming our own fear of the "other"? How can the gospel message be embodied in our relationships but also in the systems and institutions of which we are a part?*

As I reflect on the various ways in which my theology around community, identity, and power relationships was challenged during those years right after the turn of the century, I realize that I needed to go beyond asking the question of my own identity and power as a woman. I needed to ask how we as a Christian community in our brokenness could become part of the larger movement of God in the world. I needed to ask questions that created an alternative to the fear and pain felt by so many in our communities.

I was fortunate to be able to work at these questions in a practical way by being part of the peace committee of Mennonite Central Committee (MCC). We devoted one of our meetings to ask how to address the fear and systematic violence that we encountered among us. Of course, we had already wrestled with these questions over the years since MCC works in many areas where conflict and chaotic conditions are normal parts of daily life. Having heard the reports from many countries beyond the USA and Canada, we knew that many people lived daily with the threat of violence. For example, we had heard about the need for order and security in Columbia where the government and various armed groups competed for power and ordinary people became the victims. We had been asking what kind of institutions should be supported to ensure safety and security in these countries. But now the threat of chaos and disorder was coming closer to home and we began to ask the question: how could we, who believe in peace-making, be involved in building a just order beyond the church in our own society?

As a peace committee, we decided that we needed a sustained conversation over the next few years with those individuals in our congregations who were already involved in society's systems of ordering such as teachers, lawyers, politicians, police, social workers, or probation officers. We wanted to ask them about how they applied their faith to the practical decisions that they faced in their work, whether with the main stream of society, with indigenous groups, or with other minority groups among us. We wanted to hear stories in which they had found creative solutions without needing to use violence. We were asking them to reflect on which institutions in our society were necessary so that peaceful relationships among people could exist. The "MCC Peace Theology Project" grew out of these discussions.

I was asked to be part of a team of five researchers for this two-year study project beginning in January, 2003. The work consisted of a series of consultations in various parts of USA and Canada as well as many individual conversations with people directly involved in "ordering" functions within our society. A final international conference took place in Akron, Pennsylvania where the results of our theological thinking were presented and discussed. The papers presented were published in the book, At Peace and Unafraid, *the title expressing the hope we had for all peoples of the world.*

Our research group spent many hours listening and then reflecting together about what we had heard. We discovered that there were many people who felt lonely and un-affirmed in their professions because they did not fit into the traditional categories that Mennonites have seen as contributing to peace. Others expressed their discomfort when we listened to police, prison wardens, or politicians, not sure if we were compromising our traditional Anabaptist stance of nonresistance. The question that I wrestled with most was: how do we use the Bible as a resource to answer these questions?" More and more I began to see how we in the Anabaptist tradition had neglected the wisdom strand of the Bible while emphasizing the prophetic strand. My contribution to this committee was to explore the wisdom strand in Scripture more fully to see how it could help us as we "seek the welfare of the city" in which we live.

As I reflect on who is part of our church community, I realize that many of us have jobs and professions that give us authority and power within the larger structures of society. The theology of peace-making that we embrace should give practical assistance to each of us as we try to embody our peace theology in our daily lives. Much wisdom is needed to make decisions that will address both our human tendencies to colonize and dominate the other as well to fear and distance ourselves from the other. Peace-making thus requires us to grow in our own identity as compassionate loving people. But it also asks us to be both prophetic and wise in our work within institutions of ordering within our society. The essay I wrote for this project seeks to work toward that goal. It speaks specifically to peace theology as understood within the Mennonite communmity but is applical to any theology that seeks justice and peace.

***

SEEKING WISDOM IN THE FACE OF FOOLISHNESS: TOWARD A ROBUST PEACE THEOLOGY[2]

It may seem surprising that the Peace Committee which advises Mennonite Central Committee's (MCC) international program would consult with police officers, lawyers, city councilors, and social workers in order to develop a peace theology for Anabaptist-Mennonite witness in the public sphere. A second surprise, however, has been the degree to which I as a theologian and MCC Peace Committee member identified with these persons, who are active in institutions that attempt to create safety and order in society. In the questions they raise I have recognized my own fear, insecurity, and guilt in the face of injustice, disorder, and violence. Often we wish for quick solutions. Often we experience a messiness, ambiguity, or loneliness as we take risks to seek security for our neighbor and community. Or else, overwhelmed with the problems of the world, we succumb to passivity, as hope disappears and we retreat into our own comfortable, safe haven.

This identification is not surprising. I grew up in an immigrant family that had left the Ukraine after the Russian Revolution to seek security in a new land. The loss of family members and a secure home in the Ukraine subtly influenced my early years. My family had experienced the temptations that come when institutions are violently disrupted, disorder reigns, and family and friends are in constant danger in communities that once were considered safe and secure. I remember my father telling us stories of the self-defense group that decided nonresistance did not work in those revolutionary times. I remember him telling of Mennonites who joined whichever group had power at the moment, willing even to betray their brothers and sisters in the faith. But more importantly, I remember him telling us the story of his father's murder and his struggle with feelings of revenge and hate. I marveled that he finally came to a place of forgiveness and could express strong convictions, born of that very time, about nonviolence and peacemaking.

One way that my parents expressed these peace convictions was in helping to build a community in the new land, a community in which trust and freedom would reign. I remember being told of the importance of cooperative ventures in which the church took a leading role: our farm co-op, our church schools, our Mennonite burial society. I remember as a child being one of the first people to join the Mennonite Credit Union being established to serve our whole community. I also learned to trust neighbors of various nationalities and religions as I watched my father and mother interact with others in the arduous task of farming and marketing their produce. In addition, I learned to share our resources with others, particularly with the refugee and the homeless. I grew up feeling secure in my family and community, while vaguely aware of the insecurity of others.

In more recent years I have become more directly involved with persons who continue to face insecurity, danger, prejudice, and fear as part of their daily life. Some feel insecure because they have been robbed of their cultural heritage, language, and family structures, as in the case of First Nations peoples in Canada. Others, including recent refugees from Colombia, were forced to flee from their homes in the face of violence and unrest. Still others have experienced the abuse and violence that can come about in their own homes when the social safety net in our communities is ineffective. I have realized how much security and safety depend on societal institutions that provide structures and communication channels so that basic needs can be met.

During the consultations that our MCC project team conducted on security and safety, I have become aware that we often do not know how to speak theologically about building institutions to seek the common good. This means that we do not know how to call each other to faithfulness, how to counsel each other when we are afraid, how to face the hard questions that have to do with institutional power and integrity or with coercive intervention. We can speak much more comfortably in social, political, psychological, or business language, unsure of the way these relate to our theological convictions. We sit in church hearing about the "upside-down kingdom" of God, or read our MCC brochures describing the prophetic ministry that we are doing in other lands. But we wonder what these have to do with our daily work, which often focuses more directly on bringing stability and order to our communities.

One of the primary challenges we face at the beginning of the twenty-first century, therefore, is to find ways to speak theologically about the "logic" underlying the kingdom of God and the "logic" underlying our human institutions and structures. We need language that will relate the vision of transformation and peace which God's reign promises to the daily decisions we make as we go about our daily work. We need clear language that will aid our discernment as we struggle to live faithfully, seeking the common good of the society in which we live.

God's Reign and Human Institutions

> *Your kingdom come. Your will be done, on earth as it is in heaven.*
> (Matt 6:10)

Theological language contrasting "the kingdom of God" with "the kingdoms of this world" is one way that the Mennonite tradition has of expressing the relationship between God's kingdom and human institutions. This contrast implies that Christians must think and act according to a logic different from the power calculations of our social, economic, and political institutions. Christians must be nonconformed in their thinking, focusing on being in tune with the logic of Jesus Christ who lived the way of righteousness and shalom, rather than on the logic of the communal good as our society defines it. Thus a tension arises between the alternative community, the church that confesses kingdom values, and all other social institutions and their values. This tension creates a prophetic engagement with society calling all persons and institutions to repentance and to a new way of peace and justice. It fuels the missional mandate of our church communities and focuses our attention on alternative strategies and institutions that can more easily exhibit these kingdom characteristics.[3]

Problems have arisen, however, because this description may too quickly equate the kingdom of God with the church, thus creating a sharp divide between the church and other societal institutions. Furthermore, modernity has created a sharp boundary between the sacred and the secular, which has further reinforced the dualism in Mennonite two-kingdom theology and tempted churches to become triumphalistic and exclusive. They forget that churches are themselves human institutions, influenced by the dominant culture, often embodying other-than-kingdom values. When this happens, Christians are tempted to forget their own culpability in the sin of economic, political, and military institutions and may fail to bring their own everyday reality into God's probing light. In addition, they may become insulated in their communities, forgetting that the biblical vision of shalom encompasses all creation and that God is actively working in the whole world so that God's reign may be effectively realized on earth as it is in heaven. The conflict between kingdoms is then understood as a closed and static conclusion rather than an open and dynamic movement of God toward a sure eschatological fulfillment.[4]

The Mennonite tradition does include a second way to speak of this relationship. In an attempt to counter the temptations of the first approach, this way focuses on the biblical conviction that God is Lord of all creation. Therefore, some similarity exists between the logic that governs the kingdom of God and the logic by which all institutions, including the church, will be judged. From this perspective God does not work in sharp discontinuity in the church and in society more generally. The kingdom of God that is "at hand" rests on a universal hope for a redeemed creation. The church must therefore be actively engaged in society, working for the common good in ways that Jesus Christ taught and embodied. This may include working within institutions and structures whose values overlap with those of the church. As Christians, we should look for signs of God's activity in the world and align ourselves with the direction that we see God moving within our society and the world at large.

Equally subtle temptations may arise when we too quickly assume continuity between the kingdom of God and the logic underlying our political and social institutions. When the whole social order is understood as the sphere of God's activity, Christians may underestimate the need for the critical discernment and empowerment that is necessary to discern and follow God's way. They may not recognize the point when a governing institution becomes oppressive and thus acts in a manner antithetical to the logic of love and compassion that is basic to the kingdom of God. They may become arrogant, so sure of God's will that they succumb to the temptation to use violence to enforce kingdom values. In using this logic Christians may forget that Christ called the church to be a sign of the reign of God in every society and that its logic may sometimes contradict the values underlying institutional structures. Thus a need remains for some tension and duality in our language in order to point to our primary allegiance to Jesus Christ, and to our calling as a church.

In the consultations that we held during this time of discernment on issues related to security and order, I was puzzled by those who felt no tension between their work as police officers, social workers, lawyers, or scholars, and their identity as people of God. However, I was equally disturbed by those for whom the tension was so great that to work in a "secular" vocation somehow seemed to mean working in another kingdom—that is, not under God's reign. The question with which I have wrestled in these months, therefore, has been this: How shall we acknowledge both the continuity and the tension that exist when we act as citizens within our society while pledging our primary allegiance to God's reign coming on earth? What kind of logic determines how we think and act in our daily professions within institutions that may be intimately connected with the use of power and even violence?

In this search I was drawn back to the Bible and its various theological traditions. In particular, I began to reread a strand of the biblical heritage that Mennonite peace theology does not often acknowledge: wisdom.[5] I immersed myself in writings on wisdom in both testaments and soon realized that these extend far beyond the books that biblical scholars know as classic wisdom literature. In this rereading, I began to note how such writings stood beside the prophetic tradition in the larger story of God's dealing with humankind. I began to wonder if including wisdom would help us affirm a logic that connects the best knowledge humans possess, while maintaining a prophetic tension between God's logic and all lesser wisdoms. Perhaps a more robust theology of peace would emerge that would challenge the sacred/secular divide in Mennonite experience while holding all the more firmly to the cruciform shape of Jesus's way of peace. Perhaps we could discover a "way of life" that we can live within a large variety of institutions while prophetically and creatively challenging those same institutions.

The Promise of the Wisdom Tradition

> *Those who listen to me [wisdom] will be secure and will live at ease, without dread of disaster.* (Proverbs 1:33)
>
> *Keep sound wisdom and prudence… then you will walk in your way securely and your foot will not stumble.* (Proverbs 3:21-23)

In the last few centuries the biblical traditions of wisdom have had only minimal impact on theology or ethics as practiced in the West. It is only recently that historical and literary biblical studies have taken a new interest in wisdom, one that theologians and ethicists have begun to notice, and that theological writings on peace and justice have begun to draw on this source.[6] Yet the book of Proverbs, as well as other wisdom literature, draws a direct connection between wisdom, security, and safety. An overview of recent writings by biblical scholars suggests at least three reasons to hope that a study of wisdom traditions might be fruitful for our quest.[7]

First, in its mix of analysis, generalization, accusation, creativity, and freedom, biblical wisdom mirrors our own struggle with God and our communities in our quest for security, safety, and shalom for all people. Because the wisdom traditions generally begin with experience, they attend to empirical evidence and data. They then reflect on that reality by attempting to link it to the "grain of the universe"[8]—that is, the underlying unity and universality of God who is creator, sustainer, and savior of the world. In its rich variety, wisdom explores order by attending to patterns of consistency in reality, while also recognizing conflict and novelty as it opens out to new and disparate experiences. This holds promise for reflecting anew on the ambiguity of our relationships to institutions of order.

Second, Scripture often presents the language of wisdom as a "middle discourse," a language about reality that can exist between the particular language of other religions, and the particular language of Israelite and Christian faith.[9] The intellectual tradition of Israel, though operating within the constraints of its theological commitments, recognized that God had given gifts of wisdom in varying degrees to people outside of Israel. Truth and goodness, wherever they are found, were considered gifts of God—part of God's revelation to all through the testimony of nature, history, and experience. In fact, parallels to various wisdom teachings can be found in Egyptian and Babylonian wisdom. Thus wisdom speaks in a public language and is dialogical at its core. Wisdom may therefore model constructive ways of speaking about security in the public sphere.

Finally, Wisdom is one of the names that early Christians gave to Jesus. Wisdom thus merits particular attention by those of us who stand in a discipleship tradition of following Jesus. Recent study has recognized anew that New Testament writers did not see true wisdom as a rival truth to the prophetic Word or the gospel. After all, Jesus both taught and modeled for us how to live wisely in conformity with the "normative culture of the reign of God" as confessed in our worship of God, and as revealed (though in a hidden way) through creation.[10] New Testament writings recognize that seeking to follow Jesus, the Wisdom of God, into the marketplaces of our world may be risky. As the wisdom of Christ challenges the dominant values of society, it will thus (and paradoxically) require Jesus's disciples to seek safety and security in risky ways. Reflection on Jesus in relationship to larger wisdom traditions, therefore, should help us see how the prophetic and the wise meet as they challenge false understandings and false prophetic words.

To test these possibilities this paper will sample examples of the wisdom idiom embedded in a variety of literary texts in the Bible, spanning a broad range of thought about the cosmos, human nature, and social organization in relationship to peace and security.

Wisdom's Invitation: An Image of Abundance

> *Come, eat of my bread and drink of the wine I have mixed. Lay aside immaturity, and live, and walk in the way of insight.* (Proverbs 9:5-6)

> *Come to me, all you that are weary and are carrying heavy burdens, and I will give you rest. Take my yoke upon you and learn from me, for I am gentle and humble in heart, and you will find rest for your souls.* (Matthew 11:28-29)

One of the central images of wisdom in both the testaments is that of a banquet table symbolizing the abundant riches of life under the reign of God. The image expresses an invitation to all to partake of the nourishment that Woman Wisdom offers and to receive the promise of blessing and shalom that is freely given through God 's abundant generosity.[11] This contrasts markedly with the image of the foolish woman who is a flighty creature, a simpleton who cares for nothing but sits on a seat to invite passers-by indoors (Proverbs 9:13-18). That invitation leads to death instead of life.

The image of a banquet table highlights at least two aspects of the wisdom of God. Most basic is the conviction that God is generous and it is the desire of God to give abundant life to all creatures. In fact, the book of Proverbs sees wisdom as the first of creation, present with God to delight and rejoice in the human race and in the world that God had made (Proverbs 8:27-33). The New Testament testifies that God through Christ freely offers wisdom for living to everyone, including the weary and heavy laden, so that all can know what makes for life and security. Second, this image suggests that although God is generous to all, God also expects humans to make choices as to whose table they will join. Judgments must be made and choices faced in order to partake of God's goodness. These do not depend on human skill nor on human strength alone, but do require our willingness to accept the lessons that wisdom offers. For it is the wise who hear and gain in learning, but the foolish who despise wisdom and instruction (Proverbs 1:5-7).

Wisdom is thus the reflective side of our life of faithfulness to God, valuing insight and reasoning in the search for a comprehensive vision of the meaning of life. It is this image of wisdom that will guide our study as we explore its expression in a variety of genres, assumptions, expectancies, and perspectives on life. Though the texts chosen will be those that relate most directly to security and safety, the sampling of texts should also point to the scope and richness of the wisdom tradition in its various literary forms. Perhaps these morsels of insight will whet our appetite to partake of the rich nourishment that wisdom offers us.

A Conversation in Many Modes

> *Wisdom cries out in the street; in the square she raises her voice.*
> (Proverbs 1:20)

The biblical writings that invite us to wisdom's table are not of the same literary genre nor are they fully integrated with each other. Though there are biblical books that scholars specifically designate as classic wisdom texts (such as Proverbs, Ecclesiastes, Job, and several apocryphal books), the Bible also contains narratives that model wise action, parables that illuminate the wisdom of God, letters that give wise advice, and psalms and hymns that celebrate God's wisdom.[12] Therefore the interfacing of wisdom texts with each other and with other texts in the canon will be most central to our discussion. This will allow us a glimpse of the intertextual dialogue within the Bible. But more to the point, this will allow us to see how wisdom can be a mode of invitation to all people to work out the meaning of peacemaking in our human societies.

1. Stories

Many of the wisdom stories in the Bible arise out of the popular ethos of the tribe and village circle. They were probably told and retold to generations of youth and adults to inspire them to choose the way of life instead of death. Stories invite identification with their characters in the problems and situations that they encounter. For example, stories with characters like Abigail and Daniel begin with conflict situations or personal threats and gradually, through wise responses to the situations, move to a measure of peace and security. Others such as the stories of Joseph and Esther, Stephen and Paul, lead to further risk but serve to highlight how God used human decisions to further God's peace. The wisdom in these stories arises out of the reflection on these events by the story-tellers.

Throughout the centuries, many different hearers and readers of the stories have identified with the biblical characters even though they lived in quite different social orders of families, tribes, and empires. Still, many stories contain aspects that make them ambiguous models for our own ethical reflection. Waldemar Janzen has given some helpful perspectives on stories of wisdom. He points out that stories that present an exemplary action are not self-contained wholes "yielding an encapsulated and timeless ethical principle." Instead, ethical action emerges from a situation that a preceding story has shaped, and that in turn contributes to the ongoing movement of the larger narrative. Crucial to the interpretation of these stories is the intertwining of theology and ethics, creating a link between God's ordering providence and human action. In many situations it is God's generosity that redeems human actions that only partially fit with God's ways.

Janzen claims that stories operate at an ethical level prior to law.[13] Thus they invite us to reflect on values that successive storytellers have honed into paradigms of wise thoughts and actions. They help us reflect on our own experiences of life, allowing us to differentiate between wise and foolish actions. They therefore invite us to interpret our experiences in the light of the Creator God's provisions for a good life as well as help us understand our human actions in the context of the larger human story.

2. *Didactic Traditions of Wisdom*

The didactic traditions of wisdom encompass a wide variety of observations about life, ranging from the seeming naiveté of Proverbs, the pessimism of Ecclesiastes, the subversive wisdom of Jesus's teachings to the practical advice within the epistles. Ponderings on daily life by these sages begin with observations but often turn to questions about the larger design and purpose of creation and the role of humans in that creation. These sages believed that the Creator brought into being an orderly world and that divinely ordered rules for living were there for the curious and discerning to discover.

The forms in which the sages gave these teachings were invitational because of their familiarity, not unlike didactic traditions outside of Scripture. For example, a proverb is a form of teaching that is ingrained in our consciousness because of its brevity and its common sense. Poetic presentations such as those of Job inspire meditation and debate about their interpretation of life. Parables such as those in the teachings of Jesus create a metaphorical tension that leads to further reflection. The personal address of the Pauline letters creates relationships that allow the readers to receive good advice. Thus the variety of didactic forms itself invites us to reason further about God's design for our security and safety.

It is the assumptions underlying these teachings, of course, that create the ongoing debate and discussion within the wisdom literature. Unlike the prophets who directly claimed to speak God's word for specific circumstances, the sages were more impressed by the limits of their wisdom and by the mystery of God that was beyond their reach. Though they assumed that much wisdom could be distilled from everyday experience, they were also impressed by the vastness of God's work and the need for God's self-manifestation through specific revelation. Thus proverbial wisdom could concern itself with seemingly mundane instructions on table manners or on tending the flocks, while other wisdom literature such as Job and Ecclesiastes debated more comprehensive themes such as justice, suffering, the nature of God, and creation.

In the New Testament various didactic traditions lie hidden within the literary genres of gospels and epistles. Too often, therefore, we have failed to recognize them as wisdom teachings. Nonetheless, the strongest consensus of contemporary scholarship is that Jesus was a teacher of wisdom.[14] Early in life he was eager to debate with the rabbis in the temple. As Luke testifies, Jesus grew and became strong, "filled with wisdom" (Luke 2:40). In the gospel narratives he was addressed as Teacher, he gathered disciples, taught in public places, drew on Old Testament wisdom motifs, and appealed to all to follow the narrow way leading to life rather than the broad way ending in death. His parables resembled popular stories, but drew readers into deeper reflection on God and God's ways. He was recognized as a teacher greater than Solomon (Matthew 12:42) for he often turned the world of conventional assumptions upside down with his radical and wise interpretations of the tradition.[15] In the epistles there is a renewed interest in wisdom expressed in a variety of forms, including creative restatements of the gospel message as well as proverbial and parabolic wisdom containing direct advice on practical matters.

Too often, instead of leading us to discern and reflect further on wisdom in our day, these didactic traditions have been used to cut off discussion and demand immediate obedience. They have been used dogmatically and applied directly to situations that differ vastly from the biblical times. Yet in the dialogue between these various texts, some tensions remain unresolved and some questions do not receive complete answers, thus creating space for our own reflection. We are invited to discern further, to open ourselves to sustained conversation, and deeper thought. These texts, therefore, ask us not only to receive the wisdom that they contain but also to thoughtfully contribute our own insights from our own experience to the conversation.

3. The Merging of Creation Wisdom and Covenantal Wisdom

> *See, just as the Lord my God has charged me, I now teach you statutes and ordinances for you to observe in the land that you are*

> *about to enter and occupy. You must observe them diligently, for this will show your wisdom and discernment to the peoples, who, when they hear all these statutes, will say, "Surely this great nation is a wise and discerning people."* (Deuteronomy 4:5-6)

Already in the Old Testament, some biblical writers suggest that Torah, the revelation of God that Israel received from God within its own particular history, was the highest form of wisdom. The covenant that God established with the people of God included the promises to Abraham, the Law, and also the knowledge they gained through their experience of exodus from slavery. Post-exilic writings identified the Torah with wisdom itself (Ecclesiasticus 24:23), as did several of the Psalms (19, 119). However, the wisdom that comes through observation of God's work in creation and the wisdom that the people of God gain through God's liberating action in the exodus meet in rather complex ways in various writings. In response to threats against their national identity in the centuries just before the time of Jesus, scribes and sages intensified their study of the Law. As the identification of Torah with wisdom intensified, creation blessing and covenantal blessing were sometimes held in tension rather than completely identified with each other.[16] For example, as other nations appeared more and more to be enemies, tensions surfaced between openness to the wisdom of those outside the border of Israel and strong needs for identity and protection of the holy nation. But this merging of traditions had a paradoxical result: Priestly concerns for holiness through separation from the nations, and the sages' concern for openness to a wisdom that extended internationally, drew closer and closer to each other. In this context some understood law, which required immediate obedience, as wisdom personified.

Gerald Sheppard has suggested that during the late Old Testament period, wisdom became a theological category that formed a perspective from which to interpret Torah and the prophetic traditions.[17] Wisdom could show in practical terms how Torah related to its own concerns for faithful living. In addition, poetic celebrations of Woman Wisdom as the personified daughter of God emerged during this time, bringing Creation and Torah together in the figure of an attractive woman identified with God's activity from Adam to Moses (Wisd of Sol 10:1-2, 15). It is thus no wonder that early Christians explicitly made the connection between Personified Wisdom and Jesus; the later wisdom tradition was doing exactly this with Torah (Wisd of Sol 7:25-26). In using this identification, Jesus' early followers made the radical claim that Jesus Christ is the key to understanding created reality in all of its manifestations and dimensions.

Within the epistles the teachings of the apostles are understood as the wisdom of God, in contrast to "human" wisdom which strives for prestige and status and leads to ruin (1 Cor 1:18-31). The invitation to discern true wisdom became increasingly central as did the role of the Holy Spirit in giving power for that discernment. The book of Ephesians is a good example of an epistle that brings the concerns of traditional wisdom and the concerns of the gospel of Jesus into conversation with each other. Its view of salvation is repeatedly depicted as new creation, stressing the emergence of creation and salvation from the one God. Tom Yoder Neufeld suggests that Ephesians stands firmly in the wisdom tradition of "revelatory reflection," in which the author consciously reformulates and restates the apostolic deposit, while probing its implications.[18]

The merging of traditions, therefore, not only introduced continuity but also a tension into the overall category of wisdom. Do these traditions overlap completely or can one be given highest priority? Biblical literature does not answer this question by suggesting that only the people of God have wisdom. Neither does it subsume the particular experience of God's people under the general category of wisdom. Instead it recognized that foolishness is never far away from any human knowing and therefore discernment is always necessary. In addition, the biblical witness understood all wisdom to be a gift of God, thus leading to the view that only God's eschatological fulfillment would finally and fully integrate all wisdom. In the meantime, wisdom must be sought with all our minds and hearts and actions.

4. Worship Traditions of Wisdom

The worship tradition of wisdom is highly processed, somewhat removed from immediate experience, and often couched in the language of poetry, or at least placed into a context of the cult, such as the Psalter or New Testament hymns.[19] Its poetic form invites prayer, meditation, and doxology more than debate. For example, Psalm 1 is a classic wisdom psalm in its depiction of the two ways, the way of life and the way of destruction. Placed at the beginning of the Psalter, it points to wisdom as of crucial importance in the worship of God. So too Psalm 34 celebrates God's deliverance and then actively teaches how the fear of the Lord works itself out practically in the daily choices of life that the righteous make.

The Psalms are therefore a celebration of God and God's way. They encourage all to choose that righteous way because this way leads to life and blessing not only for oneself but also for the larger community. The Psalmist assumes that God and others will overhear these meditations and prayers, which reflect on God's gifts of creation, life, law, and social ordering.[20] For the Psalms rest on the twofold assumption that one can learn by wisdom how to pray and that wisdom itself is a gift of God.

It is the hymns of the New Testament that bring wisdom to its climax in the incarnation of God's Wisdom in Jesus. In these hymns creation and new creation merge in the person of Jesus Christ. Jesus becomes the key to understanding reality in all of its manifestations and dimensions (John 1, Colossians 1, Philippians 2). In worship wisdom merges with prophetic speech proclaiming God's gifts to all creation. Christ is Lord of all since he was present in creation as Wisdom. God's active and ongoing care for creation will continue until creation is completed in the gathering up of all things in the fullness of time.

He is the image of the invisible God, the firstborn of all creation; for in him all things in heaven and on earth were created, visible and invisible, whether thrones, or dominions, or rulers, or powers—all things have been created through him and for him. He himself is before all things, and in him all things hold together. (Colossians 1:15-17)

It is these convictions of God's generosity in both creation and new creation that give the church confidence to witness to the wisdom of God "in its rich variety," even to "rulers and authorities in the heavenly places" (Ephesians 3:10). A rhythm or dynamic thus underlies the wisdom traditions. It is a dynamic of receiving from God that which makes for life and then inviting others also to experience life in its fullness. It is this dynamic of receiving and giving that compels the church to enter the conversation in the marketplace and to seek the common good of the community. It is also this dynamic that counters all pride and triumphalism, creating instead a conversation at the table where all can hear an invitation both to share their wisdom and to listen to the wisdom of others.

Wisdom's Truth: Values, Insights, Convictions and Practices

> *Therefore walk in the way of the good, and keep to the paths of the just, for the upright will abide in the land.* (Proverbs 2:20)

> *For the gate is narrow and the road is hard that leads to life, and there are few who find it.* (Matthew 7:14)

Wisdom's invitation is to the narrow and hard way that leads to abundant life, also named the "way of righteousness," "prosperity," "rest," "blessing," "shalom," or the reign of God coming "on earth as it is in heaven." These terms and images hint at the vast horizon of wisdom writings on this abundant life, and on all that preserves and continues life, and on all that gives meaning and purpose to life. This includes access to necessities for physical life: land, food, and security. But it also includes ongoing family and broader social relationships, which help create the structures that make life possible.

Instead of setting down laws or rules for action for every occasion, wisdom traditions are subtle and more open. They suggest values, insights, practices, and convictions that lead to life. Though they do include some basic substantive knowledge, they realize that this knowledge must continually grow and mature as one learns to live in the way of wisdom.

Questions of security and safety are important for the abundant life toward which wisdom aims. The following convergences in the various modes of wisdom demonstrate a direction for any reflection on safety and security. They do not give final answers, yet they do present learnings from the various traditions of biblical wisdom that can challenge Mennonite peace theology as it struggles with its response to threats of violence and insecurity. In each case, one or two short proverbs or teaching distill these learnings.

> *1. Keep your heart with all vigilance, for from it flow the springs of life.* (Proverbs 4:23)

Though few have thought of the story of Cain in the fourth chapter of the Genesis as a wisdom text, it affirms the teaching in Proverbs: jealousy and anger within the individual human heart lead to insecurity for the broader human community. The storyteller is specific about the inner feelings of Cain: "Cain was very angry and his countenance fell." The comment that "sin is lurking at the door" suggests someone whose heart is filled with anger (Genesis 4:6-7). Cain's killing of his brother Abel and the ensuing curses upon him affect the whole community and are prominent elements in the stories of the succeeding generations. Classic wisdom texts later highlight these inner feelings and attitudes, placing an emphasis on the personal dimensions that create either insecure situations for individuals and communities or lead to peaceful resolutions.

"Those who are hot-tempered stir up strife, but those who are slow to anger calm contention" (Proverbs 15:18). "The greedy person stirs up strife" (Proverbs 28:25). "The fear of others lays a snare but one who trusts in the Lord is secure" (Proverbs 29:25). These proverbs arise from common sense observations but point to deeper truth about the role that the inner self plays in communal security and safety. Many of the verses use terms such as the "perverted mind," the "wicked heart," the "jealous," the "self-indulgent," and the "haughty" to indicate those inner attitudes that cause a person to refuse to learn and instead devise wicked plans that lead to violence. Yet there is also sensitivity to the loneliness within one's inner self and to the pain that others cause.

"The heart knows its own bitterness, and no stranger shares its joy" (Proverbs 14:10). "By sorrow of heart the spirit is broken" (Proverbs 15:13b). The book of Proverbs is particularly aware of how hasty words can create conflict and turmoil, and it sees the need for self-discipline to avoid the chain of violence that these words can unleash. It thus calls for prudence and thought before acting.

"Fools show their anger at once but the prudent ignore an insult" (Prov 12:16). "A fool's lips bring strife" (Proverbs 18:6). Jesus in his teachings suggests that the personal aspects of our lives are indeed crucial, for it is there that violence is born. "It is from within, from the human heart, that evil intentions come" (Mark 7:21). Jesus' teachings reiterate the importance of tending to our inner being, even suggesting that uncontrolled anger and insults are just as liable to judgment as is murder (Matthew 5:21-26). But Jesus also understands the worry, the valuing of earthly treasures, the envy, and fear that arise within the human heart. His rhetorical questions, such as: "And can any of you by worrying add a single hour to your span of life?" (Matthew 6:27) function to bring about deeper reflection on the hidden self that often lies behind violent actions.

In his practical advice James summarizes the need for gentle practices that are born within the heart. But he also recognizes that these can only come from God as a gift when one is open to receive it. Righteousness and peace follow the practice of "keeping one's heart with all diligence."

> Who is wise and understanding among you? Show by your good life that your works are one with gentleness born of wisdom. But if you have bitter envy and selfish ambition in your hearts, do not be boastful and false to the truth. Such wisdom does not come from above, but is earthy, unspiritual, devilish. For where there is envy and selfish ambition, there will also be disorder and wickedness of every kind. But wisdom from above is first pure, then peaceable, gentle, willing to yield, full of mercy and good fruits without a trace of partiality or hypocrisy. And a harvest of righteousness is sown in peace for those who make peace. (James 3:13-18)

Perhaps one aspect of security that needs further attention in Mennonite peace theology is the relationship of the personal and the social/political in responding to issues of violence and insecurity. The scientific approach to knowledge has tended to divide psychology from sociology and political science, as well as the social sciences from theology, thus narrowing our conversation about safety and security. In Mennonite congregations, separation of the domestic sphere from the public has also created barriers to talking more directly about the fear, the worry, the anger, and the trauma that help to create violent responses in our world. Attention to factors that lead to insecurity must include those that arise within the self, thus suggesting that more inclusive conversations are mandatory for those who are wise.

> *2. Whoever walks in integrity walks securely.* (Proverbs 10:9) *The righteous find a refuge in their integrity.* (Proverbs 14:32)

In the book of Proverbs righteousness and integrity are almost synonymous with the wisdom that brings security, while unrighteousness and wickedness lead to destruction. There is an assumption that individual righteous and wise persons, especially among the powerful, can uphold a pattern of life that brings security to a community (blessing) while individual foolish actions will bring disaster and conflict (curses). Solomon is the best-known model of royal wisdom within Israel, thanks to his request to God "to give your servant therefore an understanding mind to govern your people, able to discern between good and evil" (1 Kings 3:9). In the biblical corpus 1 Kings and 2 Chronicles link Solomon to wisdom just as Moses is linked to Torah.[21] The assertion of Solomonic authorship of the book of Proverbs and several of the wisdom psalms fits well with the international fame that the narrative attributes to Solomon and his wisdom. Yet his story illustrates both the blessing and the destruction that come when wisdom does not coincide with integrity.

The story of Solomon begins with the young king having a dream in which he receives the divine gift of wisdom (1 Kings 3). As the narrative progresses, wisdom and right action are associated with varied examples of creative judgment in cases of conflict (such as the famous case of two women claiming the same baby); intelligence and skill in the building of the temple and the royal retinue; overseeing of priests in service at the temple; and the ability to answer riddles and questions from the visiting queen of Sheba, who had heard of Solomon's wisdom.

Repeatedly in the narrative Solomon is also cautioned to exercise his gift of wisdom by obeying the Torah. In the end, the story faults him because "his heart was not true to the Lord his God, as was the heart of his father David.... So Solomon did what was evil in the sight of the Lord" (1 Kings 11:4, 6). The story ends with the Lord becoming angry with Solomon and raising up adversaries against him, resulting in conflict, warfare, and disaster.

In the book of Proverbs, the individual and institutional interest coincide in the language of building a "house" (24:3). Many proverbs assume contemporary social structures, of course, including the institution of kings and warriors (Proverbs 24:5, 21-22). Various spheres of order that we moderns often separate in our understanding—including cosmology, societal order, and human nature—are integrated in the notion of a righteous order.[22] In the end, however, reliance for security cannot stay with social or institutional powers because they tend to become unjust. True righteousness is evident in the response of rulers to the poor and vulnerable. Thus it is God's righteousness, with its preferential option for the poor, that judges the righteousness of any institution: "Those who oppress the poor insult the Maker, but those who are kind to the needy honor him" (Proverbs 14:31). "The Lord tears down the house of the proud, but maintains the widow's boundaries" (Proverbs 15:25).

The book of Ecclesiastes is rather cynical in its portrayal of the present social order. The writer knows that this order can easily become tyrannical in its hierarchy and its rigidity. He also recognizes the presence of war but knows that wise reflection can find better ways to solve conflict: "If you see in a province the oppression of the poor and the violation of justice and right, do not be amazed at the matter; for the high official is watched over by a higher, and there are yet higher ones over them" (Ecclesiastes 5:8). "Wisdom is better than weapons of war, but one bungler destroys much good" (Ecclesiastes 9:18).

These learnings already suggest that there is a tension between the wisdom of God and conventional wisdom, between the righteousness of God and commonly held definitions of justice. Thus wisdom's quest for discernment often takes the shape of a struggle characterized by ambiguity and even contradiction in the expected patterns of life. In this struggle divine forces of creation and chaos contend for the domination of the cosmos, resulting in threats to the processes of life. Social life mirrors this struggle. It is in times of crises that significant tensions develop, raising new questions as to which patterns of living and which institutions are in tune with God's way.

In the face of this uncertainty the people of God turned to the particular revelation of God in history, to Torah and to gospel, in order to gain more light into the mystery and purpose of God. Jesus entered this struggle and affirmed the way of justice, nonviolence, peacemaking, and reconciliation toward which earlier sages had already pointed. At the heart of his teachings was the coming of the kingdom of God and its righteousness. In many ways this righteousness challenged the conventional way of power, especially in its way of seeking security. In Jesus's teachings, power and authority did not give the right to insist on higher status or to act as a tyrant but rather gave the opportunity for service and might even lead to death for the sake of the other (Mark 10:42-45).

Thus the way of wisdom with its concern for the vulnerable and poor merged with the righteousness that Jesus defined and embodied. It is not surprising that the epistles associate "learning Christ" with "true righteousness" (Ephesians 4:24). The letter to the Ephesians admonishes Christians to learn to live as "wise" people, living righteously in a way that exposes the "unfruitful works of darkness" (5:3-20). For righteousness can be defined by its fruits, that which is "good and right and true" (5:9). Mennonite peace theology has often talked about the struggle between righteousness and unrighteousness as a struggle between the church and the world. This suggests little continuity between integrity and justice as society generally understands such virtues and the righteousness that Christians understand to be God's gift through Jesus. But if wisdom and righteousness connect more directly, we may understand both to be gifts of God, available to all who are open to learning wisdom. Any prophetic engagement will certainly require the church to name the sharp opposition between unrighteousness and righteousness. But the church must acknowledge that it too, like Solomon, has often contributed to warfare and insecurity. The church too has sought prestige and power and contributed to injustice and oppression.

If we understand wisdom as the righteousness Jesus embodied in his wise and compassionate response to the poor and vulnerable, we realize that this wisdom is a gift of God given also to reflective persons who learn through their experience. Thus Mennonite theology must continue to accept and testify to the incompatibility between justice and injustice, righteousness and unrighteousness, which is basic to true wisdom. At the same time, however, Mennonites dare not use their status as church to assert power in the public square, but rather must act wisely, choosing to act justly and compassionately for those who are most vulnerable.

3. *If your enemies are hungry, give them bread to eat; and if they are thirsty, give them water to drink.* (Proverbs 25:21; Romans 12:20)

The story of Abigail in 1 Samuel 25, which some scholars identify as a model wisdom tale, invites us to consider this practice as a way to gain security. The story begins with the foolishness of Nabal who refuses traditional tribal hospitality to David the fugitive. Abigail, a woman who is "clever and beautiful," averts the tragedy that David's revenge would have created. Going out to meet David, she takes with her rich gifts of food and drink and appeals to him to forgive. David summarizes the story in this way: "Blessed be the Lord who has judged the case of Nabal's insult to me, and has kept back his servant from evil" (25:39).

Abigail, in wisdom born of life experience and ordinary good sense, thus takes her place in the larger story of David, a story in turn linked to God's gracious purposes of blessing the whole world through God's people. Abigail chooses to preserve life by pursuing hospitality and intervening in a timely way when her family is under threat. As a result of this action she not only protects her family but builds community security and good will. Abigail moves outward from kinship hospitality to embrace the stranger, even while protecting the tribal interests to which she is committed.

In a story in 2 Kings 6:15-23, Elisha the prophet suggests that this kind of hospitality can also be extended to national enemies. He instructs the king to provide a generous feast for his enemies, thus averting further raids upon his own land. In these stories hospitality overlaps with traditional values, but moves to a deeper level when that hospitality extends not only to strangers but also enemies. Interestingly enough, Egyptian and Akkadian proverbs also assert this direction in some of their proverbs.[23]

Biblical wisdom teachings give a number of reasons for not seeking revenge. One of them is simply that the wise will not answer another's folly by being foolish themselves (Proverbs 26:5). But other reasons focus on what one's actions do to the enemy. Heaping "coals of fire" on your enemy suggests shaming them but also suggests overcoming evil with good. It points to the space that one ought to leave for God's actions, since we should not "claim to be wiser than [we] are" (Romans 12:14-21).

Jesus recommends the practice of hospitality for a yet deeper reason—the generosity of God who makes rain to fall on both the just and unjust (Matthew 5:43-45). Jesus in his earthly life rejected the way of revenge and extended hospitality. He ate with sinners, had compassion on the outsider, and forgave those who injured him. Likewise, the epistles confirm this practical alternative to revenge (Romans 12:14-21).

Mennonites have understood hospitality as a key practice of peacemaking, but have not always recognized the inclusive nature of this hospitality. In addition, they have not always understood that others beyond the church may long for exactly this kind of wisdom to overcome vengeance. Thus Mennonites must more readily seize the opportunity to witness to practices of hospitality in the public square beyond the church and enter into discussions of what it means in our present global context.

4. *For everything there is a season, and a time for every matter under heaven.* (Ecclesiastes 3:1)

The book of Esther does not explicitly mention God's action, yet the presence of God's people with their wisdom surrounds this story, in which a woman chooses wisely in moments of great insecurity and fear. Esther's great beauty allows her into the harem of the Persian king. She then uses the power structure of the Persian court skillfully in order to attain her goal, the security of her people. This goal takes precedence over any personal fear she may have had for her own life. What is striking is the advice of Mordecai, Esther's mentor. "For if you keep silence at such a time as this, relief and deliverance will rise for the Jews from another quarter, but you and your father 's family will perish. Who knows? Perhaps you have come to royal dignity for such a time as this" (Esther 4:14). Beneath these words lie subtle assumptions about God's providence and the place of human action in God's plans.

The book of Proverbs assumes that people are capable of choosing their attitudes and course of action in situations that are often ambiguous and confusing. Few of the behaviors are universally applicable. Instead the proverbs call for the flexibility of mind to determine which are appropriate for a particular situation. Statements that seem contradictory or at best confusing when we attempt to follow them dogmatically are helpful if understood as needing further discernment as to when they are most appropriate. Thus "do not speak harshly" and "do not refrain from rebuking" seem opposite but may each be appropriate for a particular time. What is crucial is not just doing right but doing right at the right time.

Though wisdom has a particular understanding of time, focusing on the present, in writers such as the authors of Ecclesiastes and Job there is also a growing discontent about limiting the results of righteous actions to this life. After all, experience clearly shows that often the wicked prosper and the righteous fail in their endeavors (Ecclesiastes 7:15). Tom Yoder Neufeld suggests that wisdom introduces an eschatological hope that "loads the present to overflowing while also seeing it as movement toward culminating the process of reconciling the cosmos in Christ, a process that began already before the beginning, so to speak."[24] Thus the heart of Jesus's message had to do with the fulfillment of time, for the reign of God is at hand. This suggests that Jesus understood wisdom's concern with God's timing and the place of human action within God's overall design. His willingness to trust God and risk even death in order to fit into God's plan is in line with the wisdom of the sages of old who also took risks in order to live in allegiance to God's reign. This becomes particularly clear in Ephesians, with its focus on reconciliation.

> With all wisdom and insight he has made known to us the mystery of his will, according to his good pleasure that he set forth in Christ, as a plan for the fullness of time, to gather up all things in him, things in heaven and things on earth. (Ephesians 1:8-10)

To discern the times in a spirit of hope thus becomes a crucial practice for the people of God as they seek to witness to God's wisdom in the marketplace. Wisdom cautions us that doing the right thing at the right time is crucial and requires discernment, but also requires hope in God's action of full reconciliation. In any Mennonite concern for security, deliberate attention to time in light of eternity will be necessary in order to know when to wait for God's action and when to act in God's name.

5. *In the fear of the Lord one has strong confidence and one's children will have a refuge.* (Proverbs 14:26)

To recognize the limitations of human life and the human inability to control its direction is part of the wisdom tradition, as is trust in God as our refuge and strength. It is the book of Ecclesiastes that reminds us most clearly of human limitations, the ambiguity of all human achievement, and the impossibility of securing anything permanent as human beings. The writer laments these limitations particularly in the area of intellectual capabilities and wisdom. "All is vanity," he cries. Ecclesiastes' unique niche among wisdom teachings seems to be to bring out exceptions to the rule, to keep wisdom honest in its reflections, and to encourage a deeper pondering of the seeming contradictions that belie God's intention and purpose in creation.[25]

Similar to the book of Job, the writer contests a world that operates according to principles of fairness and justice as defined by human rules of behavior. It delves beneath these assumptions to ask questions at the limits of human understanding. Thus the book of Ecclesiastes suggests the futility of conventional wisdom and points to the search for a deeper wisdom that does not come from mere observation of life.

The story of Joseph in Genesis 37-50 is actually a wisdom tale. It prompts similar reflections because Joseph's actions do not directly fit the outcomes in the story. It begins as a story of family strife and violence yet struggles with the broader social political question of brothers ruling over brothers. Joseph, though misunderstood, falsely accused, and even threatened with death makes decisions that preserve his own life in face of great insecurity. But these decisions also lead him to become the chief adviser to Pharaoh, because there was no one "as discerning and wise" as he. His eventual reconciliation with his brothers, who had betrayed him, was possible because he recognized God's leading beyond his own actions and could set aside revenge in favor of reconciliation. His acknowledgment of God suggests the fear of God that is the beginning of wisdom: "God sent me before you to preserve for you a remnant on earth, and to keep alive for you many survivors" (Genesis 45:7). Though the book of Proverbs seems to suggest that human logic and keen observation can discern the way of blessing that God has revealed through God's creation, it also acknowledges that the way of the foolish is the more popular course. Many do not understand the limits that God has written into creation in order to allow life to flourish for all.

The most decisive shift in focus toward God, however, occurs in the worship tradition of wisdom. It is this shift that brings a sense of security, patience, and purposeful action to those who are wise, despite the apparent flourishing of the wicked. Thus meditation and prayer in the context of the community of God's people become a crucial practice of the righteous witnessing to God and to the life that God intends (Psalms 34). A major temptation of the modern world is the dualism that would divorce secular from sacred; such a dualism in turn tends to separate intellectual activity from worship. Mennonites have not been immune to this temptation. At times, in fact, Mennonites have narrowed their operative theology to a humanistic ethic, which does not adequately acknowledge God's wisdom as beyond our human ethical understandings. Biblical wisdom suggests that the practice of worship is necessary in order to keep our wisdom honest by acknowledging the limits of its knowledge.

6. *For the message about the cross is foolishness to those who are perishing, but to us who are being saved it is the power of God.* (1 Corinthians 1:18)

Already in the stories of the Old Testament, faithful interpretation of God's way in the marketplace includes risk, suffering, and death. Daniel models wisdom in situations where the overwhelming reality is the exercise of power by foreign rulers. In Daniel's specific role as courtier, he exhibits his fidelity to the true God in his observance of Jewish food laws and in his faithfulness in prayer, despite threats to his life. The story suggests that it was God who gave Daniel wisdom and skill in every aspect of life as well as insight into dreams and visions (Dan 1:17, 5:14.). It also suggests that any power a ruler enjoys comes as a gift from God (2:36), who could also take it away. Threats to Daniel's own security, however, find their answer through trust in the "Most High God," the King over all creation, whom he served.

Daniel's story reminds us that to choose wisdom over foolishness involves risk. Temptations abound as persons struggle to choose the way of life amidst opposition and persecution. Idolatry, misuse of power, and a seeking of prestige or status are temptations of the wise as they gain in power. Being wise, therefore, may require us to go to the halls of power, but it also requires us to claim an alternative power based on faith in God the creator and sustainer of the universe. The New Testament confirms this in the story of Jesus, who in his willingness to risk death on the cross fully embodied trust in the loving God. The resurrection assures us that the power of God can bring life from death. Thus the presence of God through the Holy Spirit encourages the wise to make risky choices in the face of threats and violence, secure in the knowledge that God's power will ultimately intervene.

In the book of Acts, Stephen and Paul as well as other followers of the Way demonstrate a security based on a trust in God in their public witness. Paul knew from his own experience the "wisdom of the cross" and the "power of the resurrection," which allowed him to be confident even when there were risks of death. First Corinthians 1-2 suggests that a willingness to suffer will help discern between the wise and foolish. For the wise are those who depend fully on God's creative and redemptive power instead of conventional learning, status, or eloquent speech. The cross represents for Paul God's loving will to stand with the suffering world against the "rulers of this age," even to death (1 Corinthians 2:8). True power is thus born not of oppressive control or violence, but of solidarity in divine love. This power of the cross is revealed through the Spirit (2:10). The cross, therefore, is also the wisdom that will reconcile enemies and bring together those who are alienated. Paul reiterates this theme in Ephesians when he calls Christ Jesus "our peace," the one who has broken down the dividing wall between

Jews and Gentiles, creating one humanity in place of the two, thus making peace.

What is clear in all of these discussions is that wisdom's willingness to risk life for the other is not based on a depreciation of biological life but rather on trust that mere physical death does not present a limit to life. Rather, it is an opening to full eternal life. Eternal life, by definition, overflows for the other. Jesus Christ most directly embodies it, for the totality of his life and death took on a cruciform shape in order to bring abundant life to others. Wisdom recognizes the need to suffer on behalf of others, but it also strongly asserts that fear of death, insecurity, and violence are not God's will for humans. Thus the "wisdom of the cross" makes sense only within the larger rhythm of receiving and giving, a rhythm in which life and power are received from God, and voluntary vulnerability and risking suffering are given for the sake of the life of the other. It is this wisdom that is crucial so that teaching self-denial does not just become another way to assert power over another—another temptation to which Mennonites have not always been immune.

Conclusion: The Promise of Wisdom for Discernment of the Common Good

This sampling of various biblical texts confirms that the Bible does use the language of wisdom to describe the relationship of the logic of the kingdom of God and the logic underlying the good in our human institutions and structures. It suggests the value of human reasoning in seeking the good but also seeks to define aspects of righteousness and goodness that only those who are ready to follow wisdom's invitation can learn. It helps us understand the many persons in our pews, who like my parents, participate actively in their communities by building institutions of ordering even as they maintain a prophetic witness against all violence.

The term "wisdom" has the advantage of a broad range of meanings—from folk wisdom to royal wisdom, from personal insight to the common sense of a community, from compassionate practice to skillful calculation, from careful orderly reasoning to unpredictable revelatory knowledge. It encompasses a way of doing things as well as a way of reasoning, an attitude of the heart as well as some substantive assertions of truth. It is not limited to one area of life but plays itself out in the family circle as easily as in the royal palace. Thus wisdom is not a static, closed characteristic of the sort that a strict formula can capture, but is rather defined by particular values, attitudes, insights, and practices at particular moments in time. Foolishness is never far away; discernment is always necessary for the kind of wisdom that gains in breadth and depth as it receives new insights.

The image that most directly points to this dynamic definition of wisdom is God inviting all to a banquet of life-giving food. This invitation is open to all and no person or community can hoard it. It is God who creates and sustains life, and who knows therefore what is needed for the ongoing sustenance of all throughout God's creation. Yet anyone at any time can refuse God's invitation to partake of this nourishment. Only the indiscriminate pattern of God's gracious gift of insight allows life to continue despite human foolishness and pride.

Yet to partake of this nourishment is to take one's place at a larger table of participants, each offering the gift of wisdom to the other. The invitation can come in many forms, but the process of becoming wise is always one of receiving and giving—of receiving life, land, justice, and blessing from God, and of giving life, land, justice, and blessing to others. It is about choosing life for oneself and then acting in life-giving, generous ways toward others. It is about receiving power and then empowering others. By implication, it is also about not being violated and killed oneself while in turn refusing to inflict violence and death on others. It is about not being controlled by others, while in tum not abusing and controlling others. It is this rhythm of righteousness that creates the dynamic of life in the kingdom of God.

It is also this rhythm that sustains life in human community, thus creating an interconnection and solidarity with all people in their quest for security and safety.[26] Wisdom rejects a dualistic view of reality that would draw a strict boundary between sacred and secular wisdom, between faith and reason, or between church and the public square. It insists that God has traced a grain of wisdom through the universe, which humans are to discover and respect. Yet wisdom is keenly aware of the limits to human understanding, knowing that truth is frequently hidden from human eyes, and that only God understands fully the direction of the universe.

A tension arises when we accept this limit to wisdom and when we look more closely at the description of the security of life that we find in wisdom literature. Biblical wisdom would understand biological life as a mere starting point as it reflects on what makes for the "way of life" that we are urged to choose. For wisdom, life is that abundance which terms such as land, family, rest, and security indicate, but it also includes justice and righteousness, blessing and shalom. To receive life, therefore, is to receive the kind of life that God intends, not merely existence as it so frequently presents itself in human experience. Biblical wisdom strongly challenges lesser definitions of life, no matter who presents them.

Wise persons who understand this rhythm recognize "kairos" moments when the wise must take action and challenge lesser wisdoms. They become prophetic in their willingness to witness to life in its fullness and are empowered to suffer through the power of the Holy Spirit. In this sense, wisdom and prophetic speech intersect in their dependence on the indwelling of God's Spirit of Wisdom that we need to discern wisely as to when and where to speak and act.[27]

One can name a number of key practices as wise in the way they seek the common good or life of our world. These include interpreting situations truthfully, probing all experiences for their life-giving qualities, extending hospitality to others, forgoing revenge and forgiving the other, conscientious objection to injustice and greed, generosity and care for the needy, seeking reconciliation with the enemy, and patient waiting for God's action. How does wisdom answer the question of whether we should be involved in institutions and structures that order human life? It asks us to demonstrate practically how our engagement is determined by the rhythm of life that we have discovered in our own experience of God's grace. After all, wisdom takes seriously the importance of personal virtues and individual initiatives that witness to truth and justice within institutional structures.

This rhythm of life is also important for the way we enter into public discourse. Wisdom as understood in the Bible counters discourse that would seek a control or monopoly of the truth. This includes the power that one can exert by using the idiosyncratic language of the faith community or the selective language of a particular political institution in order to dominate the other. It counters all triumphalism, tribalism, and forceful insistence on one's own way. But it does not hide its own insights, nor shy away from sharing its distinctive interpretation of reality while inviting others to share their unique perspectives. This means that the church must learn to be dialogical and "multilingual," that is, willing to speak and listen in many languages.[28]

First, the church must be fluent in its own particular tongue, arising out of its own historical experience, where identity is forged, virtues are learned and taught, and God is worshipped. This language of worship and caring community becomes the institutional witness that points to the source of all wisdom while recognizing the limits of human wisdom.

But second, the church must also speak the language of a middle discourse "on the wall" between communities of discourse, where witness for the gospel logic and the struggle for the good intersect.[29] In that conversation Christians must participate wisely and prophetically for the sake of the abundant life of the whole community.

In the final analysis, all wisdom is accountable to God, who is both the source and sustainer of life. As Christians we can turn to Jesus Christ, who embodied wisdom in his very being, and to the Holy Spirit, who continues to enliven the whole universe, in order to learn the rhythm of wisdom. Our calling as people of God is to become wise, to speak and act according to the limits of our understanding and to trust in the promise of God, "I will bless you and make you a blessing." With that hope we can wait with eagerness for God's promise to be fulfilled, when all things will be "gathered in him, things in heaven and things on earth." In the meantime, we participate in God's rhythm of life, in tune with

Jesus and the sages of old, willing to transcend lesser wisdoms for the sake of the "wisdom of the cross." This way of life is aptly characterized as "walking in the resurrection"[30] while seeking the common good of our communities and nations.

Chapter 9 Ministry

NAMING THE ECCLESIAL CONNECTION

The courses that I taught over the years gradually shifted from questions of hermeneutics and biblical authority to questions of ecclesiology (the nature of the church). In retrospect this makes a lot of sense because the notion of "hermeneutic community" in my graduate work connects the Bible and the church in a political, sociological, and theological process. Focussing on the church gave me the opportunity to ask what kind of a church is able to faithfully discern the message that God is giving to us through the Bible. The course that I taught most consistently was "Church and Ministry," a required course in the ministry stream of the MA program in theology at Conrad Grebel University College (CGUC) in Waterloo, Ontario—a course co-taught with my husband, Gary.

Gary and I had been partners in the theological enterprise beginning with our years at Bible College when we studied Greek together and argued about the place of evangelistic meetings (or of sports) in congregational life. Our marriage has always included vigorous theological discussions each from our own context. Gary as pastor often brought issues to my attention that arose in his ministry setting. When I became part of the preaching team at the Toronto United Mennonite Church we worked even more closely in identifying themes and scriptures that were relevant for the congregation.

When it was suggested by the dean of CGUC that we teach this course together we were excited to bring our two professions closer together. Gary had finished a Doctor of Ministry degree back in Edmonton focussed on worship, particularly on how to use worship committees in the congregation. These committees were new in the 1970's and many pastors were ready to invite laypersons into the process of planning worship but were unsure of how to do this. Gary's project dissertation addressed that need. In the Church and Ministry course, Gary could speak out of his experience and pastoral theological orientation and I could bring more systematic theological frameworks to bear on the themes. My reading shifted to include many more books on the practical aspect of ministry. Now I read books on systems theories, on pastoral counselling approaches, and on leadership styles. I discovered that my previous work on authority and power was very helpful as we discussed discernment processes and conflict resolution in the congregation. Feminist theological methods also gave me critical tools to use in my analysis of congregational life and its ministry.

One of my disappointments during these years was the attendance at a Pastor's seminar, a course that was taught every year at CGUC on a variety of themes. I was asked to teach a course on Women's Voices in Theology *for one of these seminars. These seminars were usually well attended by both male and female pastors of the area. The attendance that year was dominated by females with only two male pastors attending, one of them being my son.*[1] *I was not sure how to respond to that lack of interest since the evaluations of my teaching were positive. I continue to wonder: Do men still have the preunderstanding that women's theological voices would not be valuable to them? What does that say about the future of Mennonite theology and ministry? What other voices are not being heard?*

When I became an interim co-pastor with my husband I became even more convinced that the hermeneutical community that most needs our participation as theologians is the church, both as a congregation and as networks of congregations such as a denomination. But the opposite is also true—as theologians we need the partnership of congregations to ground our theology in life experience broader than one's own and to test its relevance. Yet I do not want to define church by its organizational structures. For me the hermeneutic community of "church" has included not only the formal organization but also the small group committed to eat dinner together every month while sharing life experiences with each other, the women's Bible study and exercise group, or the phone calls between members of a prayer chain. New expressions of church may be needed that can bridge the divide between the sacred and the secular making for more holistic communal theology.

Leadership in these variety of church settings includes encouraging congregational members to listen to the word of God as mediated through the Bible. This is not an easy task because the Bible as a human book is vulnerable to misunderstanding and misuse. Its power can be harnessed to dominate and oppress as well as to save and free. I wrote the papers in this section with congregation leaders in mind who wish to create freeing, loving hermeneutic communities that are not afraid to wrestle with the Bible's meaning for our lives today. The first two are specific interpretations of biblical texts that arose out of work that I also did for ministry in a congregation. The last one is an article that Gary and I did together right after his retirement while at Anabaptist Mennonite Biblical Seminary for a semester of renewal and transition.

***

READING PSALM 139: OPTING FOR A REALISTIC READING[2]

The book of Psalms has become for me a symbolic reminder of the humanness of our Bible and the humanness of the hermeneutic community we name church. Brueggeman has pointed out that the Psalms are "not screened through the language of piety or mysticism or contemplation" but are rather the "direct" yet "stylized" language of a community that is in a covenantal relationship with God.[3] *In the Psalms lament and praise, accusation and trust lie side by side as the people of God respond to the God who is transcendent but near and accessible to the people. The psalms speak of experience but include not only the present but also the past and anticipated future experience. They are confessional statements that speak of failure or despair but also of hope, trust, and love for their God.*

To be a theologian of the church is to be someone who reflects on the language the church uses to speak to *God as well as* about *God. If the Psalms are a kind of "pattern" for such language, what would change in how we speak to God during a worship service? This question occupied me as I did interim pastoring in several churches. These churches were often in crises or at a turning point in their communal life. The challenges that they faced were conflicts around ethical issues, power dynamics within leadership, unresolved issues from the past, or differing expectations of the church's worship and communal life. At the same time, there were personal traumas and personality differences that hindered healthy relationships among congregants and leaders. How could the worship language on a Sunday morning be a conduit for the community to relate to the God whom they confessed?*

One approach that we used several times was to intentionally create our own psalm of lament as a community. We gathered comments from congregational members about their feelings and thoughts one Sunday and then wrote a litany that included those words but re-framed them in a litany interspersed by the simple hymn, "Cast thy burdens upon the Lord." We discovered that a communal worship that included ancient words from the Bible but also personal words from the present could become a healing moment for many, allowing the community to let go of the past and enter the future with hope. I include a litany, a composite of several that were used within one of our churches, created from comments by members of the congregation. It is an attempt by a hermeneutic community to embrace prayer in the Spirit of the Psalms with its honest approach to a God whom they confessed as near and open to our feelings and thoughts.

LITANY OF ACKNOWLEDGMENT AND LAMENT[4]

Voice 1: *For God alone my soul waits in silence;*
...God is my rock and my salvation,
my fortress; I shall not be shaken.
Trust in God at all times, O people,
pour out your hearts before God. (Psalm 62:5, 6–8)
Voice 2: *We pour out our hearts before you this day, O God.*
Voice 3: *Some of us bring our personal pain, our family stories, our sense of loss and discouragement and anger over the blows of life, or over our personal failures.*

All voices: ***We lament our inner personal pain.***

Voice 1: *I am tired of feeling lonely. I desire deeper and more meaningful relationships, but struggle to find the strength to be vulnerable with others.*
Voice 3: *I am disappointed that I have not taken action when I should have.*
Voice 2: *I am confused about how to act on personal beliefs.*
Voice 1: *I am frustrated that I am not able to communicate well.*
Voice 2: *I am afraid that the decisions I am making are not the right ones.*
Voice 3: *I feel that I have refused to open my heart to everyone.*
Voice 1: *I wish I could just let go of the pain that abuse has inflicted on me so that I can enter healthy relationships.*

Quartet: *Cast thy burden upon the Lord.*

All voices: ***We also pour out our communal laments to you, O God.***
We grieve what has happened in our congregation.

Voice 3: *You know, God, how much we have loved this fellowship. It has been for us:*
a place to worship you in peace and harmony
a place where we felt welcomed and comfortable and challenged
Voice 1: *a place where people held differing views, with integrity, and we seemed to be able to live with these differences*
a place of many visions of how we might serve you
Voice 2: *a place of great energy, creativity, and caring*
a good place to meet and to worship you, God.
Voice 3: *But something now feels broken, changed, damaged*

as if we have gone through a rough storm and our church vessel is thrown off course.

All Voices: ***Some of us feel troubled and disappointed.***

Voice 1: *I am disappointed that our faith does not bring us joy. We seem downcast and worried.*
Voice 2: *I am disappointed that we let our personalities get in the way of the very good things that are happening here.*
Voice 3: *I am disappointed that this congregation and its members failed to live up to its commitment to its principles, such as, peacemaking, justice and, community.*
Voice 2: *I am disappointed that I don't have more competence in dealing with conflict.*

All voices: ***Some of us feel angry.***

Voice 1: *I am concerned that some members have continued to hold onto hurts from the past.*
Voice 2: *I am tired of people who don't let go of their differences.*
Voice 3: *It pains me when we continue to question one another's motivations within our fellowship.*
Voice 1: *I am afraid of anger and don't know how to respond to it in others. I grieve the loss of connection when anger occurs.*
Voice 2: *I still find it deeply troubling that there was so much anger and meanness in the way we responded to our leaders.*
Voice 3: *I grieve that I am still angry. I grieve that my eyes are blind to the divine spark in some members of our community.*

Quartet: *Cast thy burdens upon the Lord.*

All voices: ***Some of us feel that there has been an erosion of spirituality, creativity, and respect in our congregation.***

Voice 1: *I feel sad about the state that we've gotten ourselves into.*
Voice 2: *I lament the loss of innocence.*
Voice 3: *I grieve that we were not always kind to each other.*
Voice 2: *I am concerned about our young people.*
Voice 1: *I grieve that our congregation does not always feel like a safe place for differing opinions and approaches.*
Voice 3: *The chipping away of prime values has left me with a feeling that I no longer belong. I no longer feel at ease. My sense of loyalty is diminished, and that makes me profoundly sad.*
Voice 1: *I lament that I frequently do not look forward to going to church on Sunday mornings.*
Voice 2: *I am getting old. Family members are gone from the church. Values that I have aren't shared by others. Is there a place for me here?*
Voice 3: *I lament the absence of carefree joy in the congregation.*

All voices: ***Gracious and loving and forgiving God, we have laid before you our laments, our disappointments, our tiredness, our pain, our anger. Now we want to let go of them. Embrace us God with new freedom, and new joy, and new hope for the future. We cast our burdens on you, O God.***

Quartet: *Cast thy burden upon the Lord.*

***

I wrote the article that follows to honour Waldemar Janzen, a long-term professor at Canadian Mennonite University, who first taught me to love and wrestle with the Old Testament as a vital, alive story of God's people. Over the years I have continued to value the dialogue with him, sometimes disagreeing but always respecting the insights that we each bring to the discussions.

***

Mennonites are seeking an "undisturbed, soothing religion of psychological well-being" by avoiding the realism of the Old Testament in which "God's activity cannot be disentangled from history, war and judgement."[5] These observations by Waldmar Janzen deserve our close attention because they come from a person deeply committed both to the church and to biblical studies. Janzen's suggestion that Mennonites have effectively reduced the biblical canon to the New Testament is disturbing in light of Mennonite affirmation of the authority of the whole Bible. The further implication, that somehow Mennonites have missed seeing God's real activity in the world, creates a discomfort for those of us who have insisted that biblical interpretation be, above all, practical and connected to our daily lives. Moreover, Janzen's charge, that Mennonite acculturation to the individualism and privatization of our Western world has created this reduction, flies in the face of an emphasis in Mennonite theology on community and nonconformity to the world. These observations, therefore, warrant a second look at how our understanding of the Bible, as the church's authoritative book, and our understanding of God's salvation, experienced as "well-being," relate to each other.

Janzen is right when he says that in Mennonite theology, both formal and informal, the authority of the Old Testament frequently has been superseded by the New. Many of us have accepted John H. Yoder's teachings that the Bible must be understood as a story of promise and fulfilment and that, therefore, it should be read "directionally."[6] We have affirmed the view that the New Testament goes beyond the Old, especially in its rejection of violence and in its promotion of a trajectory of peace. However, by doing this we have subtly taken away the opportunity for the Old Testament to speak an authoritative Word. After all, in our social climate the latest model of everything—whether computer, car or dishwasher—is considered to be best.

However, it may be that the problem is deeper than avoiding the Old Testament. Perhaps Janzen is detecting a general tendency among Mennonites in these early days of the twenty-first century to avoid tension and contradiction whenever they arise in our Bible reading. In fact, I suspect that there may be a pattern of superficial reading that has developed in Mennonite tradition to deal with the dissonances that come when texts don't fit with each other or don't fit with an assumed Mennonite theology. What is needed is guidance to help us discern the difference between avoidance techniques, that contribute to our "comfortable pew," and an interpretive stance, that helps us respond to the message of God communicated even in dissonant texts.

The affirmation of biblical authority in our confessions of faith does not give us adequate guidance for this task, since differing practices can grow out of the same affirmation. Therefore, we must turn to an analysis of our normal reading habits in order to see exactly what this affirmation means in practice. We must identify the customary ways of interpreting that have developed through time and be willing to evaluate the motivations and the ethics of the interpretive choices that we make as we read. The usefulness of this kind of analysis depends on our willingness to repent of those interpretive practices that serve to justify our comfortable life, rather than open us to true well-being, often named shalom in the Bible. One approach to this analysis is to note how we deal with the inherent tension in the biblical texts themselves. I have chosen Psalm 139 as a test case to help us reflect on our own reading practices and interpretive choices. The focus will be on illuminating the tensions within the text and suggesting possible implications of embracing the realism of the psalm. Perhaps this can be one way to avoid the temptation of a "soothing religion" that is not life-giving.

Why Psalm 139?

> O LORD, you have searched me and known me.
> You know when I sit down and when I rise up.... (vv. 1-2a)
>
> If I take the wings of the morning
> and settle at the farthest limits of the sea,
> even there your hand shall lead me,
> and your right hand shall hold me fast.... (vv. 9-10)
>
> For it was you who formed my inward parts;
> you knit me together in my mother's womb.
> I praise you, for I am fearfully and wonderfully made.... (vv. 13-14a)
>
> O that you would kill the wicked, O God,
> and that the bloodthirsty would depart from me.... (v. 19)
>
> Search me, O God, and know my heart;
> test me and know my thoughts.
> See if there is any wicked way in me,
> and lead me in the way everlasting. (vv. 23-24)

Tension and ambiguity lie at the heart of this psalm's poetic language and cannot be avoided by interpreters who are committed to reading the complete text as it stands in the Bible. The drastic shift in mood and theme in verses 19-22 presents challenges to the most experienced interpreter as well as to the first-time reader. How does an interpreter bring together the reflective mood at the beginning and end of the psalm with the plea for revenge in the middle. In particular, how do Mennonite interpreters, who have embraced Jesus' call to love their enemies, read this psalm? Do we excise verses 19-22 out of Psalm 139 because of our convictions on peace-making?

Psalm 139 has been one of the most difficult psalms for scholars to classify because it expresses the variety of moods and themes also present in Scripture as a whole. H. Gunkel regarded it as a "mixed type" that has "burst" the structural forms which have long been recognized in the various psalms.[7] Elements of a creation hymn, a psalm of trust, a lament, and a wisdom saying can be detected in its 24 short verses. Its connections to themes in Genesis, Job, Isaiah, and Jeremiah place it squarely into the Old Testament. Yet its understanding of human nature in the presence of God has the same kind of universal appeal that many of the parables in the New Testament have.

Not only the structural form but also the theme of Psalm 139 invites diverse interpretations, identifications, and connections. The prominence of the "I" suggests that it can easily connect with the subjectivity of our day. Yet this psalm is part of a collection of songs arising out of the communal worship of an ancient people. It is certainly one of the most personal psalms in the Psalter, exuding trust and assurance in God's presence. Yet it portrays a sense of order in the universe that names certain ways as wicked and portrays some people as bloodthirsty enemies.

This psalm is familiar to regular church attenders. We are rereaders, reading the psalm in the context of a history of interpretation that subtly influences our responses. We have read and heard this psalm many times, using it to inspire, comfort and teach each other. It is included in the biblical readings in the *Hymnal: A Worship Book*,[8] suggesting its popularity in worship settings. Choirs and soloists have sung the words of this psalm into our hearts and mind so many times that we cannot think of words such as "Search me, O God" without accompanying melodies. Settings in which meditation is encouraged, such as campfire services or family devotions, seem to suit this psalm well. And yet this psalm also has been used in arguments for the rights of the unborn, suggesting a more political context of interpretation.

Despite its popularity, most of us have not heard the whole psalm read publicly nor read the whole psalm in devotional material. There is a common discomfort with verses 19-22, no matter whether the reading focuses on a theological, psychological, or political interpretation of the text. Why is this so? Has the example of Jesus and his teachings made this kind of prayer obsolete? Or is this a case in which our search for "psychological well-being" has taken precedence over a Word from God that would shatter the barriers protecting our comfort zone?

My analysis of the interpretations of Psalm 139 will focus on three different ways in which the connection has been made between the psalm and the real world in which we live. In each interpretation we will explore the tensions that come when verses 19-22 are included in the reading. Each section will also include an example from my own experience that suggests the importance of wrestling with this tension as we seek to create shalom for ourselves and our communities.

A Theological Connection

A prevailing approach to Psalm 139 assumes that it is the presence of God in our world that creates the connection between the psalm and our reality. In fact, some interpreters would call this psalm a "doctrinal classic" because it expresses basic doctrines that have developed in the community of faith to talk about God's presence among us. Most interpreters who emphasize this approach realize that Psalm 139 is not abstract speculative thinking about God. The psalm itself concentrates on those convictions that are developed out of personal experience and expressed in the profound poetry of the psalm. Patrick Miller, for example, notes several theological topics that seem to open naturally out of the text.[9] These themes include God's omniscience and omnipresence, God's purpose and calling, God's eternal preservation and God's judgement and anger. James Luther Mays suggests that Psalm 139 is a doctrinal classic because it "portrays human existence in all its dimensions in terms of God's knowledge, presence, and power."[10]

The psalm nurtures a sense of God as the total environment within which every aspect of life, from beginning to end, finds its meaning. It is, therefore, natural to read Psalm 139 as a psalm of worship and praise. However, the very context of worship creates a tension with those troublesome words of vengeance that sit in the middle "of this otherwise marvellous, deep well of living water that is the Psalter."[11] In worship, we concentrate on praise, thanksgiving and trust. We confidently proclaim that God will protect us and keep us from evil, because God is on the throne and therefore in control of the world. As Walter Brueggemann points out, through the words we use in worship, we re-experience and re-describe "the safe world over which God presides."[12] It is this world of wellbeing, of blessing, in which we wish to live.

What is shocking in this psalm is that verses 19-22 disrupt our worship by suggesting disappointment in God's lack of intervention in the world. In fact, these verses imply that God has not yet acted with justice to make the world a safe place to be. At the same time, they give the impression that God shares our anger and will act out of vengeance to punish the enemy. As Miller puts it, these curses and imprecations against enemies sound very much "as if Archie Bunker of *All in the Family* is correct: God zaps people to get even."[13] These verses do not allow us to imagine an abstract transcendent God extending bountiful blessings from above to all God's people. Instead, they raise the question of God's presence and activity within the real world of violence in which we live. They point to a tension within our image of God that emerges whenever our safe world is shattered by experiences of war, evil, injustice, and death. These verses, therefore, raise the ultimate question about God's relationship to a world in which evil also resides. They force us to wrestle with the seemingly absent God as Elijah did in the desert. They free us to pray as Jesus did in the face of violence, "My God, my God, why have you forsaken me?" (Matthew 27:46). The questions that these verses raise lead us ultimately to the cross of Jesus who died for his enemies, while feeling forsaken by God. Wrestling with these tensions can lead us to a deeper understanding of God's ways and to a trust in a God who stands in solidarity with us in our pain. However, this deeper understanding does not come easily. Sometimes we need to be jolted out of our easy assurances before we can truly worship a God who embodies both compassion and judgment.

I will never forget the moment when, in the midst of a worship celebration, I heard my father, who has always expressed strong pacifist convictions, speak about how he "could have cursed God to his face!" The occasion was the 50th wedding anniversary celebration of my parents. Instead of focussing only on God's goodness, my dad began to recall the difficult years in Russia, just before the family immigrated to Canada. With strong emotion he remembered the struggle to believe in a God of love while standing beside his father's death bed, a father who had been murdered by a band of robbers. Yet somehow Dad was able to end his testimony with a strong affirmation that the all-knowing God had surrounded him with grace so that he finally had been able to embrace the way of love instead of vengeance. His stance of peace had never seemed as real to me as at that moment!

Psalm 139, prayed in its entirety, does not give us easy assurance that God will always make life comfortable for us. However, it encourages us to struggle with the contradictions that we see in God, until we again recognize God's presence transforming the evil among us into ways of peace.

A Psychological Connection

Some interpreters direct their attention more primarily to the individual human feelings and thoughts expressed in the psalm. In this psychological reading of the psalm, the connection to our present reality is made within ourselves. For example, Walter Harrelson suggests that this psalm focuses upon "the inner being of [humans], that sense that every man [and woman] has of being dealt with by God at every moment, whether waking or sleeping."[14] In fact, in Harrelson's view the external world hardly appears at all in this psalm. It is this very personal nature of the psalm that makes it appealing to many people in our day. We can identify with the contradictions and complications within our own hearts that this psalm expresses. Its poetic quality and its use of the personal pronoun throughout invites reflection on one's individual spiritual pilgrimage. Thus Gene Rice names this psalm "A Diary of the Inward Journey."[15] He suggests that each section of the psalm is a stage on the way to a mature spirituality. In the encounter with the Holy One the psalmist moves from flight from God, to joy of surrender to God, to a passionate self-righteous outburst, and finally to a mature realization that God must continually search and cleanse the inner heart.

Throughout the psalm we sense an ambivalence about God that feels very familiar to many of us. God is pictured as "the very life and breath of the self" while at the same time God is seen as the "scourge and nemesis" of the self, the one who searches and exposes every evil thought.[16] God's presence with us, no matter where we go, can be comforting, but also somewhat frightening as all our motives and thoughts are exposed and revealed. As Donald R. Glenn suggests, the point in Psalm 139 is not that God is everywhere in a more general way, but that everywhere we turn we are confronted by God who knows us so thoroughly, who will then also judge us.[17]

The fact that this psalm is used in Jewish worship on the day of atonement (Yom Kippur) points to a possible context for this interpretation. The purpose of the prayer seems to be personal preparation for communal worship, an introspective moment that is intended to lead to repentance and change. However, this makes verses 19-22 particularly disturbing because they seem to claim personal innocence while projecting the evil onto the enemy. The psalmist clearly disassociates himself from the wicked and bloodthirsty people and claims that he and God are on the same side.

This is not an unusual thing for us to do, as Gene Rice reminds us: "One has only to recall the intolerance, the injustice, the oppression, the violence practised with religious sanction to realize that this passionate, self-righteous outburst of the psalmist is also a fact of spiritual pilgrimage."[18] The temptation is to censor this aspect of ourselves, to cover it over with pious assertions that we have no enemies, or that this is talk of only spiritual foes, or that we already love our enemies. The honesty and courage to speak publicly subverts a tendency toward denial of the inner anger and prejudice that our pious words would not allow. In fact, the psalm seems to suggest that after this cry of revenge one is more ready to submit oneself to the searching eye of God who tests every heart for wickedness.

I remember a story from my home church which resonates with this reading of the psalm. A woman who had been hurt deeply by the words and actions of a male leader in the church participated in a service of reconciliation, designed to end the conflict. The leader asked for forgiveness and each person in the small circle assured him of their forgiveness, including the woman. However, when she got home, she recognized that the feelings of anger and mistrust were still very strong. She could not gain peace within herself until she turned around and went to the leader's home. There she confessed her lack of real forgiveness, but also said that she would like to be able to forgive him. As they began to talk about what had happened she suddenly realized that the feelings of anger had disappeared. The gift of forgiveness had come, but only after she had admitted her own inability to forgive. A life-long friendship resulted from this honest exchange.

Praying Psalm 139 in its entirety will encourage us to go beyond a superficial identification with the feelings of the psalm to probing into the unresolved hatred and anger within us. The plea for justice will then not be based on a projection of evil on to others, but will become a real wrestling with evil both within ourselves and others.

A Social-political Connection

In this third approach to the interpretation of the psalm, the connection to our reality arises from similarities in the external context, in the social fabric of our lives which include conflict and enmity. The passionate outburst in verses 19-22 becomes the vital clue to the meaning of the whole psalm. For it is these verses that bring the external world to our consciousness, that can move us from introspection to ethical action.

This focus reminds us of the "political background integral to the language of prayer."[19] In this context, the words of the psalm that cry out to God for justice are taken seriously because they echo our own experiences with "those who speak maliciously" or "those who lift themselves up against us." As Gerald Sheppard suggests, the Psalms point "to a world of intimate enemies not so different from our own."[20]

Some interpreters see this psalm as a plea of innocence in the face of false accusations. Thus Robert B. Coote suggests that this psalm is a "plea of the exploited," of those who do not easily gain justice in human courts and who therefore bring their appeal to God. When the psalm is reread from the beginning with this perspective in mind, both the mood and the character of the poem change. The agitation felt in verses 19-22 can also be sensed in the first verses as the plaintiff opens himself to the searching eye of God. In the face of accusation, only God can make a fair judgment, because God knows both the external circumstances and the innermost motivations of the plaintiff. In the first few verses, therefore, God can be understood as conducting a trial which supersedes and invalidates the trial of others. As Coote suggests, God is Perry Mason on the bench conducting a trial.[21] God is both advocate and judge as every circumstance of life and every motive is searched and examined. In the darkness of condemnation, the plaintiff moves through every aspect of his [sic] life, from birth to the present moment, asking the God whom he trusts to search out the truth.

By the time the psalmist reaches verses 19-22, he is convinced that his personal enemies are also God's enemies. Therefore, the cry for vengeance is a cry to God to protect his own interests by protecting him. In this psalm the plea of innocence and the accusation of the wicked stand side by side waiting for God's judgment. The context is injustice or conflict in the societal order. The psalmist is not satisfied that the imbalances of life will somehow be corrected in heaven. Instead, he pleads for justice now. Jesus echoes this need for God's justice to permeate present social/political reality when he teaches us to pray: "Thy kingdom come on earth as it is in heaven."

Gerald Sheppard has suggested that when the Psalms were collected in a book, they became public prayers that could be "overheard" by the enemy, thus adding a prophetic dimension to this kind of discourse.[22] The prayers clearly name injustice and evil, frustrating the denial of evil which the enemies would like to foster within the community.

My most poignant memory of Psalm 139 is of its use in a worship setting by survivors of incest and sexual abuse. They used this psalm to speak about their own innocence, particularly as they recalled their childhood experiences of abuse. For them, it was crucial that the whole psalm should be read in public worship. They wanted to express their faith that they too were wonderfully made, that no matter where they had tried to flee, God's right hand had held them fast. Yet they could also identify with the words, "O that you would kill the wicked, O God, and that the bloodthirsty would depart from me" (v. 19). It was important to proclaim publicly what had happened, to name the evil that had been done and to cry out for justice from God.

Allowing the whole community to overhear the cry for justice means that personal pain becomes a communal issue. Bringing about justice is no longer a lonely enterprise. Instead, the community can gain passion and understanding, can begin to find ways to hold the abuser accountable, while encouraging members of the community to stand with victims in their struggle for justice. Together they can now find redemptive ways to bring about that justice.

Conclusion

In our exploration of the various directions that have been taken in the interpretation of Psalm 139, we have noted the tensions that come with reading verses 19-22. The option to ignore these verses is there for all interpreters of these texts, whether they focus on their theological, psychological, or social/political aspects. The temptation to move into an idealism that does not connect with the reality of our lives is common to all readers of the text.

The canon, which we accept as Scripture, includes Psalm 139 in all its complexity, even though our hymn books and devotional books usually do not. In these prayers, human projections and human imagination are present, though intertwined with divine disclosure. The Hebrew people and the early church did not attempt to censor the human elements in the Psalms, because prayer by nature is dialogical and interactive, including both God and humans. And it is within this relationship that transformation happens, though usually not without a struggle.

Should Christans read the whole psalm in their worship? That can be dangerous if we read it as an ideal vision. However, if the psalm helps us connect to the reality of our own lives in such a way that the psalm becomes our prayer, transformation is possible. We can become open, ready to discover the God who alone can transform our imprecations and pleas of innocence into celebrations of true shalom. That kind of reading of the Psalms may be risky, but it will help us overcome the temptation toward "undisturbed, soothing religion." Instead it may lead us to a faith that is dynamic and life-giving because it is rooted in the reality of a God who responds to our human prayers in ways beyond our imaginings. Thanks be to God!

***

THE WITNESS OF WOMEN: DYING TO SIN AND RISING TO LIFE[23]

I was happy to write an article on the theme of salvation for the journal Vision. *Launched in 2000 by the Institute of Mennonite Studies (at AMBS) and CMU, this journal attempted to bridge the academic and the pastoral in order that it could become a resource for pastors and lay leaders in the church. Its purpose was to "help church leaders reflect theologically on the identity, mission and practices of the church from an Anabaptist-Mennonite perspective." Its articles were all 5–10 pages long, enabling busy pastors to keep up with scholarship on particular topics and with the experience and reflections of their peers.*

In my understanding of biblical authority, I was concerned that the Bible should be used "for the sake of salvation" as Elizabeth Schüssler Fiorenza put it. But I had never spelled out exactly what salvation meant to me, despite the fact that the traditional theories of atonement no longer expressed the fullness of meaning that that term had for me.

Memories from my childhood and youth began to flood back to me as I thought about what I could write on that theme. In early childhood I had considered myself God's child and felt warmly embraced by my family and church. For me their embrace translated into the embrace of a loving God. The Sunday School pictures of angels protecting me, of a Good Shepherd leading me, and of Jesus lovingly holding me in his arms provided me with an assurance that I did not question. The hymns assured me that my sins were forgiven and that "it was well with my soul."

But a change happened during my high school years. I attended a Mennonite high school with a theological emphasis different from my earlier experience. Special evangelistic meetings were held challenging me to convert. At the same time, crusades such as the Billy Graham crusade or the Brunk brothers crusade were held in our area. My father, who had had a dramatic conversion experience after the revolution in Russia, supported these meetings. I enjoyed the music and some of the sermons, but found it difficult to know exactly what I was to convert from. The altar calls and the pious prayers of my fellow class mates for the "unsaved" created great inner turmoil for me.

One evening at the high school evangelistic meeting I finally succumbed to the pressure and raised my hand at a meeting, ready to be "saved." The prayer with the evangelist did not bring peace to me though I did get initial assurance of God's acceptance of me. He then suggested that I go to everyone whom I had hurt in the past and ask forgiveness for the way I had wronged them. I promised I would but realized that I was not sure whom to go to and which of my relationships needed this intervention. I never did keep that promise and the guilt of the "lie" that had come within hours of being "saved" created unease in me for a long time.

The evangelist also suggested that I begin immediately to "witness" to others of my salvation. Again, I was unsure of what to do, except perhaps to get up in the general school testimony meetings and say that I now was a "real" Christian. As I left the private school and went on to Grade 13 at a public school and then Teacher's College this struggle only became greater. More and more I was faced with the inner pressure to witness but I felt that I did not have anything to witness about. What this kind of "salvation" created was a barrier between me and others, and maybe between me and God, a barrier that I did not know how to bridge.

My own youth group and congregation provided me with a safe place of social interactions and worship. But more and more I began to feel a separation between me and those beyond my narrow world of church and home. One example will illustrate this. I was anxious and nervous as I entered the elementary school in Niagara Falls where I had gotten a job teaching after one year of Teacher's College. I was unsure of my teaching ability but just as unsure about how to relate to fellow teachers. I was happy when one of the teachers invited me to eat lunch with them in a small room somewhat apart from the regular teacher's lounge. But I soon discovered that this was where the "Christian" teachers ate, those of like evangelical mind. The others from more mainline churches ate in the regular staff room. I struggled all year with the choice of where to eat, feeling uneasy in both and often alternating between rooms.

The years at Bible College were years of "salvation" for me. Immersing myself in the Bible and seeing its human qualities created a crisis for me at first, especially when my home church in its conflicts had also proved to be sinful and human. But God also became present to me and I found an assurance of God's love for me that has never left me despite my struggles with the patriarchy in the church and in the Bible. Gradually salvation began to mean inner healing as well as social healing of a community. I began to see how my feminist orientation was urging me to not merely try to find healing for myself but rather to work for the healing of our churches and communities from the trauma of exclusion and abuse.

But I also needed to come to terms with the cross and its role in our salvation. As I reflected on these experiences in preparation for writing this article, I decided to begin with the biblical story of the women at the cross and the tomb rather than with theories of atonement. I did not need an overarching all-inclusive theory to witness to God's salvation. I only needed to tell the story again of the cross and the resurrection from the perspective of the women and let the story itself be the witness. I gladly wrote this essay as my own witness to the power of the Bible to mediate God's salvation.

***

As the sun rises and sets each day, a crystal hanging in my window refracts the light in ever-changing patterns. Its various facets catch the light, and rainbow colours flicker across the walls of my study, sometimes behind me, often beside me and at times in front of me. To me, this crystal has become a symbol of the multi-faceted Bible that reflects rainbows of hope on and around us as we read its various witnesses and interpret its texts in the community of the faithful. To be effective, the crystal requires the sun—the source of illumination, a symbol of the Spirit—to cast its light first on one facet and then on another, separating into sparkling hues of red, blue, green and yellow.

One set of biblical witnesses to the good news of salvation are the women at the empty tomb. As we overhear their witness, rainbows of hope surround us. Though we do not have much information about the ongoing testimony of these women, we can note two contexts within which they experience the cross. These contexts will serve as two facets through which the meaning of Jesus' death for our salvation will be illuminated. The image of dying to sin and rising to life will connect these two contexts with the action of God in our own lives. Yet the contexts and analogies that will be explored can only be pointers to the much larger multi-faceted mystery of God's salvation for all of us.

The Context of Violence and Pain

Unlike some of his followers, these women did not run away but stayed to witness the brutality of Jesus' death and then watched the body of Jesus placed into a tomb. They knew first hand that death by crucifixion is a cruel punishment for a crime considered treason by the Roman rulers and blasphemy by many Jewish leaders. No gentle death to close a rich and full rabbinic life; this was undeniably a violent and humiliating death for the one who had pointed them to the kingdom of God.

At first glance, this context for an interpretation of the cross suggests Jesus' solidarity with all humans in suffering, and especially those who undergo violent death because of commitment to a just cause. Yet there is a more personal, theological angle involved in this death. For these women, Jesus was not a distant heroic figure. He was their leader, their friend whom they had experienced as a powerful healer and teacher. He was their Lord, the one who had often been a guest at their tables, the one whom they had accompanied to a place of terror: these women "used to follow him and provided for him when he was in Galilee" and had now "come up with him to Jerusalem" (Mark 15:41).

The perspective of these women on Jesus' death was probably markedly different from that of the rulers and officials or even of the crowd who sometimes followed and sometimes fled. Their first response would probably have taken the form of agonized questions. How could the power of the officials have overcome the power of love exhibited throughout his life by their leader? How could they go on without the one who had pointed them to God's kingdom? How could a righteous God have let this calamity happen?

Mary's words of accusation when she encountered the angels at the empty tomb point to confusion, pain and anger: "They have taken away my Lord, and I do not know where they have laid him" (John 20:13). Though few of these women's words are recorded for us, we can sense the political, the personal and the theological issues of salvation that had arisen in the face of the violence of the cross. Likely, these first interpretations of the death of Jesus were direct responses to the injustice of the execution, their horror at the sacrifice of a good and innocent life, and the separation from Jesus and God that this catastrophe seems to entail. The women may have feared for their own lives, knowing that they too were implicated in Jesus' "guilt," since they were followers of this king. Their decision to anoint the body despite the large stone protecting the grave testifies to their courage but also points to fear and a sense of weakness and aloneness in the face of such violence. One can only imagine their questions about the God who would allow this horror to happen to their leader.

Again in our day, the violence of the crucifixion has given rise to women's critical questions about lofty theories of atonement and redemption. The image of Jesus as a victim who accepted violence meekly for the sake of salvation has created doubt and anger triggered by women's feelings of powerlessness in the face of a similar violence. Mary Daly was one of the first women to express these questions directly: "The qualities that Christianity idealizes, especially for women, are also those of the victim: sacrificial love, passive acceptance of suffering, humility, meekness, etc. Since these are the qualities idealized in Jesus 'who dies for our sins' his functioning as a model reinforces the scapegoat syndrome for women."[24]

For many women today, theories of salvation that glorify sacrifice do not give hope in the face of violence they know best, the context of abuse against women and children. If Jesus' death was redemptive, is all human suffering also redemptive? Does obedience to God mean that women should negate themselves and willingly accept the violence enacted against them? Is this the path to salvation? These questions are further complicated in a theological framework that assets that God the Father willed that his child be killed. How does this act model loving parenthood?

These women point out the insidious effects of the notion that atonement for human sin can happen only through the bloody sacrifice of God's own son: this view supports the sacrifice of innocent lives even in our day, and it can be converted to the belief that suffering and death are necessary to ensure the kind of life we wish to live. Power politics and reckless consumption require victims who willingly accept their suffering. Therefore it is not difficult to understand how the glorification of innocent victimhood, and of redemption as freely chosen suffering, prepare women psychologically to acquiesce in their suffering. To believe that God willed Jesus' cruel death is to see God as violent. For women caught in a web of violence this understanding may even suggest that God abandons those who suffer.

Mennonite women theologians have entered the conversation at this point. They agree that some emphases in our salvation theologies, including our peace theology, have had a subtle influence on women's readiness to accept violence against them. As Carol Penner and Mary Schertz assert, the notion of sacrifice has taught women to "be content to suffer" and has contributed to and increased the danger of family violence among us.[25] For these women, the personal-political dimension of the cross is related to the theology of redemption that demands the sacrifice of an innocent person.

Other women respond by seeing in the cross the solidarity of Jesus with women in their suffering. Theologians such as Luise Shottroff no longer view the cross as an atoning sacrifice but rather as a political means of punishment not restricted to Jesus but suffered by all who act against injustice. Others realize that struggle for God's reign and commitment to God's will often lead to rejection and even death. As Kwok Pui Lan eloquently writes: "It is the very person on the Cross that suffers like us, who was rendered as a nobody that illuminates the tragic human existence and speaks to countless women in Asia.... We see Jesus as the God who takes the human form and suffers and weeps with us."[26] These voices lead us to ask: what image of God do we embrace? Do our theories of atonement point to a God who demands violent sacrifice?

Gayle Gerber Koontz speaks to this question of atonement by beginning with an understanding of sin that includes the sins that contribute to violence. She suggests that the sins of the weak and the sins of the powerful both need to be confronted by the cross. Pride, overreaching, exploitation and self-aggrandizement characterize the sins of the powerful, while self-hatred, shame, humiliation, uncleanness, and worthlessness characterize the sins of the weak. She goes on to suggest that sin can be defined in terms of human failure to embody Christ-like relatedness with God, neighbor, and earth. She thus sees salvation as the "restoration of Christ-like relatedness between humans and God," a wholeness that includes new life in all its fullness and rejects violence against another.[27]

How does the cross achieve this wholeness? Koontz opts for the image of the victory of God over the powers that begins with the liberating-atoning work of Christ throughout his life. This victory is ultimately the work of a Christ who incarnates a divine power that does not compel but rather empowers and invites. Jesus' healing and teaching ministry has already pointed the way. The cross becomes the ultimate symbol of reconciling love, a demonstration of the divine love that continues to love enemies even while they are sinners. We can enter into salvation by embracing this way of life ourselves as we receive a new identity in Christ. Thus we too can die to the sins of self-negation and of pride and be empowered to struggle against the evil of violence and domination. In addition, we can be drawn into a liberating community that is not bound by the evil powers. For Koontz, salvation is both social and personal, and it includes rejecting the violence that put Jesus on the cross, as well as the self-denial that would sacrifice out of a sense of worthlessness and self-negation.

Koontz admits that this view of salvation only makes sense if there is reality beyond this world and beyond history, and if God's power is ultimately victorious over death and evil. In order to trust in this view of salvation, we must therefore go to the second context: the women at the empty tomb.

The Context of Hope and New Life

It was women who were the first to be given a surprising new context in which to interpret the meaning of Jesus' death: the context of new life and therefore hope. However, this shift in context also created confusion and fear. In Mark's account, when the women encountered the empty tomb they fled from the tomb, too afraid to say anything. Why this fear? Luke gives us a hint: when the women did speak, "these words seemed to them [the Twelve] an idle tale and they did not believe them" (Luke 24:11). And why would they? After all, these were women who had a role to play in the anointing of a dead body, but not as witnesses to this new reality. (Note that in the short summary of the gospel tradition by Paul in 1 Corinthians 15:3-8, the women were not even mentioned as witnesses to the resurrection.) Yet when Jesus encountered the women on the way, they receive the mandate, "Go, tell his disciples and Peter that he is going ahead of you to Galilee, there you will see him" (Mark 16:7). And eventually the women were able to bring the good news of Jesus' risen presence to the rest of the disciples.

What created this readiness to speak with joy? First of all, the women knew that Jesus was no longer in the tomb. The empty tomb signified that Jesus was present and alive. Second, they were told that Jesus was going ahead of them to Galilee, a reminder of Jesus' powerful words and actions in Galilee. If Jesus would be present in their futures as promised, they could testify to the empty tomb. And third, they had met Jesus as the resurrected one. In Mary's case, meeting the risen Christ and receiving the surprising news that Jesus was ascending to the Father, "to my God and your God," created the clarity that she needed. Now she could say with confidence: "I have seen the Lord" (John 20:17-18). All of the women thus knew that the ignominious death had been transformed into life, not only for Jesus but also for them. The resurrection signified the vindication of the suffering but also the vindication of the message of the reign of God which Jesus had proclaimed and lived. They had not followed him in vain. The power already exhibited in Jesus' life was stronger than the power of death.

Mary Schertz's study of the atonement as presented by Luke suggests that the root metaphor for redemption is not death but life.[28] She studies Luke's view of the "divine necessity" (δει: it is necessary) and discovers that the gospel writer introduces the idea of the necessary will of God first of all in Jesus' call to ministry. It was *necessary* for Jesus to study the Torah, to receive a strong sense of purpose to proclaim the coming kingdom of God. She then goes on to show how this *necessity* was there in his healing ministry, in his feeding of the hungry and in his seeking and saving the lost. In a pair of texts at the climax of his ministry, however, Jesus chooses to remind himself and his disciples that his way of life is fraught with peril; it is not a triumphalist march to claim conventional power. He warns his followers of his coming fate (Luke 9:22, 13:33). It was *necessary* for Jesus to suffer and die.

Schertz then points to the three instances of this term in the resurrection narratives. Each comes in the context of a teaching situation where the gospel writer points out that it is necessary for Jesus to be betrayed and crucified (24:7), for Jesus to suffer and come into his glory (24:26), and for the Scripture to be fulfilled (24:44). The followers of Jesus were reminded and chided for not remembering all these necessary aspects of God's will. Thus Luke shows us that suffering does not by itself define redemption; rather it is the whole mission of God that includes but is not limited by the tragedy of the cross. As summarized by Schertz:

> For Luke, what is redemptive is the kingdom of God. People are saved and their sins blotted out when they stop resisting the kingdom and become, in turn, proclaimers and enactors of this kingdom. The conversion of individuals is possible because Jesus preached, taught, healed, exorcised demons, suffered, died, and was raised—all to announce and bring about the kingdom of God. Conversion of individuals comes about

> through the Holy Spirit and the faithfulness of believers who continue to proclaim and enact the kingdom of God in the name of Jesus.[29]

Thus it is the turning to the life of the kingdom that creates the passion and the power to enact this kingdom in one's one life and community; even though this enactment may lead to suffering for the sake of the kingdom. When life becomes the root metaphor for salvation, death has lost its sting—as Paul's letters testify.

For the Sake of Our Salvation

In Romans 6, baptism is understood as a dying to sin and rising to walk in the newness of life. Whether our primary sin is self-negation that willingly suffers or pride that engenders violence and abuse, our old self needs to be crucified so that we will no longer be enslaved to sin. In solidarity with Jesus (who did not take up violence nor did he negate his identity as Messiah), we are to consider ourselves dead to sin and alive to God in Jesus Christ. Paul goes on to say that we are not to live unto ourselves. Rather, we become slaves of another power, the power of righteousness for sanctification. The final purpose of this sanctification is eternal life in Christ Jesus.

This turn to life is one that many women can embrace, for it does not deny the brutality of the cross but places it into the context of its purpose for abundant and eternal life that the kingdom of God promises. It rejects sin in its many forms. Yet it commends a rising into a new power, the very power of love and righteousness that Jesus exhibited in his death on the cross and that God confirmed in the resurrection. This rising represents a new holiness, entering a process of sanctification that transforms our very life. This power can only be received as a gift of God freely given for the sake of our salvation.

The witness of women is often hidden until God's light creates such a rainbow of hope that no one can ignore it. The fact that women begin to play the leading roles in the final scenes of the gospel narratives is one of the surprises of the passion story. Today, rainbows of hope created by the witness of women who have read the gospel in the midst of violence are again dancing across the theological landscape, giving hope to many caught in the web of violence. Let us not ignore these voices as though they told an idle tale, for they may point us to the saving power of God exhibited in the life and death of Jesus Christ.

* * *

SEXUALITY IN THE WEDDING[30]

The first time my name appeared on the cover of book was together with Gary in the year 1980. That came about in a rather strange way. Gary and I had been asked by the Worship Series Committee of our denomination to write a booklet on "Celebrating Christian Marriage" as part of a series on leading worship. I declined because I had no experience in leading wedding rituals. Besides, Gary was used to doing his own preaching and teaching and was most comfortable writing in his own voice. When we received the edited version, I noticed that my name appeared on the cover. When I protested, the editor said it made most sense for a couple to write this booklet, and since I had probably influenced it, I deserved some credit!

Since then Gary and I have learned to preach, teach, and write together without one voice being subsumed by the other. There are various steps to our collaborative process of writing an article. We begin with brainstorming about the topic, spending time just talking and thinking about stories, books to use as background material, themes that need elaboration, and biblical passages that need exegesis. Gradually a direction emerges out of these conversations. Usually Gary does the initial writing and I do the editing and sometimes rewriting. Sometimes we each write part of an article or sermon and then put it together into a framework that emerges for us during the writing. Gary and I both enjoy the creative process. I tend to be more particular about details like spelling, grammar, proper footnotes, and scholarly analysis; Gary is the more creative writer, able to play with metaphor and story in his writings.

The article on sexuality in the wedding was written during a semester at Anabaptist Mennonite Biblical Seminary (AMBS). Gary had just retired from full-time ministry and we were taking a semester break by living in Elkhart on the campus of AMBS. The seminary needed someone to teach a leadership course for one semester and we had planned to do some research and thinking about weddings and wedding planning with some visions of writing a book together. We even had a good title for the book, Blessing Weddings: Unwrapping God's Wedding Gifts. Gary had always loved officiating at weddings and the pre-marriage preparation in which he integrated wedding planning with the counselling. Together we had officiated at a number of weddings and led marriage preparation sessions. We were convinced that as Christians we needed to look again at the wedding industry and the present cultural situation and ask why and how the church wanted to be involved in this ceremony.

The year before I had spent some time researching what our Mennonite Confessions of Faith say about marriage. I had discovered that our confessions have been more concerned with the boundary between church and "world" and how marriages affect that relationship. Little guidance was given for how the church could support and nurture healthy marriage relationships and loving families. For example, in early Anabaptist teaching the purpose of "shunning" a marriage partner who had strayed from the church's teaching was to keep the church pure. In later Confessions of Faith, concerns about marrying a partner who was not a church member, premarital sex, divorce, and homosexuality became the main themes that were addressed (abuse within marriage was not mentioned).

At the same time Gary had discovered that many pastors do not like to do weddings because of the great pressure of the wedding industry that makes a pastor into a pawn doing the will of the couple and not a pastor leading a worship service celebrating the covenant of marriage. Pastors also did not know how to deal with pre-marital sex, something that the church condemned but that many couples accepted as normal. So a book that we could write together seemed to be in the making.

Though we enjoyed the planning of the book and led several workshops on the theme, the actual writing of the book never happened. Instead, one article was published in Vision that began to deal with some of the issues. Since then we have been challenged to think more deeply about boundaries and their effect on same-sex relationships—something that we do not address in this article.[31] *We have realized how uncomfortable we as a church community are with our human bodies and their sexual desires. We now understand that the exclusion of LGBTQ couples from our marriage ceremonies is unjust and does not support LGBTQ couples as they create families and seek to be faithful to their partners. The article that follows begins a conversation that we need to have within our churches about how all of us can keep body and soul connected in our theological and ethical reflection on sexuality and marriage.*

***

The rules of the sexual dance have been changing rapidly in our society. No longer do most couples look to the church for permission, via a marriage license, to dance together sexually. Pastors no longer oversee the dance floor. However, many couples still come to pastors to preside at their weddings. They still come to the church to marry—and perhaps to look for deeper meanings for their married and sexual lives. How will we respond? How do we negotiate the changing dance floor scene?

Reflections From the Dance Floor (Gary)

I am all too aware of the overt sexuality she exudes. It frightens and disconcerts me a bit. It also excites me, enough at least to know that I need to keep my boundaries clearly in place. "Don't start fantasizing," I order myself. How then to begin the marriage preparation journey for this couple sitting before me? Especially when I know we will need to talk about their sexuality.

Jan and Eric (not their real names) have come to my office because they want me to officiate at their wedding. They come hesitantly. They bring guilt feelings. They have been living together for almost a year and cannot reconcile that fact with their upbringing and stated convictions that full sexual expression belongs only within marriage. They are Christians, and they feel they have betrayed their Christian commitment. They are tired of hiding their living arrangement from their families, and they want to commit their lives to each other in marriage.

I can see how Eric might have succumbed to Jan's sexual appeal—and for that matter, how Jan could have been attracted to Eric's strong aura of maleness. They start listing excuses for moving in together. There were economic realities. They already knew they wanted to get married, so they just started having sex a bit early. And then Jan is in tears. "Can we still get married in the church? Will you still marry us?"

In some ways the church has seen the marriage license as a license to have sex. The wedding service legitimates full sexual expression. Marriage is the boundary that regulates our sexuality. Before marriage, sex is bad. After marriage, sex is legitimized— almost regardless of how it is expressed. We have had a hard time naming sexual abuse within marriage.

But we find it difficult to be honest about sex both in marriage preparation and in the wedding service. It hovers just beneath the surface, bubbling away just out of reach of words, unnamed until someone tells a crude joke at the reception and leaves most of us embarrassed. In the way we do weddings, can we somehow deal honestly and compassionately with sexuality? Can we address sex with integrity, aware of the highly sexualized nature of our society, aware of how our society commodifies sexuality? Can we be ready to offer a wholesome vision of sexual expression?

Perhaps integrity around our sexuality is a gift the church can offer a couple getting married. But then we will have to get our act together. We have to be open about sex in the church. We have to talk about it. We have to name the blessing and the curse, how sex can wonderfully enrich our lives and how it can harm us and empty our relationships of meaning. We have to struggle as a church to understand and own our vision for a healthy sexuality. And we need to pass on our vision to our children.

But how do we make our sexuality sacred, a part of our journey with and toward God? How do we resist letting our secular society control our understanding of sexuality?

From colleagues in ministry I have heard about three possible ways of responding to a common law couple wanting to get married. Some pastors start with rules, insisting that the couple move apart and refrain from intercourse until after the wedding. Others try to ignore the issue, believing that if they don't ask, they won't have to deal with it. Others try to engage the couple about their sexual expression as honestly as they can, and from there point to a fuller, covenanted vision.

The Bible is more forthright about human sexuality than we are often able to be. Let's consider Genesis 1 and 3.

In pleasure and delight God breathes life and spirit into the human beings. "I have created relating beings," exults God, "loving beings, male and female beings.

Companionship and intimacy can replace loneliness and alienation."

God delights in seeing Adam and Eve enjoy the garden, each other's companionship, and conversation with their creator. The woman and man tend the garden, name the animals, run free and naked and unashamed, taking pleasure in each other's love and in each other's bodies. And God laughs with them in joy.

But alas, other powers also reside in the garden and in each psyche. Another spirit breathes an unwelcome discordant reality into Eden. These first mythical humans, like each of us, have a lust for power, perhaps the strongest urge of all. Power. Control. Avoidance of vulnerability. Wanting to be like God, knowing good and evil, they eat of the fruit of the forbidden tree.

Then comes the blaming. And denial. And defending the indefensible. And exploitation. And hiding from God and from each other. All hell breaks loose as they are chased out of the garden.

The intimacy is lost. These first humans are alienated from each other and from God. Their nakedness is now a source of shame, and they cover their sexual parts. In their brokenness, Eden slips out of their grasp. But is it lost forever?

If we are honest with ourselves, we will acknowledge that many of the couples—maybe even the majority—that we marry in the church are not virgins on their wedding night. We are a long way from Eden. What do we do with that reality?

Integrity starts with candor in the office, with being honest with the couple wanting to get married. Far better to deal with the reality of the couple living together before marriage than to pretend, white wedding dress notwithstanding, that they are "pure." I thank Eric and Jan for being so open and honest with me. "I think we can now talk candidly about what your living together has meant for your relationship. And my hope is that it can lead to a wedding service that has integrity."

We are now free to explore a more full-orbed vision of intimacy. Jan and Eric acknowledge that their sex drives have taken over their relationship, that they are struggling to find other intimate ways to relate to each other. They are not able to keep in touch with each other emotionally as well as they want to. They have not explored how they could include spiritual intimacy in their relationship, even though both are Christians and regularly attend church. Their friendships and social networks are not well developed. Perhaps their guilt about their living arrangement is an inhibiting factor. They are dissatisfied with various aspects of their relationship. Even their sex life is less than satisfying. Will getting married magically heal their relationship?

Marriage can contribute to healing, but not without hard work. Jan and Eric drink in that bigger picture of intimacy. Over time they begin to address areas that they have neglected in their haste to move in together. They begin to be more vulnerable to each other emotionally. They even start praying together, one of the hardest kinds of closeness to embrace, because it is so intensely intimate. I realize, as we explore this terrain in preparation for their marriage, that I am no longer conscious of the overt sexuality that first drew my notice on meeting Jan. As my relationship with her and Eric has deepened, other aspects of her identity now engage my attention.

Their wedding is honest and joyful. I can name before their families and communities their journey from living together to a relationship that is ready for the multifaceted intimacy of a healthy marriage. We freely reinsert sexuality into the service.

The Song of Songs revisits the wholesome sexuality of Eden. The song is a symphony of sensuality in five movements. It is unashamedly erotic. Gone is the violence and cover-up of a distorted Eden, replaced with a restored and full mutuality. The woman is as free as the man to make advances. Neither dominates or exploits the other.

She begins the song, and he responds.

> Let him kiss me with the kisses of his mouth!
>
> For your love is better than wine,
> your anointing oils are fragrant,
> your name is perfume poured out....
>
> I compare you, my love,
> to a mare among Pharaoh's chariots....
>
> My beloved is to me a bag of myrrh
> that lies between my breasts.
>
> My beloved is to me a cluster of henna blossoms
> in the vineyards of Engedi....
>
> Ah, you are beautiful, my love;
> ah, you are beautiful;
> your eyes are doves.
> Ah, you are beautiful, my beloved,
> truly lovely....
>
> With great delight I sat in his shadow,
> and his fruit was sweet to my taste.

> He brought me to the banqueting house,
> and his intention toward me was love. . . .
>
> How beautiful you are, my love,
> how very beautiful.
> Your eyes are doves
> behind your veil.
> Your hair is like a flock of goats,
> moving down the slopes of Gilead. . . .
> Your two breasts are like two fawns,
> twins of a gazelle,
> that feed among the lilies. . . .
>
> My beloved is all radiant and ruddy,
> distinguished among ten thousand.
> His head is the finest gold;
> his locks are wavy, black as a raven.
> His eyes are like doves. . . .
> His body is ivory work,
> encrusted with sapphires...

And finally this symphony of sensuality ends, as it must. The curtain is drawn shut, and with it the circle of intimacy between the two closes as they become one:

> Make haste, my beloved,
> and be like a gazelle
> or a young stag
> upon the mountains of spices!

Earthy, embodied, erotic, sensual, mutual—a powerful yet tender love song written in a patriarchal context, revisiting old Eden and sending waves into ever new Edens.

Jan and Eric's marriage is happy and honest, growing in the context of their congregation. They continue to learn that intimacy is God's gift to them and their gift to each other. One wonderful part of their many-faceted intimacy is enjoyment of each other's bodies in full sexual expression.

Musings From the Balcony (Lydia)

The balcony overlooks the dance floor, providing perspective on the unfolding sexual dance. The view from the balcony encourages us to reflect and ask, what is really happening here?

When I step back to reflect theologically on weddings and sexuality, I realize that most of the time I do not think about the wedding as "the liturgical ritualized celebration of the sexual union of two persons."[32] In fact, the words of the wedding service rarely speak about the mystery of sexual desire or the creative reproductive power of sexual union. Because the wedding is a worship service, we assume that the focus is on the spiritual and sacred covenant that is deeper and broader than having sex. However, what strikes me about our wedding practices is that we often leave our sexuality at the church door. We have become so comfortable with separating the sacred and the secular as we enter worship that we don't even notice that no one is speaking about physical intimacy at an event in which it should be celebrated as a gift of God.

I wonder if this separation of the sacred and secular leaves us open to the seductive power of our technological culture. That culture wants to take over our most intimate relationships and make them shallow, artificial, superficial. In our society the perfect sexual relationship is a commodity that can be acquired with the right technique or through using the right beauty product or by having so-called safe sex or by planning the most romantic wedding. The market encourages couples to enjoy sexual goods without responsibility, without outside interference, and without the burdens of a community ethic. Marriage is available to anyone who wishes for it, and if one product does not suit, perhaps another will. The wedding is in danger of becoming a counterfeit, a spectacle produced for public consumption. Sexuality has been reduced to a possession rather than experienced as a gift of God which we tend and nourish through hard work.

In earlier times, we could not so easily ignore sexuality. If a couple lived together, a baby would likely appear before long. If a woman died in childbirth, her husband needed to find a new wife in order to provide a secure home for his children. If a young man bought a farm, he sought out a wife to share the work with him. Partnership was built into the marriage relationship for economic and social reasons. Therefore, community rules could be effective in encouraging a deeper and more multifaceted relationship. Sexuality was a part of a larger whole, blessed and regulated by the community, because the community needed the family and the family needed the community.

Now couples may no longer look to the community to provide economic and social support and sanctions. What they may fail to realize is that our most profound human capability to be intimate with others and to be fruitful within our community is being crippled by a culture that converts our sexual nature into a consumer product. Couples may long for a deeper understanding of sexuality but discover that their church is afraid to speak about sexuality's power. They may wish for community support but worry that their sexual desires are not understood. They may even wish they could counter the domination of the wedding industry but do not know where to start.

Can weddings become public events that engage the community and the couple in ways that reorient sexuality toward a full-orbed practice of marriage? Can our weddings become celebratory events that establish honest marriage relationships? Can weddings speak about sexual intimacy as a gift of God that nonetheless requires an investment of our attention and effort? Can we recognize sex as a gift we will not fully enjoy if community support and encouragement are absent?

The transition from singleness into marriage is not an easy one, despite our romantic notions. We need worship rituals that acknowledge the difficulties, admitting that sexual intimacy in its fullest sense does not come easily within our society of consumerism. But above all, couples need to know that God delights in marriages in which sexual intimacy mirrors the love that God has for the church and for all humankind. The church must focus its wedding preparation and wedding services on celebrating this kind of love. Then what we say and celebrate in weddings will be good news for the dancers and for the church.

Chapter 10 Discernment

NAMING THE REWARDS OF COMMUNAL DISCERNMENT

Discernment is a word that has been used frequently in the Mennonite church to talk about decision making within our organizational structures. For lay people within the church, the notion of hermeneutic community has implied that every member of the church is entitled to be part of the decision-making process. Yet for discernment to be effective, there is an acknowledgement that in-depth analysis, a diligent research of options, biblical study, and focussed questions by leaders, must be present. Underlying this ordinary process of communal decision-making is an assumption far greater, an assumption that God is leading the process in a faith community. For many church members, this has created a crisis of faith when political maneuvering, hurtful accusations, and a silencing of voices also becomes part of the process. It is sometimes difficult to see how this embodied church made up of fallible humans can be one of the representatives of God's presence in the world.

Yet, I am hopeful that God continues to work through a human Bible, a human church, and even human individuals such as each one of us. Though I continue to understand discernment as a search for truth, I also understand that search within a context of relationships among people. Therefore it is more about trusting conversation and deep listening than about a rational decision-making process. It is more about openness and vulnerability to others than about making a judgment on the ideas of others, more a sharing of experiences than of overpowering others with our arguments, more a common search for truth than a creation of certainties. And in the final analysis it is openness to prayer and transformation that comes through our relationship to God. I therefore am committed to working at building relationships while also naming and confronting power when it becomes abusive.

My last six years of active work were spent in interim pastoring in several churches that experienced some conflict or stress for a variety of reasons. I was reminded again how powerful Jesus's prayer for unity among God's people is in the face of the many broken relationships created through the abuse and misuse of power and authority. This unity comes not from uniformity but from relationships of love. It does not dominate and oppress some members of the congregation as did the uniform dress codes for women in some Mennonite communities, the uniform theology created by one or two powerful leaders or the uniform ethics created by rigid rules and regulations. These distanced people from each other. The unity that I now strive for is more elusive, for it comes in communion and sharing of gifts, and in forgiveness and worship. Hope comes because of the many moments of unity that I have experienced in our churches both in the past and present.

At the same time as I strive for unity, I am aware of how difficult it continues to be for many people to speak their own truth into the community discernment process. Persons who have been excluded or marginalized need great courage and persistence to continue to relate to communities that systematically exclude them. What is needed is allies that stand by those excluded without taking over their unique voice. Support can be given in many ways so that these voices can be listened to as prophetic voices that can lead us to greater truth.

These reflections represent the thoughts of my senior years as I am called upon to mentor younger persons entering theological studies or ministry. The following article suggests an approach to Bible and church discernment that includes many voices, even those that are disturbing, trusting that God will lead and direct. It is a call to create unity in a community that values justice, reconciliation, and truth as it finds way to include and value each person and their gifts. The rewards for this kind of communal discernment are experienced as truthful encounters, deepened relationships, and above all an outpouring of love that moves beyond the community itself.

***

THEOLOGICAL CONVERSATIONS ABOUT SAME SEX MARRIAGE: AN OPPORTUNITY FOR THE CHUCH TO BE SCRIPTURAL IN ITS DISCERNMENT[1]

In my growing up years sexual expression was firmly connected to marriage and to child-bearing. Birth control methods such as the pill had only recently become available. In fact, my doctor rejected my request for a prescription when we were first married because he believed that intimate sex should result naturally in any children that may be conceived. Most of my friends got married right after high school, happy for the "permission" to engage in sex. The congregation of which I was a part quickly performed the marriage of a friend when it was discovered that she was pregnant (after a confession of the sin of pre-marital sex). And we assumed that marriage with the accompanying housework, home-making, and child-rearing was the best possible life for women. Men were expected to support their wives and children. Those who stayed single whether by choice or not were considered less fortunate. All of this was supported by a theology of marriage most concerned with boundaries that named sex within marriage good and sex outside of marriage bad.

Much has changed during my life time. We have learned that sex within marriage can be violent and abusive. We have discovered that singleness can be a calling and a blessing for many people. We have learned that women and men can be flexible and mutual in their roles within the family as well as in the work situation. And we have learned that families can have many different shapes, as adopted families, blended families, and intentional families become more common.

Yet one of the greatest conflict within our church and societal communities in the last twenty years has centred on the inclusion/exclusion of LGBTQ persons. Our heteronormative congregations have been trying to discern how to relate to persons whose sexual orientation is not heterosexual and/or whose gender identity does not conform neatly to a male/female binary. We, the heteronormative centre, have learned of the oppression and the violence that has silenced the LGBTQ community on the margins of society and have begun to hear of their devastating experiences in our own ecclesial communities. Far too slowly we have begun to hear the theological voices of our brothers and sisters as they too wrestle with scriptures that have been used to exclude them from the people of God. In a culture where sexuality is both celebrated and made the core of our identity, LGBTQ Christians have begun to claim their own dignity as persons made in the image of God.

In the recent past I was shocked and silenced as I heard of the horror of the murder of 49 persons, primarily LGBTQ persons, in the so-called Orlando massacre (2016). I realize that as a heterosexual Christian and particularly as one who has studied theology, I must recognize and confess my own fear of the other and my own slow acknowledgment of different genders and sexualities among us. However, if I accept my calling as a theological leader, I cannot dismiss a long ethical tradition without taking some time to see the longer view and understand the implications of a major (though very necessary) theological shift.

The following essay gives a glimpse of my own involvement in trying to be faithful to God while being open to the experiences of others in the complexity of our sexual identities and the changes within our cultural context. It presents the approach I took in leading our congregation through an educational process during our own church's discernment around same-sex marriage. The essay relies on the multi-faceted biblical traditions to speak to our uncertainties and fears in face of sexual and gender differences. It points to the multi-faceted witness and testimony of the past in order to also be open to the multi-faceted witness and testimony in the present.

Yet as I reflect on that experience, I realize that my eyes are often blinded to the power dynamics present even as I try to be faithful. The pain, betrayal, and frustration of congregational processes testify to the need for something more. Discernment is not done with biblical and theological analysis alone. What is still needed is confession, lament, and forgiveness even as we accept the differences among us.

The essay was written to honour A. James Reimer, the colleague and friend with whom I worked most closely with over the years of my career in doing theology. We first met at college and then worked together to envision the direction and purpose of the Toronto Mennonite Theological Centre (TMTC). I remember many conversations with him, not always ones in which we agreed on every aspect of our theology or on the direction that TMTC should go. However, we shared a vision that created a stimulating dialogue that both challenged and supported me in my work.

In the midst of honouring Jim, I want to also acknowledge the women and men in my various non-scholarly communities who have spent many hours of conversation with me supporting my work, often without understanding fully why scholarly work is necessary. I think of the stimulating and supportive Bible study groups in the various communities of which I was a part. I think of Irene, Marianne, and Ruth who first encouraged me to enter theological study even though they themselves were more interested in the practical work of caring for refugees, teaching children, and encouraging supportive relationships in the church. I think of the circles of women, like the book club of which I am a part, who continue to meet to talk about current issues and share personal stories. I think of Jan, Muriel, Martha, Marilyn, Michele, and Gail who through the years met with me for conversations about our callings and the obstacles that seemed to stand in our way, some that looked insurmountable. I also think of those women who spoke to me from their place of pain from often being pushed to the margins of church and society. It is these conversation partners that have convinced me that community is possible even in our differences as we acknowledge the moving of the Spirit among us.

***

One of the threats to the church in its struggle with issues surrounding same-sex marriage is the polarity that often develops within congregations, dividing faithful members from one another.[2] A wedge is driven between the church's identity as a compassionate community in "priestly-pastoral" solidarity with persons of homosexual orientation and its identity as a moral theological community, speaking a "prophetic-ethical" word to a church confused about its sexual ethics.[3] Conversations among church members about intimate same-sex relationships become battles, with appeals to different readings of the Bible justifying different ethical positions. In the process, the enormous interpretive steps that have already been taken to bridge the distance between a historical text such as the Bible and today's world are largely ignored.

Jim Reimer has rightly pointed to the need for the church, in dependence on the Holy Spirit, to move in a dynamic or developmental way "beyond" the biblical text in addressing these issues.[4] However, this can be a dangerous and risky move without some understanding of the kind of church we need to be, and the kind of theological process we need to engage in, in order to be in continuity with the Bible that we name our Christian Scripture.[5] This essay will describe one approach that moves dynamically beyond the biblical text but seeks to be in continuity with it.

Defining the Approach

Choosing a Place to Start

Stephen C. Barton has suggested a place to start in the discernment process on same-sex marriage that can keep us from shifting too quickly into arguments about biblical authority. For him the crucial question is: What kind of people do we need to be in order to interpret wisely what the Bible says? It is now "no longer the Bible which is on the dock but we who ask the question or of whom the question is asked."[6] The focus has changed from the Bible as an abstract concept to the church as a concrete community demonstrating in its life that the God of the Bible is present and active, bringing new experiences of transformation and renewal. A bridge created by the community reading and interpreting its scriptures now replaces the wedge often driven between present experience and the Bible.[7] This shift places the responsibility for the "performance" of Scripture directly on the community itself. Thus the challenge is to be a community that nurtures the virtues, skills, and practices that can create honest, truthful interpretation of both the Bible and the societal and church context.

An approach that includes the present church is dependent on the Holy Spirit being present in the midst of the congregation, and assumes that despite human failures the church too can live "in rhythm" with the Bible.[8] However, this means that churches must recover new, vital worship that does not avoid the anguish and struggle that comes when compassion and solidarity with individuals stand beside a genuine search for God's will.[9]

Choosing a Framework to Structure the Conversation

Finding a framework that could be helpful to congregations as they struggle with issues related to sexuality and family is not easy. Various elements that may be included in the discussion, such as tradition, culture, experience, and reason, tend to divide people from each other rather than create better understandings of the Bible and the context within which we read it. Thus the concrete congregational setting of a worshiping community becomes an obstacle to be overcome, not an important element in hearing the particular Word of God for our time.

Reimer points us in another direction. He insists that it is the Trinitarian God as understood from the biblical witness and as present to the whole world that must form the basis of all Christian theology.[10] This confession of God's active presence is embodied not only in the Bible but in worshiping communities that seek to discern God's leading for their daily lives. These communities thus have the opportunity to take into account God's activity in the world while not ignoring the many aspects of human involvement as easily seen within their own congregational processes of interpretation.[11]

The thesis of this paper is simple. It assumes that a broad variety of human experiences, traditions, cultural contexts, and reasoning processes are included in the multiple witnesses to God in both the Bible and our worshiping communities. However, these elements are seen not as hindrances but as gifts of God to us to enrich our understanding of God's will. In fact, the shape of the scriptures with their multiple approaches to truth can be a helpful criterion to assess the shape of our own church's theological conversation. By paying attention to the overall structure of our scriptures we will gain clues that will point to the variety of conversation partners needed in our discernment process. Yet, ultimate authority must be given to the God who is revealed in these human witnesses, present within our scriptures and within our communities of worship.

This approach is not original. In *The Creative Word* Walter Brueggemann uses the shape of the canon to look at the shape Christian education should take in our day.[12] My approach would do something similar by asking questions and making observations on the church's theological conversation about same-sex marriage based on the shape or "modes of knowledge" included in the canon that we name as our authority. After all, the term canon comes from the notion of a measuring reed or rod; and criteria for discernment are sorely needed for our contemporary theological process.

The particular modes or layers of Scripture that will be used to illustrate a "scriptural" hermeneutical process rest on a long tradition within Jewish and Christian interpretation.[13] They include "instruction from the priest, counsel from the wise and a word from the prophet" (Jer 18:18) as represented by "prophets, sages and scribes" (Matt 23:34). As Brueggemann suggests, each of these sources or agents of knowledge has a "different function in Israel, proceeds from a different epistemology, and makes a different claim."[14] Thus it can be helpful to identify each of these distinctive partners to the intertextual dialogue within the Bible in order to overhear the emphasis they bring. For it is these "parallel and persistent" modes of knowledge, operative in communal conversations throughout the centuries of scriptural formation, that can also help us test our present modes of knowledge to see if similar functions and roles are among us today.

The focus on intertextual conversation rests on the belief that the particular processes shaping the biblical text were not neutral or incidental but "confessional actions" of the community of God's people.[15] Gerald Sheppard has pointed out that as the notion of Scripture emerged during various historical periods, an engagement with earlier texts as live words of God can be detected in the later texts.[16] The interfacing of the foundational narratives, the prophetic word, and the wisdom tradition within Scripture testifies to a dynamic interpretive process that has allowed the texts to continue to have vitality, authority, and relevance for new generations in new circumstances. What continues to be important for the present theological process is that new claims be made on the grounds of both the shape and substance of the older scriptural tradition.

Recognizing the Critical Edge

In 2 Timothy 3:16, the Holy Spirit's activity is claimed as the crucial element that transforms the human words of the scriptures so that "they will be useful for teaching, rebuking, correcting and training in righteousness." Thus it would seem necessary for this same Spirit of God to be invited into congregations through prayer in order for God's Word to be discerned for the present time.

The centrality of the Psalms in the Old Testament attests most directly to the importance of the divine/human relationship in seeking direction for life. Psalm 119 is explicit in describing how prayer and attention to Scripture are related in the discernment of God's way. The Bible as a whole embodies this interaction in the way that prayer is interspersed in the Torah and gospel narratives, in the prophetic word, and in the wisdom literature. In the New Testament prayer is connected to discernment most directly in Jesus' prayers and in several stories in Acts, but throughout the epistles prayer is interwoven into the very substance of the letters.

The inherent conviction within the canon that prayer gives energy and substance to the discernment of God's will is illustrated in the prayer in the book of Ephesians. The prayer is explicit in its recognition of our human need for resources that can be given only by God. In chapter 3, for example, the writer prays that the church will grasp the "manifold wisdom of God…according to the eternal purpose which he accomplished in Christ Jesus our Lord" (verses 10-21). It begins by kneeling "before the Father through whom every family in heaven and on earth derives its name." Thus this prayer is relevant to all families in their great variety, for it is addressed to the Creator Parent who best knows our human natures and our need for intimate relationships and healthy family lives. The prayer goes on to suggest the abundance of resources available to the church through the power of the Spirit and through the presence of Christ Jesus within those who gather in Christ's name.

> I pray that according to the riches of his glory, he may grant that you be strengthened in your inner being with power through his Spirit, and that Christ may dwell in your hearts through faith as you are being rooted and grounded in love. I pray that you may have the power to comprehend, with all the saints, what is the breadth and length and height and depth, and to know the love of Christ that surpasses knowledge, so that you may be filled with all the fullness of God. (Ephesians 3:17-19)

This prayer asks for a climate of discernment that is unafraid, knowing that these gifts of the triune God are available through faith as we gather together with fellow believers (saints). The assertion that love, rather than knowledge, is the necessary element in the discernment process suggests the relational element of the theological conversation. A solidarity with each other that is rooted in Christ's love is necessary for the fullness of God to be present in the community.[17] Thus the power of the Spirit will be released in the midst of the congregation as it is rooted and established in this love.

Yet prayer as a genuine divine/human interaction is a difficult theological activity, because it cannot be controlled by us. What it does require is a placing of one's whole being, both personally and communally, into a vulnerable position before God. For Scripture does not assume that critical discernment and obedience to that discernment come easily. A kind of wrestling with God is embodied in the prayers of Job and the prayers of Jesus, in the communal struggles in Exodus and those in Acts. But the Bible does assume that fear can be cast out, as people begin to trust in God to guide them. Communal prayer thus becomes the critical edge that will enable a community to listen deeply to Scripture and to make the practical judgments that will encourage a healthy sexuality and family life in our day.

Exploring Scriptural Modes of Knowledge

The particular themes that we will overhear in these three modes of knowledge are examples of themes especially pertinent in the conversation about same-sex marriage. Thus further themes and texts can be suggested. All need testing in a theological conversation that includes today's scribes, prophets, and sages in the context of a praying community.

Hearing the Foundational Narratives: Living in covenant in order to bless all peoples

1 Corinthians 15 speaks about the gospel tradition that the Corinthians have received, in which they stand and through which they are being saved. However, Paul does not set forth this core tradition in the form of objective statements. Rather, he points to the distilled story of Jesus in the context of his own experience with Christ. My focus in this section of the paper will be on these kinds of foundational narratives—narratives about God's revelatory and saving presence passed on through the generations by the mediation of today's "priests and scribes" spawning numerous experiences of faith for hearers of that tradition. This kind of tradition functions to form communities with a strong sense of identity as God's covenant people because this heritage, though rooted in the past, is life giving for persons today.

Many Christians testify that the Bible as a whole is this kind of identity-forming material. Yet within the scriptures themselves there are books particularly noted for the core narratives they proclaim. It is probably no accident that these books have been placed at the beginning of the two testaments. Five books, named the Torah, stand at the beginning of the Old Testament and form the most authoritative part of the canon for Israel. They are the response of the priest/teacher/parent to the questions of the child/learner who asks about the rituals and practices of the community.[18] Four gospels and the book of Acts stand at the beginning of the New Testament. They form the core of the surprising gospel of the reign of God coming through Jesus, and tell the story of the spread of the good news to all peoples. Together these documents may be understood as the core identity-forming knowledge that must be passed on to the next generation in order for the community to know its reason for being. These books are largely in the form of narratives of God's active presence in creating an alternative "holy" community and transforming that community into a people through whom "all the families of the earth shall be blessed" (Genesis 12:3).

I have chosen "covenant" as the theme that connects most directly with our current questions about the meaning of marriage. It is also a central way that these core traditions speak about our identity as the people of God.[19] Included in the understanding of the covenant relationship are two central motifs: (1) redemption and salvation, based on God's loving intervention; (2) holiness, being set apart and consecrated in order to fulfill the purpose of the relationship. Thus this core tradition also includes basic laws and teachings that concretely apply the identity as God's people to the way the people are to live their daily lives in their particular context. In a sense we read a variety of "recipes" for living faithfully that concretely show them what it meant to be in covenant with God in the midst of those with other gods.[20] But included also are stories of failure and struggle as the covenant people learn and grow in their understandings and practices based on their covenantal identity.

In all of these biblical identity-forming narratives and community forming teachings it is assumed that persons are sexual beings, that they form the community of God's people as sexual beings, and that kinship and family social structures can be used to pass on the blessing of God. Genealogies, family relations, and family law are scattered throughout these core traditions. Included in the recipes are several pertaining to sexuality and family, each helping to set the people apart from the larger society as a covenant community. However, like recipes, the particulars have changed throughout the history of God's people. Eunuchs and prostitutes who once were outside the covenant have become part of the salvation story, single persons who once were deemed unfruitful are now considered gifted, and women who were once considered secondary are valued. So too polygamy, divorce laws, and uncleanness attributed to menstruation, all of which were accepted in Old Testament times, became increasingly seen as less than God-willed.

In Scripture the pattern that judges these behavioural codes is God's covenantal relationship to God's people, a relationship characterized by God's faithfulness, righteousness, and steadfast love despite human sin. In the New Testament this relationship was incarnated in Jesus, sent by God to invite all peoples into this covenant. Thus the experience that encouraged God's people to live ethically was the experience of being freed from the slavery of sin and condemnation, and of being invited into the reign of God made available through Jesus.

As we overhear this core tradition, we too must seek to answer the question about our own identity as a covenant community and our own recipes for a holy life arising out of God's redeeming activity in this place at this time. This first strand of the biblical heritage thus brings to the table those conversation partners that can explain our present church practices, including covenant ceremonies relating to family. Thus the key question becomes: What does the marriage ceremony mean? Included in our answer must be stories and concrete explanations answering further questions. What purpose do these covenants have in the larger mission of God? What is the sin from which faithfulness to these covenants saves us? And perhaps most important, how does our covenant-making shape us as a covenantal people, saved from sin and formed in holiness in order to bless all peoples? Only after these questions are explored should further questions be raised as to how the sexual orientation of the covenant partners affects the covenant relationship.[21]

The covenantal tradition embodied in Scripture will become alive in our congregations as we become vulnerable, sharing our own narratives of failure and success in embodying our commitments in our expressions of sexuality and in our formation of families. That kind of foundational knowledge will be trusted, because it will arise out of a sense of solidarity with each other and a mutual witness to a living God who continually calls us back to faithfulness. Within that context we will recognize anew which recipes for holiness best embody our covenant with God, and thus bring blessing to those around us.

Hearing the Prophetic Word: Imagining a re-alignment of relationships

The classic prophetic books in the Old Testament introduce a kind of tension into the hermeneutical interface among the books of the Bible. Their claim to truth is that they speak a new Word for a particular time as they receive it from God, a word that demands a rereading of the foundational tradition. Prophets read the signs of the times, recognize the larger eschatological plan of God present in the foundational narratives, and situate the community's current life within that larger framework. Prophets uncover and denounce sin and idolatry, but they also give a new vision for the future. Most important, they do not just urge people to go back to a former order of being but instead exercise a "prophetic imagination" to envision new ways of living out the covenant relationship with God that are more true to God's way.[22]

True prophets must be distinguished from false prophets who give false hope for a quick solution to the problems of the day. True prophets are not primarily individualistic voices, crying out their own pain or creating divisions for selfish reasons. Instead they know the tradition and can confront it critically when it is no longer life-giving for some members of the community. They suggest that God will judge the people on the key qualities of holiness that God exhibits:

justice, compassion, and mercy. Prophets are thus interested in social and political relationships; in how kings relate to the poor and the widow, liberated Israelites relate to slaves and foreigners, shepherd leaders relate to the sheep, and parents relate to their children.

Jesus embodied this prophetic voice in his proclamation of the reign of God and in his direct challenge to rigid authority structures, whether based on kinship, economic, religious, or political systems. He insisted that a re-alignment of relationships and structures will arise under God's reign. Thus children will be included, adulterers will be forgiven, the rich will be called to repentance, and the poor will be welcomed. The Pharisee is no longer the best symbol of righteousness, but rather Zaccheus who repents. The unblemished are no longer the primary symbol of holiness, but those made clean through God's healing. External washings are no longer the main vehicles of the holy; instead it is the inner state of the heart. Thus Jesus as prophet turned some cherished religious assertions and institutions upside down with his words and actions.

But this prophetic activity did not end with Jesus. In fact, prophets inspired by the Holy Spirit were recognized as among the most authoritative of the early church leaders. Paul as well as Peter could be accused of turning accepted norms of Judaism upside down. Especially important were their interpretations of the gospel for the Gentiles and their rejection of the need for circumcision as a prerequisite for inclusion in the community of faith.

Recognizing a true prophetic word in our day in regard to sexuality and family is not easy, because it is difficult to recognize which of the cultural patterns we are immersed in are no longer in line with God's kingdom. Jesse Mugambi, a theologian from Kenya, can be helpful here. He includes kinship among the variety of cultural systems and patterns requiring transformation.[23] Mugambi contends that in many societies kinship systems refer to the relational systems that we create, including not only the kind of families we form but other, more hidden relational systems that tell us whom we should relate to and whom we should avoid. Jesus understood the problems with these systems when he suggested they do not by themselves coincide with those who do God's will (Mark 3:31). Thus prophets in our day will also point out how our kinship relationships fit or do not fit with the vision of God's kingdom coming "on earth as it is in heaven."

In recent years women and racial minorities who felt excluded have challenged cultural relational patterns, insisting that they do not reflect the justice and love of God's reign. The church has begun to recognize and confront unjust power dynamics and abuse that happen even within covenanted relationships.[24] Thus it should not be surprising that in the midst of this prophetic rethinking of kinship relationships there would be a rethinking of the place of persons with same-sex orientation within our communities. As the charge of oppression and exclusion of gays and lesbians emerges, the church must address how our relationships to each other can best reflect the mercy, justice, and holiness of the covenant God.

Conversation partners who challenge us are more difficult to include at our table. We are tempted to draw boundaries based on either liberal or conservative assumptions, suggesting that the society around us has contaminated the voices of those with whom we do not agree. Though these voices do need to be tested, this testing must first of all include attending to the vision that they proclaim. Is it in line with the vision of God and God's purposes for human relationships? Are the critical words about present patterns of relationship true? Where does transformation need to happen?[25]

Today the prophetic voices ask whether God can still lead us into new paths to create different kinship patterns that more fully express both the delight and anguish of intimate relationships. These voices will finally be persuasive to the community of faith if they witness to God's way of relating to people as proclaimed by the prophets of old and as incarnated in Jesus' prophetic ministry.

Hearing the Words of Wisdom: Understanding the limitations and possibilities of our created being

The claim that wisdom teachers make is modest but clear: "Truly, the fear of the Lord, that is wisdom; to depart from evil is understanding" (Job 28:28). With this simple, practical reminder, the sages helped to construct the community of their day, using the knowledge they had gained through experience and attention to the created world. Yet wisdom's invitation is not to an easy road. In fact, the invitation is to the narrow, hard way leading to abundant life, also named the "way of righteousness," "blessing," "shalom," or the reign of God coming "on earth as it is in heaven."[26] These terms and images hint at the vast horizon of wisdom writings on this abundant life, and on all that preserves and continues life, including family relationships.

Wisdom affirms the value of human reasoning in seeking the good, but also defines aspects of righteousness and goodness that only those ready to follow wisdom's invitation can learn. The classic wisdom books include a broad range of knowledge, from folk wisdom to royal wisdom, from the common sense of a community to personal insight, from compassionate practice to skillful calculation, from careful orderly reasoning to unpredictable revelatory knowledge. Thus wisdom invites everyone to the table, but places all of this knowledge under the one who is the Creator of all that makes for life.

Wisdom literature is the most varied and is often considered the least authoritative of the three modes of knowledge in the Bible. Instead of describing events in terms of divine intervention as much of Scripture does, or setting down divine laws for every occasion, wisdom traditions are subtle and more open.[27] They suggest values, insights, practices, and convictions born of experience that lead to life. They realize knowledge must continually grow and mature as one learns to live in the way of wisdom. Foolishness is never far away, and discernment of God's way is always necessary. Thus the book of Proverbs assumes that people are capable of choosing their attitudes and course of action in situations that are often ambiguous and confusing. Few of the behaviours are universally applicable. Instead, the proverbs call for the flexibility of mind to determine which are appropriate for a particular situation at a particular time.

However, in some wisdom writings, such as Job and Ecclesiastes, a kind of deconstructive mode seems to dominate. "All is vanity," says the writer of Ecclesiastes, "a chasing after wind" (Eccl.1:14). The sages were aware of the limitations of language to speak of ultimate reality and struggled with the ambiguity they observed in much of life's experience. But in the end they accepted their solidarity with all humans in their ongoing search for wisdom. Even amidst their reflections on the fundamental questions of human existence, they stayed connected with the practical, mundane concerns of everyday life. They even wrestled with claims to knowledge from those outside the community, discerning what could be used in a practical way to build their own community.

Perhaps the most startling aspect of wisdom literature is the way some New Testament writers interpret Jesus as the Wisdom or "Sophia" of God. The book of Ephesians, also written in the wisdom tradition, suggests that through Jesus "God has made known to us the mystery of his will…as a plan for the fulness of time, to gather up all things in him, things in heaven and things on earth" (Ephesians 1:9-10). This is a rather presumptuous claim based on an eschatological hope in God's ultimate plan. Ephesians is clear that central to that plan is reconciliation—reconciliation of God with people and of those far off with those nearby. Thus the wise are called to be reconcilers, because they know the love of God that surpasses all knowledge and the grace of God toward all our human efforts. The wise, therefore, are called to be peacemakers in order to break down boundaries and to build bridges between people.

Sages are much needed in our theological conversation about same-sex marriage. For the wise are humbled because of their solidarity with all people in their human frailty, yet they are convinced that God knows the mystery of the universe. They are open to examining the knowledge about sexuality gained through physical, psychological, and sociological studies, yet they are also aware of the limitations of these studies in determining ethical choices. They recognize the need for reconciliation, but understand the need to wait for God's timing.

Though not speaking directly to issues of family, aspects of the classical wisdom texts create some analogies and precedents for the present process of discernment. For example, the book of Job wrestles with issues where experience does not fit with traditional answers of faith. The Song of Solomon, with its suggestion that humans' delight in each other and desire for each other has its own integrity, may be a helpful counterpart to Genesis, with its emphasis on child bearing. So, too, both Proverbs and the practical elements in Paul's letters are important, for they assume that boundaries are needed to protect the vulnerable and to resist the temptation to abuse God's gift of sexuality.

Thus we must ask: What possibilities do the wise see in light of the traditional form of family and the issues raised by our changing society? What limitations do they see in our nature as human beings? What kind of knowledge do they view as dangerous, and why? For it is the wise who challenge us to be practical in our discussion of the shape of families and to avoid creating false polarities, false hierarchies, and false religious boundaries. The wise ask us to admit our conflicts and differences, and they challenge us to find a way of unity that moves toward the reconciliation of all. The wise will finally be persuasive to the community of faith if they witness to both the limitations and the possibilities of our humanness in light of God the Creator and Jesus the Reconciler of us all.[28]

The Possibility of Unity while Discernment Continues

As the church listens to the various witnesses to God from the past, its members may recognize the various modes of knowledge in the theological discussion today, each fulfilling a particular function and role. Yet we know that people are often drawn to one aspect of knowledge to the relative neglect of others. Within ourselves too, we find these various witnesses vying with each other, each wanting to insist that theirs is the only approach to truth. Yet, if we confess the authority of the Bible, we know that all these resources are included within its pages and therefore must be brought into our discernment process.

Scriptural interpretation requires a re-reading of each part of the canon in light of the other so that each text relevant to a particular topic can give its distinctive message.[29] A dynamic is thus created that opens us to new insights and new learnings for our day, no matter where we begin in the process. So, too, in the theological conversation each mode of knowledge brings new questions and insights as that process continues. Transformation is possible because the various contributions will challenge, support, modify, supplement, or at times even contradict each other as they function within the framework of the scriptures to address a particular issue.

How, then, do we come to any decision about practical issues of the day? Will questions about same-sex marriage ever be settled? Questions about biblical interpretation for practical issues have always been settled by the larger interpretive community of a particular historical period. Similarly, in this particular historical moment congregations, larger church groupings, and finally the whole global church will be called on to make decisions in regard to same-sex marriage. However, premature closure that tends to squelch the distinctive voice of one or the other of the scriptural modes of knowledge will create divisions rather than fruitful conversations.[30]

We must therefore not base our unity on an initial agreement on all issues but on the gift of God's presence among us, continually leading us to further truth. We can be confident that in the context of a worshiping community we will in God's own time discern God's Word so that the priestly, the prophetic, and the wise knowledge of the church can be united. Our challenge is to journey in hope, and with Abraham and the early church to claim the promise that our discernment will lead to reconciliation and blessing for "all the families of the earth." Thus fear is cast out, and God's love will create the climate needed for faithful scriptural discernment.

***

Afterword

GOD OF MANY NAMES[ii]

I include a hymn as a closing reflection in this book. It is in communal singing that Mennonites have traditionally expressed their theology in an integrated way, seeking to bring heart and mind and body together. The hymn I have chosen is a joyful prayer that embodies the unspoken longing of my whole being—to sense the moving of God's Spirit in the midst of each hermeneutic community. Prayer is relational, suggesting that God is a relational God, a radical concept in a post-Christendom world where the transcendence of God as well as the immanence of God is questioned. I suggest that naming God in prayer and praise is a relational action that changes us and our perception of others. And through prayer God's love is made manifest to us as we hear again God's word to us through Jesus: "I do not call you servants any longer because a servant does not know what the master is doing; but I have called you friends because I have made known to you everything that I have heard from my Father." [iii] *I am confident that becoming "friends" with God and with each other creates the kind of community where discernment can happen in "rhythm" with God—in this time and in this place. It is a place where knowledge can increase and shalom spills over into the surrounding communities.. I can therefore end this chapter with a shout of "Hallelujah" trusting that any partial naming of God that we do is a response to the One who first of all named us "Beloved." Thanks be to God!*

ii Brian Wren, in *Praising a Mystery*, in *Hymnal, A Worship Book,* #77. Words: Brian Wren © 1986 Hope Publishing Company, Carol Stream, IL 60188. All rights reserved. Used by permission.

iii John 15:15.

God of Many Names

God of many names
Gathered into One,
In your glory come and meet us,
Moving endlessly becoming,
God of hovering wings,
Womb and birth of time,
joyfully we sing your praises
Breath of life in every people–

God of Jewish faith,
exodus and law,
in your glory come and meet us,
joy of Miriam and Moses!
God of Jesus Christ,
Rabbi of the poor,
joyfully we sing your praises,
crucified, alive forever–

God of wounded hands,
Web and Loom of love,
In your glory come and meet us,
Carpenter of new creation.
God of many names,
gathered into One,
Joyfully we sing your praises,
Moving, endlessly becoming–

Hush, hush, Hallelujah!
Shout, shout, hallelujah, hallelujah!
Sing, sing, hallelujah, hallelujah, God is love!

Endnotes

CHAPTER 1

1. Parker J. Palmer, "Now I Become Myself," posted March 31, 2001. www.yesmagazine.org/issues/working-for-life/now-i-become-myself.
2. Harder and Harder, "Called, Discerned and Blessed."
3. Based on the well-known definition of vocation by Buechner in *Wishful Thinking: A Theological ABC.*
4. Mark 16:7.
5. This paper was first published in "Reaching for a Blessing," in Swartley and Keener, *She Has Done a Good Thing*, 23-30, and reprinted with minor editorial changes.
6. Doris Weber was the first woman ordained in the Western Ontario Mennonite Conference in 1979. Martha Smith Good was the first woman ordained in the Mennonite Conference of Ontario and Quebec in 1982. These three conferences integrated in 1988 to become the Mennonite Conference of Eastern Canada.
7. First published in Weaver-Zercher, *Minding the Church: Scholarship in the Anabaptist Tradition,* 193-207, and reprinted with minor editorial changes.
8. Denck's observation has been quoted many places, including in Yoder, "The Hermeneutics of the Anabaptists," 27.
9. *Complete Writings of Menno Simons*, 605.
10. I explored this notion in my MTh thesis, "Hermeneutic Community: A Study of the Contemporary Relevance of an Anabaptist-Mennonite Approach to Biblical Interpretation."
11. Yoder, "The Hermeneutics of the Anabaptists," 21-22.
12. See Brueggemann, *Interpretation and Obedience: From Faithful Reading to Faithful Living*, 41-69.
13. I elaborate on this approach in my book *Obedience, Suspicion and the Gospel of Mark: A Mennonite-Feminist Exploration of Biblical Authority*, esp. 1-24.
14. Ibid., 104-15.
15. See for instance my response to Mary Schertz, in Yoder, ed., *Peace Theology and Violence Against Women*, 25-28.
16. Harder, "Biblical Interpretation: A Praxis of Discipleship."
17. See Harder, "Postmodern Suspicion and Imagination."
18. See the use of this image in "Response to Mary Schertz," *Peace Theology and Violence Against Women*, 25-26.
19. Unpublished reflection on ministry, 2015.
20. Insert in bulletin of the Toronto United Mennonite Church on Thanksgiv-

ing Sunday, October, 2007.

21. Celia Hahn, *Growing In Authority; Reliquishing Control: A New Approach to Faithful Leadership.*

CHAPTER 2

1. "Hermeneutic Community: A Study of the Contemporary Relevance of an Anabaptist-Mennonite Approach to Biblical Interpretation." MTh thesis, Newman Theological College, 1984, 153-161.
2. Ephesians 4:11-13, 15-16. (author's italics)
3. 1 Corinthians 14:29, 31; 1 Corinthians 15:1-2.
4. Matthew 18:18.
5. First published in Koontz and Swartley, *Perspectives on Feminist Hermeneutics*, 46-55, and reprinted with minor editorial changes.
6. Koontz, "Preface" in *Perspectives on Feminist Hermeneutics*, 7-9.
7. Collins, "Feminist Theology at the Crossroads," 344. Note also the way Fiorenza points to the importance of the communal base in *Bread Not Stone*, 41-42.
8. Russell, "Authority and the Challenge of Feminist Interpretation" in *Feminist Interpretation of the Bible*, 142.
9. Hans-Georg Gadamer, *Truth and Method*, 271-274.
10. Ruether, "Feminist Interpretation: A Method of Correlation," in *Feminist Interpretation of the Bible*, 112.
11. Fiorenza has begun this work in her book *In Memory of Her*.
12. Habermas, *Theory and Practice*, 1-40; *Knowledge and Human Interest*.
13. This is particularly true in theological education. However, women are beginning to articulate their struggle to gain a valid place in the theological process. See The Cornwell Collective, *Your Daughters Shall Prophesy: Feminist Alternatives in Theological Education*.
14. *In Memory of Her*, xxiii.
15. Ricoeur elaborates on these theories in a number of books and articles. Among the most helpful are: *Interpretation Theory: Discourse and the Surplus of Meaning* and "Naming God".
16. Mudge, "Paul Ricoeur on Biblical Interpretation" in *Essays on Biblical Interpretation*, 4-5.
17. McFague, *Metaphorical Language: Models of God in Religious Language*, 4-7. For an example of feminists working at the question of God language particularly in worship see Clark, Ronan and Walker, *Image-Breaking /Image-Building*.
18. McFague, *Metaphorical Language*, 4-9.
19. First published in *MCC Women's Concerns Report* No. 76, 1-2, and reprinted with minor editorial changes.
20. Schneiders, *Women and the Word.*
21. First published as "Response" to Mary Schertz in Elizabeth G. Yoder, ed. *Peace Theology and Violence Against Women*, 25-28 and reprinted with minor

editorial changes.

22. Elizabeth G. Yoder, ed., "Preface" in *Peace Theology and Violence Against Women*, v.
23. Ibid., 1.
24. See the extensive overview of the relationship of John H. Yoder and the Mennonite church and its peace theology in *Mennonite Quarterly Review*, vol. 89, no. 1.
25. Yoder's ministerial credentials were taken away in 1992, the same year that the conference proceedings were published.
26. Brueggeman speaks of biblical interpretation as "homemaking" in his book *Interpretation and Obedience*, 8. Note also the way he uses the metaphor of God and the people of God as homemakers in chapter 13, "Welcoming the Stranger," 290-310.

CHAPTER 3

1. First published in *The Church as Theological Community: Essays in Honour of David Schroeder,* 199-220, and reprinted here with minor editorial changes.
2. Sawatsky, "Words becoming Flesh: The Life and Thought of David Schroeder," in *The Church as Theological Community*, 3-21.
3. See my article "Hermeneutic Community: A Feminist Challenge" in chapter 2. There I propose that both Mennonite and feminist hermeneutics acknowledge two poles in the interpretive process. By linking past faith—knowledge with present faith—experience in the hermeneutical community, Mennonites have tended to recognize the contributions of both text and interpreter in determining the meaning of the text for contemporary life. I suggest that a feminist hermeneutic challenges us to more clearly define the shape of the hermeneutical community. It challenges us to look more closely at the tradition that provides the pre-understanding, as well as the institutions and language that affect the communication process among the members. This paper takes the next step in analyzing this process.
4. Harold Bender's focus on discipleship as essential to Anabaptism has had considerable influence on Mennonite theological writings and preaching. For him discipleship expressed the inseparability of belief and practice, faith and life. See "The Anabaptist Theology of Discipleship."
5. Klaassen, "Anabaptist Hermeneutics: Presuppositions, Principles and Practice," in *Essays in Biblical Hermeneutics: Anabaptist-Mennonite Perspectives,* 10. See also the essay in the same volume by John H. Yoder, "The Hermeneutics of the Anabaptists."
6. Swartley uses this expression in his concluding article, "Afterword: Continuity and Change in Anabaptist-Mennonite Interpretation," in *Essays in Biblical Interpretation*, 327.
7. A key book on this subject is Russell, *Feminist Interpretation of the Bible.* See particularly the article by Sakenfeld, "Feminist Uses of Biblical Materials," 55-64, for an understanding of how women have countered the way the Bible is used to justify their traditional place in Western culture. The focus on the *function* of text, on how the texts have been used not only for salvation but also for oppression, is central for both liberation and feminist scholars.
8. When we think concretely there must be a specificity about our observations. In this preliminary sketch I am basing my observations on my own and other women's experience of life and theology in Mennonite congregations in Canada in the past few decades.
9. In his book, *Mark: The Way for All Nations*, Swartley has recognized the theme of the "way" in Mark. He has, however, not studied the stories of

women in relation to this theme.

10. Fiorenza, *In Memory of Her*, 50
11. It is important to recognize a pluralism in feminist theology and to avoid reducing the contribution of the individual writers to several stereotypical characterizations. However, a number of elements can be identified which are shared by a large group of feminist writers. Margaret A. Farley has named the underlying principle for a feminist hermeneutic "the conviction that women are fully human and are to be valued as such." See: "Feminist Consciousness and Interpretation of Scripture," in *Feminist Interpretations of the Bible*, 44. This includes the related principles of equitable sharing and mutuality between women and men.
12. Gayle Gerber Koontz points out the ambivalence which women, who first attended the Anabaptist-Mennonite consultation to draw together Mennonite women scholars to discuss Bible and theology at Associated Mennonite Biblical Seminaries in Elkhart, Indiana (Summer, 1986), had about their work. See "Preface" in *Perspectives on Feminist Hermeneutics.*
13. Di Brandt has recognized the contradiction between the Mennonite emphasis on the "priesthood of all believers" and the silence of women in the church. She points out that the language of submission and obedience and "brotherhood" speak of arbitrary privilege and power of one group of people over another. See "The Silence of Women Is a Goal of Pornography," 11.
14. Barbara Hilkert Andolsen outlines how feminist ethicists are struggling with the traditional understanding of "agape" as self-giving love and sacrifice in the context of women's experience. See "Agape in Feminist Ethics." For an example of a Mennonite woman's struggle with the dilemma of self-denial interpreted as self-sacrifice, see Hartzler, "Choosing to Be Honest Rather Than Good," 7-9.
15. Fiorenza has pointed out the implications of maintaining this duality between the domestic sphere and the public sphere: "Wherever the 'private sphere' of the patriarchal house is sharply delineated from that of the public order of the state, women are more dependent and exploited; while in those societies in which the boundaries between the household and the public domain are not so sharply drawn, women's positions and roles are more equal to those of men." *In Memory of Her*, 86.
16. I have been told on a number of occasions that I was lucky I could study theology purely for pleasure. The implication clearly was that I did not need to be responsible for the theology of the church but could study for personal enjoyment and enrichment.
17. There are many studies of the disciples in Mark. See for example, Best, *Disciples and Discipleship* and Swartley, *Mark: The Way for All Nations.* Some important studies that provide a corrective to the above by focusing more

directly on the women disciples in Mark are: Malbon, "Fallible Followers: Women and Men in the Gospel of Mark," Fiorenza, *In Memory of Her*, 316-323, and Munro, "Women Disciples in Mark?"

18. This question can be studied from various historical and literary perspectives. Historical questions would include the following: Were there in fact women among the immediate associates of Jesus? Were women considered disciples by the early Christian community of which Mark was a part? Does Mark, as a redactor, accept women as disciples? Do the women represent a specific group in the early church? I will try to understand how women fit into the theology of discipleship in Mark's narrative account. Historical and more complex literary questions form a necessary background to our subject, which the limits of this paper will not allow me to explore as thoroughly as is necessary. Nor can I speak of how discipleship is described in the other gospels.
19. Best prefers to see the Twelve as normally signifying the wider group of followers rather than seeing Mark place a deliberate emphasis on the Twelve as the only disciples. He understands Mark as deliberately widening the tradition with its focus on the Twelve. See Best, *Disciples and Discipleship*, 103.
20. Ibid., 133.
21. Malbon, "Fallible Followers," 30.
22. Best, *Disciples and Discipleship*, 5.
23. Both Fiorenza, *In Memory of Her*, 320, and Munro, "Women Disciples in Mark?" 231, understand this inner circle in terms of commitment and leadership and would include the women in Mark 15 as a parallel inner circle to the male leaders.
24. See Best, *Disciples and Discipleship*, 103.
25. Rhoads and Michie, *Mark as Story*, 129, includes women within the group of characters called the "little people."
26. Munro, "Women Disciples in Mark?" 226. Androcentrism implies that the texts are "reflective of the experience, opinion, or control of the individual male writer but not of women's historical reality and experience." Fiorenza, *In Memory of Her*, 108.
27. In *Memory of Her*, 143-144.
28. Here I differ from Munro who sees a redactional silencing in Mark in which women's prominent role is obscured. See Munro, "Women Disciples in Mark?" 234-236.
29. Swartley points out that in Mark fear and amazement function as the opposite of understanding. See *Mark: The Way for All Nations*, 200.
30. Ringe has interpreted this story as told in Matthew and Mark by focusing particularly on the gifts and ministry that the woman gives to Jesus. She says, e.g., "Her gift was not the submission or obedience seen as appropriate

for women in her society, but rather the gift of sharp insight—the particular insight of the poor and outcasts.... Her gift was also the gift of courage...." See "A Gentile Woman's Story," in *Feminist Interpretation of the Bibl*e, 71-72.

31. Fiorenza, *In Memory of Her*, xiv.
32. Luise Schottroff has uncovered the historical evidence in the writings of Josephus and Tacitus which points to the danger of death for women who mourned the death of one who was crucified. "Maria und die Frauen am Grabe Jesu."
33. Rhoads and Michie, who coined this phrase for the women in Mark's narrative, have also characterized them as "flat" characters with several consistent traits unlike the Twelve who are "round" characters with conflicting traits. See, *Mark as Story*, 122-136.
34. Ibid., 132-133.
35. Malbon, "Fallible Followers," 41-42.
36. I am accepting the ending in v. 8 as the ending by the original author. The added endings give us the viewpoint of the early church. It is interesting that Fiorenza, as well as most male commentators, do not want to recognize this flight of the women as disobedience to the command of the angel. See *In Memory of Her*, 322. This does not fit the picture of the women as paradigms of true discipleship. However, if women are to be seen as responsible agents in history, they must also be seen as those who are tempted and sometimes fail. I would concur with Boomershine and Bartholomew, who feel that the dominant tone of the ending is negative. It brings to the fore the "powerful conflict between responsibility and fear ." See "Mark 16:8 and the Apostolic Commission," 237.
37. Malbon suggests that the significance of the women's silence is found "in the outward movement of the text from author to reader." See "Fallible Followers," 45. As the narrator's story ends and reaches the point of silence, the hearer/reader's story begins. It is lime for the reader to act and speak, thus continuing the line of followers. Swartley points out that the Gospel shows us the direction of discipleship but does not close the challenge. It is left open for them and for us to finish the mission begun by Jesus, the Christ, the Son of God. *Mark: The Way for All Nations*, 198.
38. Malbon, "Fallible Followers," 26.
39. Swartley uses these three terms to summarize the emphasis of these passages. *Mark: The Way for All Nations*, 140.
40. Schneiders, "Evangelical Equality: Religious Consecration, Mission and Witness," 298-300, speaks of the superior/inferior paradigm for human relations which is prevalent even in our notions of equality. She points out that in looking at Jesus we can see both the refusal to dominate as well as the refusal to be dominated. Discipleship may then mean the refusal to accept

both the under or the over position in the accepted social hierarchy.

41. Though we cannot directly equate or correlate the experiences of women disciples as portrayed by Mark with women's role in the hermeneutical community today, we can draw parallels because of the patriarchal nature of both societies. However, other factors such as class and race must also be considered in the way we identify with both female and male disciples. Though women, as female, may identify themselves as marginalized, as scholars they may share the advantages of the male elite and often also belong to the privileged who have financial power. Men, as male, may identify themselves as the privileged but as Mennonite scholars in the ecumenical scene, they may see themselves as marginalized. In particular social situations we may need to identify with both women and me as presented in Mark.
42. First published in *The Conrad Grebel Review* (Winter, 1992), 17-32, and reprinted with minor editorial changes.
43. Harder, *Dancing through Thistles in Bare Feet: A Pastoral Journey*, 70-71.
44. *Conrad Grebel Review* 10, no.1, 217-221.
45. For me, this latter approach is not as helpful, probably because I enjoy the "left brain" analytical approach to knowledge that is often represented as a "male" approach. I am also convinced that both men and women can develop both sides of their brains.
46. "Katie Funk Wiebe reflects on the conference: 'In a Mennonite Voice: Women Doing Theology,'" 211.
47. Ibid., 210.
48. Swartley, *Slavery, Sabbath, War and Women.*
49. Fiorenza, *In Memory of Her*, 99-241.
50. Fiorenza, "The Ethics of Biblical Interpretation: Decentering Biblical Scholarship."
51. Schneiders, "Feminist Ideology Criticism and Biblical Hermeneutics," 9.
52. Zikmund, "Feminist Consciousness in Historica1 Perspective."
53. "Disciple," *Interpreter's Dictionary of the Bible*, vol. 1, 845.
54. For example, in a narrative analysis of the Gospel of John the disciples are discussed as models with whom the readers may identify. However, specific reference is made only to those who are a1so known as part of the group of 12. Women followers such as Mary and Martha as well as other followers such as Lazarus are discussed under the category of minor characters. Culpepper, *Anatomy of the Fourth Gospel*, 115-125 and 132-144.
55. Schneiders, "Feminist Ideology Criticism and Biblical Hermeneutics," 8.
56. Gadamer in his book *Truth and Method* has drawn attention to these preunderstandings, pointing out that they can be called tradition. Tradition for him is that ongoing intersubjective, social process which precedes and is implicit in all individual activity. It is the stream of life in which we stand

and within which things are perceived and understood. Individual textual interpretation is shaped by this dynamic community process in which tradition is formed and reformed.

57. Swartley, *Essays on Biblical Interpretation: Anabaptist-Mennonite Perspectives*. Note particularly the essays in Part I, 5-114.
58. Thistlethwaite and Engel, eds., *Lift Every Voice: Constructing Theologies from the Underside*.
59. Yoder, "The Hermeneutics of the Anabaptists," 27.
60. Fiorenza, "The Ethics of Biblical Interpretation," 8.
61. Koontz, "A Theologian's Companions."
62. Koontz, "The Liberation of Atonement," *Mennonite Quarterly Review*, 190-192.
63. Ringe, "Reading from Context to Context: Contributions of a Feminist Hermeneutic to Theologies of Liberation," 283.
64. For example, Williams, "The Color of Feminism," 164-165.
65. Sakenfeld, "In the Wilderness Awaiting the Land: The Daughters of Zelophehad and Feminist Interpretation," 190.
66. For example, Trible in her book, *Texts of Terror* highlights the stories of Hagar, Tamar, the unnamed concubine, and the daughter of Jephthah, all stories that have not been central to our theology in the past.
67. Fiorenza, "For the Sake of Our Salvation…" in *Bread Not Stone.*
68. This change can be seen in the discussion of doctrinal language by Lindbeck, *The Nature of Doctrine*.
69. Trible, *God and the Rhetoric of Sexuality*, 3.
70. Schneiders, "Feminist Ideology Criticism and Biblical Hermeneutics," 7.
71. Kermode, *The Genesis of Secrecy*, 16-147.
72. Swartley, *Slavery, Sabbath, War and Women*, 224.
73. "The Footwashing in JN 13 and its relation to the Synoptic Gospels," 279-308.
74. Ibid., 299-300, fn. 45.
75. Weiss, "Footwashing in the Johannine Community," 313; Seim, "Roles of Women in the Gospel of John.," 73.
76. Fiorenza, *In Memory of Her*, 330.
77. Schneiders, "Women in the Fourth Gospel and the Role of Women in the Contemporary Church," 42.
78. Schneiders, "The Foot Washing (John 13: 1-20): An Experiment in Hermeneutics."
79. Segovia, "John 13: 1-20: The Footwashing in the Johannine Tradition."

CHAPTER 4

1. Fiorenza, "The Ethics of Biblical Interpretation."
2. First published in Esau, ed., *Understanding Ministerial Leadership: Essays Contributing to a Developing Theology of Ministry,* 70-81, and reprinted with only minor editorial changes.
3. "No Longer Innocent," 3.
4. Harder, "Women doing theology: Individual Voices in Chorus," 1.
5. This approach resembles reader-response criticism because it consciously examines the way we as readers tend to determine the meaning of the Gospel. My reading assumes a reader who wishes to know the will of God as revealed through the reading of the Bible. For an exploration of the method see: Anderson and Moore, *Mark and Method*, chapter 3.
6. Malbon, "Disciples/Crowds/Whoever: Markan Characters and Readers," 104.
7. Munro, "Women Disciples in Mark?"; Fiorenza, *In Memory of Her*, 316-323.
8. Fiorenza, *In Memory of Her*, 320-321.
9. Throughout this essay I am concurring with many scholars who would assume that verse 8 is the original ending of the Gospel of Mark. Note the endings in both the NIV and the NRSV. A number of scholars suggest that the abrupt ending asks the reader to respond in line with the challenges presented in the story thus far. See, for example, Tolbert, *Sowing the Gospel*, 295.
10. Narrative critics have pointed out how Mark's story settings provide an overall framework for the action. The whole story is presented to us as a journey from Galilee to Judea. The geographical settings thus begin to symbolize different parts of Jesus' life. Galilee is thus associated with powerful teaching and healing (Mark 1-9), while Judea is associated with confrontation and death (Mark 10-15). See Rhoads and Michie, *Mark as Story*, 63.
11. Schottroff, *Maria und die Frauen am Grabe Jesu*, 3-25.
12. See Fiorenza, *In Memory of Her*, 322; Boomershine, "Mark and the Apostolic Commission," 225-39.
13. Previously published in Heisy and Schipani, eds., *Theological Education on Five Continents: Anabaptist Perspectives,* 103-112, and reprinted here with only minor editorial changes.
14. Heisy and Schipani, eds. *Theological Education on Five Continents: Anabaptist Perspectives*, 3.
15. Hansell, "The Seminary as a Learning Organization: A Systems Approach," 3.
16. Heisey and Schipani, eds., *Theological Education on Five Continents*, 5-35.
17. Brueggeman, "The Legitimacy of a Sectarian Hermeneutic," 41-69.

18. An example: Rowland, "In this Place: The Centre and the Margins in Theology."
19. Brueggeman, "The Legitimacy of a Sectarian Hermeneutic," 43.
20. Ibid., 29.
21. First published in *Conrad Grebel Review* 13, no. 2 (1995), 152-156 and reprinted with minor editorial changes.
22. Hauerwas, *Against the Nations: War and Survival in a Liberal Society*, 17.
23. Hauerwas, *After Christendom? How the Church Is to Behave If Freedom, Justice, and a Christian Nation Are Bad Ideas*, 130-31.
24. Ibid., 127.
25. Ibid., 148.
26. Ibid.,18.
27. Hauerwas, *Christian Existence Today: Essays on Church, World, and Living in Between*, 11.

CHAPTER 5

1. First published in *Mennonite Quarterly Review,* vol. LXXI, no. 2, 267-283 and reprinted with minor editorial changes.
2. Snyder, *The Anabaptist Vision: Theological Perspectives*, v.
3. *Mennonite Quarterly Review,* vol. LXVIII, no. 2.
4. Yoder, "The Hermeneutics of the Anabaptists," 291-308.
5. Klaassen, *Anabaptism: Neither Catholic nor Protestant*, 47.
6. Perry Yoder, "The Role of the Bible in Mennonite Self-Understanding," 77.
7. Roth, "Community as Conversation," 46.
8. Murphy and McClendon, "Distinguishing Modern and Postmodern Theologies," 191-212.
9. See for example the essays in Burnham, ed., *Postmodern Theology: Christian Faith in a Pluralist World.*
10. Tracy, *Plurality and Ambiguity: Hermeneutics, Religion, Hope*. Page #s?
11. Ibid., 49-50.
12. Ibid., 66.
13. Ibid., 60.
14. Ibid., 76.
15. See Segovia and Tolbert, *Reading from This Place*, vol. I and II for examples of feminist and liberation theologians who challenge the objectivity of Western theology.
16. Tracy, *Plurality and Ambiguity: Hermeneutics, Religion, Hope*, 78.
17. Ibid., 79.
18. Klassen and Klaassen, *The Writings of Pilgram Marpeck*, 71.
19. *Complete Writings of Menno Simons*, 207-08.
20. Yoder, "Ethics and Eschatology," 124.
21. Yoder, *The Priestly Kingdom: Social Ethics as Gospels*, 47.
22. Ibid., 48-49.
23. Brueggemann, *Texts Under Negotiation: The Bible and Postmodern Imagination*, 17.
24. Note my exploration of discipleship in previous chapters "Discipleship Reexamined: Women in the Hermeneutical Community," "Biblical Interpretation: A Praxis of Discipleship," and "The Mutuality of Ministry."
25. Note an exception to that pattern in Schertz, "Interpretation as Discipleship: Luke 24 as Model," 115-39.
26. Brueggemann, *Texts under Negotiation*, 12-17.
27. Ibid., 12-13.
28. Ibid., 19
29. Ibid., 26.
30. Ibid., 19-20.

31. Ibid., 21-22.
32. See also the essays in Roth, *Refocusing a Vision.*
33. Sawatsky,"The Quest for a Mennonite Hermeneutic," 1-3.
34. Janzen, "A Canonical Rethinking of the Anabaptist-Mennonite New Testament Orientation," 90-95.
35. Note my response to what I consider false alternatives that are sometimes set out for theologians: an intertextual approach that listens to the "other" outside of the community vs. an intra-textual approach that concentrates on dialogue within the community. See Holland, "How Do Stories Save Us? Two Contemporary Theological Responses," in *Conrad Grebel Review* 12 (Fall 1994) and my response to it in *Conrad Grebel Review* 12 (Spring 1994).
36. Malbon, "Fallible Followers: Women and Men in the Gospel of Mark."
37. First published in Hoekema and Kuitse, *Discipleship in Context*, 43-60 and reprinted with minor editorial changes.
38. Ibid, vii.
39. Wenger, *Complete Writings of Menno Simons*, 339.
40. 1 Corinthians 3:11.
41. The order in which I am treating these themes comes from the order in which I became aware of them in my reading. However, the order also roughly corresponds to the shifts in emphases in Menno's own thinking, evident if one compares his earlier writings as an evangelistic preacher to his later more apologetic and defensive writings.
42. The primary interest in this paper is not the historical genesis of Menno's theology, though I will at times indicate some of the probable roots of Menno's thinking. Rather this paper analyzes the strengths and weaknesses of Menno's theology in order to help us to reflect on our own theology and how it lays a foundation for the church of today. Both the process and the content of his theology are therefore important.
43. See Isaak, "Menno's Vision of the Anticipation of the Kingdom of God in his Early Writings."
44. A relationship to medieval penitence theology could be suspected in this concrete call to repentance. See Voolstra, "True Penitence: The Core of Menno Simons' Theology." So too the terms Spirit and flesh remind us of the general reform climate in which alternatives to Catholic views of authority were looked for in spiritualistic visions as well as in the literal letter of the scriptures.
45. Menn Simons, *Complete Writings*, 101.
46. Ibid., 90, 108, 691.
47. Ibid., 106-107.
48. Ibid., 158.

49. Bornhauser, *Leben und Lehre Menno Simons: Ein Kampf um das Fundament des Glaubens*, 54.
50. This foundation was crucial in the context of the Münsterites and their new revelations as well as in the context of the Catholic church and its reliance on tradition. See Isaak, 64-65.
51. Voolstra, "True Penitence: The Core of Menno Simon's Theology," 394.
52. Menno Simons, *Complete Writings*, 101.
53. Ibid., 164.
54. Loeschen, *The Divine Community: Trinity, Church and Ethics in Reformation Theology*, 11.
55. Menno Simons, *Complete Writings*, 108.
56. Ibid., 204.
57. Ibid., 115-116.
58. Ibid., 156.
59. Ibid., 125.
60. Ibid., 116.
61. Ibid., 597.
62. Isaak suggests that "Menno's theology is mainly a theology of the new creation or the anticipation of the kingdom of God. He accepted the cross reluctantly and never stopped complaining about it. Suffering and the cross did not become an explicit characterization until 1554 in his reply to Gellius Faber." See, *The Heavenly Jerusalem has Descended Upon this Earth*, 229.
63. Menno Simons, *Complete Writings*, 221.
64. Ibid., 772.
65. Ibid., 439.
66. Ibid., 148.
67. Ibid., 145.
68. Ibid., 967-968.
69. Ibid., 564.
70. Ibid. 299-300.
71. Ibid., 601.
72. Stoesz, "The New Creature: Menno's Understanding of the Christian Faith," 181.
73. Menno Simons, *Complete Writings*, 335-336.
74. Depperman, *Melchoir Hoffman: Social Unrest and Apocalyptic Visions in the Age of Reformation*, 214-217, 220-240.
75. *Die Wiedertauffer in Münster,* Stadtmuseum Münster, *Katalog der Eröffnungsausstellung vom I October 1982 bis 27 Februar 1983,* 159-160.
76. Menno Simons, *Complete Writings,* 427-440.
77. Weingart has summarized various interpreters of Menno who suggest that Menno considered the material body sinful, arising out of a gnostic view

which separates the mind and the body. There is certainly an ambiguity here that needs more study. However, I think Menno is more influenced by the strong dualism in biblical literature between those living in the Spirit and those living according to the flesh. See Weingart, "The Meaning of Sin in the Theology of Menno Simons."

78. Menno Simons, *Complete Writings*, 427.
79. Ibid., 191.
80. A sermon preached in Oct. 2002 at one of the regular "Wine Before Breakfast" worship services for grad students at Wycliffe College in Toronto, Ontario.

CHAPTER 6

1. Consultation on Issues of Power and Authority in the Mennonite Church held in Waterloo, Ontario, May 24, 1997.
2. First published in Benjamin W. Redekop and Calvin W. Redekop, eds., *Power, Authority and the Anabaptist Tradition,* 73-94 and reprinted with minor editorial changes.
3. Ibid. 155-173.
4. An acknowledgment of diversity in the historical origins of Anabaptism in recent years has contributed to an acknowledgment of diversity in theological development within Mennonite writings. For a historical analysis, see Stayer, Packull, and Deppermann, "From Monogenesis to Polygenesis: The Historical Discussion of Anabaptist Origins." For an overview of the diverse approaches to theology among contemporary Mennonites, see Reimer, "AnabaptistMennonite Systematic Theology."
5. This term is used by the philosopher Wittgenstein in delineating his notion of "language-games." See Wittgenstein, *Philosophical Investigations,* part 1, par. 67and following. See also Thiselton, *The Two Horizons*, 373-79, and Keightley, *Wittgenstein*, 31-40.
6. The reinterpretation of the sacraments during the Reformation is one illustration of the debate surrounding the relationship of spirit and matter. See Rempel, *The Lord's Supper in Anabaptism.*
7. Redekop and RedeKop, *Power, Authority and Anabaptist Tradition*, Chapter 3.
8. See Isaac, "Menno's Vision of the Anticipation of the Kingdom of God in His Early Writings."
9. Ibid.,70.
10. *Complete Writings of Menno Simons*, 554-56.
11. Ibid., 562.
12. Menno followed Melchoir Hoffman in a spiritualistic Christology in which Jesus received his flesh directly from God and became human "in Mary," not "of Mary."
13. Menno Simons, *Complete Writings*, 93.
14. Ibid., 967-68.
15. C. Arnold Snyder discusses variations of this view of the church as sacrament in the various Anabaptist groups. See *Anabaptist History and Theology: An Introduction*, 251-364.
16. Menno Simons, *Complete Writings*, 129.
17. Ibid. 202.
18. Goertz, "The Confessional Heritage in Its New Mold: What Is Mennonite Self-Understanding Today?" 1.

19. For a discussion of women in Anabaptism, see Snyder and Hecht, *Profiles of Anabaptist Women: Sixteenth Century Reforming Pioneers*; for a discussion of economic sharing, see Stayer, *The German Peasants' War and Anabaptist Community of Goods*; for the movement toward a more egalitarian *Gemeindetheologie,* see Klaassen, *Anabaptism: Neither Catholic nor Protestant.*
20. Hubmaier, "A Christian Instruction" in *Anabaptism in Outline, Primary Sources,* 214.
21. Note the development of elements of church order and structure in the quotations of Anabaptists in ibid.,118-39.
22. Snyder, *Anabaptist History and Theology*, 299-303.
23. Klaassen, *Anabaptism in Outline*, 211.
24. Menno Simons, *Complete Writings*, 193.
25. Ibid., 198.
26. Snyder, *Anabaptist History and Theology*, 181-83.
27. See Redekop and Redekop, *Power, Authority and the Anabaptist Tradition*, Chapter 3.
28. Loewen, *One Lord, One Church, One Hope, and One God*, 81.
29. Menno Simons, *Complete Writings*, 198.
30. Loewen, *One Lord, One Church*, 44.
31. Goertz, "The Confessional Heritage," 4-5.
32. See Bender, *The Anabaptist Vision.*
33. Ibid., 34.
34. Roth, "Living Between the Times: 'The Anabaptist Vision and Mennonite Reality' Revisited, in *Refocusing a Vision*," 51. The focus in this paper is on those Mennonites primarily affected by the recovery of the "Anabaptist Vision" symbolized by Bender's influential essay. This would include Mennonite Church Canada and Mennonite Church USA. See Herschberger, *The Recovery of the Anabaptist Vision*, and the evaluation of this recovery fifty years later in *Conrad Grebel Review* 12, no. 3 and 4.
35. J. R. Burkholder speaks about the importance of Hershberger's works by suggesting that all denominational resolutions and position statements from the 1940s to the 1960s reflect the Hershberger consensus "with no significant deviations." See Burkholder, *Mennonite Peace Theology: A Panorama of Types*, 10.
36. Hershberger, *War, Peace, and Nonresistance*, 266.
37. Ibid., 1.
38. Ibid., 187.
39. Hershberger, *The Way of the Cross in Human Relations*, 43.
40. Hershberger, *War, Peace, and Nonresistance*, 53.
41. Ibid., 169.
42. Hershberger, *Way of the Cross in Human Relations,* 348.

43. Ibid., 353.
44. See Niebuhr, *Christ and Culture*, esp. Chapter 2.
45. Yoder, *The Politics of Jesus.Page #s?*
46. Ibid., 134-61.
47. Ibid., 145.
48. Ibid., 157.
49. Yoder, *The Royal Priesthood: Essays Ecclesiological and Ecumenical*, 10.
50. Yoder, *Politics of Jesus*, 162-93.
51. Ibid., 180.
52. Ibid., 209.
53. Yoder, *The Priestly Kingdom*, 155-66.
54. Ibid., 157.
55. Yoder, *The Royal Priesthood*, 146-47.
56. See Driedger and Kraybill, *Mennonite Peacemaking: From Quietism to Activism* for a more sociological analysis of the changes occurring in the Mennonite community amidst the vagaries of time and place. See particularly 87-107, where the debates between responsible engagement with society and separatist approaches are described.
57. Loewen, "Peace in the Mennonite Tradition: Toward a Theological Understanding of a Regulative Concept," 106-112.
58. Kaufman, *Nonresistance and Responsibility and Other Mennonite Essays*, 52.
59. Loewen, "Peace in the Mennonite Tradition," 111.
60. This critical stance can be seen in his article "Anabaptist Vision and Mennonite Reality."
61. Several conferences have been organized by Mennonite women around the theme "Women Doing Theology" in the last few years. These witness both to the sense that women have had of being the "other" and to the growing acceptance by women of the responsibility of articulating publicly their own theology. See *Conrad Grebel Review* 10 (Winter 1992); *Mennonite Quarterly Review* 65 (April 1994); and *Conrad Grebel Review* 14 (Spring 1996) for the published papers of these conferences.
62. See Esau, "Recovering, Rethinking, and Re-imagining: Issues in a Mennonite Theology for Christian Ministry," in *Understanding Ministerial Leadership*, 1-26.
63. Janzen, "A Canonical Rethinking of the Anabaptist-Mennonite New Testament Orientation," 94-5.
64. Burkholder, *The Problem of Social Responsibility from the Perspective of the Mennonite Church*; Gordon Kauffman, *In Face of Mystery: A Constructive Theology*. The writings of both of these theologians have been marginalized in Mennonite institutions because of their deviation from the accepted norm.
65. First published in *Conrad Grebel Review* 19, no. 3 (Fall 2001), 13-32 and

repirned with minor editorial changes.

66. Schneiders, "The Footwashing (John 13: 1-20): An Experiment in Hermeneutics," 84.
67. A basic description by Sandra Schneiders of these three models has been the main stimulation for this discussion. See "Evangelical Equality and Religious Consecration, Mission and Witness."
68. The length of this essay precludes an analysis of power as understood and practiced in the Mennonite community. See the earlier essay in this chapter for that analysis.
69. Schneiders explains the various notions of equality in her article, "Evangelical Equality and Religious Consecration, Mission, and Witness."
70. Schneiders, "The Footwashing," 85.
71. See Greenleaf, *On Becoming a Servant-Leader* for an example.
72. See Findlay-Chamberlain. "Keeping the Balance… Staying Healthy as Helpers," *Women's Concerns Report*, no. 115.
73. See Pence Frantz, "Women Bearing the Cross of Discipleship," *Women's Concerns Report*, 89 as an example of the struggle women have with a Mennonite theology of service that has been most directly connected to cross-bearing and suffering.
74. John Howard Yoder has also suggested that these passages relativize and undercut the order of the society of the time. See *The Politics of Jesus*. However, Yoder focuses on "revolutionary subordination," suggesting that overdoing the celebration of liberation was the problem and that the "tactic" of subordination is crucial in these passages. I submit that the tactic was limited to Paul's human insights, and that the more crucial theological and ethical insight was the limit put on the hierarchical structures by suggesting that only God is truly the master.
75. Interestingly enough, the notion of Mennonite "voluntary service" was originally a way for Mennonites to respond to a demand for service that assumed a servitude model. The U.S. and Canadian governments assumed that they had the right to ask every male citizen to serve in the army. The Mennonite church argued for "alternative" ways of service such as in psychiatric hospitals or forestry units so that young men could serve both country and God.
76. *Confession of Faith in a Mennonite Perspective*, 53-54.
77. Harder, "Biblical Interpretation: A Praxis of Discipleship."

CHAPTER 7

1. First published in "The Bible as Canon and as Word of God: Exploring the Mystery of Revelation," *Conrad Grebel Review* 19, 52-65 and reprinted with minor editorial changes.
2. Reimer, "Revelation and Authority," 7.
3. Webster, *Holy Scripture*, 11-12.
4. Froehlich, "The Inspired Word of God: Authority and Inspiration," 14.
5. A good overview of this process is found in Bird, "The Authority of the Bible," 33-64.
6. Halbertal, *People of the Book*, 1.
7. Sanders, *From Sacred Story to Sacred Text*, 4.
8. Bird, "The Authority of the Bible," 49.
9. Placher explores this in his book, *Narratives of a Vulnerable God.*
10. Webster, Holy Scripture, 14.
11. I have explored biblical interpretation as discipleship in my book, *Obedience, Suspicion and the Gospel of Mark.*
12. Yoder, *To Hear the Word*, 85-106.
13. Childs, *Old Testament in a Canonical Context*, 15.
14. Yoder, *To Hear the Word*, 100.
15. In this section I am indebted to the discussion of "Word of God" by Schneiders in *The Revelatory Text*, 27-59.
16. First presented in Akron, Pennsylvania at an MCC's Peace Committee Meeting in 2008.
17. Klassen, "Reflecting on conflict and peace," 34.
18. Bryant, Harrison, and Reimer, *On Spirituality: Essays from the Third Shi'i Muslim Mennonite Christian Dialogue*, 219.
19. Friesen and Schlabach, *At Pease and Unafraid: Public Order, Security, and the Wisdom of the Cross.* A recent historical overview of Mennonite peace theology also provides helpful background. See Koontz, "Peace Theology in Transition: North American Mennonite Peace Studies and Theology, 1906-2006."
20. Schlabach,"Beyond Two- vs One-Kingdom Theology: Abrahamic Community as a Mennonite Paradigm for Christian Engagement in Society."
21. Friesen and Schlabach, *At Peace and Unafraid*, 153.
22. Note how these relationships expanded. See Martin, "MCC And Iran," 1-2.
23. See "Iran Hostage Crisis," *Wikipedia*, last modified July 25, 2017, https://en.wikipedia.org/wiki/Iran_hostage_crisis.
24. This sentence came from an unpublished lecture by Jon Hoover. He elaborates on this in his essay, "An Anabaptist Perspective on Conversing with Muslims."

25. See Boase, *Islam and Global Dialogue: Religious Pluralism and the Pursuit of Peace*. The definition of pluralism is much in dispute as seen in this book.
26. J. Daryl Byler, "For Such a Time as This: An MCC Perspective on Iran," http//mcc.org/stories/such-time-mcc-perspective-Iran, May 2, 2008.
27. Legenhausen, "Islam and Nonviolence."
28. As quoted by Legenhausen in *Islam and Nonviolence*. Though this quote referred to a particular time of peace making among Arabs, it may be that it could be applicable to all the religions of the book.

CHAPTER 8

1. A series of enlarged periodicals that explores these notions is published by Mennonite Church Canada. One example is Steve Heinrichs, ed., "Wrongs to Rights."
2. First published in Friesen and Schlabach, *At Peace and Unafraid: Public Order, Security and the Wisdom of the Cross*, 117-152 and reprinted with minor editorial changes.
3. For an overview of this trend toward the prophetic see Driedger and Kraybill, *Mennonite Peacemaking: From Quietism to Activism*, 150-52.
4. My reflections in this and following paragraphs owe a debt to Schlabach, "Beyond Two- Versus One-Kingdom Theology: Abrahamic Community as a Mennonite Paradigm for Engagement in Society."
5. However, note two contributions on wisdom and peace theology by Douglas Miller and Tom Yoder Neufeld in Grimsrud and Johns, *Peace and Justice Shall Embrace: Power and Theopolitics in the Bible; Essays in Honor of Millard Lind.*
6. Note for example the almost complete neglect of the classical wisdom texts in the biblical index of Yoder and Swartley, *The Meaning of Peace: Biblical Studies*, 279-87.
7. I recognize that there is a great deal of debate among scholars as to what constitutes wisdom writing and how wisdom should be defined. However, for our purposes I will deliberately use a very broad definition. For an extensive survey of the varied wisdom tradition and the extensive secondary literature see Murphy, "Wisdom in the Old Testament," *Anchor Bible Dictionary*, 6: 920-31.
8. This term comes from Yoder, "Armaments and Eschatology," 58.
9. Sheppard, "Biblical Wisdom Literature at the End of the Modern Age." Middle discourse may take the place of middle axioms as understood by John H. Yoder because it can include the practice of speaking as well as to the substance of what is spoken. See Friesen's essay in *At Peace and Unafraid*, 37-83.
10. Schipani, *The Way of Wisdom in Pastoral Counseling*, 39.
11. This fits well with Pamela Leach's emphasis on the "abundant resourcefulness" of God 's creation, challenging ideologies that promote scarcity and competition. See *At Peace and Unafraid*, 104.
12. Though a chronological study of the development of the wisdom traditions would be helpful, in this preliminary overview we will take a more canonical approach to our quest. See Janzen, "A Canonical Rethinking of the Anabaptist-Mennonite New Testament Orientation," 107.
13. Ibid., 64-66.

14. Borg, "Teaching of Jesus," in *Anchor Bible Dictionary*, 3:806.
15. Borg, *Meeting Jesus Again for the First Time: The Historical Jesus & the Heart of Contemporary Faith*, 27-32.
16. Janzen, *Old Testament Ethics: A Paradigmatic Approach*, 195.
17. Sheppard, "Wisdom as a Hermeneutical Construct: A Study in the Sapientializing of the Old Testament," 13.
18. Neufeld, *Ephesians*, 364.
19. Davidson, *Wisdom and Worship.*
20. Gerstenberger, "Practicing the Presence of God: The Wisdom Psalms as Prayer."
21. Sheppard, "The Relation of Solomon's Wisdom and Biblical Prayer," 11.
22. Perdue, "Cosmology and the Social Order in the Wisdom Tradition," 271.
23. Klassen, *Love of Enemies: The Way to Peace, Overtures to Biblical Theology*, 34-35.
24. Neufeld, *Ephesians*, 51.
25. Murphy, "The Sage in Ecclesiastes and Qoheleth the Sage," 271.
26. "Holy interconnectedness" is Brueggeman's term; see *The Creative Word: Canon as a Model for Biblical Education*, 81. "Inclusivity" and "indivisibility" are terms Pamela Leach uses for the coming together of all people, since all wisdom has its source in one Creator God.
27. Wisdom of Solomon 7:27 already suggests that Wisdom is but one; she passes into holy souls and makes them friends of God and prophets.
28. Note Friesen's work on this multilingual practice in his essay in *At Peace and Unafraid*, 55-56.
29. Walter Brueggemann, *Interpretation and Obedience: From Faithful Reading to Faithful Living.*
30. This phrase was used in the Schleitheim Confession of 1527, though it was interpreted in a rather dualistic manner. See Loewen, *One Lord, One Church, One Hope, and One God: Mennonite Confessions of Faith in North America: An Introduction*, 79.

CHAPTER 9

1. Harder, "Gifts of the Red Tent: Women Creating," 95.
2. First published in Gordon Zerbe, *Reclaiming the Old Testament: Essays in honour of Waldemar Janzen*, 128-137 and reprinted with minor editorial changes.
3. Brueggeman, *The Creative Word*, 93.
4. Shortened and adapted from a litany written by and for a congregation.
5. Janzen, "A Canonical rethinking of the Anabaptist-Mennonite New Testament Orientation," 91-95.
6. Yoder, *The Priestly Kingdom: Social Ethics as Gospel*, 9.
7. Gunkel, as quoted in Bullard, "Psalm 139: 'Prayer in a Stillness,'" 141-150.
8. *Hymnal: A Worship Book*, # 823.
9. Miller, *Interpreting the Psalms.*
10. Mays, *Psalms*, 425.
11. Miller, *Interpreting the Psalms*, 150.
12. Brueggemann, *The Message of the Psalms*, 26.
13. Miller, *Interpreting the Psalms*, 152.
14. Harrelson, "On God's Knowledge of the Self-Psalm 139," 261.
15. Rice, "A Diary of the Inward Journey," 63.
16. Harrelson, "On God's Knowledge of the Self," 263.
17. Glenn, "An Exegetical and Theological Exposition of Psalm 139," 181.
18. Rice, "A Diary of the Inward Journey," 66-67.
19. Gerald T. Sheppard, "'Enemies' and the Politics of Prayer in the Book of Psalms," 82.
20. Ibid., 80.
21. Robert B. Coote, "Psalm 139," 36.
22. Sheppard, "'Enemies' and the Politics of Prayer," 78-79.
23. First published in *Vision* 7 (2006), 14-21 and reprinted with minor editorial changes.
24. Daly, *Beyond God the Father*, 77.
25. E. Yoder, *Peace Theology and Violence against Women* is a record of the first attempt of Mennonite theologians to name this concern.
26. Lan, "God Weeps with Our Pain," 230.
27. Koontz, "The Liberation of Atonement."
28. Schertz, "God's Cross and Women's Questions: A Biblical Perspective on the Atonement."
29. Ibid., 206.
30. First published in *Vision* 9, no.1 (Fall 2008), 33-40 and reprinted with minor editorial changes.
31. See the chapter on discernment for further thoughts on same-sex marriage.

32. Willimon, *Worship as Pastoral Care*, 127.

CHAPTER 10

1. First published in Jeremy Bergen, et al., *Creed and Conscience*, 27-45 and reprinted her with minor editorial changes.
2. I am focusing on same-sex marriage rather than the variety of sexual orientations for several reasons. First of all, marriage has been the traditional way that intimate relationships have been ordered and blessed in the Christian community. Second, there is much biblical material to begin this discussion, including words of Jesus. Third, how exceptions to the ordering are perceived, such as widows, eunuchs, celibate persons, singles "burning with desire," etc. can add to the conversation with their very presence within the Bible.
3. I am using the terms as Reimer uses them in *Mennonites and Classical Theology: Dogmatic Foundations for Christian Ethics*, 516.
4. Ibid., 513-15.
5. Bible, Scripture, and canon each emphasize different aspects of the book claimed as authoritative within the church. However, in this paper I will use these terms interchangeably to describe the final shape of this book as it is used today within our congregations. Ibid., 513-15.
6. Barton, *Life Together*, 66-67.
7. This is congruent with the Anabaptist-Mennonite emphasis on the hermeneutic community. See Murray, *Biblical Interpretation in the Anabaptist Tradition*, 157-83.
8. I assume that congregations use the Bible differently than seminaries or schools do, and that they therefore provide a unique environment for scriptural interpretation. However, this is not primarily a theory vs. practice kind of difference. Rather, congregations use a wide variety of methodologies that intermingle to provide the content of the conversation. In addition, the power of the interpretations comes about in a more poetic way (through the hymns, prayers, sermons and personal experiences that are shared). Thus the Bible is used in ways not as methodologically precise as in the scholarly environment.
9. This statement arises out of my personal experience in the Toronto United Mennonite Church in their discernment process. See, "Letters," *Canadian Mennonite* 7, no. 15 (August 4, 2003).
10. Reimer points to this most clearly in "Confessions, Doctrines and Creeds" in *Mennonites and Classical Theology*, 355-71.
11. One scholarly book that is helpful in the way it assumes God's active presence is Johnson, *Scripture Discernment: Decision Making in the Church*. See also his discussion of homosexuality in the church, 144-48.
12. Brueggemann, *The Creative Word: Canon as a Model for Biblical Education*.

Brueggemann brings together the emphases of two authors who wrote groundbreaking works on canonical criticism: James A. Sanders, with his focus on the process of canon formation (*Torah and Canon*) and Childs *(Introduction to the Old Testament as Scripture)* who has focused on the final form of the text.

13. Ibid., 8-10. In this paper I suggest that the threefold form of the Old Testament is also present in the New Testament, though not nearly as clearly defined.
14. Ibid., 9.
15. Ibid., 3.
16. Sheppard, "Wisdom as Hermeneutical Construct."
17. That some Christians are not able to be fully part of the process of discernment testifies to the fear of each other that is still controlling the conversation. For eloquent pleas to open this conversation to homosexual Christians, see the periodical *Dialogu*e (Minneapolis) produced by the Brethren/Mennonite Council for Lesbian and Gay Concerns, and Kreider, *The Cost of Truth: Faith Stories of Mennonites and Brethren Leaders and Those Who Might Have Been.*
18. Exodus 12:26, 13:8; Deuteronomy 6:20-21.
19. The term "covenant" is used in the *Confession of Faith in a Mennonite Perspective* for marriage (72) and also for the church (40).
20. The imagery of "recipe" comes from Perry Yoder, who is writing the Believers' Church Bible Commentary on Leviticus. Note the most explicit texts on homosexual activity in the Old Testament are found in the Holiness Code, a series of recipes for living in covenant with God. In the New Testament these come within Paul's letters.
21. I differ here from those who begin with a theology of sexuality based on the creation account in Genesis (e.g., Willard Swartley, *Homosexuality: Biblical Interpretation and Moral Discernment*). I do not think that sexuality is one of the more significant pointers to God's design for human interactions and thus should not be our starting point. In fact, the Bible is androcentric in many of its parts reflecting the culture of the times. However, we do need to work out a theology of sexuality in a secondary way from an understanding of the divine/human relationship that includes all persons as sexual beings and strives to reflect God's redeeming activity in all our sexual relationships.
22. Walter Brueggemann is one author who has brought "imagination" to the fore in the prophet's role. See his book, *The Prophetic Imagination.*
23. "Theology of Reconstruction and the Peace Churches," a lecture given at the Toronto Mennonite Theological Centre in 1999. Other systems that he identified were politics, which he defined as the distribution of social influence, and economics as the distribution of resources, opportunities, and

privileges.

24. One of the earliest examples of this new consciousness is the discussion in Elizabeth G. Yoder, ed., *Peace Theology and Violence Against Women*.
25. A voice that needs to be listened to is the one asking how the fruitfulness of same-sex unions would be expressed. What is the place of children within our families? What does this mean in a context where birth control has already created many more choices for the shape of families among heterosexual unions? How have our families changed because of the possibility of fertility treatments/technologies and adoption that create new parenting possibilities for heterosexual partners, single persons who wish to parent as well as same-sex couples?
26. My own more detailed study of the wisdom tradition is summarized in "Seeking Wisdom in the Face of Foolishness: Toward a Robust Peace Theology." See Chapter 8.
27. One author who speaks about homosexuality in terms of wisdom traditions is Choon-Leong Seow. See his "A Heterotextual Perspective."
28. David Schroeder clearly identifies the inadequacy of both the church's present theological statements and the arguments by homosexual Christians. See his article "Homosexuality: Biblical, Theological and Polity Issues."
29. Janzen, "A Canonical Rethinking of the Anabaptist-Mennonite New Testament Orientation," 108-10.
30. Other denominations besides Mennonites struggle to be the church in their dialogue on same sex marriage. For a good example see Dunn and Ambridge, *Living Together in the Church: Including our Differences*.

Bibliography

Anderson, Janice Capel and Stephen D. Moore, eds. *Mark and Method.* Minneapolis: Augsburg, 1992.

Andolsen, Barbara Hilkert. "Agape in Feminist Ethics." *Journal of Religious Ethics* 9 (Spring 1981): 69-83.

Barton, Stephen. *Life Together.* Edinburgh and New York: T & T Clark, 2001.

Bender, Harold. "The Anabaptist Theology of Discipleship." *Concern*, no.18 (July,1971): 36-44.

Bergen, Jeremy M., Paul G. Doerksen and Karl Koop, eds. *Creed and Conscience.* Kitchener, ON 2007.

Best, Ernest. *Disciples and Discipleship.* Edinburgh: T. & T. Clark Ltd., 1986.

Bird, Phyllis. "The Authority of the Bible." *The New Interpreter's Bible,* Vol. 1: 33-64.

Boase, Roger, ed. *Islam and Global Dialogue: Religious Pluralism and the Pursuit of Peace.* Burlington, VT: Ashgate Publishing, 2005.

Boomershine, Thomas E. and Gilbert Bartholomew. "Mark 16:8 and the Apostolic Commission." *Journal of Biblical Literature* 100 (Summer 1981): 225-239.

Borg, Marcus J. *Meeting Jesus Again for the First Time: The Historical Jesus & the Heart of Contemporary Faith.* San Francisco: HarperSanFrancisco, 1994.

Borg, Marcus J. "Teaching of Jesus." *Anchor Bible Dictionary*, 3: 806.

Bornhauser, Christoph. *Leben und Lehre Menno Simons: Ein Kampf um das Fundament des Glaubens.* Bielefeld, Germany: Neukirchener Verlag, 1973.

Brandt, Di. "The Silence of Women Is a Goal of Pornography." Mennonite Reporter, 24 June 1985, 11.

Brueggemann, Walter. *The Creative Word: Canon as a Model for Biblical Education.* Philadelphia: Fortress Press, 1982.

Brueggemann, Walter. *Interpretation and Obedience: From Faithful Reading to Faithful Living.* Minneapolis, Minn.: Fortress Press, 1991.

Brueggemann, Walter. "The Legitimacy of a Sectarian Hermeneutic." *Interpretation and Obedience: From Faithful Reading to Faithful Living*. Minneapolis: Fortress Press, 1991, 41-69.

Brueggemann, Walter. *The Message of the Psalms.* Minneapolis: Augsburg Press, 1984.

Brueggemann, Walter. *The Prophetic Imagination*, 2nd ed. Philadelphia: Fortress Press, 2001.

Brueggemann, Walter. *Texts Under Negotiation: The Bible and Postmodern Imagination.* Minneapolis: Fortress Press, 1993.

Bryant, M. Darrol, Susan Kennel Harrison, A. James Reimer, eds. *On Spirituality: Essays from the Third Shi'i Muslim Mennonite Christian Dialogue.*

Kitchener, ON: Pandora Press, 2010.

Buechner, Frederick. *Wishful Thinking: A Theological ABC*. San Francisco: Harper &Row, 1973.

Bullard, John H. "Psalm 139: 'Prayer in a Stillness'," in *Society of Biblical Literature 1975 Seminar Papers*, vol. 1, edited by George MacRac, 141-150. Missoula: Scholars Press, 1975.

Burkholder, J. Lawrence. *The Problem of Social Responsibility from the Perspective of the Mennonite Church*. Elkhart, IN: Institute of Mennonite Studies, 1989.

Burkholder, John Richard. *Mennonite Peace Theology: A Panorama of Types*. Akron, Pa.: Mennonite Central Committee, 1991.

Burnham, Frederick B., ed. *Postmodern Theology: Christian Faith in a Pluralist World*. San Francisco: Harper and Row, 1989.

Byler, J. Daryl. "For Such a Time as This: An MCC Perspective on Iran." http// mcc.org/stories/such-time-mcc-perspective-Iran, May 2, 2008.

Childs, Brevard S. *Introduction to the Old Testament as Scripture*. Philadelphia: Fortress Press, 1979.

Childs, Brevard. *Old Testament in a Canonical Context*, London, UK: SCM Press, 1985.

Clark, Linda, Marian Ronan and Eleanor Walker. *Image-Breaking /Image-Building*. New York: Pilgrim Press, 1981.

Collins, Sheila D. "Feminist Theology at the Crossroads. "*Christianity and Crisis* (Dec. 14, 1981): 342-347.

Confession of Faith in a Mennonite Perspective. Scottdale, Pennsylvania: Herald Press, 1995.

Coote, Robert B. "Psalm 139," In *The Bible and the Politics of Exegesis*, edited by David Jobling, Gerald T. Shephard and Peggy L. Day, 33-38. Cleveland: Pilgrim Press, 1991.

Cornwall Collective. *Your Daughters Shall Prophesy: Feminist Alternatives in Theological Education*. New York: Pilgrim Press, 1980.

Culpepper, R. Allan. *Anatomy of the Fourth Gospel*. Philadelphia: Fortress Press, 1983.

Daly, Mary. *Beyond God the Father*. Boston: Beacon Press, 1973.

Davidson, Robert. *Wisdom and Worship*. The Edward Cadbury Lectures. London, Philadelphia: SCM Press and Trinity Press International, 1990.

Depperman, Klaus. *Melchoir Hoffman: Social Unrest and Apocalyptic Visions in the Age of Reformation*. Edinburgh: T&T Clark, 1987.

Dunn, Greig and Chris Ambridge, eds. *Living Together in the Church: Including our Differences*. Toronto: ABC Publishing, 2004.

Driedger, Leo and Donald B. Kraybill. *Mennonite Peace-making: From Quietism to Activism*. Scottdale, Pa.: Herald Press, 1994.

Esau, John. "Recovering, Rethinking, and Re-imagining: Issues in a Mennonite Theology for Christian Ministry." In *Understanding Ministerial Leadership: Essays Contributing to a Developing Theology of Ministry*, edited by John Esau, 1-26. Text Reader Series 6, Elkhart, Indiana: Institute of Mennonite Studies, 1995.

Esau, John H. ed. *Understanding Ministerial Leadership: Essays Contributing to a Developing Theology of Ministry*. Text Reader Series 6, Elkhart, Indiana: Institute of Mennonite Studies, 1995.

Farley, Margaret A. "Feminist Consciousness and Interpretation of Scripture." In *Feminist Interpretations of the Bible,* edited by Letty M. Russell, 41-51. Philadelphia: Westminster Press, 1985.

Findlay-Chamberlain, ed. Keeping the Balance. . .Staying Healthy as Helpers." *Women's Concerns Report* No. 115.

Fiorenza, Elisabeth Schüssler. *Bread Not Stone.* Boston: Beacon Press, 1984.

Fiorenza, Elisabeth Schüssler. "The Ethics of Biblical Interpretation: Decentering Biblical Scholarship." *Journal of Biblical Literature*, 107 (1988): 3-17.

Fiorenza, Elizabeth Schüssler. *In Memory of Her*. New York: Crossroad, 1984.

Frantz, Nadine Pence, "Women Bearing the Cross of Discipleship," *Women's Concerns Report* 89 (March-April, 1990): 1-2.

Friesen, Duane and Gerald Schlabach. *At Pease and Unafraid: Public Order, Security, and the Wisdom of the Cross.* Scottdale, PA: Herald Press, 2005.

Froehlich, Karlfried. "The Inspired Word of God: Authority and Inspiration." In *The Bible as Word of God,* edited by Terence E. Fretheim and Karlfried Froehlich, 11-22. Philadelphia: Fortress Press, 1998.

Gadamer, Hans-Georg. *Truth and Method.* London: Sheed and Ward, 1975.

Gerstenberger, Erhard S. "Practicing the Presence of God: The Wisdom Psalms as Prayer." In *To Hear and Obey: Essays in Honor of Frederick Carlson Holmgren*, edited by Bradley J. Bergfalk and Paul Edward Koptak, 20-41. Chicago, Ill.: Covenant Publications, 1997.

Glenn, Donald R. "An Exegetical and Theological Exposition of Psalm 139." In *Essays in Honor of Charles Lee Feinberg*, edited by John S. Feinberg and Paul D. Feinberg, 161-188. Chicago: Moody Press, 1981.

Goertz, Hans-Jürgen. "The Confessional Heritage in Its New Mold: What Is Mennonite Self-Understanding Today?" In *Mennonite Identity: Historical and Contemporary Perspectives*, edited by Calvin Wall Redekop and Samuel J. Steiner, 1-13. Lanham Md.: University Press of America, 1988.

Goosen, Rachel Waltner. "Defanging the Beast: Mennonite responses to John Howard Yoder's Sexual Abuse." *Mennonite Quarterly Review* Vol LXXXIX (January, 2015): 7-80.

Greenleaf, Robert K. *On Becoming a Servant-Leader.* San Francisco: Jossey-Bass Publishers, 1996.

Grimsrud, Ted and Loren J. Johns, eds. *Peace and Justice Shall Embrace: Power and Theopolitics in the Bible: Essays in Honor of Millard Lind.* Telford, Pa.; Scottdale, Pa.: Pandora Press U.S.: Herald Press, 1999.

Habermas, Jürgen. *Knowledge and Human Interest.* Boston: Beacon Press, 1968.

Habermas, Jürgen. *Theory and Practice.* Boston: Beacon Press, 1983.

Hahn, Celia. *Gaining Authority: Relinquishing Control: A New Approach to Faithful Leadership*. Lanham, Maryland: Rowman and Littlefield, 1994.

Halbertal, Moshe. *People of the Book*. Boston: Harvard University Press, 1997.

Hansell, Eugene. "The Seminary as a Learning Organization: A Systems Approach." Unpublished paper presented to Board of Trustees and Faculty of Associated Mennonite Biblical Seminaries, June 3, 1993.

Harder, Gary. *Dancing through Thistles in Bare Feet: A Pastoral Journey.* Waterloo, ON and Scottdale, PA: Herald Press, 2008.

Harrelson, Walter, "On God's Knowledge of the Self--Psalm 139." *Currents in Theology and Mission* 2 (1975), 261-265.

Hartzler, Tina. "Choosing to Be Honest ·Rather Than Good." *Festival Quarterly* 13 (Summer 1986), 7-9.

Hauerwas, Stanley. *After Christendom? How the Church Is to Behave If Freedom, Justice, and a Christian Nation Are Bad Ideas.* Nashville: Abingdon Press, 1991.

Hauerwas, Stanley. *Against the Nations: War and Survival in a Liberal Society.* Minneapolis: Winston Press, 1985.

Hauerwas, Stanley. *Christian Existence Today: Essays on Church, World, and Living in Between*. Durham, North Carolina: The Labyrinth Press, 1988.

Heinrichs, Steve, ed. Wrongs to Rights, *Intotemak*, July, 2016.

Heisey, Nancy and Daniel Schipani eds. *Theological Education on Five Continents: Anabaptist Perspectives.* Strasbourg, France: Mennonite World Conference, 1997.

Hershberger, Guy F. ed. *The Recovery of the Anabaptist Vision.* Scottdale, Pa.: Herald Press, 1967.

Hershberger, Guy F. *War, Peace, and Nonresistance.* Scottdale, Pa.: Herald Press, 1969.

Hershberger, Guy F. *The Way of the Cross in Human Relations.* Scottdale, Pa.: Herald Press, 1958.

Hoekema and Kuitse, eds. *Discipleship in Context*. Occasional Papers #18, Elkhart, IN: Institute of Mennonite Studies, 1997.

Holland, Scott. "How Do Stories Save Us? Two Contemporary Theological Responses." *Conrad Grebel Review* 12 (Spring 1994), 131-53.

Hoover, Jon. "An Anabaptist Perspective on Conversing with Muslims." In *Evangelical, Ecumenical, and Anabaptist Missiologies in Conversation: Essays in Honor of Wilbert R. Shenk,* edited by James R. Kraybill, Walter Sawatsky and Charles E. Van Engen, 120-129. Maryknoll, NY: Orbis Press.

Huebner, Harry, ed. *The Church as Theological Community: Essays in Honour of David Schroeder.* Winnipeg, MB: CMBC Publications, 1990.

Hymnal: A Worship Book. Elgin: Brethren Press; Newton: Faith and Life Press; Scottdale: Mennonite Publishing House, 1992.

Interpreter's Dictionary of the Bible. New York and Nashville: Abingdon Press, 1962.

"Iran Hostage Crisis." *Wikipedia*. Last modified July 25, 2017. https://en.wikipedia.org/wiki/Iran_hostage_crisis.

Isaak, Helmut. "The Heavenly Jerusalem has Descended Upon this Earth". Amsterdam: PhD thesis, 1989.

Isaak, Helmut. "Menno's Vision of the Anticipation of the Kingdom of God in his Early Writings." In *Menno Simons: A Reappraisal,* edited by Gerald R. Brunk, 57-72. Harrisonburg, Virginia: Eastern Mennonite College, 1992.

Janzen, Waldemar, "A Canonical Rethinking of the Anabaptist-Mennonite New Testament Orientation" in *The Church as Theological Community* edited by Harry Huebner, 90-95. Winnipeg: CMBC Publications, 1990.

Janzen, Waldemar. *Old Testament Ethics: A Paradigmatic Approach.* Louisville, Ky.: Westminster /John Knox Press, 1994.

Johnson, Luke Timothy. *Scripture Discernment: Decision Making in the Church.* Nashville: Abingdon Press, 1996.

Kauffman, Gordon. *In the Face of Mystery: A Constructive Theology.* Cambridge: Harvard University Press, 1993.

Kaufman, Gordon. *Nonresistance and Responsibility and Other Mennonite Essays.* Newton Kansas: Faith and Life Press, 1979.

Keightley, Alan. *Wittgenstein, Grammar and God.* London: Epworth Press, 1976.

Kermode, Frank. *The Genesis of Secrecy.* Cambridge, Mass.: Harvard University Press. 1979.

Klaassen, Walter. "Anabaptist Hermeneutics: Presuppositions, Principles and Practice." In *Essays in Biblical Hermeneutics: Anabaptist-Mennonite Perspectives* edited by Willard Swartley, 5-10. Elkhart, IN: Institute of Mennonite Studies, 1984.

Klaassen, Walter, ed. *Anabaptism in Outline: Primary Sources*, Kitchener, ON: Herald Press, 1981.

Klaassen, Walter. *Anabaptism: Neither Catholic nor Protestant*. Waterloo, Ont.: Conrad Press, 1973.

Klassen, Arli., "Reflecting on Conflict and Peace," *Canadian Mennonite* (Jan. 25, 2007), 34.

Klassen, William and Walter Klaassen, trans. and eds. *The Writings of Pilgram Marpeck*. Scottdale, Pa.: Herald Press, 1978.

Klassen, William. *Love of Enemies: The Way to Peace, Overtures to Biblical Theology.* Philadelphia: Fortress Press, 1984.

Koontz, Gayle Gerber. "A Theologian's Companions." *The Window,* April, 1982, 1-2.

Koontz, Gayle Gerber. "The Liberation of Atonement." *Mennonite Quarterly Review*, 63/2 (April, 1989): 190-192.

Koontz, Gayle Gerber. "Peace Theology in Transition: North American Mennonite Peace Studies and Theology, 1906-2006." *Mennonite Quarterly Review* 81/1, 77-96.

Koontz, Gayle Gerber and Willard Swartley, eds. *Perspectives on Feminist Hermeneutics,* Occasional Papers No. 10. Elkhart, Indiana: Institute of Mennonite Studies, 1987.

Kreider, Roberta Schowalter, ed. *The Cost of Truth: Faith Stories of Mennonites and Brethren Leaders and Those Who Might Have Been*. Kulpsville, PA: Strategic Press, 2004.

Lan, Kwok Pui. "God Weeps with Our Pain." *East Asian Journal of Theology* 2 (1984): 228-232.

Leach, Pamela. "Gadfly Citizenship: Faithful Public Practices beyond the National Security Model." In *At Peace and Unafraid,* edited by Duane K. Friesen and Gerald W. Schlabach, 83-116. Scottdale, PA., Waterloo, ON: Herald Press, 2005.

Legenhausen, Hajj Muhammad. *"Islam and Nonviolence." www.Islamicinsights.com/religion/clergycorner/islam-and-nonviolence.html.* Posted Feb 24, 2008.

Lindbeck. George A. *The Nature of Doctrine*. Philadelphia: Westminster Press, 1984.

Loeschen, John R. *The Divine Community: Trinity, Church and Ethics in Reformation Theology.* Kirksville, Missouri: Sixteenth Century Journal Publishers, 1981.

Loewen, Howard. *One Lord, One Church, One Hope, and One God.* Elkhart, IN: Institute of Mennonite Studies, 1985.

Loewen, Howard. "Peace in the Mennonite Tradition: Toward a Theological Understanding of a Regulative Concept." In *Baptism, Peace and the State in the Reformed and Mennonite Tradition*, edited by Ross T. Bender and Alan P. F. Sell, 106-12. Waterloo, ON Wilfred Press.

Malbon, Elizabeth Struthers. "Fallible Followers: Women and Men in the Gospel of Mark." *Semeia* 28 (1983), 29-48.

Malbon, Elizabeth Struthers. "Disciples/Crowds/Whoever: Markan Characters and Readers." *Novum Testamentum* 28, No. 2 (1986): 104-130.

Martin, Ed. "MCC And Iran." *Peace Office Newsletter* 31, No. 3 (July-Sept. 2001): 1-2.

Mays, James Luther. *Psalms*. Louisville: John Knox Press, 1991.

McFague, Sallie. *Metaphorical Language: Models of God in Religious Language.* Philadelphia: Fortress Press, 1982.

Miller, Patrick. *Interpreting the Psalms.* Philadelphia: Fortress Press, 1986.

Mudge, Lewis S. "Paul Ricoeur on Biblical Interpretation." In *Essays on Biblical Interpretation,* edited by Paul Ricoeur, 1-40. Philadelphia: Fortress Press, 1982.

Munro, Winsom. "Women Disciples in Mark?" *Catholic Biblical Quarterly* 44 (1982): 225-241.

Murphy, Nancey and James William McClendon Jr., "Distinguishing Modern and Postmodern Theologies," *Modern Theology* (April 1989): 191-212.

Murphy, Roland. "The Sage in Ecclesiastes and Qoheleth the Sage." In *The Sage in Israel and the Ancient Near East,* edited by John C. Cammie and Leo G. Perdue, 263-271. Winona Lake, Ind.: Eisenbrauns, 1990.

Murphy, Roland E. "Wisdom in the Old Testament." *Anchor Bible Dictionary*, edited by David Noel Freedman. New York, N.Y.: Doubleday, 1992, 6:920-31.

Murray, Stuart. *Biblical Interpretation in the Anabaptist Tradition*. Kitchener, ON: Pandora Press, 2000.

Neufeld, Thomas R. Yoder. *Ephesians,* Believers Church Bible Commentary. Scottdale, PA and Waterloo, ON: Herald Press, 2002.

Niebuhr, H Richard. *Christ and Culture.* New York: Harper and Row, 1951.

Palmer, Parker J. *Let Your Life Speak: Listening to the Voice of Vocation.* Hoboken, New Jersey: John Wiley & Sons, 2000.

Perdue, Leo G. "Cosmology and the Social Order in the Wisdom Tradition." In *The Sage in Israel and the Ancient Near East,* edited by John C. Cammie and Leo G. Perdue, 457-478. Winona Lake, Ind.: Eisenbrauns, 1990.

Pipkin, Wayne ed. *Essays in Anabaptist Theology*. Elkhart, Indiana: Institute of Mennonite Studies, 1994.

Placher, William. *Narratives of a Vulnerable God.* Louisville, Kentucky: Westminster John Knox, 1984.

Redekop, Benjamin W. and Calvin W. Redekop, eds. *Power, Authority and the Anabaptist Tradition.* Baltimore and London: John Hopkins University Press, 2001.

Reimer, A. James. "Anabaptist-Mennonite Systematic Theology." *Ecumenist* 21, no.4 (May-June, 1983): 68-73.

Reimer, A. James. *Mennonites and Classical Theology: Dogmatic Foundations for Christian Ethics*. Kitchener, ON: Pandora Press, 2001.

Reimer, A James. "Revelation and Authority: Shi'ah-Mennonite Dialogue II." *Conrad Grebel Review* 24, No.1 (Winter, 2006): 4-11.

Rempel, John. *The Lord's Supper in Anabaptism.* Waterloo, ON: Herald Press, 1993.

Rhoads, David and Donald Michie, *Mark as Story.* Philadelphia, PA: Fortress Press, 1982.

Rice, Gene. "A Diary of the Inward Journey." In *Journal of Religious Thought* 37, no. 2 (1980-1981): 63-67.

Ricoeur, Paul. *Essays on Biblical Interpretation.* Philadelphia: Fortress Press, 1982.

Ricoeur, Paul. *Interpretation Theory: Discourse and the Surplus of Meaning.* Fort Worth, Texas: Texas Christian University Press, 1976.

Ricoeur, Paul. "Naming God." *Seminary Quarterly Review,* Vol. XXXIV (Summer, 1979): 215-227.

Ringe, Sharon. *"A Gentile Woman's Story." In Feminist Interpretation of the Bible,* edited by Letty Russell, 71-72. Philadelphia: Westminster Press, 1985.

Ringe, Sharon. "Reading from Context to Context: Contributions of a Feminist Hermeneutic to Theologies of Liberation," In *Lift Every Voice: Constructing Christian Theology from the Underside*, 283-292. San Francisco: Harper and Row, 1990.

Roth, John D. "Community as Conversation." In *Essays in Anabaptist Theology*, edited by H. Wayne Pipkin, 35-40. Elkhart, IN: Institute of Mennonite Studies, 1994.

Roth, John D. ed. *Refocusing a Vision*. Goshen, Ind.: Mennonite Historical Society, 1995.

Rowland, Christopher. "In this Place: The Centre and the Margins in Theology." In *Reading From This Place: Social Location and Biblical Interpretation in Global Perspective*, edited by Fernando F. Segovia and Mary Ann Tolbert, 169-182. Minneapolis: Fortress Press, 1995.

Ruether, Rosemary Radford. "Feminist Interpretation: A Method of Correlation." In *Feminist Interpretation of the Bible,* edited by Letty M. Russell, 111-125. Philadelphia: Westminster Press, 1985.

Russell, Letty M., ed. *Feminist Interpretation of the Bible.* Philadelphia: Westminster Press, 1985.

Sabbe, M. "The Footwashing in JN 13 and its relation to the Synoptic Gospels," *Ephemerides Theologicae Lovaniensis*, 58 (December,1982): 279-308.

Sakenfeld, Katherine Doob."In the Wilderness Awaiting the Land: The Daughters of Zelophehad and Feminist Interpretation." *Princeton Seminary*

Bulletin, 9/3 (1988): 179-196.

Sakenfeld, Katherine Doob. "Feminist Uses of Biblical Material". In *Feminist Interpretation of the Bible*, edited by Letty M. Russell, 55-64. Philadelphia: Westminster Press, 1985.

Sanders, James. *From Sacred Story to Sacred Text.* Minneapolis, Minnesota: Augsburg Press, 1987.

Sanders, James A. *Torah and Canon*. Philadelphia: Fortress Press, 1972.

Sawatsky, Rodney. "The Quest for a Mennonite Hermeneutic." *Conrad Grebel Review* 11 (Winter 1993), 1-3.

Sawatsky, Rodney. "Words becoming Flesh: The Life and Thought of David Schroeder." In *The Church as Theological Community: Essays in Honour of David Schroeder,* edited by Harry Huebner, 3-21. Winnipeg, MB: CMBC Publications, 1990.

Schertz, Mary H. "God's Cross and Women's Questions: A Biblical Perspective on the Atonement." *Mennonite Quarterly Review* 68 (April 1994): 194-208.

Schertz, Mary H. "Interpretation as Discipleship: Luke 24 as Model." In *The Church as Theological Community,* edited by Harry Huebner, 115-39. Winnipeg: CMBC Publications, 1990.

Schipani, Daniel S. *The Way of Wisdom in Pastoral Counseling.* Elkhart, Ind.: Institute of Mennonite Studies, 2003.

Schlabach, Gerald W. "Beyond Two vs. One -Kingdom Theology: Abrahamic Community as a Mennonite Paradigm for Engagement in Society." *Conrad Grebel Review* 11, no 3 (fall, 1993): 187-210.

Schneiders, Sandra M. "Evangelical Equality: Religious Consecration, Mission and Witness," *Spirituality Today* 38 (Winter 1986): 298-300.

Schneiders, Sandra M. "Feminist Ideology Criticism and Biblical Hermeneutics." *Biblical Theology Bulletin*, 19/1 (January 1989) 3-10.

Schneiders, Sandra. "The Foot Washing? (John 13: 1-20): An Experiment in Hermeneutics." *Catholic Biblical Quarterly* 43 (1981): 84-87.

Schneiders, Sandra. *The Revelatory Text. Francisco, California:* HarperSanFrancisco, 1991.

Schneiders, Sandra. *Women and the Word.* New York: Paulist Press, 1986.

Schneiders, Sanders. "Women in the Fourth Gospel and the Role of Women in the Contemporary Church." *Biblical Theology Bulletin*, 12/2 (April 1982): 35-45.

Schottroff, Luise. *„Maria und die Frauen am Grabe Jesu."* *Evangelische Theologie*, 42 (Jan/Feb, 1982): 3-25.

Schroeder, David. "Homosexuality: Biblical, Theological and Polity Issues" In *To Continue the Dialogue: Biblical Interpretation and Homosexuality,* edited by C. Norman Kraus, 62-75. Telford, PA: Pandora Press US, 2001.

Segovia, Fernando R. "John 13: 1-20, The Footwashing in the Johannine Tradition." *Zeitschrift für die neutestamentliche Wissenschaft,* 74 (1983): 31-51.

Segovia, Fernando R. and Mary Ann Tolbert. *Reading from This Place, Vol. I and II.* Minneapolis: Fortress Press, 1995.

Seim, Turid Karlson."Roles of Women in the Gospel of John." In *Aspects of the Johannine Literature*, edited by Lars Hartman and Birger Olsson, 55-73. Upsala: *Collectanea Biblica*, 1987.

Seow, Choon-Leong, "A Hetrotextual Perspective." In *Homosexuality and Christian Community edited by Choon-Leong Seow,* 19-24. Louisville: Westminster John Knox Press, 1996.

Sheppard, Gerald T. "Biblical Wisdom Literature at the End of the Modern Age." In *Vetus Testamentum Supplements* 80 (2000): 369-398.

Sheppard, Gerald T. "'Enemies' and the Politics of Prayer in the Book of Psalms." In *The Bible and the Politics of Exegesis* edited by David Jobling, et al. 61-82. Cleveland: The Pilgrim Press, 1991.

Sheppard, Gerald T. "The Relation of Solomon's Wisdom and Biblical Prayer," *Toronto Journal of Theology* 8, no. 1 (1992), 7-27.

Sheppard, Gerald T. "Wisdom as a Hermeneutical Construct: A Study in the Sapientializing of the Old Testament. *Beiheft Zur Zeitschrift Für die Alttestamentliche Wissenschaft,* Vol. 151. Berlin; New York: Walter de Gruyter, 1980.

Snyder, Arnold C. *Anabaptist History and Theology: An Introduction.* Kitchener, Ont., Pandora Press, 1995.

Snyder, Arnold, ed. "The Anabaptist Vision: Theological Perspectives." Themed issue of *Conrad Grebel Review.* Vol. 13, No.1, Winter, 1995.

Snyder, C. Arnold and Linda Huebert Hecht. *Profiles of Anabaptist Women: Sixteenth Century Reforming Pioneers, Studies in Women and Religion* vol. 3, Waterloo, Ont.: Wilfred Laurier Press, 1996.

Stayer, James M. "The Anabaptist Revolt and Political and Religious Power." In *Power, Authority and the Anabaptist Tradition* edited by Benjamin W. Redekop and Calvin W. Redekop, 50-72. Baltimore and London: John Hopkins University Press.

Stayer, James M. *The German Peasants' War and Anabaptist Community of Goods.* Montreal: McGill-Queen's University Press, 1991.

Stayer, James M., Werner O. Packull, and Klaus Deppermann. "From Monogenesis to Polygenesis: The Historical Discussion of Anabaptist Origins". *Mennonite Quarterly Review* 49 (April, 1975): 83-121.

Stoesz, William B. "The New Creature: Menno's Understanding of the Christian Faith." In *Essays in Anabaptist Theology* edited by H. Wayne Pipkin,

175-197. Elkhart, IN.: Institute of Mennonite Studies, 1994.

Swartley. Willard, ed. *Essays in Biblical Hermeneutics: Anabaptist-Mennonite Perspectives.* Elkhart, IN: Institute of Mennonite Studies, 1984.

Swartley, Willard. *Homosexuality: Biblical Interpretation and Moral Discernment.* Scottdale, PA and Waterloo, ON: Herald Press, 2003.

Swartley, Willard. *Mark: The Way for All Nations*. Scottdale, PA: Herald Press, 1979.

Swartley. Willard. *Slavery, Sabbath, War and Women*. Scottdale, Pa. and Kitchener, Ont.: Herald Press, 1983.

Thiselton, Anthony C. *The Two Horizons: New Testament Hermeneutics and Philosophical Description With Special Reference to Heidegger, Bultman, Gadamer, and Wittgenstein.* Grand Rapids: Eerdmans, 1980.

Thistlethwaite, Susan Brooks and Mary Potter Engel, eds. *Lift Every Voice: Constructing Theologies from the Underside*. New York: Harper & Row, 1990.

Tolbert, Mary Ann. *Sowing the Gospel.* Minneapolis: Fortress Press, 1989.

Tracy, David. *Plurality and Ambiguity: Hermeneutics, Religion, Hope.* San Francisco: Harper and Row, 1987.

Trible, Phyllis. *Texts of Terror.* Philadelphia: Fortress Press, 1984.

Trible, Phyllis. *God and the Rhetoric of Sexuality.* Philadelphia: Fortress Press, 1978.

Voolstra, Sjouke. "True Penitence: The Core of Menno Simons' Theology." *Mennonite Quarterly Review* 62 (1988): 387-400.

Weaver-Zuercher, David. *Minding the Church: Scholarship in the Anabaptist Tradition,* Telford, PA: Pandora Press U.S and Scottdale, PA: Herald Press, 2002.

Webster, John. *Holy Scripture*. Cambridge, England: Cambridge University Press, 2003.

Weingart, Richard. "The Meaning of Sin in the Theology of Menno Simons." In *Essays in Anabaptist Theology* edited by H. Wayne Pipkin, 157-174. Elkhart, IN: Institute of Mennonite Studies, 1994.

Wenger, J.C. ed. *The Complete Writings of Menno Simons*. Translated by Leonard Verduin. Scottdale, Pa.: Herald Press, 1956.

Weiss, Harold. "Footwashing in the Johannine Community." In *Novum Testamentum,* 21/4 (1979): 298-325.

Wiebe, Katie Funk. "Katie Funk Wiebe reflects on the conference: 'In a Mennonite Voice: Women Doing Theology.'" *Conrad Grebel Review* Vol. 10, No. 2, (1992), 209-213.

Williams, Delores S. "The Color of Feminism." *Christianity and Crisis*, April 29, 1985. 164-165.

Willimon, William. *Worship as Pastoral Care*. Nashville: Abingdon Press, 1979.

Wink, Walter. *The Bible in Human Transformation.* Philadelphia: Fortress Press, 1973.

Wittgenstein, Ludwig. *Philosophical Investigations.* Translated by G.E.M. Anscomb. New York: Macmillan Publishing Co., 1968.

Yoder, Elizabeth G., *ed. Peace Theology and Violence Against Women.* Elkhart, Ind.: Institute of Mennonite Studies, 1992.

Yoder, John H. "Anabaptist Vision and Mennonite Reality." In *Consultation on Anabaptist-Mennonite Theology*, edited by A.J. Klassen, 1-46. Fresno, Calif.: Council of Mennonite Seminaries, 1970.

Yoder, John H. "Armaments and Eschatology," Studies in Christian Ethics 1, no\. I (1988): 43-61.

Yoder, John H. "Ethics and Eschatology," *Ex Audita* 6 (1990): 119-128.

Yoder, John H. "The Hermeneutics of the Anabaptists," *Mennonite Quarterly Review* 41 (Oct. 1967), 291-308.

Yoder, John H. *The Politics of Jesus: Vicit Agnus Noster.* Grand Rapids, Michigan: Eerdmans, 1994.

Yoder, John H. *The Priestly Kingdom: Social Ethics as Gospels.* Notre Dame, IN.: University of Notre Dame Press, 1984.

Yoder, John H. *The Royal Priesthood: Essays Ecclesiological and Ecumenical.* Grand Rapids, Michigan: Eerdmans Press, 1994.

Yoder, John Howard. *To Hear the Word.* Eugene, Oregon: Wipf and Stock, 2001.

Yoder, Perry B. and Willard M. Swartley, eds. *The Meaning of Peace: Biblical Studies, Studies in Peace and Scripture.* Louisville, Ky.: Westminster /John Knox Press, 1992.

Yoder, Perry. "The Role of the Bible in Mennonite Self-Understanding." In *Mennonite Identity: Historical and Contemporary Perspectives*, edited by Calvin Wall Redekop and Samuel J. Steiner, 69-82. Lanham, N.Y.: University Press of America, 1988.

Zerbe, Gordon, ed. *Reclaiming the Old Testament: Essays in Honour of Waldemar Janzen.* Winnipeg, Manitoba: CMBC Publications, 2001.

Zikmund, Barbara Brown. "Feminist Consciousness in Historica1 Perspective." In *Feminist Interpretation of the Bible.* Letty M. Russell, ed., 21-29. Philadelphia: Westminster Press, 1985.

Selected Writings of Lydia Neufeld Harder

"The Bible as Canon and as Word of God: Exploring the Mystery of Revelation." Conrad Grebel Review 24, No. 1 (2006): 52-65.

"Becoming a Church that Listens to God's Word, *Canadian Mennonite,* Vol. 2, no. 24, (1998): 6-7.

"Biblical Interpretation: A Praxis of Discipleship," *Conrad Grebel Review* 10, no. 1 (1992): 17-32.

"Dialogue with Hauerwas." *Conrad Grebel Review* 13, no. 2 (1995): 152-156.

"Discipleship Reexamined: Women in the Hermeneutical Community." In *The Church as Theological Community: Essays in Honour of David Schroeder,* edited by Harry Huebner, 199-220. Winnipeg, MB: CMBC Publications, 1990.

"Formal Theological Education: The Centre and the Boundaries." In *Theological Education on Five Continents: Anabaptist Perspectives*, edited by Nancy Heise and Daniel Schipani, 103-112. Strasbourg, France: Mennonite World Conference, 1997.

"Gifts of the Red Tent: Women Creating." Afterword, Conrad Grebel Review 23, no. 1, (2005): 91-95.

"Hermeneutic Community: A Study of the Contemporary Relevance of an Anabaptist-Mennonite Approach to Biblical Interpretation." MTh thesis, Edmonton, Alberta: Newman Theological College, 1984.

"Hermeneutic Community: A Feminist Challenge." In *Perspectives on Feminist Hermeneutics* edited by Gayle Gerber Koontz and Willard Swartley, 46-55. Occasional Papers No. 10, Institute of Mennonite Studies, 1987.

"In Search of God's Kingdom Incarnate: Power and Authority in Mennonite Theological Development." In *Power, Authority and Domination in the Anabaptist-Mennonite Tradition.,* edited by Ben Redekop and Calvin Redekop, 73-94. Baltimore and London: John Hopkins University Press, 2001.

"Menno's View of Jesus." In *Theological Education on Five Continents: Anabaptist Perspectives* edited by Nancy R. Heisy and Daniel S. Schipani, 103-112. Strasbourg, France: Mennonite World Conference. 1997.

"The Mutuality of Ministry: A Dialogue with Mark." In *Understanding Ministerial*

Leadership: Essays Contributing to a Developing Theology of Ministry edited by John H. Esau, 70-81. Text Reader Series 6, Elkhart, Indiana: Institute of Mennonite Studies, 1995.

"Naming Myself a Theological Scholar in the Anabaptist Tradition." In *Minding the Church: Scholarship in the Anabaptist Tradition, edited by David*

Weaver-Zercher, 193-207. Telford PA: Pandora Press U.S. and Scottdale, PA: Herald Press, 2002.

"No Longer Innocent" *Sophia* (Winter, 1995), 3.

Obedience, Suspicion and the Gospel of Mark: A Mennonite Feminist Exploration of Biblical Authority. Waterloo, ON: Wilfred Laurier Press, 1998.

"Our God-talk: Images, Idols, Metaphors and Masks." *MCC Women's Concerns* Jan/Feb. 1988, 1-2; 9-10.

"Postmodern Suspicion and Imagination: Therapy for Mennonite Hermeneutic Communities," *Mennonite Quarterly Review* LXXI, No. 2 (1997): 267-283.

"Reaching for a Blessing." In *She Has Done a Good Thing,"* edited by Mary Swartley and Rhoda Keener, 23-30. Scottdale, PA: Herald Press, 1999.

"Response to Mary Schertz." In *Peace Theology and Violence Against Women* edited by Elizabeth G. Yoder, 25-28. Elkhart, Ind.: Institute of Mennonite Studies, 1992.

"Response to Scott Holland." *Conrad Grebel Review* 12, no. 3 (1994): 324-327.

"Seeking Wisdom in the Face of Foolishness: Toward a Robust Peace Theology." In *At*

Peace and Unafraid edited by Duane Friesen and Gerald W. Schlabach, 117-152. Waterloo, ON and Scottdale, PA: Herald Press, 2005.

"Singing a Subversive Song of Hope." *Conrad Grebel Review* 19, No. 3 (2001): 13-32

"Theological Conversations about Same Sex Marriage: An Opportunity for the Church to be Scriptural in its Discernment in *Creed and Conscience: Essays in Honour of A. James Reimer* edited by Jeremey Bergen, Paul G. Doerksen and Karl Koop, 27-45. Waterloo, ON: Pandora Press, 2007.

"The Witness of Women: Dying to Sin and Rising to Life." Vision 7, No/1 (2006), 14-21.

"Women Doing Theology: Individual Voices in Chorus." *Women's Concerns Report,* No. 121 (July-August, 1995): 1-2

Gary Harder and Lydia Neufeld Harder "Loved, Blessed and Freed to Hear God's Call." *Vision*, Vol.12, No.2 (2011), 28-35.

Gary Harder and Lydia Neufeld Harder, "The Perils and Delights of Leading Congregational Discernment." *Vision* Vol. 8, No. 1 (2016), 54-62.

Gary Harder and Lydia Neufeld Harder, "Sexuality in the Wedding." *Vision,* Vol.9, No. 2 (2008) 33-40.

Acknowledgments

The author and the publisher are grateful for the permission from the following publishers to include previously published articles in this volume.

CMU Press (CMBC Publications)

"Discipleship Reexamined: Women in the Hermeneutical Community." In *The Church as Theological Community: Essays in Honour of David Schroeder*, edited by Harry Huebner, 199-220. Winnipeg, MB: CMBC Publications, 1990.

"Reading Psalm 139: Opting for a Realistic Reading." In *Reclaiming the Old Testament: Essays in honour of Waldemar Janzen*, edited by Gordon Zerbe, 128-137. Winnipeg: CMBC Publications, 2001.

Conrad Grebel Review

"The Bible as Canon and as Word of God: Exploring the Mystery of Revelation." *Conrad Grebel Review* 19, no. 1 (2006): 52-56.

"Biblical Interpretation: A Praxis of Discipleship." *Conrad Grebel Review* 10, no. 1 (1992): 17-32.

"Dialogue with Hauerwas." *Conrad Grebel Review* 13, no. 2 (1995): 152-156.

"Singing a Subversive Song of Hope." *Conrad Grebel Review* 19, no. 3 (2001): 13-32.

Herald Press

"Naming Myself a Theological Scholar in the Anabaptist Tradition." In *Minding the Church: Scholarship in the Anabaptist Tradition*, edited by David Weaver-Zercher, 193-207. Telford PA: Pandora Press U.S. and Scottdale, PA: Herald Press, 2002.

"Reaching for a Blessing." In *She Has Done a Good Thing*, edited by Mary Swartley and Rhoda Keener, 23-30. Scottdale, PA: Herald Press, 1999.

"Seeking Wisdom in the Face of Foolishness: Toward a Robust Peace Theology." In *At Peace and Unafraid*, edited by Duane Friesen and Gerald W. Schlabach, 117-152. Waterloo, ON and Scottdale, PA: Herald Press, 2005.

Institute of Mennonite Studies

“Hermeneutic Community: A Feminist Challenge,” In *Perspectives on Feminist Hermeneutics*, edited by Gayle Gerber Koontz and Willard Swartley, 46-55. Elkhart, Indiana: Institute of Mennonite Studies, 1987.

“Menno’s View of Jesus: The Foundation of a New Reality.” In *Discipleship in Context*, edited by Alle Hoekema and Roelf Kuitse, 103-112. Elkhart, IN: Institute of Mennonite Studies, 1997.

“Response to Mary Schertz.” In *Peace Theology and Violence Against Women*, edited by Elizabeth G Yoder, 25-28. Elkhart, IN: Institute of Mennonite Studies, 1992.

“The Mutuality of Ministry: A Dialogue with Mark.” In *Understanding Ministerial Leadership: Essays Contributing to a Developing Theology of Ministry*, edited by John H. Esau, 70-81. Elkhart, Indiana: Institute of Mennonite Studies, 1995.

“The Witness of Women: Dying to Sin and Rising to life.” *Vision* 7, no.1 (Spring, 2006): 14-21.

Gary Harder and Lydia Neufeld Harder. *“Sexuality in the Wedding.” Vision* 9, no.1 (Fall, 2008): 33-40.

John Hopkins University Press

“Power and Authority in Mennonite Theological Development.” In *Power and Authority and the Anabaptist Tradition* edited by Benjamin W. Redekop and Calvin W. Redekop, 73-94. John Hopkins University Press, 2001.

Mennonite Central Committee

“Our God-talk: Images, Idols, Metaphors and Masks.” *MCC Women’s Concerns Report* January/February (1988): 1-2, 9-10.

Mennonite Quarterly Review

“Postmodern Suspicion and Imagination: Therapy for Mennonite Hermeneutic Communities.” *Mennonite Quarterly Review* 71, no. 2 (1997): 267-283.

Mennonite World Conference

“Formal Theological Education: The Centre and the Boundaries.” In *Theological Education on Five Continents: Anabaptist Perspectives*, edited by Nancy Heise and Daniel Schipani, 103-112. Strasbourg, France: Mennonite World Conference, 1997.

Pandora Press

"Theological Conversations about Same Sex Marriage: An Opportunity for the Church to be Scriptural in its Discernment," In *Creed and Conscience: Essays in Honour of A. James Reimer* edited by Jeremy M. Bergen, Paul G. Doerksen and Karl Koop. 45-62. Waterloo, ON: Pandora Press, 2007.

Miscellaneous

The author also wishes to thank Paul Doerksen and Gordon Zerbe at CMU Press for their encouragement and work in bringing this volume to completion.